Empire and Identity

Central European Studies

Charles W. Ingrao, senior editor
Gary B. Cohen, editor

Empire and Identity

Biographies of the Austrian State Problem in the Late Habsburg Empire

Fredrik Lindström

Purdue University Press
West Lafayette, Indiana

Printed in the United States of America.

Library of Congress Cataloging-in-Publication Data

Lindstrom, Fredrik, 1965–
Empire and identity : biographies of the Austrian state problem in the late Habsburg empire / Fredrik Lindstrom.
p. cm. — (Central European studies)
Includes bibliographical references and index.
ISBN-13: 978-1-55753-464-4 (alk. paper)
ISBN-10: 1-55753-464-0 (alk. paper)
1. Austria—Politics and government—19th century. 2. Austria—Politics and government—20th century. 3. Austria—Intellectual life—19th century. 4. Austria—Intellectual life—20th century. 5. Austria—Biography. I. Title.
DB80.L56 2008
943.6'04410922—dc22 2007042129

To Maria, Samuel, and Alva

Contents

Acknowledgments

This book began as a doctoral dissertation at Lund University, Sweden, and was finished in 2002. During the years in which I worked on the original dissertation, I received help and advice from many people, too many to enumerate here. However, I incurred a special debt to Professor Sven Tägil of Lund University, who supported my work during its early years, when few people in the Swedish historical profession could see the point of studying a long defunct Central European empire. My doctoral adviser, Professor Rune Johansson, of Linköping University, was also crucial for the continuing work on my dissertation. There were many others at the Department of History in Lund who during these years commented on and discussed my seminar papers with me. I thank them all.

During that time I worked extensively in archives in Vienna, and to some extent in Germany. In Vienna, Professor Fritz Fellner supported my work in many ways, always ready to read my drafts and discuss them with me. Dr. Peter Urbanitsch was also an important discussion partner. And a special thanks is extended to Dr. Franz Adlgasser, who often spent time discretely enlightening me on the peculiarities of Austrian society and culture, which my Scandinavian world view made me blind to. I also thank Dr. Ulrich Weinzierl, who generously spent time with me to read and comment on the part of my book concerning Hugo von Hofmannsthal. There were many others in Vienna to whom I owe thanks for their friendliness and willingness to give help and advice. A special thanks to Marianne de Maré, who during all my visits to Vienna and the two prolonged stays in which I was accompanied by my family helped me in numerous ways to settle in and to solve all the practical problems of daily life in a foreign country. In the Hofmannsthal-Archiv in Frankfurt am Main, Ellen Ritter helped me find my way in the scholarship and archival materials on Hofmannsthal. I thank her also for reading and commenting on the part of my work concerning Hofmannsthal. And I extend a special thanks to Luboš Velek, of Prague, who helped me to locate relevant materials from the archives of this old Habsburg city, and also for copying and sending this information to me.

I am very grateful for all the help and advice I received at the archives in Vienna. The staff of the Staatsarchiv, including its library, the Haus-, Hof-, und Staatsarchiv and the Wiener Stadt- und Landesbibliothek, all helped me during the several years of my work there. Also many thanks are extended to the staff of the archive of the

German Foreign Ministry, where I worked during its last few months in Bonn, and to members of the German Bundesarchiv in Berlin. I also thank members of the staff of the Austrian National Library in Vienna, who over the years have become like longtime acquaintances.

During the years since finishing my dissertation, I have revised and extensively reworked the original text. This has been a lonely job and was carried out in my own time. This also means that all the remaining mistakes are my own. Also, unless otherwise stated, all translations from German into English are my own. However, I must thank Professors Gary Cohen and Charles Ingrao, editors at the Purdue University Press, for encouraging me and giving me important suggestions on how to proceed with the revision. I also thank them for their patience. Many thanks to James Keating for improving the language of the book, and Carol Bifulco for preparing the manuscript for publication. I also want to thank the Frankfurt Goethe-Museum (Frankfurt am Main), the Austrian National Library (Vienna), the Kreisky-Archiv (Vienna), and Professor Fritz Fellner (Vienna) for permission to publish the pictures included in this book.

The main financial support for this project came from the Department of History at Lund University, which financed my Ph.D. studies. I also received substantial support from the Erik-Philip Sörensen Foundation. Several foundations were essential for financing my many trips to Austria and Germany: the Crafoord Foundation; Lars Hierta Foundation; the Royal Academy of Letters, History and Antiquities; the Letterstedt Foundation; the Per Westling Memorial Foundation; and the Uno Otterstedt Foundation. I express my gratitude to all these institutions.

Foreword

This book by the Swedish historian Fredrik Lindström makes an important contribution to a growing body of scholarship which is reassessing elite and popular thinking about the Habsburg state during the last decades before 1918. The recurring political crises in various provincial diets, in the Austrian and Hungarian parliaments, and in the ministerial councils deeply impressed observers at the time, both at home and abroad. Since the end of World War I, those political crises have also captured the attention of scholars interested in explaining the collapse of the monarchy. In the successor states of the monarchy and beyond, historians focused on the rising national loyalties during the late nineteenth century and the apparently irresolvable conflicts both among the nationalities and between them and the state, all of which was fuelled and exacerbated by growing democratizing pressures. In this oft-repeated narrative, the rigid dualist state structure, which was devised in the 1860s but based on old traditions of imperial prerogative and bureaucratic authority, could satisfy neither nationalist aspirations for self-government nor the growing demands for democratization. Unable to resolve the domestic political conflicts and fearing the growing nationalist agitation on both sides of the southeastern borders, the emperor and his chief officials responded to the international crisis of July 1914 with the conviction that they had to defend militarily the monarchy's continued status as a Great Power as an indispensable part of the Habsburg state's *raison d'être*.

In conventional accounts, the combination of seemingly insoluble domestic and foreign dilemmas persuaded the monarchy's leadership to take the enormous risk of entering into a major war and eventually to pay the ultimate price with the exhaustion of the state's military, material, and moral resources and the loss of popular loyalty after four years of brutal warfare. Yet despite the manifold internal conflicts and external threats which had existed for years before 1914, it still took a prolonged war and significant changes of attitudes during those four years among the population, domestic elites, and foreign statesmen to seal the state's doom. Research from the last twenty-five years points to the continuing ability of most political parties and interest groups in the Austrian and Hungarian halves of the monarchy before 1914 to work within the existing state institutions and to employ intricate modes of ostentatious protests, patient negotiation, and complex compromises, both major and minor. This scholarship also shows that, even after 1900, the Habsburg state, its laws, and the emperor commanded considerable loyalty among both the general population and a wide spectrum of political elites, despite the many unresolved demands and grievances.

Historians today are engaged in vigorous debate and inquiry about how attitudes and loyalties to the Habsburg state were actually changing during the last decades before 1918; how and to what extent the general population and political and intellectual elites identified with the Austrian, Hungarian, or joint Habsburg state; and what they hoped or expected the character of the state to be in the future. We have known for decades that few people in the monarchy had given up on the state before 1914, but just what notions people actually had about their relationship with the monarchy and about its future has been little studied until recently.

In the present book Fredrik Lindström offers intellectual and political biographies of three pairs of prominent Austrian German figures: the ministerial official and prime minister Ernest von Koerber, paired with the historian Heinrich Friedjung; the poet and playwright Hugo von Hofmannsthal, paired with his friend, the poet and diplomat Leopold von Andrian; and the law professor, parliamentarian, and finance minister Josef Redlich, paired with the political theorist, parliamentary librarian, and socialist party leader Karl Renner. Lindström focuses on these six figures' critiques of the existing Austrian state structure and their desires to change its character and identity, its official and popular political cultures, and the state's modalities for representing the needs, desires, and cultures of its peoples. In one form or another, all of these men engaged with the political or legal issues of the Austrian state problem, as it was understood in their time; and each tried in his own way to shape the state and how the citizenry could relate to it. At the same time, all of them also thought deeply about the larger issues of Austrian culture and identity and what it should mean to be an Austrian and a citizen of the Habsburg state. Lindström makes it indelibly clear that each of the six was deeply committed to accepting the monarchy as a political and cultural system as they worked to reconfigure and reform its system of governance and, thereby, preserve it for the future. Their analyses of how the state functioned and how it might be improved and strengthened illuminate the broader political discourse of Austria in this era, to which these six personalities made important contributions.

—Gary B. Cohen

INTRODUCTION

Biographies of the Austrian State Problem

> "[The book about Austria] will become a work that . . . describes and explains the origins and development of 'the Austrian problem' and how the rulers with the assistance of the peoples turned it into 'the Austrian chaos.' . . . If I succeed in properly explaining the origins, character, and effects of this chaos, then surely it will be easy to demonstrate how we can overcome it and again forge a stable and durable order."[1]
>
> Josef Redlich (1915)

Josef Redlich, one of the main personalities of this book, spent a large part of his life trying to understand what he variably called "the Austrian problem," or "the Austrian problem of the state and empire." When writing the letter from which the above quotation is taken, a few months after the outbreak of World War I, Redlich still felt confident that he would also participate in the political work of finding and realizing a solution to this problem. In 1906, he had taken the step from the academic study of it (he was a noted expert in constitutional and administrative law) to the political sphere in which it existed. During the following years, Redlich had engaged politically with this problem, an engagement that peaked in his leading-role activities in the Imperial Commission for Administrative Reform of the Austrian state in 1911–1914. During the war years his participation remained strong, but it also went through many changes resulting from the difficulties he suffered as a result of the upheavals of the war. During this time he also worked intensely on the book he mentions in the above quotation. However, when the first volume of this grand attempt at laying bare the foundations of the Austrian problem was published in 1920, Redlich noted in the foreword that because of the dissolution of the Habsburg empire in 1918, the purpose of his work had changed decisively and was now one of pure historical scholarship.[2] One might argue, however, that despite this change, the work has retained a special quality as a result of its origins as a work aiming to find the solution to a problem that was strongly present in the life of its author.

In its subject, the present book is closely related to this main scholarly work of Josef Redlich. What I refer to as the Austrian state problem has two main aspects. First, it concerns the problems of institutional adaptation that the multinational imperial Austrian state experienced during the accelerating modernization process of the nineteenth and early twentieth centuries. Especially important here are the political effects of this process, which can be defined broadly as the twin tendencies of the democratization and nationalization of society. Inherent to the modernization process, together they put severe stress on the political institutions of the old Austrian Obrigkeitsstaat. Under the heading of the "nationality problem," this problem has received a great deal of attention in historical scholarship.[3] However, interest has mainly been centered on nationalism and the political movements leading to the erection of nation-states on the ruins of the empire in 1918, and less on the problem of the multinational *state* as such.[4] As a search for the origins of the present, this is also completely understandable because of the dominant role of the sovereign nation-state in Europe during the twentieth century. At the beginning of the twenty-first century, however, the time might have come for a more unmediated interest in the multinational state as such, a cognitive interest that is also more directly akin to that of Josef Redlich's.

I find that the second aspect of the Austrian state problem as defined here is its "softer" side, the side pertaining to questions of culture, mentality, and identity. Because I approach the Austrian state problem as it was addressed at the center of the empire, in the German-speaking elite culture centered on Vienna, this mainly becomes a problem of imperial mentality and of Austrian culture and identity. These two different aspects of the Austrian state problem will be introduced in the two main sections that follow this introduction.

The method of the present investigation into the problem is biographical. It departs from the above suggested special quality of Josef Redlich's strong personal engagement with the Austrian problem. As I will demonstrate, all the six individuals represented in this book approached the Austrian problem as a problem of identity; to different degrees, they all experienced it as a problem of personal identity, as an existential problem. Furthermore, they all acted politically, in a broad sense, to remedy what they experienced as a collective identity crisis around 1900. In certain regards, this focus on identity highlights the similarities to the strong contemporary focus on national identity in the politics and society of the late Habsburg empire; the general problem is here only transposed into a variety of elements focusing on the interrelatedness of empire and identity.

The book consists of six biographies, grouped into three pairs with one main character and one secondary character in each. The three dual biographies aim at treating a certain field of tension in responses to the Austrian state problem, but the whole set of six biographies also have several interrelations that cut through this arrangement. The three pairs also have different foci concerning the two main aspects of the Austrian state problem as described above. Part one, containing the dual biographies of Austrian career civil servant and Minister President Ernest von Koerber and that of historian Heinrich Friedjung, as well as part three, containing those of the professor of law and German-Liberal politician Josef Redlich and of political theorist and Social Democratic politician Karl Renner, each has its main focus on the Austrian state problem proper, i.e., the political institutional development of the imperial Austrian state under the process of modernization. Part two, however, containing the dual biographies of poet and dramatist Hugo von Hofmannsthal and poet and career diplomat Leopold von Andrian, has its main focus on the problem of Austrian culture and identity.

The purpose of the present work is to examine the Austrian state problem in the late Habsburg Empire through the investigation of six different positions on this problem and responses to it. This also means that the aim is to go into greater depth with the problem than to achieve a generalizing overview of it. Consequently, as a point of departure for these investigations I present below a historical overview of the problem, which is later examined in depth. Also, my focus is on the state problem in a more narrow sense, leaving politics and the interest groups and organizations of civil society on the margins of the investigations. Indeed, these studies aim in part to demonstrate the centrality of the state as regards politics and political reform in late Imperial Austria, as well as to the shaping of individual life careers in Austrian society. The aim will be to delineate the role of the state in the six individual—in a broad sense—political projects examined, and especially the different purposes and meanings attributed to this state. Together they will create a network of mutually different but interrelated positions on this problem, which will demonstrate several central fields of tension inherent in the Austrian state problem in the late Habsburg Empire.

Besides this main purpose, there is also a secondary and more directly biographical purpose with these studies. Although the main analytical flow of the present work runs from the biographies to their common focus, the Austrian state problem, there is also a secondary effect of this common focus throwing light on the individual biographies. The biographies of this book are concentrated political biographies (in a wide sense), focusing on the attempts of these individuals to interact with and contribute to shaping the polity and collectivity that they were part of. Often the political engagements of these six individuals also cast an interesting light on the products of their artistic and scholarly works, which through the present approach are placed in a political context. The biographies will be briefly introduced in the last section of this introduction.

1. The Problem of the Austrian State and People(s)

The state is the central institutional organizational development of European history in the past millennium. This is the finding of a large body of scholarship in the social sciences and history on the problem of the state.[5] The development of the state in Europe has gone through a series of phases, the decisive one having taken place in the eighteenth century (though it can sometimes be traced back as far as the sixteenth century) when competition between European states reached such a level that an extended control of the resources of the respective states became increasingly important. The foundation of the Theresian-Josephinian Austrian state in the mid- to late-eighteenth century falls well within a general European pattern; in some regards the Austrian situation even seems to be in the avant-garde of developments at this time. In the next phase, that of the development of constitutional foundations and popular legitimacy for the growing state following the French Revolution and the Napoleonic Wars, the Austrian state, however, was on the late side in developments. The Metternichian regime ensured that early in this period the Austrian state hardly followed developments at all, but in the second half of the nineteenth century and in the early twentieth century, the Austrian state had to struggle to catch up and adapt to developments in a more hurried fashion. This phase is characterized by a move toward democracy, but is also strongly shaped by nationalism. The dual pressure of the democratization and nationalization of European society on the Austrian state and the failure by Austrian statesmen to seriously deal with this pressure for change made this phase as a whole, I would argue, into a drawn-out state crisis[6] that found its solution only by the dissolution of the multinational empire in 1918. Consequently, however, during this era there was also a constant focus on the Austrian state problem, which will be partly dealt with in this book.[7]

Taking a closer look at the development of the Austrian state from the eighteenth century until 1918,[8] we can find that the point of departure is clear enough: it is the Pragmatic Sanction of 1713, ensuring the "eternal bond" between the different lands of the Habsburgs, which constitutionally (to use an anachronism) laid the foundation of the imperial Austrian state. The Pragmatic Sanction was cited until 1918 as part of the constitutional foundation of the Austrian state and also of the Austro-Hungarian Empire. The state reforms of Maria Theresia, starting in the 1740s, then laid the actual foundation for the later development of the Austrian state institutions. At this time the central administration was founded by focusing many old princely authorities in the different lands of the Habsburg dynasty into a small number of central state institutions in Vienna. Under Joseph II this concentration was further enhanced, and the state also increased its direct intervention in Austrian society, thus ensuring the growth of this central administration. Notable already at this time is that the Hungarian administration never was integrated completely in this central state apparatus in Vienna, thus prefiguring the formation of the later Dual Monarchy already during this phase of intense centralization policies. On the state bureaucracy beyond the central chancelleries in Vienna, it should be noted that at this time it consisted only of a system of supervisory state organs on a middle level (Kreise), which rested on a fully traditional structure of aristocratic estates, townships and the like, not coming into direct contact with the population.

The Theresian-Josephinian state then basically existed as created at this time until 1848. It had, however, received a new constitutional foundation in 1804 through the proclamation of the unified Austrian Empire, encompassing all lands remaining under the Habsburgs. The phase of constitutionalism, of giving the European state at least partly a foundation of popular legitimacy and popular representation, only gathered momentum in Austria in 1848. Great changes occurred in this year and the following, giving Austria her three (!) first constitutions. Of these the Kremsier Constitution of 1849 primarily deserves mentioning. It was, as Josef Redlich would never tire pointing out, the only time in the history of Austria where all her peoples had together worked out a solution to the Austrian problem. It was never actually put in force, but much of the content was taken over into the March Constitution of 1849—also called the Stadion Constitution, after the interior minister who authored it—which was promulgated by imperial decree. This constitution was, in the following years, only partly realized in actual institutions until full neoabsolutism took over in early 1852. The main importance of this "early constitutionalism" (Brauneder), with the Kremsier Constitution as an example of fully developed constitutionalism, was that it created a model for later developments. The following neoabsolutist phase, however, was extremely important for the development of the Austrian state in a more narrow sense, because the period 1849–1859 saw the complete reconstruction of the state administration under the interior minister, Alexander Bach. Originally realizing a newly invented, unified, and homogeneous system of state administrative districts for the whole of the empire (including Hungary), this reform broke with the traditional forms of administration through the lands and aristocratic estates. An administration was implemented on two levels (Gubernium and Bezirke) that reached all the way down to the local level. This was the first centralized Austrian bureaucracy that had direct contact with the entire population, and after its retreat from Hungary in 1859 and 1860 it continued to function as the basis for the Austrian Verwaltung until 1918 (and beyond).

A dismantling of the neoabsolutist system was begun in 1859. However, Austria reached a new state of equilibrium only in 1867 in the so-called December Constitution (simultaneously with the creation of the Dual Monarchy), which then served as the constitutional framework for the Austrian half of the Dual Monarchy until its dissolution in 1918. In 1860 and 1861 the October Diploma and the February Patent, two decreed constitutions, had been attempted first. Formally speaking, the December Constitution was amended only on the basis of these earlier constitutions, but in fact it broke decisively with the one-sided monarchical system of these earlier constitutions. The December Constitution realized the fundamental quality of "high constitutionalism" (Brauneder) that could be found in the Kremsier Constitution, i.e., dividing power and legitimacy between monarch and popular representation. The latter, the central parliament in Vienna, had a rather limited curial representation, but was reformed in a series of steps (1873, 1882, 1896) until reaching equal and universal male suffrage in 1907. However, on the level of the Länder (provinces), which had been restored in their traditional shapes after the neoabsolutist period, the provincial diets continued to be elected on the basis of curia until 1918. The system of constitutional monarchy was built on a fundamental divide between state and society, having the monarch and government representing the former and the parliament representing the latter. In this system there existed no parliamentarism; the government was appointed by and responsible to the monarch, not to the parliament. There was only a strictly juridical ministerial responsibility. However, the budget rights and the legislative powers of parliament in effect meant that the government needed parliamentary support. The result was a creeping parliamentarization, expressed in several governments from 1868 to 1895 and then again in the early period of universal male suffrage; this phase began with a renewed move toward parliamentarization by the government of Max Vladimir von Beck in 1906–08.

The Verwaltung was also reformed in the 1860s, though not in its fundamental structure. Instead of the Bezirksamt of neoabsolutism, in which all authority on the lower levels of the administration had been concentrated (in the absence of political autonomy), the Bezirkshauptmannshaft, a somewhat larger unit, was now made the fundamental element of the new structure of administration. It was combined with a system of autonomous municipalities (Gemeinde), which carried a great part of the burden of the administration proper, allowing the primary state organs to step back to a somewhat less marked interventionism. The autonomous municipality had been one of the more important parts of the Stadion Constitution of 1849 never to be realized, and it was now finally realized in the Reichsgemeindegesetz of 1862. More important, the Länder (provinces) were restored and given a dual role of state administration on the intermediary level (Statthalterei, Land) and popular representation on the provincial level (Landtag). All in all, these changes created a dual system of state and autonomous administration that would become a constant subject of political struggles and reform attempts in the late Imperial Austria. I would like to emphasize this "vertical" dimension in the politics of late Imperial Austria, which I think needs to be upgraded in relation to the more thoroughly examined "horizontal" nationalities problem acted out between centers and peripheries.

One element of the Austrian administrative structure that after 1848 led a shadow existence was the old Theresian Kreis. The Kremsier parliament of 1848–49 aimed at using these intermediate administrative entities (larger than Bezirke, smaller than Länder) for the crucial role of organizing the Austrian nationalities. The idea was to attempt to create (mainly) nationally homogeneous Kreise, which, as the Länder, would later be a carrier of popular representation and also state administration. The Stadion Constitution as well as neoabsolutism intended to put them in use, the latter as exclusively state organs, but the Kreis was one of the many institutional elements of the Austrian state that simply faded out under neoabsolutism. After 1867, the reintroduction of Kreise was a repeatedly discussed measure for finding a solution to the most diverse problems in Austria, ranging from administrative overload in the Bezirkshauptmannschaften and Länder to canceling out in a centralist way the influence of the autonomous administration, and again, as in Kremsier in 1848–49, to acting as a central element in solving the nationality problem.

In a study focusing on the Austrian state problem, the nationality problem cannot be left unattended, but neither can it be given extensive treatment. It will here mainly be addressed in its interface with the state institutions. Viewed from the perspective of the state, the nationality problem also seems intricately interwoven with the problem of historical Austrian federalism. In the early phases of the Austrian state, nationalities as such were hardly even an issue for the state. The traditional estates of the different provinces were the relevant representatives of the Austrian people. The Theresian and Josephinian reforms in the eighteenth century practically eradicated the influence of these estates without, however, abolishing them. They therefore remained a traditionally legitimate focal point in society for resistance against the state. As such, they were crucial in the early phases of constitutionalism as carriers of the popular will. The legacy of the estates of the different Habsburg lands had resulted in a fundamental "differentiated federalism" (Brauneder) that was completely eradicated only during the short neoabsolutist era (1849–1859), which created a new and completely homogeneous system of administrative districts instead of the historical provinces of Austria with their varied rights and prerogatives. In the October Diploma of 1860, the historical provinces were reinstated as the main political-territorial structure of the Habsburg Empire. The creation of the Dual Monarchy in the so-called Ausgleich ("Settlement") of 1867 was in a way only the final elevation of the largest and politically weightiest of the historical Austrian lands (Hungary). The population of the historical provinces of Austria were also as a rule multinational, and this became increasingly important after 1848. The national conflicts in Austria raged hottest within individual provinces. Furthermore, during the Dual Monarchy federalism became a position associated with the non-German nationalities in Austria, as the historical Länder were often made a vehicle for these national movements. Conversely, attempts to hold federalism down, i.e., centralism, was often viewed as a German position.

The nationality problem as such emerged as a problem for the state only in 1848. Ironically, this was also when a "peoples' parliament" (Redlich) came very close to realizing a solution worked out among representatives of the Austrian nationalities. After the Kremsier parliament had been struck down by a renewed monarchical assertion of power in 1849, neither the state nor any central popular representation again came close to realizing a similarly far-reaching solution. However, national-political solutions on lower levels would indeed be worked out during the last decades of the monarchy and in several cases also implemented (Moravia, Bukovina, Galicia, and Budweis districts in Bohemia, among others). The Austrian solution chosen in 1867 was not to recognize the national groups as carriers of collective political rights, but instead to recognize nationality as an individual quality (§19 of the December Constitution). The Austrian state remained firm on the question of having a nationally neutral, i.e., supranational, character and the bureaucracy attempting with moderate success to fulfill its functions by aiming to transform itself into a truly supranational, multilingual organization that could interact with a population of nationally varied individuals.

However, the social self-organization within the bounds of the national groups and the formation of national-political parties on all levels, as well as the widespread national takeover of first the autonomous administration and then increasingly of the lower echelons of the state administration, arguably created a mounting pressure for a political recognition of the national groups. This was the official stance taken by the multinational Social Democratic party at the party congress in Brünn in 1899 as Karl Renner first appeared with his later famous solution to the Austrian problem, building on exactly this same element. These proposals were responses to political developments in Austria. Since the early 1890s, provincial parliamentary bodies in Austria had been plagued by obstruction because of national conflicts. Obstructions also nearly paralyzed the central parliament in Vienna for several years after the violent parliamentary clash between German and Czech nationalists during the Badeni crisis in 1897. They intermittently appeared until 1914 and seriously affected the functioning of this central representative body in Austria. This development also had the more general effect of weakening the expectations that a solution to the Austrian state problem could be worked out from "below" among the national groups and political parties, which in its turn led to a general strengthening of the role of the only organization in Austria, the Josephist Verwaltung, that was unified and powerful enough to be able to affect developments significantly.

Almost simultaneously with Renner's and the Social Democrats' stand for an evolution of the Austrian political system in the direction of a nationally based popular sovereignty, Ernest von Koerber was appointed Austrian minister president.

Koerber's solution to the Austrian problem was definitely one building on the old Obrigkeitsstaat, but at the same time it was much more innovative than the literature on late Imperial Austria recognizes. Nevertheless, in its fundamentals it was also the exact opposite of the Social Democratic solution, aiming, as I will argue in part one below, at reconstructing and buttressing the supranational Austrian *state* instead of letting the principle of nationally popular sovereignty guide developments. Karl Renner's solution, however, did not follow the fully developed principle of nationally popular sovereignty laid down in the Brünn program, but actually, as I will argue in part three, it seems to move on a middle ground between this solution and Koerber's modernized Josephism. In part three, Josef Redlich's solution will hold center stage, a solution that also moved on this middle ground. Just as Renner did, Redlich tried to find and help realize a solution that could stabilize the relationship between the supranational unitary Josephist state and the multinational and federally organized Austrian society. However, whereas Renner basically propagated the same solution to the Austrian problem during the last two decades of the monarchy, Redlich's solution developed substantially from the early years of the century until his prominent appearance in Austrian politics during 1917–18.

These different solutions to the Austrian problem can to a degree be approached with Max Weber's model of legal rule (legale Herrschaft) as the model of government in a modern society, in a Rechtsstaat, which is a theoretical model developed during this same time period. Weber's model is characterized by a tension between bureaucratic leadership and political leadership, where the former is seen as a necessary element in an efficiently functioning, stable and predictable modern political system, while the latter is necessary to make this system creative, dynamic, and capable of adapting to social change. To Weber, bureaucracy was absolutely necessary in a modern society, but ideally it should be only an instrument in the hands of political leaders based in parliament. However, the almost indestructible elements of bureaucracy also have an inherent tendency to usurp power, to turn "political," and to realize such development that Weber terms the "pathology of legal rule." It is also in this light that one should see Weber's application of the concept of charismatic leadership as an element in legal rule; as a way to infuse a modern bureaucratically structured political system with vitality and dynamism.[9]

We can make several observations on the Austrian state problem around 1900 with this model. First, it should be noted that what Weber terms "political leadership" was in Austria inherently weak, but the bureaucratic leadership of the Josephist Verwaltung was strong and firmly established.[10] This structural tendency toward a pathological development of the Austrian state in the direction of the rule of bureaucracy was indeed the crucial problem in Josef Redlich's political project, and it was not unimportant in that of Karl Renner's. Redlich strove throughout his career to expand and reinforce the institutional framework of political leadership, in terms of both local self-government and parliamentary government. However, from early on he also realized the important role played by the Austrian state and bureaucracy in supplying a basic stability and unity in the heterogeneity and diversity that characterized the multinational, federally organized Austrian society. Renner was much less disturbed by the risk, in Weberian terms, of a pathological development of the Austrian state and at an early stage gave this state and its bureaucracy a central place in his solution to the Austrian problem. But he also strongly focused on the need for self-government and especially national autonomy as necessary to infuse new vitality and dynamism into this Austrian state.

A second reflection regards there being more than a structural element favoring bureaucratic rule in Austria. Especially in the monarchy's last two decades, bureaucrats were often openly turned into political leaders, thus in Weberian terms making the pathological development of the Austrian state acute. Ernest von Koerber was an example of a Weberian bureaucrat turned "political" leader.

A third reflection on Weber concerns the tendency of all the individuals examined here to look for the solution to the Austrian problem in a charismatic leader. However, in late Imperial Austria this hoped-for leader was usually someone coming from within the bureaucratic structures, which probably mirrors the fundamental weakness of political leadership in Austria. The abilities of Alois Lexa von Aehrenthal were experienced by many people in late Imperial Austria, along with nearly all the individuals examined here, as the archetype of a dynamic leader who could break through the deadening weight of established, petrified bureaucratic structures, though he was himself an imperial diplomat, i.e., a bureaucrat in the Weberian sense.

By viewing Koerber in the Weberian light as a "political" bureaucrat heralding a pathological development of the Austrian state, we find a fourth reflection here, acute: that of applying Weber's model to such a heterogeneous polity as Imperial Austria. Weber's model seems to presuppose a national state characterized by at the very least a minimum of unity in society. The society Weber theorizes about is just like late Imperial Austria, suffocated by bureaucracy, but it is not like Austria threatened in its existence by national and territorial cleavages in society of the type that might very well lead to the breakup of the state. We thus find that Koerber's bureaucratic project and Renner's (and sometimes even Redlich's) rather strong emphasis on the state are defined somewhat differently. In fact, one might deepen this Weberian problem into the more general and open-ended problem of unity and diversity (or unity in diversity). Although they have different emphases, the political projects of Koerber, Redlich, and Renner all moved in this general field of tension, seeking a certain balance through which the Austrian state could be maintained as it simultaneously adapted itself to accelerating social change and released the powers in society.

In an extension to this fourth reflection on Weber, I find it beneficial to consider James Shedel's fundamental questioning of the relevancy of using a Weberian model for understanding the problem of state and society in late Imperial Austria. Shedel formulates his interesting argument as a criticism against the view of crisis dominating in the perspective on the Austrian Fin-de-Siècle as put forward by Carl Schorske and many others. Shedel wants to view Vienna 1900 not as a crisis, but simply as "the product of a developmental continuity defined by the concept of the *Rechtsstaat*." He argues that the Habsburg Monarchy had been defined since Joseph II by a dual legitimacy, both traditional (divine) and modern, building on the rule of law; the latter was born in the legalistic and rational spirit of the Enlightenment. The dynasty from this time viewed itself as within the law, but not above it, and the ruling emperor was viewed as "the first servant of the state." Furthermore, as Shedel puts it, "The Josephist spirit of the *Rechtsstaat* and the state as responsible for a progressively regulated social order was reified in the bureaucracy from Joseph onward, so that both the master and the servants of the dynastic state were bound by law." In Shedel's view, the Rechtsstaat served as a stabilizing framework that gave late Imperial Austria the capacity to adapt to rapid social change while simultaneously maintaining a basic continuity in the development of state and society.[11]

Shedel's argument has direct effects on the view of the development of the Bürgertum and the liberal movement, as well as politics as such, in late Imperial Austria. First, he emphasizes that the Austrian bourgeoisie developed in close rapport with the state, either serving the state or viewing it as the protective shell within which it functioned. Second, Austrian Liberalism also developed *with* the state rather than *against* it; the creation of a constitutional monarchy in 1867, in which bourgeoisie and the monarch shared power, went a long way in satisfying the Austrian Liberals. Furthermore, toward the end of the century Austrian Liberals increasingly moved into the state apparatus simultaneously as they were marginalized in popular politics; the Liberal Bürgertum retained much of its influence in society through positions in the Verwaltung and judicial system, as well as in universities, business, and the arts. Third, and most important in this context, the history of reliance on the state colored the whole of political life in Austria. As Shedel writes, "Grievances and projects for reform were habitually directed to [the state] following the pattern developed under Josephist and traditional paternalistic models of government." Shedel also observes that this function of the state in Imperial Austria made it serve as a container of the nationality conflicts, ensuring that these conflicts were in the main conducted through legal and parliamentary channels, seldom erupting into open violence.[12] I believe Shedel's perspective is an important corrective to the traditional Weberian view of these things. The peculiarities of the Austrian Rechtsstaat and Josephist Verwaltung partly canceled out the opposition between bureaucratic and political leadership in late Imperial Austria.

Shedel's argument concludes by returning to the problem of the Fin de Siècle as crisis, pointing out that the choice of an artistic pursuit in the strongly state-promoted arts sector of late Imperial Austria is difficult to construe as an expression of alienation, as did Carl Schorske; it was sooner a vote of confidence in the liberal Rechtsstaat. Similarly, I would like to press on the political side of Shedel's argument and point out that this development had created a peculiar political culture in which parliamentary politics existed in symbiosis with a sort of "politics through the bureaucracy" at both the local and central levels of government. That is, there was a marked tendency in Austrian society to expect ostensibly political matters to be dealt with through direct contact with a Beamte (or minister) rather than through an elected representative or representative body. I would argue that on the scale of the whole of society, this created a fundamental trust in and reliance on the state to take the lead in important questions and to act on behalf of the well-being of the entire population. Indeed, the old imperial state was emphatically not always seen as a problem; it was as often seen as part of the solution to the problems experienced in Austrian society in the early twentieth century.

Before moving on to deal with the "soft" side of the Austrian state problem, I must briefly address one more aspect of the Austrian state problem proper, the problem of the Dual Monarchy. After 1867, the Austrian state in a more narrow sense was also part of a larger structure, the Austro-Hungarian Empire, or, as some insisted, it was laterally related to another and equal state (Hungary) in a Realunion. Most important, the way this arrangement should be described was intensely contested during the whole Dual Monarchy; the Austrian view of a unified empire, a Gesamtsstaat, gradually gave way to the Hungarian view of a union between two equal states. However this arrangement was viewed, it resulted in a rather complicated system of government. Austria and Hungary each had a government of its own, appointed by the emperor, which ruled internally under the provisions of a constitution and in rapport with the parliament. Apart from these institutions, there were also three common ministers: the foreign minister, the war minister, and the finance minister. Foreign relations and the imperial army were defined constitutionally as common to both halves of the monarchy, in a strict sense a purely monarchic reserve. However, as was usual in a constitutional monarchy, this prerogative was partly canceled out because decisions in these domains for budgetary reasons needed the approval of the two parliaments through the so-called delegations (a parliamentary body elected jointly by the parliaments). The conflicts over this arrangement intensified after 1900 and played an important part in several of the careers examined in this book. The constitutional treaty laying the foundation to this arrangement, the Ausgleich, also needed renegotiation in certain parts every ten years, which ensured that it would be contested at regular intervals.

2. Empire and Austrian Identity

Austrian identity and imperial mentality are two aspects of the same phenomenon. Today this interrelationship is merely a charming aspect of Austrian mentality. It might be slightly annoying to Austria's neighbors, especially those who were formerly part of the empire, but in the main it is a harmless cultural relic. A hundred years and more ago things were different. At that time, this mentality was the cultural expression of an actual imperial structure of domination centered on Vienna and the Austrian core lands.[13] Before tracing the historical-structural matrix supporting this cultural phenomenon, I wish to point out that this view of the Austrian identity contains an implicit view of the empire as ruled exclusively by a German-Austrian elite. Furthermore, it also contains the notion that only the German-Austrians identified with the empire, while all the other nationalities did not. This view is not wholly false, but historically it is only partially accurate; in late Imperial Austria, centralism was usually identified by the non-German nationalities as a policy of German domination. Nevertheless, the long historical presence of the Habsburg monarchy in Central Europe created much more complex patterns of identification than can be captured by such a simple dichotomy.

If we concentrate on the German-Austrian center of the empire, however, two main views exist of the identity of the people inhabiting this center. First is an Austrianist view, maintaining that the long history of the Habsburg monarchy had turned the German-speaking population of its center into a nationality, or indeed, a nation of its own, an Austrian nation.[14] The second view maintains that the German-Austrian center remained firmly German throughout history and became more so in the nationality conflicts of the late Habsburg Monarchy.[15] These views both exist historically as competing views of the Austrian identity, and they still exist today.[16] The problem of the Austrian identity appears in different ways in most of the biographies in this book; Leopold von Andrian most clearly represents the Austrianist position, and Heinrich Friedjung the most pronounced Germanist position. Andrian maintained a basic view of the Austrian identity (or Austrian idea) as fundamentally shaped by its history of multinational cohabitation with several other central European peoples and by its conflicts with Germany since the mid-eighteenth century. Friedjung took a German national view, maintaining that the German-Austrians of the Habsburg Empire primarily remained tied to the larger German nation and had an important historical mission of carrying German civilization to Central and southeastern Europe.

However, although the Austrianist position was shaped by its hostility to Germany, the Austro-German tradition represented by Friedjung was also marked by its feeling of superiority vis-à-vis the Prusso-German tradition that dominated in the German Empire; the German-Austrians of this persuasion had been severely traumatized by the defeat in war against Prussia and the subsequent exclusion of Austria from Germany in 1866. The long-standing hegemony of Vienna and Austria within the Holy Roman Empire is arguably the historical-structural matrix behind the dual imperial mentality present in both these positions (directed both toward Germany and the non-German eastern dominions of the Habsburg Empire). Although the Germanist view of the Austrian identity tends to discard the notion of an Austrian nation or nationality before 1945, I think both Friedrich Heer and Ernst Bruckmüller in their very different ways have demonstrated that an Austrian consciousness can be traced further back into history. Furthermore, the concept of Austria has an even longer history that reflects the historical-structural matrix that contributed to the formation of an Austrian consciousness beginning at the latest in the Josephine era in the late eighteenth century.[17]

A fundamental characteristic of the concept of Austria over time is the dualism it exhibited throughout history between, on the one hand, the two core duchies, the two "Austrias," and on the other the dynastic, imperial concept of Austria, the "House of Austria" and the "Monarchia Austriaca." The narrower of these concepts referred not only to the duchies of Upper and Lower Austria; it was also sometimes extended to a great part of the Hereditary Lands of the Habsburgs.[18] The imperial concept of Austria departs radically from this concept after the rise of the Habsburg dynasty, beginning around 1500. In the sixteenth and seventeenth centuries, this concept of Austria carried ambitions to fill the role of a Universal Monarchy.[19] The great move eastward in the late seventeenth century, when Prince Eugene of Savoy led the (re-)conquest of the eastern lands of the empire from the Ottomans, reinforced this imperial meaning of the concept. In the eighteenth century, the concept began to change into that narrower but still imperial concept centering on the Central European lands of the Habsburg dynasty. The Enlightenment project of the centralized imperial Austrian state, with a civilizing mission in Central and southeastern Europe, was carried by the new imperial bureaucracy founded by Empress Maria Theresia (1740–1780) and expanded into a highly efficient instrument of reform by Emperor Joseph II (1780–1790). In this period, dualism between the two concepts of Austria also crystallized, and that is of interest here. What could perhaps be called an elite consciousness of Imperial Austria was formed in Vienna during the late eighteenth century. It was in many ways a by-product of the enlightened centralization project of Joseph II. This enlightenment elite viewed as "Austrian" all that was contained within the borders of this Josephist imperial state, but the actual social and cultural bases of this elite were much narrower.[20] As Ernst Bruckmüller has demonstrated, this elite, the later so-called Hofratsnation, was in the main an outgrowth of the Austrian state and was constituted by a culturally broad German group that socially belonged to the upper and middle classes of a geographically small area centered on Vienna.[21]

In the period 1804–1867, there was an "Austrian Empire." In 1804, Franz of Habsburg decreed himself to be "Emperor of Austria," a derivative title built on princely and royal titles already gathered under the Habsburg crown. However, this era also saw the first attempt to build an Austrian consciousness within this Austrian Empire to reinforce its popular legitimacy.[22] Nevertheless, starting with the revolution of 1848 the Austrian Empire went through a prolonged period of crisis, which was ended with a new stability after the creation of the Dual Monarchy, Austria-Hungary, in 1867. In the beginning of this phase, during the neoabsolutism of the 1850s, the Austrian Empire acquired a unified character for a short spell; it was in fact the only all-out attempt ever to unify and modernize the empire. However, as will be demonstrated in this book, the experience of a sudden retreat ten years later from this centralized and unitary ideal of empire was also a strong formative experience for the Austrian political elite and shaped its self-understanding during the following generations.

The decisive impulse for the final retreat from Hungary in 1867 was the defeat in the Austro-Prussian war of 1866. This latter event was also the end point of a long struggle for the supremacy in Germany between Austria and Prussia. Historically, Austria had been the first of the German powers and exercised the leadership in the Holy Roman Empire. But since the War of the Austrian Succession in the 1740s, Prussia had been challenging this position. Austria successfully fought off the challenge again and again, the last time in the early 1850s. In fact, the early 1850s saw not only the direct imperial rule of Vienna over the Austrian Empire in its entirety, but also the ambitious attempt of Austrian Minister President Felix Schwarzenberg to establish a great mitteleuropäische customs union, encompassing both the Austrian Empire and Germany, under the leadership of Austria; in effect, this was a reestablishment of Austrian power in Germany and in Central Europe. However, only somewhat more than a decade later, in 1866 Austria was defeated in war by Prussia and was instead locked out of the new Germany of Bismarck's kleindeutsche Lösung.[23]

This latter event might very well have been the most decisive blow for an Austrian self-understanding that historically to a great extent had been defined by the leadership in the Holy Roman Empire. The closing of the Dual Alliance between Bismarck's German Empire and Austria-Hungary in 1879 can be viewed as the reestablishment of a weak version of the old German-Roman Empire.[24] However, this solution did not end the uncertainty in Austria about the relationship between Austria and Germany. The memory of Austrian leadership in Germany would continue to be a fundamental problem for the Austrian self-understanding at least until 1945.[25] From 1866 to 1938, many German-Austrians could imagine Austria as a part of Greater Germany, but when they did so, they also imagined this empire as at the very least co-ruled from Vienna.

Ernst Bruckmüller has observed that the concept of Austria as used in the period of the Dual Monarchy reflected three different meanings: First, it signified the two duchies of Austria; second, the western half of the empire; and third, the whole of the empire. Bruckmüller then observes that this shifting, ambivalent concept of Austria seems to have been reflected only in the identity and self-understanding of the German-Austrian inhabitants of the empire. Bruckmüller continues: "An Austrian consciousness in a socially broader and deeper sense probably developed earliest among the German-Austrians, a fact that after the outbreak of the nationality struggles automatically hindered such a consciousness to spread to the non-German nationalities."[26] Ernst Bruckmüller is one of the few who has systematically studied the problem of Austrian identity historically in terms of its social base, or, as he himself puts it, in terms of *Nation Österreich*.[27] The results of his work seem to strengthen the assertion that one can trace a (rudimentary) Austrian identity far back into history and to corroborate the assertion made at the beginning of this section, that this Austrian identity was tied to the development of an imperial mentality. As described above, there was a dualism in the Austrian identity from early on, a dualism that with time assumed the form of a spatially rather inflated German-Austrian identity. As the Austrian nation evolved, it did so in interaction with an imperial state.

3. The Biographies

My way of approaching the Austrian state problem biographically, or more specifically, through dual biographies, goes back on an ancient model. Plutarch's *Lives* was a series of biographies presented in pairs, one Roman statesman and one Greek statesman, with the purpose of presenting and exploring existential and moral problems. As Timothy Duff has demonstrated in a recent work on Plutarch's *Lives*, these works in practice also have the purpose of exploring problems of cultural identity. Duff notes about dual biographies "that the parallel structure encourages comparison and contrast between paired Lives, a process that itself illuminates and clarifies the moral questions at their core."[28] I believe that there is a special quality in the very approach of juxtaposing, comparing, and contrasting parallel lives that is potentially productive for historical research, especially if it is used as an instrument in the investigation into a concrete historical problem. In comparison with the existing modes of using biography as a vehicle for historical study—such as the contextual biography or the collective biography—I believe that the model of using a small number of biographical studies centered on a historical problem is a very flexible and potentially useful way of developing biography as a method of historical research.[29] In the end, of course, the method must be judged on what it achieves.

The six biographies of the present work all interact to different degrees in the overall purpose of investigating the Austrian state problem and the problem of Austrian identity in the late Habsburg Empire. The basic structure of (three) dual biographies contributes to focusing this effect around a few central fields of tension in the historical problem investigated, though the network of interactions between the different life careers is much too multifaceted to be captured in any simple formula. Rather, the six different positions throw light on one another, as different voices can do in musical counterpoint, facilitating multidimensionality in the analysis of the Austrian problem. Nevertheless, while briefly introducing the biographies below, I will also point out the main fields of tension and the central problems that I have wanted to focus on with my approach.

The main character of the first dual biography is Ernest von Koerber (1850–1919). Koerber was born on 6 November 1850 in Trient (Trento), South Tyrol, where his father was on one of the stations of his state service. He was sent to the boarding school of the Theresianum in Vienna at the age of nine, where he stayed on into the first part of his law studies at the University of Vienna. Not long after receiving his doctorate in 1873, Koerber embarked on a civil service career that in 1896 would reach the highest position in the Austrian civil service, first Sektions-Chef in the interior ministry. After this, a career as an imperial minister followed suit, the pinnacle of which was the five-year-long government headed by Koerber in the years 1900–1904.[30] Koerber's social background was firmly anchored in the civil and military service elite of Austria(-Hungary), and, as will be argued below, Koerber even identified himself to such an extraordinary degree with the Austrian imperial state and its bureaucracy that his political project is best understood as a strongly personalized quest for the reconstruction and modernization of the supranational Josephist Rechtsstaat.

Heinrich Friedjung (1851–1920), the secondary character of the first dual biography, was born in Rostchin (Roštín) Moravia on 18 January 1851. His family moved to Vienna when he was a child, where Friedjung lived the greater part of his life. He studied at the Akademisches Gymnasium and the Benediktinergymnasium in Vienna. Beginning in 1868, he studied mainly history at the universities of Prague, Berlin, and Vienna. At the latter university he received his doctorate in 1873, after which he served as a professor at the Handelsakademie in Vienna until 1879. In that year, Friedjung was fired from this post by the Liberal minister of education, Karl von Stremayr, a result of his public political engagement for the Young-German National-Liberal movement of these years. After this, he supported himself as a publisher, journalist, and historian, becoming so successful in the latter two fields that he could support himself as an independent professional for the rest of his life.[31] Friedjung's life career would develop in the borderland between history writing, journalism, and politics,[32] a career that in its latter phases also repeatedly brought him in touch with Ernest von Koerber. With Koerber he had an interesting dual relationship, both as a historian interested in writing about the statesman Koerber, and as an active political journalist who viewed Koerber as the carrier of a political program that might just point Austria in the direction Friedjung wanted.

His politics were markedly German-national throughout his life. However, at the center of his life project was the problem of the identity of the German-Austrians. Over time, this preoccupation gradually led Friedjung to develop a strongly affirmative stance on the Habsburg monarchy as a sort of German mission in Europe. Nevertheless, the basic field of tension in the Austrian state problem studied in the first dual biography developed between German nationalism and Josephist supranationalism. Another important field of tension here transcends the form of the dual biographies and involves Koerber and Joseph Redlich (and Karl Renner): It is the one between state and society, developing between the supranational Austrian state and multinational Austrian society during the process of political modernization, i.e., the problem of the multinational Josephist state in the age of democracy, setting the Josephist Beamte against a Liberal (and a Social Democratic) political project of multinational popular sovereignty.

The second dual biography has the poet and dramatist Hugo von Hofmannsthal (1874–1929) as its main character. Hofmannsthal was born into a prominent family of industrialists and financiers in Vienna on 1 February 1874. Hofmannsthal's great grandfather Isaak Löw Hofmann (1759–1849) had come from Bohemia to Vienna in 1788, where he became a prominent member of the Grossbürgertum and an important member of the Jewish community. Löw Hofmann was ennobled in 1827 as Edler von Hofmannsthal, which became the name of his descendants. In the following generations, the Hofmannsthals completed the assimilation to the Catholic Viennese Grossbürgertum. Hugo von Hofmannsthal attended the Akademisches Gymnasium in Vienna and then started the traditional law studies of his family and class at the University of Vienna. In 1895 he changed to studies of philology, and in 1899 he received his doctorate. Already during his studies at the Akademisches Gymnasium in the early 1890s, Hofmannsthal had become an instant success as a Wunderkind poet and was included in the Jung-Wien circle. His major breakthrough as a dramatist came in 1903 with the success of his play Elektra (after Sophocles), directed by Max Reinhardt, in Berlin, after which he successfully supported himself as an author.[33]

Hofmannsthal's lifelong struggle with the problem of an Austrian culture and identity will here be juxtaposed to the life career of Hofmannsthal's youthful friend Leopold von Andrian (1875–1951). Andrian represents a purely Austrianist position on the problem of Austrian culture, though Hofmannsthal had a much more complex position on this matter. Andrian early appointed himself Hofmannsthal's "Austrian conscience," watching over his friend's uncertain balance act on the borderline between German culture and "true" Austrian culture, as Andrian would have it. Ironically, the arch-Austrian Andrian was born in Berlin on 9 May 1875, but the family soon moved to the city, Vienna, that would become very important to Leopold's strong identification with Austria. The Andrian family was an old and prominent Austrian baronial family, von Andrian zu Werburg. Andrian first attended the Jesuit school of Kalksburg outside Vienna as an internist and then moved to the Schottenstift Gymnasium in the city of Vienna. In the 1890s he belonged to the Jung-Wien circle together with Hofmannsthal, when he also wrote one of the paradigmatic texts of this group, the novel *Der Garten der Erkenntnis* (1895). In the second half of the 1890s, Andrian finished his law studies and then entered into a diplomatic career that took him to different parts of the world during the next ten years.[34]

In 1911, Andrian became consul general in Warsaw in the Russian part of Poland, a posting that would become closely tied to his struggle for the Austrian identity during the war years, a struggle that will be followed as a counterpoint to Hofmannsthal's simultaneous political activities during these years in part two below. The central problem treated in part two is one of Austrian (cultural) identity. There is also a field of tension between parts one and two, between Andrian and Friedjung, who constitute the mutually most distant points in an identity landscape that is ordered by the fundamental conflict of the Austrian identity as culturally something wholly separate from Germany, as an Austrian nation (Andrian), or as an integrated part of a larger German cultural community, a part of the German nation (Friedjung).

The third and last dual biography has the professor of constitutional and administrative law, historian, and Liberal parliamentarian Josef Redlich (1869–1936) as its main character. Redlich was born on 18 June 1869 in Göding (Hodonin), Moravia, into a German-Jewish family of prominent industrialists. In 1878, at the age of nine, he moved to Vienna with his brother, where the two of them attended school. Just like Friedjung and Hofmannsthal, Redlich attended the school of the German-Liberal Bürgertum, the Akademisches Gymnasium, and later he studied law at the University of Vienna. His years of study, 1887–1891, also entailed studying at the universities of Tübingen and Leipzig. His law studies were followed by the usual period of state service, in Redlich's case at the Statthalterei in Brünn (Brno), capital of his home province, Moravia. After some hesitation with regard to his choice of a career, in the latter half of the 1890s Redlich concentrated on constitutional history. He became an authority in the field of English constitutional and administrative history, and in later years he had a full-blown academic career in the United States, topped off by a professorship at Harvard in 1926. Redlich's first marriage, in 1897, entailed his conversion to Protestantism. Late in life Redlich then also converted a second time, to Catholicism (in 1931).[35]

The main focus in the present work will stress Redlich's political career from 1906 to 1918 as a Liberal parliamentarian, and his parallel scholarly interest in the history of the Austrian imperial state. The latter resulted in the publication from 1908 to 1929 of a series of works on the history of modern multinational Austria, which will here be read as a part of Redlich's intense preoccupation with the problem of bringing the multinational Austrian state into modernity, into the age of democracy.

Redlich had become acquainted with Karl Renner (1870–1950) in the late 1890s when the two were moving in the same circles of Liberal and Social Democratic student societies in Vienna. Renner was born in Unter-Tannowitz (Dolní Dunajovice) into a family of small landowners in the mixed German-Czech province of Moravia on 14 December 1870. The family was firmly of peasant stock and equally firmly of German origin, as he would emphasize in his memoirs. Karl's father went bankrupt in 1885, after which to a great extent he had to fend for himself, which he did with great success, even financing his studies at the Gymnasium in Nikolsburg (Mikulov) through his own income. Drawn early into the circles of Social Democracy, he was diligently active in various educational activities within the labor movement. Renner would also study law at the University of Vienna in the late 1890s. He received his doctorate in 1898, and the year before he had accepted a post as a librarian in the library of the parliament. In the years 1897 to 1907, Renner led a sort of double existence as a civil servant and as a political writer under different pseudonyms. In the latter year he took a full step into politics when he was elected to the Austrian parliament as a representative of the Social Democratic party, after which began a remarkable political career that was topped off with his role as a founder of two Austrian republics in 1918 and 1945.[36]

The present approach to Renner will mainly limit itself to the period from 1897 to 1918 and will examine his preoccupation with the problem of bringing the imperial Austrian state into the age of democracy through his writings and actions at that time. Running in counterpoint to the primary examination of Redlich's political project, Renner's approach to this problem will also fill the function of illustrating and examining the problem of devising a democratic solution for the multinational state, a problem that to different degrees and in different ways was also affected by the imperial mentality and the German-Austrian cultural identity of both Redlich and Renner. Although their views of the Austrian state initially were similar, during World War I the political affinity between them on the question of multinational democracy would open up into a decisive difference between their conceptions.

As already stated, the focus of the investigation is on how the Austrian state problem was addressed at the center of the empire in the German-Austrian elite culture centered on Vienna. A further narrowing down of the focus is surely evident by now, but it has not yet been directly addressed. The individuals chosen belong, with one exception, to a sort of broad Liberal, progressive political spectrum in late Imperial Austria, ranging from the liberal Josephist Koerber, through the bürgerliche Liberals (of varying shapes and forms) Friedjung, Redlich, and Hofmannsthal, and over to the moderate Social Democrat Renner. This selection came about gradually through the focus of work on the Austrian state problem during a historical period of intensive modernization, a time of social and institutional change. In my view, the most interesting attempts to approach the problems created by these processes and to find solutions to them were made by people with varying types of progressive world views who therefore tried to find solutions moving with and adapting to these changes, not solutions that merely aimed to control or hinder them. Nevertheless, in the end this is a study of six different positions and responses to the Austrian state problem in the early twentieth century. Ultimately, the range and representativity of this study must be judged by the reader.

Notes

1. Josef Redlich in a letter to Hermann Bahr, 31 January 1915. *Dichter und Gelehrter. Hermann Bahr und Josef Redlich in ihren Briefen 1896–1934*, Fritz Fellner, ed. (Salzburg: Verlag Wolfgang Neugebauer, 1980), 104.
2. Josef Redlich, *Das österreichische Staats- und Reichsproblem. Geschichtliche Darstellung der inneren Politik der habsburgischen Monarchie von 1848 bis zum Untergang des Reiches.* 2 vols. (Leipzig: Der neue Geist Verlag, 1920/1926), here 1:XIII.
3. There is a wealth of works in this field. One standard work is Robert Kann, *The Multinational Empire: Nationalism and National Reform in the Habsburg Monarchy 1848–1918*, 2 vols. (New York: Columbia University Press, 1950). Another is Adam Wandruszka & Peter Urbanitsch, eds. *Die Habsburgermonarchie 1848–1918*, vol 3: *Die Völker des Reiches* (Vienna: Verlag der österreichischen Akademie der Wissenschaften, 1980).
4. That Robert Kann's half-century-old work on the Multinational Empire (cited above) retains its relevance, has much to do with its being one of the few works that does not sever the tie between the state problem and the nationality problem. Although the emphasis lies on the latter, Kann treats these two problems together. The problem of the multinational state is addressed more directly inVolume 7 of *Die Habsburgermonarchie 1848–1918*, Peter Urbanitsch and Helmut Rumpler, eds. *Verfassung und Parlamentarismus* (Vienna: Verlag der österreichischen Akademie der Wissenschaften, 2000).
5. For theoretical perspectives on the state and its historical development, see, for instance, Charles Tilly, ed. *The Formation of National States in Western Europe* (Princeton: Princeton University Press, 1975); idem, *Coercion, Capital, and European States, AD 990–1990* (Oxford: Blackwell, 1990); idem, *European Revolutions 1492–1992* (Oxford: Blackwell, 1993). See also Margaret Levi, *Of Rule and Revenue* (Berkeley: University of California Press, 1988); idem, *Consent, Dissent, and Patriotism* (Cambridge: Cambridge University Press, 1997). Compare Michael Mann, *The Sources of Social Power*, 2 vols. (Cambridge: Cambridge University Press, 1986/1993), and Wolfgang Reinhard, *Geschichte der Staatsgewalt. Eine vergleichende Verfassungsgeschichte Europas von den Anfängen bis zur Gegenwart* (München: Verlag, C.H. Beck, 1999).

6. Alan Sked argued for quite the opposite view in his revisionist account, *Decline and Fall of the Habsburg Empire 1815–1918* (London: Longman, 1989), i.e., that in the whole period 1815–1918, the Habsburg Empire was really threatened in its existence only in the revolution of 1848. The relative stability Sked identifies in the period 1849–1918 can also, as here, be viewed as a low-intensive state crisis, which, however, was never serious enough to bring about real and sorely needed reforms of the Austrian state.
7. The institutional development of the European state, with a mass of detail from the actual European states, is followed in brilliant fashion by Reinhard, *Geschichte der Staatsgewalt*, passim.
8. I have here opted for a bibliographical note for the whole treatment of the development of the Austrian state on the following pages. For a general Austrian history of the period 1700–1918, see Charles Ingrao, *The Habsburg Monarchy, 1618–1815* (Cambridge: Cambridge University Press, 1994); Sked, *Decline and Fall*; Robert Kann, *A History of the Habsburg Empire, 1526–1918* (Berkeley: University of California Press, 1974). On the era of Maria Theresia and Joseph II, see also *Was blieb von Joseph II.? Eine Dokumentation Internationales Symposion Melk 1980* (St. Pölten-Wien: Niederösterreichisches Pressehaus, 1980); Erich Zöllner, ed. *Österreich im Zeitalter des aufgeklärten Absolutismus* (Vienna: Österreichischer Bundesverlag, 1983); Richard Plaschka, Grete Klingenstein Georg, eds. *Österreich im Europa der Aufklärung. Kontinuität und Zäsur in Europa zur Zeit Maria Theresias und Josephs II*, 2 vols. (Vienna: Verlag der österreichischen Akademie der Wissenschaften, 1985); Ritchie Robertson & Edward Timms, eds. *The Austrian Enlightenment and its Aftermath. Austrian Studies 2* (Edinburgh: Edinburgh University Press, 1991). On the Austrian state problem in the period 1804–1848, see Wolfgang Häusler, "Kaiserstaat oder Völkerverein? Zum österreichischen Staats- und Reichs-problem zwischen 1804 und 1848/49," in *Was heisst Österreich? Inhalt und Umfang des Österreichbegriffs vom 10. Jahrhundert bis heute*, Richard G. Plaschka, Gerald Stourzh, und Paul Niederkorn, eds. (Vienna: Verlag der österreichischen Akademie der Wissenschaften, 1995), 221–254. On the late Habsburg monarchy, see also the multivolume work of the Austrian Academy of Sciences, *Die Habsburgmonarchie, 1848–1918,* vols. 1–6, Adam Wandruszka & Peter Urbanitsch, eds. and vol. 7, Helmut Rumpler & Peter Urbanitsch, eds. (Vienna: Verlag der österreichischen Akademie der Wissenschaften, 1973–2000) at present 7 volumes. See especially vols. 2 (*Verwaltung und Rechtswesen*), 3 (*Die Völker des Reiches*) and 7 (*Verfassung und Parlamentarismus*). On constitutional history, see especially Wilhelm Brauneder, *Österreichische Verfassungsgeschichte* (8th ed., Vienna: Manz, 2001), Ernst Hellbling, *Österreichische Verfassungs- und Verwaltungsgeschichte* (2nd ed., Vienna: Springer-Verlag, 1974), and also the above-mentioned vol. 7 of *Die Habsburgmonarchie 1848–1918.* Regarding the more specific problem of the constitutional monarchy, see Ernst Wolfgang Böckenförde, "Der Verfassungstyp der deutschen konstitutionellen Monarchie im 19. Jahrhundert," in idem, *Moderne deutsche Verfassungsgeschichte (1815–1918)* (Cologne: Kiepenheuer & Witsch, 1972). Concerning the period 1848–1867, the above cited work of Josef Redlich, *Das österreichische Staats- und Reichsproblem*, remains important. In time for the 150th jubilee in 1998, several works on the revolution of 1848 were published, for instance, Lothar Höbelt, *1848. Österreich und die deutsche Revolution* (Vienna: Amalthea-Verlag, 1998), and Pieter Judson, *Wien brennt! Die Revolution von 1848 und ihr liberales Erbe* (Vienna: Böhlau Verlag, 1998). On the neoabsolutist period, see Johann Waldenegg, and Christoph Berger, *Mit vereinten Kräften! Zum Verhältnis von Herrschaftspraxis und Systemkonsolidierung im Neoabsolutismus am Beispiel der Nationalanleihe von 1854* (Vienna: Böhlau Verlag, 2002), and Hans Loew, *Alexander Freiherr von Bach* (unpublished dissertation, University of Vienna, 1947). On

the Austrian *Verwaltung*, see Brauneder, *Österreichische Verfassungsgeschichte*, and the abovementioned vol. 2 of *Die Habsburgmonarchie 1848–1918, Verwaltung und Rechtswesen*. See also the magisterial work by Friedrich Walter, *Die österreichische Zentralverwaltung* (Vienna: Holzhausen, 1934–71 [Veröffentlichungen der Kommission für neuere Geschichte Österreichs]), and Jirí Klabouch, *Die Gemeindeselbstverwaltung in Österreich, 1848–1918* (Vienna: Verlag für Geschichte und Politik, 1968). Social histories on the Austrian Verwaltung are scarce; for two examples, see Waltraud Heindl, *Gehorsame Rebellen: Bürokratie und Beamte in Österreich 1780 bis 1848* (Vienna: Böhlau Verlag, 1991), and Karl Megner, *Beamte. Wirtschafts- und sozialgeschichtliche Aspekte des k.k Beamtentums* (Vienna: Verlag der österreichischen Akademie der Wissenschaften, 1985). Generally on the nationality problem, see the references in note 3 above. For a few important specialized works from the past few decades, see John W. Boyer, *Political Radicalism in Late Imperial Vienna. Origins of the Christian Social Movement 1848–1897* (Chicago: University of Chicago Press, 1981); idem, *Culture and Politial Crisis in Vienna. Christian Socialism in Power, 1897–1918* (Chicago: University of Chicago Press, 1995); Emil Brix, *Die Umgangssprachen in Altösterreich zwischen Agitation und Assimilation* (Vienna: Böhlau Verlag, 1982); Gary B. Cohen, *The Politics of Ethnic Survival: Germans in Prague, 1861–1914* (Princeton: Princeton University Press, 1981); Bruce M. Garver, *The Young Czech Party, 1874–1901, and the Emergence of a Multi-Party System* (New Haven: Yale University Press, 1978); Lothar Höbelt, *Kornblume und Kaiseradler. Die deutsch-freiheitlichen Parteien Altösterreichs, 1848–1918* (Vienna: Verlag für Geschichte und Politik, 1993); Pieter, M. Judson, *Exclusive Revolutionaries: Liberal Politics, Social Experience and National Identity in the Austrian Empire, 1882–1914* (Ann Arbor: University of Michigan Press, 1996); Jirí Koralka, *Tschechen im Habsburgerreich und im Europa 1815–1914: sozialgeschichtliche Zusammenhänge der neuzeitlichen Nationsbildung und der Nationalitätenfrage in der böhmischen Ländern* (Vienna: Verlag für Geschichte und Politik, 1991); Jan Kren, *Die Konfliktgemeinschaft. Tschechen und Deutsche 1780–1918* (Munich: Oldenbourg Verlag, 1996); Gerald Stourzh, *Die Gleichberechtigung der Nationalitäten in der Verfassung und Verwaltung Österreichs, 1848–1918* (Vienna: Verlag der österreichischen Akademie der Wissenschaften, 1985). On the problem of the Austro-Hungarian political system, see Éva Somogyi, *Der gemeinsame Ministerrat der österreichisch-ungarischen Monarchie 1867–1906* (Vienna: Böhlau Verlag, 1996). In regard to the struggle over the interpretation of this structure, see the article by Gerald Stourzh, "Der Dualismus 1867 bis 1918: Zur staatsrechtlichen und völkerrechtlichen Problematik der Doppelmonarchie," in Helmut Rumpler & Peter Urbanitsch, eds. *Die Habsburgermonarchie 1848–1918*, vol. 7 (Vienna: Verlag der österreichischen Akademie der Wissenschaften, 2000). On the Badeni crisis, see Berthold Sutter, *Die Badenischen Sprachenverordnungen von 1897*, 2 vols. (Graz: Böhlau Verlag, 1960/65). And on Austrian Social Democracy, see Hans Mommsen, *Die Sozialdemokratie und die Nationalitätenfrage im habsburgischen Vielvölkerstaat* (Vienna: Europa-Verlag, 1963), and Peter Kulemann, *Am Beispiel des Austromarxismus. Sozialdemokratische Arbeiterbewegung in Österreich von Hainfeld bis zur Dollfuss-Diktatur* (Hamburg: Junius Verlag, 1979).

9. On Max Weber's model of legale Herrschaft, see, for instance, Reinhard Bendix, *Max Weber—Das Werk. Darstellung—Analyse—Ergebnisse* (Munich: Piper, 1964), 317–47. On Charisma, see ibid., 247–50.
10. On this, see John W. Boyer, "The End of an Old Regime: Visions of Political Reform in Late Imperial Austria," *Journal of Modern History* 58, No. 1 (1986): 159–193.
11. See James Shedel, "*Fin de Siècle* or *Jahrhundertwende*. The Question of an Austrian Sonderweg," in *Rethinking Vienna 1900*, Steven Beller, ed. (New York and Oxford: Berghahn

Books, 2001), 80–104 (quotations on 90–91). Shedel refers to Heindl, *Gehorsame Rebellen*, for the central argument here on the bureaucracy as the carrier of the Josephist spirit of the Rechtsstaat.

12. This part of Shedel's argument is developed in Shedel, "*Fin de Siècle* or *Jahrhundertwende*," 93–98. The argument on the Liberals retaining their influence beyond the 1890s, through their positions in the Verwaltung, had been advanced by Shedel in 1981; see James Shedel, *Art and Society. The New Art Movement in Vienna 1897–1914* (Palo Alto, CA: Society for the Promotion of Science and Scholarship, 1981), 48–50, 60–61.
13. As far as I know, apart from very few exceptions this mental structure has never been properly addressed in historical scholarship. Nevertheless, in a patriotically engaged treatment of the Austrian identity by Friedrich Heer, *Der Kampf um die österreichische Identität* (Vienna: Böhlau Verlag, 1981), the latent imperial mentality, or perhaps even imperial Phantomschmerz (Klemperer), is obvious enough, even as late as in the second half of the twentieth century. As a remnant structure in the interwar era and later, this mentality has been addressed by Fritz Fellner and Klemens Klemperer. See Fritz Fellner, "Die Historiographie zur österreichisch-deutschen Problematik als Spiegel der nationalpolitischen Diskussion," in *Österreich und die Deutsche Frage im 19. und 20. Jahrhundert*, Heinrich Lutz & Helmut Rumpler, eds. (Munich: Oldenbourg Verlag, 1982), 33–59, and idem, "The Problem of the Austrian Nation after 1945," in *Journal of Modern History* 60 (1988): 264–289. Both these articles have recently been reprinted in Fritz Fellner, *Geschichtsschreibung und nationale Identität. Probleme und Leistungen der österreichischen Geschichtswissenschaft* (Vienna: Böhlau Verlag, 2002), 145–172, 185–209. See also Klemens Klemperer, "Das nachimperiale Österreich, 1918–1938: Politik und Geist," in Lutz & Rumpler, eds. *Österreich und die deutsche Frage*, 300–317.
14. For the Austrianist position, see especially Ernst Bruckmüller, *Nation Österreich. Kulturelles Bewußtsein und gesellschaftlich-politische Prozesse* (Vienna: Böhlau Verlag, 1996), and Heer, *Der Kampf um die österreichische Identität.*
15. For the Germanist position, see Fellner, *Geschichtsschreibung und nationale Identität.*
16. This was demonstrated in the 1980s and early 1990s when a heated intellectual debate on the problem of an Austrian identity or nation was conducted; it can be viewed as an Austrian *Historikerstreit.* It started before the Waldheim affair, but then became entwined with this debate. For the central contributions to the debate, see Gerhard Botz & Gerald Sprengnagel, eds. *Kontroversen um Österreichs Zeitgeschichte. Verdrängte Vergangenheit, Österreich-Identität, Waldheim und die Historiker* (Frankfurt am Main: Campus Verlag, 1994); Karl Dietrich Erdmann, *Die Spur Österreichs in der deutschen Geschichte. Drei Staten, zwei Nationen, ein Volk?* (Zürich: Manesse Verlag, 1989); Gerald Stourzh, *Vom Reich zur Republik. Studien zum Österreichbewusstsein im 20. Jahrhundert* (Vienna: Edition Atelier, 1990); Herwig Wolfram & Walter Pohl, eds. *Probleme der Geschichte Österreichs und ihrer Darstellung* (Vienna: Verlag der österreichischen Akademie der Wissenschaften, 1991); and the works by Fritz Fellner quoted above. For an interesting perspective on the German-Austrian identity, the findings of which partly cancel out the nationalist logic of the opposing camps of the above-quoted *Historikerstreit*, see Jörg Kirchhoff, *Die deutschen in der Österreichisch-Ungarischen Monarchie. Ihr Verhältnis zum Staat, zur deutschen Nation und ihr kollektives Selbstverständnis (1866/67–1918)* (Berlin: Logos Verlag, 2001).
17. Generally on the question of the formation of national identities in Europe, see Benedict Anderson, *Imagined Communities. Reflections on the Origins and Spread of Nationalism* (London: Verso, 1983); Ernest Gellner, *Nations and Nationalism* (Oxford: Blackwell, 1983); and Eric Hobsbawm, *Nations and Nationalism since 1780* (Cambridge: Cambridge University Press, 1990). On Austrian nation-building, see William T. Bluhm, *Building an Austrian*

nation. The Political Integration of a Western State (New Haven: Yale University Press, 1973), and Peter J. Katzenstein, *Disjointed Partners: Austria and Germany since 1815* (Berkeley: University of California Press, 1976). On Austrian national identity, see especially Bruckmüller, *Nation Österreich*, and Heer, *Der Kampf um die österreichische Identität*. On the ambivalence of Austrian identity vis-à-vis Germany, see Peter Thaler, *The Ambivalence of Identity: The Austrian Experience of Nation-Building in a Modern Society* (West Lafayette, Ind.: Purdue University Press, 2001), and Matthias Pape, *Ungleiche Brüder. Österreich und Deutschland 1945–1965* (Cologne: Böhlau Verlag, 2000). On the history of the concept of Austria, see Plaschka et al., eds. *Was heißt Österreich?*, and Erich Zöllner, *Der Österreichbegriff. Formen und Wandlungen in der Geschichte* (Vienna: Verlag für Geschichte und Politik, 1988).

18. On the history of the concept of Austria, see Plaschka et al., eds. *Was heißt Österreich?*, Wolfram & Pohl eds., *Probleme der Geschichte Österreichs*, and Zöllner, *Der Österreichbegriff*.
19. On this, see Alfred Kohler, "Die europäische Bedeutung des Begriffs 'Casa de Austria'," in *Was heißt Österreich*, Plaschka et al., eds., 135–147, and Zöllner *Der Österreichbegriff*, 55ff.
20. On this elite consciousness of Austria, see Grete Walter-Klingenstein, "Was bedeuten 'Österreich' und 'österreichisch' im 18. Jahrhundert? Eine begriffsgeschichtliche Studie," in Plaschka et al., eds. *Was heißt Österreich?*, 149–220.
21. See Bruckmüller, *Nation Österreich*, on the origins of the "Hofratsnation." Bruckmüller developed his view from the first edition of *Nation Österreich* in 1984 through several intermediate stages, later specifying it by emphasizing the socially broader, but almost exclusively *German*-Austrian character of the social basis of this Austrian consciousness. See here also Ernst Bruckmüller, "Die Frage nach dem Nationalbewußtsein in der österreichischen Geschichte unter sozialhistorischem Aspekt," in Wolfram & Pohl, eds. *Probleme der Geschichte Österreichs*, 53ff. (*"Thesenkorrektur"*); Ernst Bruckmüller, "Österreichbegriff und Österreichbewußtsein in der Franzisko-Josephinischen Epoche," in Plaschka et al., eds. *Was heißt Österreich?*, 255–288; and Ernst Bruckmüller, "Die Entwicklung des Österreichbewußtsein," in *Österreichische Nationalgeschichte nach 1945. Die Spiegel der Erinnerung: Die Sicht von innen*, vol. 1, Robert Kriechbaumer ed. (Vienna: Böhlau Verlag, 1998), 369–396.
22. See Häusler, "Kaiserstaat oder Völkerverein?" on the period of the Austrian empire. See Heer, *Der Kampf um die österreichische Identität*, especially 171ff, for the important role this period plays in the modern conception of an Austrian nation. See also Felix Kreissler, *Der Österreicher und seine Nation: Ein Lernprozeß mit Hindernissen* (Vienna: Böhlau Verlag, 1984) in regard to this.
23. On the history of Austria and the German question, see, for instance, the anthologies on this problem by Robert Kann & Friedrich Prinz, eds. *Deutschland und Österreich. Ein bilaterales Geschichtsbuch* (Vienna: Jugend und Volk, 1980); Heinrich Lutz & Helmut Rumpler, eds. *Österreich und die deutsche Frage im 19. und 20. Jahrhundert* (Munich: Oldenbourg Verlag, 1982); and Helmut Rumpler, ed. *Innere Staatsbildung und gesellschaftliche Modernisierung in Österreich und Deutschland 1867/71–1914. Historikergespräch Österreich—Bundesrepublik Deutschland 1989* (Vienna: Verlag für Geschichte und Politik, 1991).
24. See Isabel F. Pantenburg, *Im Schatten des Zweibundes. Probleme österreichisch-ungarischer Bündnispolitik 1897–1908* (Vienna: Böhlau Verlag, 1996), on this identity aspect of the Dual Alliance.
25. On this, see Heer, *Der Kampf um die österreichische Identität*, for instance, 394ff. As Fritz Fellner has argued, the *Gesamtdeutsche* view of the interwar era was an ideology centered on an attempt to reconstruct and reassert the role of Austria (and Vienna) in Germany and in

Central Europe. See Fritz Fellner, "Die Historiographie zur österreichisch-deutschen Problematik," passim, and idem, "Heinrich von Srbik—'Urenkelschüler Rankes,'" in Fellner, *Geschichtsschreibung und nationale Identität*, 330–345.

26. Bruckmüller, "Österreichbegriff und Österreichbewußtsein," 286.
27. Bruckmüller, *Nation Österreich.*
28. See Tim Duff, *Plutarch's Lives: Exploring Virtue and Vice* (Oxford: Clarendon Press, 1999), 1–10, 287–309 (quotation on 10).
29. For a recent, excellent anthology on the theory and method of the scholarly biography, see Hans Erich Bödeker, ed. *Biographie Schreiben* (Göttingen: Wallstein Verlag, 2003). On the development of the biography, see Hans Erich Bödeker, "Biographie. Annäherungen an den gegenwärtigen Forschungs- und Diskussionsstand," in idem, *Biographie Schreiben*, 9–63; Hans Jürgen von Berlepsch, "Der Wiederkehr des 'wirklichen Menschen' in der Geschichte. Neue biographische Literatur," in *Archiv für Sozialgeschichte* 29 (1989): 488–510; Christoph Gradmann, "Geschichte, Fiktion und Erfahrung—kritischen Anmerkungen zur neuerlichen Aktualität der historischen Biographie," in *Internationales Archiv für Sozialgeschichte der deutschen Literatur* 17:2 (1992): 1–16. See further the anthologies, T.C.W. Blanning, ed. *History and Biography. Essays in Honour of Derek Beales* (Cambridge: Cambridge University Press, 1996). For a very inspiring treatment of the practice of contextual biography, see Anthony J. La Vopa, "Doing Fichte. Reflections of a Sobered (but Unrepentant) Contextual Biographer," in Bödeker, *Biographie Schreiben.* Thomas Söderqvist is an eloquent advocate for the return to existential biography; see Thomas Söderqvist, "Wissenschaftsgeschichte à la Plutarch. Biographie über Wissenschaftler als Tugendethische Gattung," in Bödeker, *Biographie Schreiben* 285–325, and his biography of scientist Niels Jerne, idem, *Science as Autobiography: The Troubled Life of Niels Jerne* (New Haven: Yale University Press, 2003). For a very interesting development of the biographical approach in historical studies, see Lloyd S. Kramer, *Lafayette in Two Worlds. Public Cultures and Personal Identities in an Age of Revolutions* (Chapel Hill, N.C.: University of North Carolina Press, 1996).
30. There are several biographical articles on Koerber; see, for instance, Richard Charmatz, "Ein moderner Ministerpräsident. Dr. Ernest von Körber," in idem, *Lebensbilder aus der Geschichte Österreichs* (Vienna: Danubia-Verlag, 1947); Heinrich Friedjung, "Ernest von Koerber," in *Neue österreichische Biographie,* vol. 1, Anton Bettelheim, ed. (Vienna: Amalthea Verlag, 1923), 23–43; Alexander Novotny, "Ministerpräsident Ernest von Koerber (1850–1919)," in *Gestalter der Geschicke Österreichs*, Hugo Hantsch, ed. (Innsbruck-Vienna: Tyrolia Verlag, 1962), 485–500. See also the references below in part one.
31. For biographical information on Friedjung, see Franz Adlgasser & Margret Friedrich, "Einleitung," in *Heinrich Friedjung. Geschichte in Gesprächen. Aufzeichnungen 1898–1919*, idem, eds. 2 vols. (Vienna: Böhlau Verlag, 1997).
32. On Friedjung the historian-politician-journalist, see Fritz Fellner, "Heinrich Friedjung—Ein österreichischer Ahnherr des 'Oral History,'" in Fellner, *Geschichtswissenschaft und nationale Identität*, 293–322.
33. Biographical data on Hofmannsthal can be found in Matthias Mayer, *Hugo von Hofmannsthal* (Stuttgart: Metzler, 1993), and Werner Volke, *Hugo von Hofmannsthal. Mit Selbstzeugnissen und Bilddokumenten dargestellt von Werner Volke* (Reinbek bei Hamburg: Rowohlt Taschenbuch Verlag, 1967). There is no proper full-scale biography of Hofmannsthal. However, see Ulrich Weinzierl, *Hofmannsthal. Skizzen zu einem Bild* (Vienna: Zsolnay Verlag, 2005), for the best attempt yet to provide one.
34. For biographical information on Andrian, see, for instance, Ursula Prutsch & Klaus Zeyringer, "Einleitung," in idem., eds. *Leopold von Andrian (1875–1951). Korrespondenzen,*

Notizen, Essays, Berichte (Vienna: Böhlau Verlag, 2003), 19–28, 91–105, 235–49, 485–502, 649–61, 745–54. See also Ursula Renner, *Leopold von Andrians 'Garten der Erkenntnis.' Literarisches Paradigma einer Identitätskrise in Wien um 1900* (Frankfurt am Main: Verlag Peter Lang, 1981), and Horst Schumacher, *Leopold Andrian. Werk und Weltbild eines österreichischen Dichters* (Vienna: Bergland Verlag, 1967).

35. For biographical information on Redlich, see Fritz Fellner's biographical chapters framing Redlich's diary, in Josef Redlich, *Schicksaalsjahre Österreichs 1908–1919. Das politische Tagebuch Josef Redlichs*, 2 vols., Fritz Fellner, ed. (Graz: Böhlau Verlag, 1953/1954). See also, Amy Ng, *Nationalism and Political Liberty: Redlich, Namier, and the Crisis of Empire* (Oxford: Clarendon Press, 2004), 11ff.
36. See the three biographies of Renner: by Jacques Hannak, *Karl Renner und seine Zeit. Versuch einer Biographie* (Vienna: Europa-Verlag, 1965); by Walter Rauscher, *Karl Renner. Ein österreichischer Mythos* (Vienna: Ueberreuter, 1995); and by Siegfried Nasko & Johannes Reichl, *Karl Renner. Zwischen Anschluß und Europa* (Vienna: Holzhausen, 2000). See also Karl Renner, *An der Wende zweier Zeiten. Lebens erinnerungen von Karl Renner* (Vienna: Danubia-Verlag, 1946).

PART ONE

Ernest von Koerber (Heinrich Friedjung)

The Problem of the Austrian State

One day in mid-May 1919, the historian and journalist Heinrich Friedjung was probably browsing through the showrooms of the Dorotheum auction house in central Vienna. After leaving the Franz Josef room on the first floor, where the auction of furniture and household goods of the late former imperial Austrian minister president, Ernest von Koerber, was in progress, Friedjung would have gone up to the second floor. When he stepped into the Rössler room, nothing could have kept him from examining the books on display there. Friedjung had at this time been cultivating a many-layered interest in Ernest von Koerber for nearly twenty years, and he would not have missed out on his possibly only chance of examining Koerber's library. He would have searched for the inscribed copy of Friedrich Naumann's *Mitteleuropa*, his interest in Koerber's relationship to Naumann being fired by his own involvement with Naumann four years earlier. And when finding it, he would no doubt have flipped through its pages looking for notes in the margins or underlined passages.[1] One reason why Friedjung was probably there in the Dorotheum on one of those days in May 1919 was the strong interest in Koerber he had generally exhibited in these weeks and months. Friedjung had written the obituary on Koerber that had been in one of the largest liberal Viennese papers, the *Neues Wiener Tageblatt*, and he mingled in the illustrious crowd at Koerber's funeral, something of a parade of the old imperial bureaucratic elite.[2] During the time following Koerber's death on 5 March, Friedjung also conducted interviews with people who had been close to Koerber, trying to get information about his secretive private life and attempting to trace the whereabouts of his papers and correspondence.[3] Since the turn of the century, Friedjung had been meeting fairly regularly with Koerber, mainly in the course of his work as a political journalist, and he had also made and saved notes on these conversations.[4] One of Friedjung's last finished writing projects was actually a biographical article on Koerber, and he had also collected a lot of material in connection with this Austrian statesman. Friedjung had at least in part collected this material for the day-to-day use of his journalism. Nevertheless, judging from the mass of material, I find it also plausible that Friedjung was intending in some form to write more about Koerber. However, Friedjung survived Koerber for only somewhat more than a year and left only the biographical article behind as a finished work, which was published posthumously.[5]

Friedjung's biographical article on Koerber became the end point of his twenty-year-long preoccupation with this important Austrian statesman, a preoccupation that cannot be defined neatly as either historical or political. Friedjung's careers as a political journalist and as a historian ran parallel at least from around 1890, and they were closely interwoven. The bond between them was political, in a broad sense.[6] Because Friedjung's overt engagement in politics ended in the mid-1890s, we are tempted to view the dual tracks of Friedjung's career thereafter as a continuance of politics by other means. However, it was politics of a special sort, what could be called identity politics, that drove Friedjung to delve deeply into Austrian history, especially into the critical period from 1848 to 1866, and to engage in day-to-day political journalism, especially in questions crucial to the development of Imperial Austria, such as the relationship to Germany and the grave internal conflicts that increasingly marked Austro-Hungarian domestic politics during the course of the Dual Monarchy. Sometimes, as with Koerber, Friedjung's attempt to fashion a new historical narrative on the development of Austria fused completely with his day-to-day political writing. In instances such as these, a special quality of Friedjung's life-project becomes discernible: Friedjung attempted to write the history of Austria simultaneously as he was partaking in the enactment of this narrative, attempting to influence the course of this history as it was unfolding.

1. Heinrich Friedjung: History and Identity

During his lifetime Friedjung was known foremost as a historian and a journalist. But viewed in retrospect as a historic person, his political engagement seems to dominate, or at least to compete seriously with his image as a historian. This effect at least in part arises from Friedjung's actual partisan political activities in the 1870s and 1880s. However, there is also a definitive effect of this type in the Friedjung affair of 1909. Although his link with politics during these two periods was wholly different in character, I believe also that the latter type should be included in the category of political engagement. Especially, as will be demonstrated here, Friedjung during later years acted repeatedly in ways very similar to the Friedjung affair, i.e., trying to influence political developments by engaging directly with the top decision makers. However, Friedjung's overt political engagement fell mainly in the early part of his life. First mentioned here should be his engagement in the Jungdeutsch National-Liberal revival in Austria in the late 1870s and into the 1880s, which peaked in his collaboration on the German national Linz Program of 1882, together with Georg Schönerer, Viktor Adler, Engelbert Pernerstorfer, and others. Because of his Jewish origins, Friedjung was ousted from the increasingly anti-Semitic, radical national wing of the German Liberals in the late 1880s, after which he more and more drifted away from direct political engagement. In the first half of the 1890s, Friedjung was a member of the City Council of Vienna (1891–95) on a Liberal platform, after which he left direct political work.[7] Friedjung's historical scholarship went back to his studies in the late 1860s and early 1870s, but it received its definite focus on contemporary history only under the impression of his political engagement. After the late 1870s it was firmly focused on contemporary political history, and in his work he extensively relied on the method of interviewing the political actors. He thus established a great many relationships with individuals involved in Austrian and German politics from 1848 to 1866, which was the period on which he wrote most profusely. Moreover, he also became acquainted with a great many persons in influential positions during the last two decades of the Habsburg Monarchy. In the latter period, the fusion of historical scholarship and journalism became most evident because Friedjung used these contacts for information in his day-to-day political journalism and also for his writing of contemporary history.[8] Initially, he had financed his historical work through journalism, but after his *Der Kampf um die Vorherrschaft in Deutschland 1859–1866* (1897) had been a huge commercial success,[9] he had no problem financing his continuing work as a historian. Friedjung became a widely read and acclaimed historian, both by professional historians and by the general public.

Friedjung's parallel activities in the fields of political journalism and historical scholarship were mirrored in his interest in the question of (political) partisanship versus (historical) truthfulness, which in Friedjung's case seems to have generated a tension that propelled his very successful dual career forward.[10] While working on his history of Austria, 1848 to 1860, the identity basis of his "partisanship" became visible. Friedjung here noted that "It is not fair to ask of the narrator of contemporary events that he should refrain from partisanship, especially not when dealing with events relating to his own Heimat, which often touch his innermost feelings. No feeling human being can hope to approach such matters impartially."[11] Later Friedjung criticized what he called "philosophical history," for missing the important identity aspects of historical narration.[12] The alternative presented by Friedjung was "narrative history" which takes its point of departure in a universal human need to go over and retell experienced events and upheavals. Friedjung wrote, "After a

Heinrich Friedjung in the 1890s; Austrian National Library, ÖNB/Sign. RV3494B

shattering event, men need to act out this event again with the assistance of a knowledgeable guide."[13]

This therapeutic recounting of past events prescribed by Friedjung is not done by just anyone for any arbitrary group: it is a question of personal and collective identity. In fact, it is not difficult to discern Friedjung himself behind the above reflections on the writing of history. The "Heimat" he cannot avoid, or even the Heimat he *is obliged* to treat in a partisan manner is his own German-Austrian Heimat with its difficult historical role between Germany and the Habsburg Empire. The "shattering events" that he must go over again and again for his own sake and for the sake of his fellow German-Austrians were the failure in 1848–60 to renew the leading role of the Austrian Germans in Germany *and* in the imperial Austrian state and their subsequent exclusion from Germany in 1866. These events are also the subject of Friedjung's two main historical works, *Österreich von 1848 bis 1860* and *Der Kampf um die Vorherrschaft in Deutschland, 1859–1866*. The unparalleled success of the latter, not least in the German Reich, was probably due to its function as a way of making sense of whom and what we are and how it came to be that Germany was divided.

Twenty years earlier, the quality of existentially based identity therapy in Friedjung's approach to Austrian history had been directly discernible. In the political tract *Der Ausgleich mit Ungarn* (1877), Friedjung dealt in a more unmediated manner with the questions he would later deal with as a historian. In this work, he despaired over the lack of unity and direction that characterized Austria after the exclusion from Germany (in 1866) and the retreat from Hungary (in 1867). Friedjung's criticism of the confused and unclear political arrangements in Central Europe after the events of 1866–67 peaked in an existential outburst, which I believe is essential for the understanding of Friedjung's political engagement up to 1918. Friedjung wrote: "For the simple reason that I want to be a whole human being, I also want to be citizen of a single state. I want to have only one fatherland because I have the need to dedicate myself fully to my state. . . ."[14]

Twenty years later, when he published *Der Kampf um die Vorherrschaft in Deutschland*, Friedjung had found a new stability in his identifications, something that was not least due to political developments. As Friedjung saw it, the closing of the Dual Alliance with Germany in 1879 was a first step in the right direction, retying Austria's old bonds with Germany. The later change in the internal Austrian regime in 1899, from a government leaning in the Slavic-federalist direction to a succession of governments with more German-centralistic orientations, was entirely to Friedjung's liking. From this time on we can observe a new type of political engagement in Friedjung. Journalistically, he opposed the conservative, in Friedjung's eyes Russian-oriented, foreign minister, Agenor Goluchowski and put his pen in the service of men he judged as leading Austria in the right direction. Alois Lexa von Aehrenthal and Ernest von Koerber were two of those who from now on attracted his support.

◆

> It would not be proper to distance myself from a state that I believe fills the function of the defense line of the German nation toward the East and the South. If the [Habsburg] Monarchy does not remain true to this mission, then the Germans are also freed of their duty toward her. For forty years I have repeatedly loudly and clearly said as much.[15]

Continuity in his political convictions of the type Friedjung declares here, on the eve of World War I, finds no unequivocal support among his biographers.[16] However, a close reading of Friedjung's development seems to affirm and reinforce the impression of continuity. His deep pessimism about Austria, as expressed in his political tract *Der Ausgleich mit Ungarn* (1877), had already evaporated in 1880,[17] and this is best explained by the interceding event of the Dual Alliance, formed between Germany and Austria-Hungary in the fall of 1879. In 1877 Friedjung recommended to German-Austrians that they retreat from their historical Greater Austrian role and focus on their German identity. By 1880, however, Friedjung argued the very opposite, that the German-Austrians should identify completely with the Habsburg Empire, that they should look upon the empire as their own essentially German creation, with the function being the bearer of German civilization and prosperity, not only internally, but also beyond the borders of the empire, to the Balkans.[18]

The explanation for this shift is probably because, as Friedjung saw it, in the period 1866–79, the Habsburg Empire simply did not fulfill its German mission. But with the closing of the Dual Alliance, Friedjung experienced this bond as having been tied anew, and from this time on he fully fused his German-Austrian identity with the cause of the imperial Habsburg state. The bond between Austria and Germany created by the Dual Alliance was nevertheless rather weak and uncertain. This uncertainty continued to plague Friedjung and to propel his political project forward. He viewed the Dual Alliance as only the first step on the road to the "reunion" of the two "German" Great Powers in Europe following an unfortunate period of German division after the "civil war" ("Bruderkrieg") in 1866, and as the first step for the German-Austrians toward regaining their balance, their identity, and redefining their role in Europe after the disaster of the latter year.

We can follow the continuity of this stance throughout Friedjung's historical scholarship and political writing from the time shortly after the closing of the Dual Alliance all the way up to the fall of 1918. Two instances that can be especially highlighted here are Friedjung's meetings with the recently retired German Reichskanzler Otto von Bismarck in 1890 and his meeting with the serving Reichskanzler Theobald von Bethmann Hollweg in 1915. The first case was an interview Friedjung made during the research for his book *Der Kampf um die Vorherrschaft in Deutschland*. During this interview he focused strongly on a rather peripheral aspect of Bismarck's actions in 1879, the rather vague and never realized plans of extending the Dual Alliance into some sort of political union between Germany and Austria-Hungary. During the interview, Friedjung intensified his questioning along this line even though he got little response from Bismarck. If Friedjung in 1890 had to content himself with attempting to construct the Dual Alliance of 1879 as the lost opportunity of German (re)unification, his meeting with Bethmann Hollweg in 1915 was meant to contribute to the realization of such a (re)union during the extraordinary conditions of the ongoing war. Friedjung appeared in Berlin at this time as a representative of a German-Austrian elite network that wanted to use the Mitteleuropa euphoria of these years to bring about a union between the two empires, but Friedjung's own appearance in this role also has its background deep in his own personal history.[19]

Despite this basic continuity, changes in Friedjung's stance were manifest in how his historical attention drifts over time. In the 1880s and 1890s, he is still uncertain enough about the future of the Austrian Germans in order to delve deeply into this problem, going over the events that led to the identity crisis again and again and subsequently writing an excellent book on the question. *Der Kampf um die Vorherrschaft in Deutschland 1859–1866* is suffused by the notion that Austria was (and still is) morally inferior to Germany. This inferiority had its roots in the Counter Reformation, which according to Friedjung broke the spirit of Austrian culture and led it into absolutism and Catholic mysticism. In Prussia, though, the culturally progressive and individualist Protestantism secured a healthy development of society. Maria Theresian and Josephist Enlightenment reformism in the eighteenth century could have made the difference for Austria, but they sadly remained only historical parentheses. Under Metternich, things turned bad again, and the failure of the liberal bürgerliche Revolution in 1848 extinguished the last hope before the confrontation in 1866. In this year, according to Friedjung, the bill for hundreds of years of neglect was presented.[20]

Friedjung can be said to have closed a chapter in his therapeutic recounting of the past around the turn of the century. His final treatment of the failure of Austria was his biography of Ludwig von Benedek (1901), the general who commanded the Austrian army at Königgrätz in 1866, which in a very effective way cuts to the heart of these matters. Friedjung here recounts the story of a very able and loyal servant of the emperor, who after the defeat at Königgrätz was made to carry the full blame for the larger, true failure of the imperial regime. What Friedjung presents in this work becomes a very acute criticism of the regime of Franz Joseph and an extension of his previous criticism of the moral degeneration of Austrian culture.[21] However, the Benedek biography definitely marked the end of a phase in Friedjung's therapeutic recounting of the Austrian past. Already in the conclusion to *Der Kampf um die Vorherrschaft in Deutschland 1859–1866* (1897), Friedjung looked forward to a new era in the history of Austria and Germany, when the generation directly involved in the German "Bruderkrieg" had passed away.[22] However, his basic optimism about Austria's "new start" after the cathartic defeat of 1866 had been tempered somewhat by that internal regime, which had been established simultaneously with the beneficial German alliance of 1879. Eduard Taaffe's minister presidency from 1879 to 1893, building on a coalition of Slavic, conservative, and clerical parties and shutting out German-Austrian National-Liberalism, was seen by Friedjung as a partial restoration of the old system that had already demonstrated its historical failure.[23] But in exactly this regard another political change shortly before the turn of the century brightened Friedjung's prospects considerably.

The fall of the Badeni government over intense German national resistance in 1897 and then the fall of the following Slavic-conservative government under the Bohemian aristocrat Franz Thun in 1899 signaled a political shift in Austrian internal politics to an imperial regime resting on the centralistic high bureaucracy mainly supported by German-oriented political parties. This is at least the way Friedjung will later read this change, viewing 1899 as the most important year after 1879 for the political development of Austria.[24] After this time, Friedjung's skepticism about Austrian culture was markedly lessened. His belief in Austria was strengthened to the degree that he judged the prospects for a historical rise of the Austrian Germans, also vis-à-vis "Prussia," as definitely improved. The political shift of 1899 can be read rather clearly in the drift of Friedjung's historical imagination, because in the early years of the new century he took a deep interest in that last great period of German-Austrian rule over a centralized Austrian empire in the 1850s. In *Österreich von 1848 bis 1860* (1908/12),[25] the moral degeneration of Austria is no longer a pressing concern. Its two finished volumes deal more with the potential of the authoritarian-centralistic regime of the 1850s for regaining the hegemonic role of the Austrian Germans in Central Europe. Friedjung now sees his own role more as one to repair the deficit of appreciative studies of modern Austrian history. The affirmative stance with regard to Austria is clear, and in this work Friedjung actually carries out a broad rehabilitation of Austrian culture in the Vormärz period.[26] He also maintains much of his earlier idealization of the bürgerliche Revolution of 1848 in this work, but tends now to see these events more as centrifugal and reactionary dangers from the nationalities and provinces for the future of Austria.

The harsh centralist reaction beginning in 1849 thus receives a rather favorable treatment from Friedjung. But his main interest is invested in the modernizing authoritarian centralism of the 1850s, which he sees as carrying forth the Liberal Josephist inheritance in important regards. The new Austrian minister president in late 1848, Felix Schwarzenberg, has too much of the reactionary aristocrat and opportunist about him for Friedjung's taste. Notwithstanding this, Friedjung still cannot keep from attentively following his attempts to reestablish the effective rule of Vienna over both Germany and the Habsburg dominions. Apparently Friedjung senses that had Schwarzenberg not died prematurely, he could have become the inverted Bismarck, so to speak, and realized Friedjung's grandest hopes for the Austrian Germans.[27] Besides the political maverick Schwarzenberg, several diligent domestic reformers hold center stage in Friedjung's narrative: Franz Stadion, Alexander Bach, Karl Ludwig Bruck, and Anton Schmerling. Of these, Bach and Bruck are the most important. Especially Alexander Bach can be said to epitomize the historical dilemma Friedjung finds himself in because of his allegiance to liberalism, on the one hand, and his identification with the empire as a vehicle for the German-Austrian mission in Central Europe on the other. Bach came out of simple circumstances, and his family had a history of liberal, democratic engagement in the Vormärz era. During the revolution of 1848, Bach went through a gradual change that led him to take up government posts under Felix Schwarzenberg and thus to abandon his Liberal-bürgerliche friends and ideals. Friedjung cannot wholly approve of this behavior, but he is still full of admiration for what Bach accomplished as minister of the interior during the 1850s, especially his creation of the centralized and unified administration that ruled the whole of the Habsburg Empire for a decade in the mid-nineteenth century. The "Bach-hussars," Alexander Bach's handpicked gendarmes and administrators, who swarmed over the country and replaced locally anchored officials, were seen as forces of occupation in many parts of the empire, not least in defeated Hungary. Friedjung's evaluation of this system is ambivalent, but his admiration shines through even his critical comments.[28]

Karl Ludwig von Bruck represents another aspect of Friedjung's expectations, those of the realization of an economic Mitteleuropapolitik, ideally the realization of a customs union between Austria(-Hungary) and Germany, which extended to the Balkans and the Orient. As minister of trade, and later as finance minister, Bruck would be the driving force behind such a policy in the early 1850s, a policy that effectively came to a halt after the premature death of Schwarzenberg. Bruck's name belongs to those that Friedjung intones throughout his career as historical guiding images for Austria, especially during his own Mitteleuropa engagement during World War I.[29] Another hero of Friedjung is Anton Schmerling, who makes only a lesser appearance in *Österreich von 1848 bis 1860.*[30] Schmerling's really great historical role came only after the sea change in 1860, when the authoritarian centralism of the previous decade was dismantled. At this time he was appointed minister president over a constitutional, but still essentially centralized, Austrian Empire. Schmerling is another character that attracted Friedjung's attention as a result of his ambiguity between Liberalism and imperial bureaucratic centralism. Friedjung's judgment of Schmerling at the beginning of the new century comes out most clearly in his exchange with the French historian and specialist on Austria-Hungary, Louis Eisenmann. Friedjung would always hold Eisenmann's work in high esteem, but he had strong reservations about Eisenmann's partisanship for the Hungarians and the Czechs, and, as Friedjung never tired of repeating, his lacking appreciation of the work of the Liberal, German-Austrian bureaucracy. Eisenmann's reply to Friedjung's criticism is defensive, but he confronts Friedjung on certain questions, for example on the historical judgment of Schmerling:

> I readily admit that I have shown more of the reverse side of Schmerling's policies, but I think you exaggerate when you say that I have been through and through unfair in my judgment of him. You defend him by saying that he held the unity of the empire higher than he did Liberalism. That might be so, but what if this unity could be achieved only through true Liberalism?[31]

Eisenmann's question hits the core of Friedjung's dilemma, and Friedjung shows here just how far he at this time has gone in his identification with the old system of German-Austrian bureaucratic rule over the Habsburg Empire.

The change in Friedjung's historical interests at the beginning of the new century also finds strong resonance in his interests in contemporary political developments during the same period. He most certainly already appreciated the importance of the political shift of 1899 when Ernest von Koerber was appointed minister president in January 1900, but initially he was marking time; on the one hand he was hesitant regarding Koerber's qualities, and on the other he was expecting Koerber's career as a minister president, as so many other minister presidents in Austria at this time, to be rather short.[32] But in the following years his identification with Koerber grew, and it remained strong even during Koerber's years of retirement (1905–15). After Aehrenthal was appointed foreign minister in late 1906, Friedjung's relationship to this Austrian statesman was also intensified. In their conversations, Friedjung repeatedly brought up Koerber's name, intimating that Koerber must surely be the best choice for Austrian minister president in Aehrenthal's eyes and also in his own. In one of these conversations with Aehrenthal, Friedjung warmly declared himself to be "for Koerber," maintaining that Koerber like no other Austrian minister president had a talent for upholding the order while he unwaveringly upheld the constitutional freedoms.[33] This description also seems to delineate Friedjung's ideal balance between the constitutional freedoms of Liberalism and the order of (German-Austrian) centralist bureaucratic rule over the empire.

There are many indications that Friedjung saw Aehrenthal (as foreign minister) and Koerber (as Austrian minister president) as the political combination of his choice, the team that could have realized Friedjung's dream of the historical rise of the Austrian Germans, a combination, however, that despite Friedjung's diligent lobbying was never realized. Especially interesting in the context of Friedjung's historical scholarship during this period is the dual relationship we can discern between his political engagement in Aehrenthal and Koerber, on the one hand, and his writing on Austria of the 1850s on the other. Friedjung's expectations of Koerber actually seem to feed on his historical image of Alexander Bach. They both filled the role of the able administrator of a difficult empire, resembling one another especially in the balance between Liberalism and bureaucratic rule, which also answered to an unstable compound in Friedjung's own political persuasions.[34] In the same way, Friedjung tended to view Aehrenthal as the Schwarzenberg of his own time, perhaps his last chance of seeing that great historical mission of the Austrian Germans being fulfilled. Friedjung also approached the dynamic, but in important regards markedly conservative, not to say reactionary, Bohemian aristocrat Aehrenthal in the same careful, wary way as he had treated Schwarzenberg in his book.[35] It was as if he saw them both as highly potent but somewhat unreliable instruments to fulfill his own hopes. Friedjung also wrote profusely on Schwarzenberg during the same time he supported Aehrenthal's politics journalistically.[36]

In his relationship with Aehrenthal, Friedjung's fusion between politics and historical scholarship would become ever more accentuated. The already thin line between the two fields dissolved as Friedjung saw the opportunity for his historical vision of the rise of the Austrian Germans to be realized; during the Bosnian annexation crisis, he finally passed this line and even tried to step into the role of a historical actor himself. During World War I, he made a new attempt, engaging himself as a political activist for Mitteleuropa. However, his engagement was to no avail, and in the face of the defeat of his historical vision, Friedjung in his last years made a full circle and returned to the critical, self-therapeutic treatment of the weaknesses of Austria. This historic-therapeutic quality is evident in the only two works Friedjung began, and finished, after the dissolution of the empire. The first of these, the biographical article on Emperor Franz Joseph,[37] is critical and written in the tradition of *Der Kampf um die Vorherrschaft in Deutschland 1859–1866* as an investigation into the weaknesses of the "old system," this time of the recently dissolved Dual Monarchy. The second, the biographical article on Ernest von Koerber, deals with the able and morally untouchable individual who struggled patriotically and unselfishly in these adverse Austrian circumstances.

Friedjung on Koerber

"Ernest von Koerber was a descendant of one of those families of officers and civil servants that in a certain sense were serving as the backbone to old Austria, supplying the state with a long row of prominent men."[38] Thus begins Friedjung's recounting of Koerber's life-career. This statement essentially reflects what Friedjung had found out about Koerber's family background from his interviews and research during the weeks and months after Koerber's death. Friedjung found a family that almost exclusively consisted of military men and civil servants who had been stationed in different places throughout the empire and who had married across nationalities, but usually within the service: "The father and the grandfathers, just like the other close relatives of Koerber, belonged to this social strata, the air of which Koerber breathed from early youth until his career as a minister." Koerber particularly had many Hungarian relatives, which almost seems to make the family archetypally Austro-Hungarian.[39] Koerber was sent to a boarding school in Vienna at an early age, the Theresianische Akademie, the school par excellence for children of the governmental elite. "In those educated at the Theresianum, you invariably make the observation that they have been deprived of their youth. They seem emotionally cold, and they have loosened their ties to their families," Friedjung mused on the effective forming of future state servants in this elite school as he was interviewing Koerber's friend Friedrich Stadler in April 1919. Stadler told him that Koerber was silent, not to say secretive, about his background and his private life. But he loved to talk about political matters, Stadler went on. You only had to ask him about some event during his time in office, and he would recount it comprehensively and with a mass of detail. The relationship to Hungary was a favorite subject, and, Stadler added, "His knowledge in administrative matters was astounding." Stadler concluded that Koerber's "interests were completely dominated by public issues" and that "he devoted himself fully to his activities as a civil servant."[40]

Friedjung had under a long stretch of years gradually composed a picture of Koerber, from impressions and information received from Koerber personally and from several of his colleagues in the bureaucracy.[41] The picture of Koerber that emerges is one of strong, almost total identification with the Austrian state and its Verwaltung. Koerber has gone so up in "the service" that he almost comes across as an organic part of it, which in part seems because he was practically born into it, and also because it seems to have filled his life almost completely. His family background and schooling made his sociocultural milieu nearly identical with the Austrian(-Hungarian) state service, and Koerber never married. All this probably led Friedjung to conclude in his biographical article "that Koerber was possessed by a single consuming passion for public affairs, for the state, to which he unselfishly and eagerly devoted all his outstanding talents."[42]

When Friedjung turns to the turbulent events of Koerber's first minister presidency, the peak of his career, Friedjung has a somewhat different emphasis from both later and contemporary commentators: Friedjung focuses on the Hungarian problem, i.e., the problem of the relationship between the two parts of the monarchy, as Koerber's central concern during these years.[43] The background to this impression of Friedjung's can actually be found rather early in the overwhelming focus on the Hungarian question in his conversations with Koerber during the years 1900 to 1905.[44] The preoccupation with Hungary and with the "Gesamtstaat," in effect with constitutional questions, is the most frequent single theme in their conversations during the following years, especially those of 1903–05, when the Hungarian crisis erupted openly. Koerber played a central role in this crisis, especially from the summer of 1903 until the spring of 1904. In Friedjung's view, Koerber was a bastion against the onslaught of the Hungarians and of the Czechs, against the unity of the empire.[45] Friedjung especially appreciates what he views as the other side of the coin, Koerber's success in making peace between the German parties and the emperor after the hostility that had been caused by German national excesses during the Badeni conflict of 1897.[46]

However, in exactly this matter of Koerber's stance on the nationality question, Friedjung was forced to revise his judgment of Koerber over time. Friedjung had from early on observed Koerber's strong emphasis on the importance of constitutional continuity. In the late biographical article, he summed up Koerber's position: "Fundamental to his speeches and the advice he personally gave the emperor was the idea that the constitutional continuity, this priceless good for state and people, must be maintained."[47] Friedjung had received a deeper understanding of Koerber's stance on this question when he met him in November 1916, in the midst of Koerber's attempt to launch the political program of his second minister presidency. Friedjung was intensely involved in the German national revival in Austria during the world war, and he saw things primarily in this national-political perspective. Friedjung consequently tried to influence Koerber to carry out a coup d'état in favor of the German national program, which should establish the German identity of Austria: "I told him that it would mean missing the world-historical moment not to act decisively now." But Koerber was not impressed. Furthermore, Friedjung noted, Koerber seemed strangely preoccupied with the question of administrative reform during this "world historical moment." During the conversation, Koerber developed his stance on the constitution, saying that it was not only the question of constitutional legitimacy that hindered him from carrying out a coup d'état, but also the primary need for a thorough reform of the state through a complete administrative reform. Friedjung seems genuinely puzzled. His image of Koerber had been disturbed: "This part of his discourse made the impression on me that he saw things less from a political perspective than from a civil servant's point of view. . . . However, it would be wrong, I think, to upset his calculations. . . . With his great experience and serious sense of mission, the road chosen by him might also take us to our goal."[48]

Friedjung here recognized the fundamental political difference between himself and Koerber: his own German national interpretation of the role of the empire, and Koerber's unmediated "Austrian," Josephist interpretation. For Koerber, the Austrian state and the imperial Austro-Hungarian state in its entirety had a value of their own, a value that was invested in its constitution and institutions, and not least in its Verwaltung. While Friedjung's identity was grounded in the Heimat of the Austrian Germans, projecting this national group on the larger canvas of the empire and its historical mission, Ernest von Koerber identified himself primarily with an institutional structure that in itself did not automatically serve any special group within that society it framed. Rather, Koerber identified with that supranational Rechtsstaat, which he considered the best framework for the multinational Austrian society.

It could be Friedjung's belated recognition of the above difference between him and Koerber that made him describe Koerber as linking Austria to "a middle course" and to de-emphasize his German orientation in his late biographical article.[49] Here he even went so far as to conclude this: "As the only Austrian minister president of his era, Koerber had without hesitation laid down a comprehensive national and constitutional program, which guided his actions with great consequence. . . . Undisturbed by resistance from the left as well as the right, he went his own way."[50] As Friedjung believed, though, Koerber's way might also have led to Friedjung's own goal. This perception probably arises from the very fact that the reinforcement of state and bureaucracy in Koerber's program was something of a goal of its own. As Max Weber observed in general terms around this same time, the modern bureaucracy and the class of bureaucrats it created was—in Wolfgang Mommsen's words—"prepared to serve virtually any master, whatever his origins and whatever his objectives."[51]

In the extension, this opened up the prospect of using the Austrian Verwaltung, for example, as an instrument of the German imperial domination of Central Europe and beyond. Moreover, because a basic German element had been present in the Austrian state nearly from its beginnings, at the latest from the reign of Joseph II, the Austrian bureaucracy might nevertheless be predisposed to think and act exactly that way. However, Koerber himself would not have agreed with Weber's analysis. He would have seen the Rechtsstaat as a stabilizing structure that precisely counteracted arbitrariness and abuse in the wielding of power within Austria; in Koerber's view the Austrian Verwaltung was "objective." Even so, Friedjung may very well have been strengthened in his conviction that Koerber also followed the "German" tendency of the Josephist tradition by a letter he had received from Koerber a few years before the World War. Koerber had written this: "Despite the geographic distance between us, you have remained a loyal companion. You see, I have reread the first part and then for the first time read the second part of your work on Austria, 1848–1860, and I owe you greatly for the spiritual and inspiring hours I have received from this reading. . . . I assure you that the expression of so many sound ideas and opinions has done me good."[52] The mutual interest in and appreciation of the modernizing, authoritarian centralism of the 1850s does at least signal a certain common ground in Friedjung's and Koerber's view of the purpose of the imperial Austrian state.

2. Ernest von Koerber and the Austrian State Problem

The historical image of Koerber is strangely lopsided. It is almost completely focused on his first minister presidency in 1900–04, beyond this also incorporating his return to government positions in 1915–16 and to some degree integrating his prehistory as a very prominent Beamte in the years before his first ministerial appointment in 1897. His image almost completely lacks a private side. In this regard Koerber rather makes the impression of having been a nonperson outside of the civil service and his ministerial career. This is in part surely the result of no Koerber Nachlass having survived; thus very little private material is available to historians.[53] But this general image also in a very striking way corresponds to the lopsidedness identified by Friedjung in Koerber's *life*. Friedjung never uses the word, perhaps because the phenomenon was so common in Franz Joseph's Vienna, but his description of Koerber sounds peculiarly like the ideal typical Josephist Beamte, who devoted himself exclusively to the service, forsaking a private life to serve the state. It is interesting that Koerber's actual life also looks like the ideal type of bureaucrat created by Max Weber, an ideal type created at this very time. As the German political scientist Wolfgang Reinhard has noted, although Weber's ideal type was modeled on the Prussian bureaucracy, the oldest model for a Weberian bureaucrat can actually be found in the so-called Hirtenbrief ("pastoral letter") of 1783 by Joseph II, an instruction to the newly created Austrian bureaucracy.[54]

My own general impression after having collected and studied extensive material in connection with Koerber is that his life was virtually equal to the service and that off duty it was very withdrawn and puritanical. Of course he continued to socialize in political and especially governmental circles after his resignation as minister president in 1904.[55] However, his more intimate social intercourse seems to have taken place on a personal basis or in rather small groups, often at his home or the home of the other person(s).[56] When Koerber traveled extensively in Europe (and once to South America) after his retirement, he usually went with a single companion, his cousin Béla Szillay, and his descriptions of his days in letters to a friend, Jakob Herzog, during these travels make them look as the private continuance of the ascetic, focused life of a Josephist (or Weberian) Beamte, the days beginning early and being filled with long walks or other healthful activities at the spa he was staying in at the moment.[57] But Koerber's extremely withdrawn lifestyle after 1904, when he was financially secure (with a generous lifelong minister pension) and plenty of leisure time, was also most certainly a conscious choice of his own, a choice that can be understood as an expression of his Josephism: During this time, Koerber was still a civil servant in retirement, and as such he should continue to observe the rules of conduct of a Beamte (rules that he himself had done his best to maintain while active), not least because he could be called on by the emperor to once again serve the Austrian state in a prominent position. This also explains why Koerber almost completely disappeared from the public view from 1905 to 1915, appearing only intermittently in his one official function as vice-president (stellvertretende Kurator) of the Austrian Academy of Sciences. The perspective on Koerber as having been primarily identified with the Austrian state, that he was first and foremost a Josephist Beamte, affects the view of his historical role.

Koerber's Solution to the Austrian Problem

The Koerber government was one of the very few exceptions in late Imperial Austria to a pattern of relative slovenliness in the running of state affairs. The five years of his government were a veritable explosion of governmental activity, which has attracted a special sort of scholarly attention. His contemporaries viewed him as a "modern minister president," and the only two later works wholly focusing on Koerber have attempted to assign him a place in the grand narrative of the modernization of Europe.[58] To Alexander Gerschenkron, the author of one of these later accounts, Koerber's program in its entirety was a "program for economic development. . . . what is more, it was to be a spurt of economic development initiated and carried out by the state. . . ." According to Gerschenkron, Koerber's aim was no less than to ignite a "great spurt" in the Austrian economy that would make Austria catch up with the economic development of Western Europe.[59] Gerschenkron's focus lies completely on one of those aspects that are generally viewed as signifying Koerber's modernity, the large-scale investment program in infrastructure (such as railroads, canals, and harbor facilities), and his work is a much-needed account of a previously neglected and important aspect of Koerber's modernization policy. However, Gerschenkron's focus lies exclusively on this economic political aspect of Koerber's policies, thus unreasonably inflating its importance in Koerber's overall program. Moreover, Gerschenkron seems to make an unreflected jump from his finding Koerber to be a liberal modernizer to also viewing him as being a proponent of democracy and parliamentarism. This problem of the political quality of Koerber's policies is exactly addressed by the other main account of Koerber.

Alfred Ableitinger's interpretation of Koerber focuses on the summer of 1900 and Koerber's attempt to use constitutional reform to find a way out of fin-de-siècle Austria's paralyzing general political crisis.[60] According to Ableitinger, Koerber responded to nationalistic conflict and parliamentary breakdown by attempting to refashion the political base of the Austrian state. Centered on a progressive electoral reform, Koerber's plan aimed at letting new (ideally nonnationalistic) groups in Austria shape the composition of the new parliament. According to Ableitinger, Koerber's reform in its extension aimed at no less than creating a new identity basis for Austria, making the western half of the Habsburg Empire into something resembling the ideal of the nation-state. However, as Ableitinger himself realized, his progressive interpretation of Koerber is placed in question by the apparent authoritarian strains in Koerber's plan. First, the planned but never realized constitutional reform was to be implemented in a constitutionally dubious way, through imperial decree. Second, the reform itself contained clear antiparliamentarian measures conforming to the old monarchic principle of constitutional monarchy, rather than to the principles of popular sovereignty and parliamentarism.[61] Thus Ableitinger goes further than Gerschenkron in identifying the political character of the so-called Koerber Plan, without, however, being able to produce a comprehensive account of Koerber's political program. Some of the weaknesses in Alfred Ableitinger's and Alexander Gerschenkron's interpretations of Koerber's political program are explained by their analytical determination to see Koerber as a progressive, not just as any type of a progressive, but one molded in their own post-1945 liberal-democratic nation-state image.

However, it is possible to retain the progressive view of Koerber and to see his political program in a basic modernization perspective, simultaneously viewing him in the context of his own time and place. The point of departure here is that Koerber's political program should be viewed as strongly colored or even defined by Koerber's primary identity as a Josephist Beamte. With this point of departure, John W. Boyer's article on "visions of reform in late Imperial Austria" can supply us with the larger picture of Koerber's role. Boyer's article deals with three major models of imperial reform in the years before 1914. Besides Arch-Duke Franz Ferdinand's conservative dynastic-corporate reform plan and the progressive plans for reforming the imperial Austrian state through the popular sovereignty of the Christian Social and Social Democratic mass parties, Boyer has identified a third major model of reform: that of administrative reform. The large-scale Imperial Commission for Administrative Reform (Verwaltungsreformkommission) launched in 1911 represents Boyer's model of administrative reform. The initiative had come from Liberal parliamentarian Josef Redlich in 1909, but the commission was mainly staffed by members of the high bureaucracy. Some of its members viewed the goals of the commission mainly in practical terms: to make the bureaucracy more efficient and in tune with the times. But its core saw the project in a wider frame of reference: as the search for a new political mode of operation for the Austrian state, where the Verwaltung and the parliament, in conjunction, faced the challenge of creating a modern Austrian Wohlfahrtsstaat. This state was to be led or at least guided by the reformed bureaucracy.[62]

This model of administrative reform departed from the strong position and tradition of bureaucratic rule in Austria. The fragmentation of the model of popular sovereignty in Austria made a modernized Verwaltung a serious political alternative to or, at least as the commission tended to view itself, as a partner to the model of popular sovereignty. The predecessors of this model reach all the way back to the Josephist bureaucracy of the eighteenth century, but more recent forefathers can be found in the modernizing and authoritarian bureaucratic rule under Alexander Bach in the 1850s and the early constitutional centralism under Anton Schmerling in the first half of the 1860s. There is little doubt that Ernest von Koerber's political project should be located squarely within this tradition. Koerber was a part of this Josephist tradition of the high liberal bureaucracy, which found its last great expression in the administrative reform commission. If we view Koerber with Boyer's glasses, it is not difficult to see how Koerber's liberalism and progressiveness fits in perfectly with that authoritarian streak identified by Alfred Ableitinger. In early twentieth-century Austria, because of both historical tradition and the current political situation, the option of making the Josephist bureaucracy take the lead in the modernization of society was simply feasible and close at hand.

In its actual combination of elements, the timing with which it was implemented and especially in the determination with which it was driven forward, Koerber's program was his own creation. But it was also tied to the Josephist tradition in such an intimate way that sometimes Koerber looks more like an automaton executing the Josephist legacy of the Austrian state than an individual making autonomous decisions. Reading about Joseph II and his state reforms after coming from the study of Koerber gives us an uncanny feeling of having heard it all before. This effect stems to a great extent from the simple fact that Joseph II created the original Austrian Verwaltung; he not only shaped its esprit de corps, but he also became a living example of the Josephist Beamte. However, we would like to have this feeling further explained, for example, by concrete evidence divulging that Koerber was a great admirer of Joseph II, but no such evidence can be found, and most probably it does not exist. The reason for this may rather be indirect: in part Koerber's training at the Theresianum had inculcated these values and norms in him, and in part because the bureaucracy had a memory of its own, both of a social character and in terms of procedures and norms laid down in administrative regulations that sometimes went all the way back to Joseph II himself. In the latter, it is interesting to note that Koerber's administrative reform policies contain measures that quite concretely look like attempts to reconstruct lost modes of operation of the original Josephist Verwaltung.[63]

Even more important in this regard was probably the Bach era, a period just coming to an end as Koerber entered the Theresianum in 1859, only 15 years before Koerber entered the Verwaltung in 1874. In the Bach era, a whole new administrative structure had been put in place, one that had to be filled by a completely new corps of civil servants. Bach also did his utmost to inculcate a new esprit de corps, a Berufsethos, in this newly created organization; it has been judged that his ideal of the unitary Verwaltung as the carrier and guarantor of the unitary Austrian state actually came to suffuse the new civil service corps. Also, Bach organizationally strengthened the unity and centralism by making the interior ministry more directly involved also in those newly created lower levels of the administration that now came into direct contact with the population. One expression of the aim to enable the central administration to enforce its will locally was the creation of the gendarmerie, the organization that has come to be closely identified with the Bach system. Koerber's father, Joseph von Koerber, was an officer in the gendarmerie, which interestingly makes Koerber the son of a "Bach-Hussar." At the time Koerber entered the service, the Austrian Verwaltung was most probably still an organization strongly marked by the formative experience of the Bach era.[64]

Bach's administrative system and reforms are also echoed strongly in Koerber's administrative policies. Most notably, the fundamental structure of Koerber's large administrative reform proposal of 1904 was that of making the proposed new secondary level Kreis organization into just the type of instrument that Bach's original plans had envisaged to strengthen the unity of the central administration and to make it control also the lower levels of this administration more closely. Koerber's program of making the primary level, the Bezirkshauptmannschaften, into a system with more numerous and geographically smaller districts also echoes Bach's system of many small Bezirksämter in close contact with the local population. Here also is the case of the inspection system implemented by Koerber in 1900, which echoes Bach's plans of making the later-abolished Kreis into just such a supervisory instrument, enabling the interior ministry to closely supervise the administration's lower levels. Furthermore, when Koerber reorganized the interior ministry in 1900, he created a new "controller" function, i.e., he assigned a civil servant (the first Sektions-Chef) to more or less supervise the whole of the ministry's agenda, and this civil servant reported directly to the minister (Koerber himself). A sign of the importance attached by Koerber to the Bach legacy was that he especially recruited Anton Pace from outside the ministry to fill this post. Pace was a longtime editor of the Josephist bible, *Ernst Mayerhofers Handbuch für den politischen Verwaltungsdienst*, a work originating in the Bach era and that had collected all the regulations and administrative knowledge of the Josephist Verwaltung between its covers.[65]

Perhaps the single most important instance of this historical continuity behind Koerber's project is the high priority the Josephist tradition gave to shaping the individual civil servants and to tying them closely to the state. Joseph II lay behind the original act documenting this general European trend toward bureaucratization, his Hirtenbrief of 1783, which contained wide-ranging instructions on how the Austrian Beamte should conduct them within and without the service, a document that has been identified as bearing a strong resemblance to Max Weber's ideal type of the bureaucrat created in the early twentieth century.[66] Historically, documents like the Hirtenbrief had a dynamic, action-oriented character. Joseph II created and shaped a new instrument for his reforms through the original Hirtenbrief, and similar documents appear in the history of the Josephist Verwaltung at critical junctures. A most important instance here was the very similar administrative instruction Alexander Bach issued on his appointment as Austrian interior minister in August 1849, when he was about to start his far-reaching program of re-creating the Austrian Verwaltung after the revolution of 1848. The aim was also of a fundamental nature: to reestablish the Austrian state at a time when it had almost gone under.[67]

Koerber issued two such basic administrative instructions; the first in January 1900 and the second in November 1916. Both were signals setting off his two attempts to set the Austrian state on a new course. The one in 1916 came in a very critical situation for Austria during World War I, but it was issued only a few days before Franz Joseph's death, which cut short Koerber's second minister presidency, and it was never followed by the intended program. The instruction in January 1900 can also be seen to have come at a critical juncture: After intensive nationalist conflict since the Badeni crisis of 1897, in part leading to the paralysis of the Austrian parliament, the Austrian state as created in 1867 to contemporaries most probably looked more or less finished.[68] Koerber's instruction of 1900 was the signal starting a comprehensive program for refashioning the Austrian state, a program that was based on an extensive administrative reform program, but that also operated on the constitutional and political institutional level. In a general way, Koerber's response can be compared with that of Alexander Bach fifty years earlier. Although his political project for all practical purposes was over in 1904—he never again had an opportunity as he did in 1900–1904 to shape developments in a more fundamental way—it should nevertheless be noted that he continued to view himself as a minister president in waiting. Consequently, he continued to be an influence indirectly. It is, for example, possible to view the imperial administrative reform commission during the years 1911–14 as being tied to Koerber's program because it was staffed by a whole group of civil servants that had served in Koerber's interior ministry in

1900–1904, partly in central roles in his administrative reform program. One of them was the chairman of the commission, Erwin von Schwartzenau, who was also appointed interior minister by Koerber in his second government in 1916 and who intended to carry on with the administrative reform project at this time.[69]

Both Ableitinger and Gerschenkron noted the administrative reform program in their accounts of Koerber, but they failed to see it as a central element in Koerber's solution to the Austrian problem.[70] However, although administrative reform was a defining component in this project, it was not restricted to measures in this field. On the contrary, Koerber's program was guided by its overarching, truly Josephist aim to reconstruct and reassert the political role and identity of the Austrian state, which had been deeply affected by the internal political conflicts within Austria and between Austria and Hungary in the late nineteenth century. On a basic level, this meant reconstructing the mode of operation of the political system of the Austrian state and, by extension, of the imperial Austro-Hungarian state according to the blueprints laid down in the constitutional acts of 1867–68. Especially Koerber's legalistic stance on so many questions should be seen in this light. Moreover, this stance ultimately rested on the fundamental notion of Austria as a Rechtsstaat and the Verwaltung as the "objective" instrument of this Rechtsstaat. In the last instance, it was this Rechtsstaat that should be salvaged and reconstructed.

In such a view of Koerber's aims, both his investment program (Gerschenkron) and his constitutional reform plan (Ableitinger) would be fitted into a larger picture; they would be viewed as part of a more fundamental program of bringing the multinational Austrian state through its crisis and in extension into that modern world of liberal-democratic Wohlfahrtsstaaten that was taking shape at the time. Koerber's solution was, I would argue, fundamentally that of reconstructing and buttressing the historical supranational state as a framework for a modern multinational society. There are three central documents for understanding Koerber's program. First, the constitutional reform plan for Austria of 1900 that Ableitinger focused on in his account of Koerber; second, a proposal made by Koerber shortly after his resignation in January 1905 for setting the whole empire on a new constitutional footing; and third, the large-scale reform proposal for the Austrian Verwaltung Koerber presented in December 1904. They also reflect Koerber's activities as being played out on different institutional levels, from the Austrian Verwaltung, via the Austrian state to the empire as a whole. In these three reform proposals, Koerber's aims for the reconstruction and revitalization of the political system of the multinational empire are summed up. I have presented this reading of the Koerber plan in great detail elsewhere.[71] Here I will merely sum up my earlier argument and develop it on a few points. The constitutional reform plan will be treated first and most comprehensively because it indubitably contains the key to Koerber's larger plans for regenerating the Austrian constitutional monarchy.

The Constitutional Reform Plan

The constitutional reform plan of 1900 aimed at adapting the dual political system of the constitutional monarchy to the social and political changes that had taken place in Austria since the 1860s. Its main element, a new, markedly progressive electoral law was geared at creating a parliament that better reflected the actual social and ethnic composition of Austria. In the process, it also eliminated electoral distortions in favor of the Germans, a national group that had been promoted by the original electoral law of 1867 and that were still so in 1900. Koerber thought he was creating an all-Austrian parliament through this reform, where nationalist conflict would be displaced by the "normal" social cleavages, as elsewhere, in modernizing Europe. Koerber's parliament would be elected by three "curiae": 60% of the seats by universal suffrage, 20% by a new, modern interest group called Intelligenz, and the last 20% by one called Industrie. From Koerber's argumentation, it seems probable that he wanted to create a Liberal-bürgerliche parliament representing Austria's multinational (in practice mainly Czech-German) Bildung und Besitz, which, however, rested on a firm, majoritarian basis of multinational (also, in practice, mainly Czech-German) Social Democracy. Liberals and Social Democrats would thus mutually serve to stabilize a progressive, reformist parliament, which Koerber judged would be an ideal partner of his own Liberal Josephist government. The state was also given a stronger unitary shape through a second element of the constitutional reform, a new language law. This law expanded the use of all languages in interaction with the Austrian Verwaltung, but it simultaneously made German the main internal administrative language. Koerber argued that this was necessary to secure the unity of the Austrian state. Through these two elements of the reform, he attempted to stabilize and harmonize the two main factors of the Austrian political system of constitutional monarchy, the monarchic government and the popular parliament.

As Alfred Ableitinger concluded in his analysis of the constitutional reform plan, Koerber came down strongly on the side of the monarchic principle, rejecting parliamentarization (and in extension the principle of popular sovereignty). Ableitinger views this as a fundamental problem with a plan he otherwise judges as strongly progressive. However, Koerber's choice of the monarchic principle was not conservative; it was guided by a Josephist conviction that the multinational Austrian society could not be ruled through parliamentarism, that a unitary political force independent of the nationally fragmented parliament was needed that could function to stabilize and guide political developments in Austria. Furthermore, Koerber did not completely reject popular sovereignty; he only restricted it to its proper sphere of activity according the system of constitutional monarchy. Indeed, his interpretation was more in harmony with the existing constitution than had been an outright attempt to introduce parliamentarism and the principle of popular sovereignty, because the Austrian December Constitution of 1867 built on a dual monarchic and popular legitimacy. This also made the Austrian political system into a dual structure, where government and state stood across a constitutional divide from parliament and people, and it was this dual structure Koerber attempted to modernize. He did not try to follow what in retrospect looks like the "natural" irreversible process of rising popular sovereignty that led to the establishment of the democratic, parliamentarian nation-state as the universal (Western) ideal.

Erich Wolfgang Böckenförde has meticulously analyzed the concept and practice of constitutional monarchy, judging that it had an inherent tendency either to develop into full popular sovereignty or to regress back into full absolutism. However, he sees an exception to this instability where there existed a fundamental historical legitimacy grounded in the long history of the polity in question. Here it can be argued that Koerber could make a strong case for a modernized constitutional monarchy, since the Austrian state had a longer and more stable historical legitimacy to build on than most other European states. [72] It was arguably this historical legitimacy that lay behind Koerber's legalism and emphasis on the importance of constitutional continuity; the historically legitimated Rechtsstaat was perhaps the most stable foundation to be found on which a modern multinational polity could be built.

Beyond this main aim of the constitutional reform, it also contained measures "trimming" the political system, making it more efficient and giving it increased capacity to further a modernization of Austrian society. Through the restriction of the sphere of operation of the emergency paragraph (§14) of the December Constitution to true state emergencies, Koerber deprived government of its capacity to conduct daily business without parliament, a possibility that had been much abused in the past few years. Through a change in the business order of the lower house of parliament, Koerber correspondingly, restricted the possibility (of the parliamentarians) of obstructing the legislative process. It could be said that he disarmed both the two main factors (government and parliament) in the Austrian political system and made them more dependent on mutual cooperation.[73] The need of the mutual cooperation would also further the regeneration and modernization of the dual system of constitutional monarchy; although falling short of parliamentarism, it would arguably force the government into a true cooperation with parliament in the modernization of Austria.

In the almost triumphant final lines of the report attached to the reform plan, Koerber concluded with these words: "The unity of the state is expressed more clearly and effectively in the new lower house of parliament [Abgeordnetenhaus] than it has ever been before."[74] His way of formulating this main result of the reform also makes it evident what comes first: it is the Austrian state that is Koerber's primary concern; the Austrian people are to be remodeled to fit and to interact better with the Austrian state. Koerber's Austrian state idea looks more like a direct reflection of the state and of the old imperial structure of domination than of any group within it, be it German, Hungarian, Slavic, aristocratic, proletarian, or whatever. Simultaneously, Koerber's plan had a clear progressive, if somewhat paternalistic, tendency that might have had a noticeably positive effect on the development of some sort of democratic multinational politics. At the very least, it could have functioned to stabilize constitutional politics in the Austrian multinational setting.

As it were, Koerber's constitutional reform plan was laid ad acta in the Imperial Chancellery (Kabinettskanzlei) in July 1901. Most probably Franz Joseph no longer found such drastic measures necessary after having seen Koerber's parliamentary triumphs during the spring and the passing of the large investment bill after diligent parliamentary work in the beginning of June 1901. Koerber always maintained that the "spirit of the constitution guided his reform," but notwithstanding this, as Ableitinger stressed, it was clearly unconstitutional in its planned mode of implementation. Nevertheless, it should also be noted here that Koerber quite seriously saw his planned unconstitutional measure as *restoring* the constitutional foundations of the state.[75] In view of his documented legalism, indeed, how he tended to view constitutional continuity as vital for the Austrian state, the planned coup d'état should be taken as an indication of how serious he experienced the situation in 1900. In Koerber's perception, at least, it was probably on par with the situation confronted by Alexander Bach in 1849.

As Alfred Ableitinger has pointed out, because constitutional reform was never implemented meant that Koerber had to continue working in much the same way as he had delineated in his plans, but with the existing parliament. He did this fairly consistently throughout his minister presidency. At the beginning of each parliamentary session, Koerber presented a full working program. The large-scale infrastructural investment program of 1901, which is at the center of Gerschenkron's interpretation, was only the most sensational in a steady stream of legislative proposals that filled the parliamentary agenda. At the opening of parliament on 22 February 1900, Koerber made an archetypal presentation of this kind. As he would do many times later, he began by saying that he saw it as his most important mission to restore the working relationship between the government and parliament. He then continued with a characterization that would eventually form a standard element of his repertoire: "The government is no party government. . . . In our case that is no empty word. The great parties of this house are mostly national. . . . However, we appeal to the objectivity and unprejudiced attitude of all the parties because Austria is no nationally unitary state." After having established the way the cooperation between government and parliament should be seen, Koerber spoke at great length about the very extensive legislative program that the government and parliament were going to resolve together.[76] Taking a step back and viewing Koerber's administration in its entirety, we find that its striking characteristic is this insistence on actually attempting to force the parliament to work. Koerber repeatedly opened and closed the parliament

Plenary Hall of the Lower House of the Austrian Parliament, mid-1890s; Nachlass Josef Redlich, courtesy of Fritz Fellner, Vienna

and used every possible means to make it work—to "domesticate" it, as one observer termed it—every means except forming a permanent alliance between the government and some faction of the parliament.[77]

Even though Koerber opposed *parliamentarism*, he did not oppose *parliament*. On the contrary, he wanted to promote parliament as a crucial element of the Austrian political system. Koerber very effectively demonstrated this in the symbolic action of making one of his very first official visits in his capacity as Austrian minister president to the first speaker of the Austrian parliament, Victor von Fuchs.[78] Koerber started off his minister presidency with a meeting between the heads of the two main factors of the Austrian political system, thus signaling the centrality of this relationship. Furthermore, as the head of government Koerber worked very actively with his counterparts in parliament. The tendency of his constitutional reform plan is echoed in the way he interacted with parliament.

Koerber began his minister presidency by attempting to overcome the conflict between the Czech and German parties in a series of conciliations conferences (Verständigungskonferenzen) held in February and March 1900. Here he tried to bridge the gap between the moderate National-Liberal parties of these two peoples, which he wanted to give a central place to in his political program. Koerber kept on inviting to such conferences until 1903, but with diminishing returns. Instead, he soon started working directly with the parties to the conflict. The German-Liberals viewed Koerber as "their" minister president, in contrast to the "Czech" Franz Thun; Koerber thus had the wanted support of the German-Liberals from the start. He therefore focused his energies on winning the Czech National-Liberals: he brought one of their numbers, Antonín Rezek, into his government as Landsmannminister (representative of the Czech people). Koerber also had several personal contacts with leading personalities in the Czech camp and tried to meet their political demands. Koerber's efforts here should be seen against the backdrop of strong sentiments among the Czech Liberals at the time, that Austria should be governed by a Czech-German Liberal coalition; such a constellation fit well with Koerber's ideals of a Liberal-Social Democratic parliament.[79]

The constitutional reform plan is also echoed in Koerber's attempt to win the trust of the Social Democrats. He kept in contact with their party executive through Engelbert Pernerstorfer and made a general effort at ending all government persecution of the Social Democratic party. An interesting instance of this cooperation was when Koerber brought in the young Social Democratic theorist Karl Renner as an informal adviser on the question of electoral reform. As John W. Boyer has pointed out, the Social Democrats demonstrated a surprising degree of trust and confidence in the "objectivity" of the central ministries and this tendency was markedly reinforced under Koerber, who actively worked to win the Social Democrats for his plans. This also fits well with the program exhibited in Koerber's constitutional reform plan: Koerber viewed the Social Democrats as the coming dominant mass party in the Austrian parliament and accorded them a central place in his political plans.[80]

Notwithstanding this, in the spring of 1900 Koerber chose to support the Social Democrat's main competitors, the Christian Socials, as the hegemonic party in the imperial capital of Vienna. The municipal franchise reform he sanctioned in March 1900 and recommended for imperial sanction in practice gave the city of Vienna over to the Christian Socials until 1918. Koerber here argued, and Franz Joseph agreed, that the Christian Socials was the best political foundation to be found for the imperial capital after the collapse of the formerly hegemonic Liberals. In fact, Karl Lueger's views on the Austrian political system corresponded to a marked degree with Koerber's. As John W. Boyer observed, "one of the few real political beliefs that Karl Lueger held throughout his life was a conviction that the Austrian parliament had to function in regular and predictable modes, not only to protect the 'people' against the state, but also to protect the state against the 'people'. . . . Lueger viewed the parliament as a co-equal partner with the civil service in managing the Austrian political system."[81] Koerber had therefore found a good partner in the Christian Socials, though he tended to prefer the Social Democrats as the Austrian-wide, state-supporting mass party.

Ernest von Koerber as Minister President; Austrian National Library, ÖNB/Sign. NB901985B

Despite his focus on gaining the support of the Liberals and the two large democratic mass parties, Koerber's own political preferences are probably best disclosed by the closest thing he came to a political alliance: the German-Liberal wing of the Great Landowners curia, the Verfassungstreue Grossgrundbesitz. The ideology of this party, based on a narrow, elite interest group, was old-Liberal and Great-Austrian and therefore in important regards very close to the Liberal Josephism of Koerber himself. At an early stage this party unilaterally declared its members to be in support of Koerber's program, and Koerber collaborated closely but informally with them until the end of his minister presidency.[82] I believe the staunch support of this party indicates a not-negligible support for Koerber in broad sections of the imperial (both aristocratic and bureaucratic) elite, who saw Koerber as a potential restorer of the power of the imperial Austrian state.

Although Koerber's attitude to parliament was positive, his fundamental focus on the restoration of the Austrian state comes across in the way he primarily saw the parliament as a state-supporting institution. Indeed, Koerber referred to that stable parliamentary grouping he wanted to create as his "state party." I believe that the somewhat eclectic and sometimes directly self-contradictory way Koerber built his parliamentary support (Czechs and Germans, Social Democrats and Christian Socials, Liberal nationalists and multinational Social Democrats, Social Democrats and aristocratic large-land owners) testifies to his efforts that most of all tried to harmonize (if not pacify) parliament. The large-scale infrastructure project that Gerschenkron focused on in his study of Koerber is the policy equivalent to Koerber's way of building parliamentary support; with this project Koerber was able to make parliament work harmoniously and in basic unity for one-and-a-half years. However, his own choice would have been to remold parliament into a more harmonious whole *before* setting off on such policies. As Lothar Höbelt observed, Koerber was, in spite of this, very successful in normalizing Austrian parliamentary politics after the breakdown of parliament in the Badeni conflict, though in the end he paid a heavy price for this himself.[83] By 1904, Koerber had alienated most of the parties that had constituted the parliamentary support he had tried to build at the beginning of his minister presidency.

The Administrative Reform Plan

Coming as it did at a time of waning parliamentary support, Koerber's large-scale administrative reform project in the fall of 1904 gives the impression of a bureaucratic regime finally revealing its true colors. Indeed, toward its end the Koerber government increasingly relied on the Verwaltung to rule Austria. However, as I have tried to demonstrate above, the parliament played a crucial role in Koerber's project. Furthermore, administrative reform had been central to Koerber's project from the start of his ministry. This focus on the Verwaltung can be found in Koerber's first act as interior minister, the administrative instruction of 20 January 1900 that was issued to all personnel of the internal administration of Austria, Koerber's first Hirtenbrief. Just like his second Hirtenbrief (of 1916), it is squarely focused on the overriding duty of the civil servants to abide strictly to the existing laws; the civil servants were instructed to treat every individual they came into contact with impartially and to work conscientiously and diligently for the well-being of the population, to take their own initiatives to make the presence of the Verwaltung felt locally. In this way they would further the standing and influence of the Verwaltung in the local community. Koerber also emphasized that the civil servants must never let their political convictions interfere with their work. Koerber's second Hirtenbrief (of 1916) even more strongly focused on the strict observance of the law as the foundation for the relationship between state and people and the duty of the Verwaltung to guarantee the unity of these two entities, the unity of the "Gesamtheit," as Koerber expressed it in this second basic instruction.[84]

In Koerber's two Pastoral letters, the core of his administrative reform project becomes apparent: its basic aim is the regeneration of the Austrian Rechtsstaat through the renovation of its "objective" instrument, the Josephist Verwaltung. This aim is not in contradiction to the aim discernible in the constitutional reform plan; it is complementary. If the constitutional reform plan primarily focused on the renovation of one factor of the Austrian constitutional monarchy, the parliament, the administrative reform plan focused on its other main factor, the government (in the sense of its executive arm, the Verwaltung). As I have described elsewhere,[85] Koerber was very active in modernizing and centralizing the Verwaltung and making it more efficient from the beginning of his ministry. Through measures such as centralizing the whole of the internal administration, the issuance of an administrative periodical (*Verordnungsblatt des Ministerium des Innern*) containing every administrative instruction that had been issued, and an inspection system that should exercise control to ensure that these instructions were followed also locally, Koerber arguably tried to make the whole Austrian Verwaltung work in a unified and predictable fashion, in effect to move as one organism controlled from its center, the interior ministry in Vienna.

The administrative reform proposal presented to parliament in November 1904 and published a few weeks later came at the end of five years of administrative reform work. The reform proposal reveals the aims of this ongoing project: to centralize the internal administration and to give it a more direct influence in society by subordinating the autonomous administration on the level of the Länder and the Gemeinden to the state administration. A crucial aspect of Koerber's reform was the creation of a link between the previously separate state and autonomous administrations in the shape of joining these two structures through the creation of mixed state *and* popular representative organs with a state civil servant at the head. If anything, this proposed measure served only to alienate the political parties even more from Koerber,[86] but it would also have served to restore the unity of the Rechtsstaat, which had been fragmented because of the increasing politicization of local and provincial autonomous organs.

One aspect of the reform reveals that the administrative reform was also intended to complement the constitutional reform plan in another, more direct way. The reform shifted the weight of the administration to a new intermediary level of administrative organs, the Kreis, placed between the Länder (provinces) and the Gemeinden (municipalities). On this level, and possibly also on the next lower level of Bezirke, would be introduced new representative bodies, mixed bodies led by a state civil servant (Kreishauptmann, Bezirkshauptmann). Through this reform, arguably, Koerber transposed his constitutional reform to the grassroots of the Austrian political system; the proposed elected assemblies (Bezirkstag and Kreistag) at these levels would, of course, constitute a relocation of the weight of popular representation away from the thoroughly politicized bodies of the Gemeinden and Länder. In this way, the projected Verwaltungsreform would function as an instrument to first cleanse the administration of politicization and then to break up the institutional bases of the national political parties of Austria. It would mean a sort of fresh start for the relationship between the state and popular representation at the lower levels.

Koerber himself was doubtful about the wisdom of so blatantly putting a state civil servant at the head of the popular representations; although he finally refrained from insisting on this change, he argued that giving these organs a mixed character would be enough to create the wanted effect of cooperation between state administration and popular representation.[87] In any event, the general thrust of the reform was bureaucratic leadership, or guidance of popular representatives. It fits well with Koerber's ideas about the important role the Verwaltung should play in the local community. The administrative reform would have contributed to securing the foundation of Koerber's reinforcement of the constitutional divide between the government and the parliament that he so insistently tried to uphold throughout his ministry, thus truly setting the Austrian state on a new footing.

The Question of Imperial Unity

The third reform proposal made by Koerber came only after his resignation in early 1905 when he proposed to the emperor to reform the constitutional structure of the Dual Monarchy.[88] However, similar to the administrative reform proposal, this reform plan summed up Koerber's endeavors to secure imperial unity during the foregoing years. Koerber's striving for imperial unity can also be seen as an extension of his project to reconstruct the imperial Austrian state. Since 1867 the question of the unity of the Habsburg monarchy had been the focus of constitutional political struggles between Austria and Hungary and between the emperor and foremost his Hungarian governments. In Austria the accepted view was that a superstructure existed above the two states of the monarchy, a unitary imperial state, but in Hungary the dominant view was that no such superstructure existed and that the monarchy was more or less a union of two states with a common monarch, army, and foreign office. The strong Bach legacy in the Austrian Verwaltung probably ensured that a strong view of the ideal unity of the whole imperial state had been reproduced within its ranks. It can therefore be assumed that probably more than most Austrians, Koerber was convinced of the existence of a unitary empire, a Gesamtstaat as he would always call it, above the two subunits of the empire.[89]

Koerber's ideal of a Gesamtstaat led to conflicts with both the common foreign minister, Agenor Goluchowski, and toward the end of his minister presidency also with the Hungarian Minister President István Tisza; in Koerber's view, both of these crucial actors in the imperial political system in their different ways contributed to the gradual dissolution of the Gesamtstaat.[90] The conflict with Goluchowski had begun early, but received its decisive impulse from Goluchowski's handling of the signing of an international treaty (the Brussels sugar convention) in 1902. The conflict hinged on Goluchowski's use of three signatories for Austria-Hungary: one for Austria, one for Hungary, and one for the monarchy as a whole. The formula used was "pour l'Autriche & pour la Hongrie." Koerber and many others viewed this as an act that gave international recognition to Hungary and Austria as two separate states, therefore serving to dissolve the unity and international identity of the Habsburg Empire. Koerber fought Goluchowski on this point until the end of his minister presidency, though it is very doubtful if it was Koerber who had made the correct constitutional interpretation; in any event, Koerber again acted to restore the spirit of the constitutional acts of 1867 and 1868 in the practice of the political system, and in the process also to reinforce the unity of the imperial Austro-Hungarian Gesamtstaat.

Koerber's main grudge with Goluchowski was that he did not act as the head of the "common government," in effect as a sort of Austro-Hungarian Reichskanzler. Koerber's acute sense of an absence of the unifying force of such a common government made his conflict with Goluchowski intensify in the summer of 1903, when the conflict with Hungary over the army question was ignited. Koerber maintained that Goluchowski should have taken the lead and forced the two governments (Austrian and Hungarian) into line. As it were, Koerber was obliged to play this role himself, which, of course, was not accepted in Hungary. However, in the relationship between the two states of the monarchy, Koerber and the Hungarian minister president from 1899 to 1903, Kálmán Széll, had successfully cooperated and stabilized the Dual Monarchy. As it seems, Koerber had even been handpicked as Austrian minister president into a system of government designed by Széll and Franz Joseph in the summer of 1899, building on the close cooperation between the Monarch and his two minister presidents. This system had been implemented to overcome the internal conflicts in both Hungary and Austria in the late 1890s, as well as the conflicts between the two part states of the monarchy at this time; it was referred to as the Széll-Koerber pact during the following years. In the Ausgleich negotiated between Széll and Koerber during 1902, this pact was even institutionalized in a constitutional device written into the Ausgleich, the so-called loyalty clause, which guaranteed the mutual loyalty of the two governments.

As long as this system was in place, the political system of the Dual Monarchy worked in an acceptable way, which let Koerber focus on the domestic Austrian situation and on administrative reform. However, the whole arrangement collapsed in the summer of 1903 with the igniting of the conflict over the imperial army; Széll fell from power in Hungary, and the Ausgleich was never ratified. Koerber responded by handing in his resignation, probably because this development meant the collapse of the system of government he had worked within from the beginning of his minister presidency. From this point on, Koerber was involved in a drawn-out constitutional conflict with the Hungarian government, and indirectly with both Goluchowski and Franz Joseph. The conflict began with a contest of willpower between Koerber and Franz Joseph, which ended with Koerber having his way; he remained at the head of the Austrian government, and in September 1903, Franz Joseph issued the army declaration of Chlopy, guaranteeing the unity of the imperial army and thus rebutting the Hungarian attempt at greater influence over this army. In fact, the Chlopy declaration can be seen as a constitutional device replacing the lost loyalty clause, contributing to reinforcing the unity of the monarchy.

However, the real import of this declaration turned out to be of limited scope. Already in the fall of 1903, the newly appointed Hungarian minister president, István Tisza, again raised the question. During the spring of 1904, he launched a new provocative project of equipping the Hungarian territorial army (the Hónved) with artillery. This meant that until the late spring of 1904, Koerber was continually involved in a running conflict with both Tisza and Goluchowski, desperately trying to win over Franz Joseph enough to get his opinion, but ending up practically isolated within the leading strata of the empire. During the spring of 1904, in several documents and meetings Koerber expressed his view of the seriousness of the threat against the unity of the monarchy. In the process he gave expression to his own view of the essential unity of the Gesamtstaat, a view that peaked in his assertion, about the need to defend "the great Austrian state idea, which encompasses the whole of the Monarchy." Also on this level the strong presence of the Bach legacy in Koerber's political project was finally revealed.

In the final analysis, the emperor was also to blame for the drift away from the basic constitutional laws of the empire that Koerber tried to reverse. Franz Joseph should have defended the union of 1867 much more decisively and guarded his function as a true monarch above the two states of the empire. Koerber had already told Heinrich Friedjung this much in September 1900: "His point of view must be that he is not only the Emperor of Austria, not only the King of Hungary, but that he is also the representative of the Gesamtstaat."[91] As Koerber saw it, the double failure of the monarch and the common government to serve as guarantors of this Gesamtstaat had created so much confusion since 1867 that it was evermore difficult to see a road back to the basics of those constitutional acts. During his first minister presidency, Koerber worked hard at reconstructing the mode of operation of this Austro-Hungarian political system, first through the Széll-Koerber pact and then on his own. However, shortly after his resignation, Koerber drew the logical conclusion from his failure. In the memorandum he now presented to the emperor, Koerber recommended that the whole empire be set on a new constitutional footing: "The Crown should issue a declaration that it considers the whole of the constitutional legislation of 1867 to be untenable. Therefore it would be necessary to carry out a revision." He suggested that this revision of the common laws of 1867 should be made by the Austrian and Hungarian governments together, and that the national opposition in the Hungarian parliament should be closely involved in the work in order to accommodate the Hungarian interests in the new constitutional laws and thus secure future stability.[92]

3. Koerber in Context

The Koerber Plan should in my view be seen as a Josephist project of reforming the Austrian state and making it fit for a new age. Koerber's project was conservative in the way it fell back on the December Constitution of 1867 and the system of constitutional monarchy. However, in the multinational Austrian context a reconstruction and reinforcement of the supranational state and its separation from multinational society must also be seen as a viable way forward. I would argue that this was the gist of Koerber's project, and that this project *in itself* must be seen as a progressive project—in this last aspect my view does not differ from the interpretations of Alexander Gerschenkron and many others. However, at this point several questions arise; for instance, about the place of Koerber's project within the imperial regime, its relationship to the imperial elite, and its political ideals and goals.

First of all, Koerber's project should be located in the political system of the empire. Koerber was here restrained by structural limitations; the action radius of the Austrian minister presidency was limited by its dependence on coordination with the Hungarian minister president, as well as its subordination to the common foreign minister and, of course, to the emperor. Koerber's stable relationship with Hungarian Minister President Széll until the summer of 1903 and the firm support of Franz Joseph gave him a strong position from which to realize his program. However, after this time his conflict with the Hungarian government together with his earlier conflict with Foreign Minister Goluchowski and the waning support of the emperor greatly narrowed his options. The spectacle of rampant conflicts within the imperial leadership from the summer of 1903 was caused by Koerber's refusal to accept the loss of initiative. Nevertheless, Koerber's opposition to the other leading factors of the imperial regime at this time should not obscure his being part of this regime; Koerber shared in important regards the values and goals of the imperial elite. Furthermore, the tradition within the elite that he himself belonged to, Liberal Josephism, gave his program a certain German tendency. Here we will consider how these contextual factors might affect the judgment of Koerber. Last we will review how his program was restated in his short second minister presidency in 1916.

Koerber and the Imperial Regime

The Josephist bureaucracy had a dual tradition, so to speak. There was a Liberal and a Conservative Josephism, the one going back to people like Schmerling and Bach and to the original Enlightenment Josephism of the eighteenth century, the other going back to Emperor Franz I and Metternich, and with the minister of education after 1848, Count Leo Thun, as an important forerunner.[93] As a Liberal Josephist, Koerber was a leading proponent of a strongly state reformist tradition that had a strong position in the Austrian bureaucracy, also in its last decades. In a work written after the dissolution of the Habsburg monarchy, Josef Redlich even pointed to Koerber as *the* most prominent Liberal Josephist in the last decades of imperial Austria.[94] However, Redlich had at an earlier date also received the opinion from within the Austrian high bureaucracy that Koerber was very controversial within the imperial elite. Redlich had been told that Koerber was seen as "ultraradical" and counted among the left liberals, and that this was an important reason for his being barred from government posts for a long time after 1904.[95]

What we have with Koerber then is arguably a radical proponent of the Liberal Josephist tradition who was elevated to one of the most powerful positions in the late Habsburg Empire. It is perhaps no wonder that he created a stir at the time and that he has later received that special sort of scholarly attention that tends to view him in the larger context of the history of Europe during the era of "modernization" in the late nineteenth and the twentieth centuries. Nevertheless, it may very well have been something of a coincidence that he was elevated to this position at all. Franz Joseph had probably become aware of the brilliant young Beamte in the ministry of trade already in the early 1890s.[96] This would have given Koerber a place on Franz Joseph's list of candidates for higher office in the empire. However, it seems probable that Franz Joseph primarily saw Koerber as having a specialized competence, which made him suitable to fill important posts on the level of the resort ministries. Koerber was first made minister of trade (in 1897) and then interior minister (in 1899). The latter was arguably his ideal position, where he could have served the emperor well for a long time. However, the rapid turnover of governments in the late 1890s then suddenly propelled the able Josephist bureaucrat into the highest position of the state, as Austrian minister president. Once here, Koerber was in a position to develop a program that in retrospect looks like one of the few chances of bringing about real change in the late Habsburg Empire. Although Koerber's project was progressive, and most certainly too radical for many members of the imperial elite, it certainly emanated from this same elite.

Ernest von Koerber in 1890; Austrian National Library, ÖNB/Sign. Pf7298C2

One interesting example that might elucidate the problem of the place of Koerber's project within the imperial elite was his political relationship with the Bohemian aristocrat Alois Lexa von Aehrenthal, a prominent diplomat and Austro-Hungarian foreign minister from 1906 to 1912. Aehrenthal's development from the mid 1890s betrays an almost identical view of the need to strengthen the unity of the empire as that demonstrated by Koerber after 1900. The origins of Aehrenthal's constitutional politics lay in his spell as Chef de Cabinet to Foreign Minister Gustav Kálnoky in the first half of the 1890s.[97] After Kálnoky's fall in 1895, Aehrenthal would have to wait until his own appointment as foreign minister in 1906 to again have the possibility of affecting matters directly. However, during the period in between, which also encompasses Koerber's minister presidency, Aehrenthal also worked very actively to counteract what he perceived as the gradual dissolution of the Dual Monarchy under Agenor Goluchowski. At times it even looked as though Aehrenthal and Koerber were involved in a concerted effort.

The most obvious instance of this apparent cooperation was the conflict between Aehrenthal and Goluchowski during the spring of 1904, practically simultaneous with and very similar in substance to Koerber's heated conflict with both Tisza and Goluchowski during 1903–04. Aehrenthal, who was ambassador to Russia at the time, refused to sign a treaty in the way Goluchowski demanded, "Pour l'Autriche & pour la Hongrie." Aehrenthal argued in a very Koerber-like manner that this mode of procedure was equal to dissolving the international political identity of the empire.[98] Both in its overall structure and in the detail of Aehrenthal's argument, the similarity to Koerber's constitutional politics is striking. Moreover, the two of them also expressed mutual admiration; Koerber seems to have viewed Aehrenthal as potentially a strong hand that could effectuate change at the top of the imperial political system, and Aehrenthal saw Koerber as a guarantor of stability in the government of crisis-ridden Austria.[99]

However, their consensus on the need to strengthen the unity of the empire was joined to strongly contrasting views about the internal political organization of this imperial state; also, their fundamental ideological convictions could hardly be more contrasting. Aehrenthal's concept in the international politics of restoring the old Dreikaiserbündnis between the three Central and East European empires was not just a foreign policy. It was an attempt to anchor at the international level conservative antidemocratic and anti-Liberal politics.[100] Aehrenthal proposed to use armies to stabilize the three empires internally; armies that were to function as a guarantee for the monarchic principle as the system of government.[101] Thus Aehrenthal's aim was to use the international system to support a reactionary conception of the internal political system in Austria-Hungary. During the political crisis in 1900, when Ernest von Koerber presented his constitutional reform plan to the emperor, Aehrenthal had also aired his views on this question. Instead of Koerber's emphatic attempt to *reform* the parliament, Aehrenthal had preferred to *eliminate* it.[102] Koerber's respect for the parliament was diametrically opposed to Aehrenthal's attitude. Another example was their strongly contrasting attitudes in regard to the Inter-Parliamentarian Union. Where Aehrenthal would have liked to send in the troops, Koerber was a benefactor.[103]

Among the differences between Koerber and Aehrenthal could also be mentioned Aehrenthal's basic concept of a return to basing the Austro-Hungarian political system on an ethnic hierarchy with the Germans and the Hungarians in power, which he presented in two memorandums to the emperor in 1898–99 as the solution to the current political crisis. As concluded above, Koerber was more intent on removing the electoral distortions in favor of the Germans and making parliament reflect truly Austrian, nonnationalist opinions in society. Aehrenthal's conception was also building rather one-sidedly on strengthening the role and function of the foreign minister, turning him into a focal point for both the internal and external politics of the monarchy, a true Reichskanzler. In this area Koerber did something that Aehrenthal would actively discourage as foreign minister: Koerber tried to make the Austro-Hungarian system work by establishing a close relationship between the Austrian and the Hungarian minister presidents, even anchoring this relationship in the two parliaments through the loyalty clause in the Ausgleich treaty. As Aehrenthal saw it, the systemic relationship should be a purely vertical one; Koerber seems to have worked in the direction of giving the whole imperial state a stronger constitutional and parliamentary structure.[104]

Notwithstanding these evident and fundamental differences between Koerber and Aehrenthal, Koerber's basic adherence to the *monarchic principle* of constitutional monarchy made his political program into a potential complement to Aehrenthal's. Furthermore, the Austrian state tended to become a goal in itself in Koerber's Josephist project; this bureaucratic stance made Koerber's project liable to be placed in the service of purposes exterior to it. In this context, Koerber's strengthening of the state and the Verwaltung receives a somewhat different meaning than the one imputed to it in a progressive reading of Koerber: it could *also* have served as bureaucratic stabilizer and control instrument for a reactionary political project, as it were, a complement to those professional armies Aehrenthal imagined would keep order in the empire of the Habsburgs. The parallel to the 1850s is illuminating: the Liberal Alexander Bach became just such an instrument of neoabsolutist rule during the course of the 1850s. Also like Koerber, Bach was drawn into this modernizing-reactionary project by a charismatic leader, Bohemian aristocrat Felix Schwarzenberg, who personally reclaimed control over the empire after the upheavals of the revolution of 1848–49.

Koerber and the Problem of German Nationalism

The strong force of German nationalism also put Koerber's program to the test. In the previous chapter Koerber's political project was described as supranational, aiming in a truly Josephist manner for the reconstruction and reinforcement of the supranational state. Koerber's distance to the different national parties was equal; he attempted to make a stable state-supporting parliamentary grouping emerge without letting this "state-party" have a direct, parliamentarian influence on government. However, it was also remarked earlier that Koerber's project tended to be judged as somehow German-oriented through its very centralism. This problem will here be looked at in the broadened context of the field of tension of German nationalism generated in the relationship between Austria-Hungary and Imperial Germany.

At least from the late 1890s, the Imperial German government began to get seriously worried about the long-standing Slavic federalistic dominance in Austria, Germany's ally in the internationally evermore isolated Dual Alliance. The fear grew that Austria-Hungary might change its identity, so to speak, from a German empire to a Slavic empire. In the latter, a change of alliance from Germany to Russia was also envisioned, leaving Germany alone and surrounded by enemies. This fear appeared for the first time openly in the Imperial German government in the late 1890s. In the end it was the government of Bohemian aristocrat Franz Thun with its strong leanings in a Slavic and federalistic direction that finally in 1898 made the Reich-Germans throw all other considerations overboard and interfere in the internal affairs of their ally, attempting to overthrow the Czech-dominated Thun government. Foreign Minister Bülow argued more or less openly that the question of the Austrian government's national leanings was a question of Reich-German national interest; Ambassador Eulenburg in Vienna did his utmost to bring home this point with Franz Joseph while the Reich-German press was whipping up a German national frenzy.[105] This crisis in the Dual Alliance brought its identity-based character to the fore. The officials of the German foreign ministry, in Vienna and at home, responded almost as if the internal politics of its ally was a domestic Imperial German affair.[106] This highly subjective experience of an impending, fundamental identity change in their ally marked the German foreign ministry deeply. In Ambassador Eulenburg's reports of the following years, there is an ever-present watchfulness, which occasionally tips over into reproaches for the "infidelity" of Franz Joseph a few years earlier.[107]

The German national pressure exerted on Austria from Imperial Germany during the late 1890s interacted with a grave internal conflict between the German and the Czech parties, the so-called Badeni conflict, that had begun in the spring of 1897. It originated in an attempt by Minister President Kasimir Badeni to solve the conflict in Bohemia by expanding the sphere of use of Czech as an administrative language, an old demand of the Czech parties; and it ended by a deafening eruption of German nationalism that paralyzed the Austrian parliament (and vandalized it physically).[108] Together, these two almost identical national-political fields of tension with some delay brought about what looks like a system shift in the government of Austria; a period of attempts to appease and integrate the Slavic parties, and particularly the Czech parties, into the political order of Imperial Austria ended and was followed by a long series of governments that had a centralistic orientation and were therefore viewed more favorably by the German parties. This is not a clear-cut matter, but both the Reich-German Foreign Ministry and the German and Czech parties of Austria tended to interpret the events of the summer and fall of 1899 in this way. As recounted earlier, Heinrich Friedjung interpreted the political shift of 1899 from a German national perspective as the most important event for the Germans of Austria after the closing of the Dual Alliance twenty years earlier.

It was at this point that Ernest von Koerber came into the picture. Although Koerber had been minister of trade in the short-lived Gautsch government in the winter of 1897–98—a bureaucratic government that had tried to get matters under control after the sudden collapse of the Badeni government under pressure from German national excesses in late November 1897—it was his appointment as interior minister after the resignation of Franz Thun in the fall of 1899 that really set off his career in the Austrian government. It is important to note here that Koerber came into play as part of the solution to the internal political crisis at this time. Although this solution contained an effort to appease the German parties, it was not identical with such a move. It was arguably a much more fundamental attempt to reconstruct the whole imperial system of government, and, as discussed above, it rested on an understanding between Franz Joseph and the newly appointed Hungarian minister president, Kálmán Széll, who had been chosen at this very time to end a corresponding political crisis in Hungary. To judge from the evidence, Koerber was handpicked as Austrian interior minister in this system of government. It seems probable that his reputation as a very able bureaucrat landed him with the mission of reconstructing and reasserting the Josephist Verwaltung as a stabilizing structure in the political system of Austria; he was then unexpectedly appointed Austrian minister president only a few months later as the crisis in government dragged on throughout the winter of 1899/1900.

As the interior minister in the short-lived Clary government in October 1899, Koerber immediately felt the German national pressure from the Reich. In contacts with the German embassy, he expressed his hope that both the German-Austrian parties as well as their "foreign sympathizers" ("ausländische Gesinnungsgenossen") would observe moderation and not make the work of the new government more difficult than it already was. Simultaneously, Koerber intimated that such a Beamtenministerium as that of Manfred Clary (and later his own, of course) should be preferable for both the German-Austrians and Imperial Germany in comparison with preceeding governments.[109] Shortly after having been appointed Austrian minister president in mid-January 1900, Koerber had his first meeting with the influential political journalist, Heinrich Friedjung. During this meeting, he disappointed Friedjung in his hopes for a firm German course in the government of Austria from then on by stating that a restoration of the dominating position of the German parties in Austria, "as before 1879," was impossible.[110] For the same reasons, the

Reich-German opinion of Koerber was initially at best lukewarm. Notwithstanding Ambassador Eulenburg's victorious report in November 1899 of "the new German course of Franz Joseph, which he personally confirmed to me,"[111] the reports from the German embassy in Vienna continued to show a certain reserve during the following year. The new Koerber government did not live up to the high Reich-German expectations on an openly German-oriented government; Eulenburg thus waited for the next natural development, the exchange of Koerber's Beamtenministerium for a German coalition government that should guide Austria in the right direction through the necessary political reforms and confront the Czech opposition more decisively.[112] However, already at the end of the year 1900 Eulenburg had come to accept the Koerber government as a positive force for the Dual Alliance.[113]

In the last years of his minister presidency, Koerber achieved a high stability in the evaluation of the German foreign ministry. An important part of this development was due to Koerber's role in a perceived basic German-Czech field of conflict in Austria (that was also pro- and anti-German Empire), which was confirmed and reinforced by the conflict his government developed with the obstructing Czech parties in parliament. In early 1903, the newly appointed German ambassador Karl von Wedel therefore maintained that "it definitely lies in our interest to support Herr von Koerber as far as only we can."[114] In the summer of 1904, Chancellor Bülow confirmed the reading of his ambassador, stating that "from our point of view we can only wish that Herr von Koerber remains in charge of the Austrian government. We know what we have with Koerber, and we can rely on him."[115]

Behind the imperial German evaluation of Koerber lay the traumatic experience of a perceived impending identity change in its partner, Austria-Hungary, in the last years of the old century. This experience revealed the identity-based character of the Dual Alliance as perceived in Berlin, which in some instances took an openly Great-German shape. In Berlin the international diplomatic relationship between Germany, Austria-Hungary, and Russia was perceived as being linked to domestic political constellations within Austria, tying Slavic-federalistic politics in Austria to a Russian orientation and German-centralistic politics to a German orientation. In this field of tension, Ernest von Koerber's centralist, supranational political program of strengthening the Austrian state initially seemed of dubious value in Berlin. But not least through its escalating confrontation with the Czech obstruction tactics in the Austrian parliament, this program could be fit into the Imperial German perceptions as pro-German.

Nevertheless, the perception in Berlin of Ernest von Koerber as pro-German did not originate in Koerber's own convictions, and neither did Koerber's political program have a German-national bias. However, in the wider perspective of the international system of alliances in Europe, this did not much matter. Similar to the case of Aehrenthal discussed above, Koerber's political program of strengthening the Austrian state could through the Dual Alliance be made to play a pro-German role. As such it was consequently also perceived among the Slavic peoples of Austria, to which Koerber's supranational state had a strangely German flavor. This was not only Koerber's dilemma; it was a basic problem of the whole Josephist tradition. This tradition had always emphasized the centralized German-speaking bureaucracy in Vienna as the core of the Austrian supranational state. Furthermore, it was a tradition colored by its roots in the German Enlightenment. Frederick the Great's Prussia had, for example, been an important source of inspiration for Joseph II and his followers. Therefore one might, perhaps, say that the Josephist tradition had always wanted to modernize Austria in a German *manner*, but not to Germanize it. All of this resulted in an inherent German ambivalence in the Austrian state idea, an ambivalence that was especially pronounced in the Liberal Josephist tradition that Koerber adhered to.

Koerber's Second Minister Presidency (1916)

When Ernest von Koerber returned to state service during World War I, the conjunctures of Reich-German attempts to influence the domestic politics of Austria were high once again. In this way 1915–16 were peculiarly like the time span leading up to Koerber's first minister presidency. However, the fields of tension generated by German nationalism were stronger at this later time. Moreover, they were fused into one concentrated Great-German national movement under the concept of Mitteleuropa. The Reich-German government during the early part of the war gradually got deeply involved in plans for an economic and possibly military union between the two Central European empires; they were driven on in this endeavor by the extremely activistic German nationalism of the Reich-German ambassador to Vienna, Heinrich von Tschirschky; and they were strongly supported by several networks of German-Austrian politicians, bureaucrats, industrialists, and intellectuals in Austria, who also connected directly with their opposite numbers in the Reich.[116]

The Reich-German Liberal politician Friedrich Naumann formulated the political vision—though not the concept itself—that collected all these strands of activity and gave them direction in his October 1915 book, *Mitteleuropa*. However, he had already formulated his program in late February 1915, after a ten-day trip through Austria-Hungary, where he met many important people, and had propagated it widely ever since. It seems probable that Naumann got the inspiration for his idea during the trip itself.[117] This fits well with Naumann, that Mitteleuropa is strongly influenced by the Austrian experience of the multinational empire; Naumann only added an emphasis on the need for German leadership in central and southeastern

Europe. In this way Naumann tried to bridge the gulf between Reich-German and Austrian-German interests. As it turned out, the Liberal Josephist Ernest von Koerber was also attracted by Naumann's vision.

Koerber was initially involved to some degree in one of those German-Austrian elite networks that formed at the end of 1914, the Marchet-Baernreither group, where he most certainly encountered one of its most active members, Heinrich Friedjung. However, when he was appointed common finance minister in early February 1915, Koerber disappeared from this group.[118] Naumann nevertheless met up with Koerber during his visits to Vienna later in 1915; they discussed the political problems of the war, and Koerber apparently got engaged for Naumann's vision.[119] Koerber read *Mitteleuropa* immediately after having received the book from Naumann and wrote back: "Your newest work *Mitteleuropa* has in its entirety given me enormous inspiration. Especially your efforts to view our land without bias and to disarm misconceptions that from time to time damage our relations have made you deserve our most sincere thanks. Let's hope, for the well-being of the allied states, that our common goals are soon reached."[120]

Behind Koerber's contributions to the discussions in the Common Ministerial Council during 1915, we can discern Naumann's influence and the contours of Mitteleuropa; on the one hand, Koerber is preoccupied with securing the Balkans as an economic sphere of influence for Austria-Hungary, and on the other he argues openly that Austria-Hungary should lean economically on Germany both during and after the war.[121] Koerber also supported territorial annexations to Austria-Hungary, though he simultaneously warned that such a policy would have problematic effects on the Austrian state idea, because "the character of the monarchy and her many hundreds-of-years-old historical mission—to function as a bridge between east and west—will be decisively altered" if territorial acquisitions are made.[122] Nevertheless, when Koerber was appointed Austrian minister president in October 1916, Naumann would have great expectations of him to further Mitteleuropa and the intergovernmental negotiations on the union between Austria-Hungary and Germany.[123]

Both Friedrich Naumann and Heinrich Friedjung played important parts in that process of lobbying, which in the early fall of 1915 made the Reich-German government adopt Mitteleuropa as the concept to solve the problem of restructuring Europe that at the time seemed to present itself to the victorious Central Powers. In November 1915 an intergovernmental conference took place in Berlin, where the Reich-German and the Austro-Hungarian leadership tried to work out a common perspective on these things.[124] However, what the meeting unequivocally made clear was that the Reich-German government in 1915 still carried that same view of Austria-Hungary as a German Empire threatened in its identity by its Slavic nationalities that Foreign Minister von Bülow had already presented to Franz Joseph in 1898. In the Reich-German memorandum on the conference and in the diplomatic note dispatched to Vienna a few days later, the Reich-German government demanded assurances that the Austro-Hungarian government would take steps "through which an increasing Slavicization of Austria is hindered and through which the German element in Austria . . . is again ensured its leading role."[125] The comparison with the attitude of the German foreign ministry in the crisis of the Dual Alliance in 1898–99 is interesting. In both of these acute situations, the German foreign ministry seems to have operated with a similar identity-based view of the Dual Alliance.

This growing pressure from the Reich was welcomed by most German-Austrian political parties, which viewed Mitteleuropa as the solution to their difficult position within Austria. However, members of the Austro-Hungarian bureaucracy, sensing the dangers of losing in sovereignty to the powerful neighbor, resisted these developments. Furthermore, the diplomatic note dispatched from Berlin after the conference of November 1915 was viewed as an intrusion into Austro-Hungarian internal affairs. In these less-than-ideal conditions, the negotiations dragged on until October 1918, but the pressure from Imperial Germany reached its climax in 1915/16.[126]

When Koerber reappeared in the political arena in early 1915, there were already established perceptions and expectations of him as pro-German.[127] He soon started appearing as a serious candidate of ambassador Tschirschky for a leading function in Austria, and he continued to be a favorite candidate of Tschirschky's up to his actual appointment as Austrian minister president in October 1916. Tschirschky had become increasingly activistic and wanted Berlin to intervene directly in the Austro-Hungarian leadership questions to ensure that the people supported by Berlin, one of whom was Koerber, would lead the necessary restructuring of Austria-Hungary into a German-led empire.[128] Ironically, the imperial German foreign ministry received help from unexpected quarters, when on 21 October the serving Austrian minister president Karl Stürgkh was assassinated by the prominent Austrian Social Democrat Friedrich Adler, a deed that paved the way for Koerber's reappointment. The news of Koerber's subsequent appointment to the Austrian minister presidency consequently created great expectations in Berlin. He was fully expected to speed up the negotiations on a union between Austria-Hungary and Germany.[129]

◆

When Koerber was appointed Austrian minister president a second time, in late October 1916, in many ways it actually seems like he was picking up where he had left off in December 1904. However, the Ausgleich question dominated completely during the first few weeks as the old treaty from 1907 ran out with the end of 1916. That the new treaty be settled rapidly was a precondition for the continuing negotiations on a union between the allied empires. Koerber's demand for a revision of the Ausgleich treaty therefore met strong reactions in Berlin. Austro-Hungarian Ambassador to Berlin Gottfried Hohenlohe wrote an agitated, almost panic-stricken report to his superior, Foreign Minister Stephan Burian, about these reactions. Burian sent the report on to Koerber, who replied calmly: "Although I acknowledge the repercussions my move has on the relationship between the Monarchy and the German Empire, the new Austrian government must simply take the treaty under renewed consideration and also consider whether the treaty will be acceptable to the Austrian parliament."[130] Koerber was thorough with the Ausgleich treaty; he traveled to Budapest, where he came into conflict with István Tisza; he reviewed the documentation Stürgkh had left behind; and he requested reports from the former finance minister, Leth, and the former minister of trade, Spitzmüller.[131]

After having established control over the Ausgleich question and dealt with a few other acute matters, Koerber turned to the question of a Verwaltungsreform. When in mid-November Friedjung visited Koerber and unsuccessfully tried to influence him in a German national direction, he found the newly appointed Austrian minister president absorbed by the question of a complete reform of the Austrian internal administration.[132] The project of administrative reform was intertwined already with the formation of Koerber's new government, since Erwin von Schwartzenau, the old chairman of the administrative reform commission of a few years earlier, had been appointed interior minister. Koerber and Schwartzenau immediately began to organize the work in this field during the first days of November.[133] Schwartzenau, for his part, had worked during 1915 to retain the commission as a permanent interministerial conference, that is, as a wholly bureaucratic operation.[134] It seems probable that this was the road Koerber and Schwartzenau were now also proceeding along in late 1916.

Furthermore, in the Austrian Council of Ministers of 18 November, Koerber presented an administrative instruction on the fundamental code for the behavior of civil servants, his second Hirtenbrief. The instruction was issued to every part of the administration, not only to the internal state administration, but also to the other ministries and the whole finance administration, the post and telegraph administration, the state railways, the forest and mining authorities, and so on. It was also issued to the press and published in several papers in the first days of December. Koerber's second Hirtenbrief focuses squarely on the foundation for the relationship between the state and the people, the strictest observation of the law; thus the core of the Rechtstaat came to the fore under pressures from the Great War.[135]

Three days after Koerber issued his Hirtenbrief, the old emperor, Franz Joseph, died. Tschirschky's successor, the newly appointed German ambassador, Botho von Wedel, reported on a conversation with Koerber shortly afterward, that "the unexpected death [of the emperor] has torn his program to pieces and brought him into an extremely difficult situation."[136] Koerber's program may have been shaken by the death of the old emperor, but as usual, Koerber made an emphatic attempt to control the situation. Immediately he requested that the new Emperor Karl should without delay take the oath on the Austrian constitution, to swear to uphold the law and to govern in accordance with it.[137] Koerber's attempt to force Karl's hand was intended to secure Rechtskontinuität in the sensitive early days of the new imperial regime. As Koerber saw it, this was crucial to secure continuity and legitimacy and to dispel the feeling of uncertainty that had arisen upon the death of the old emperor.[138]

Instead of ensuring constitutional continuity and legitimacy, this request initiated Koerber's fall. Koerber's move was not received well by the young emperor and his advisers, who wanted to make their own decisions in these questions.[139] Furthermore, when Koerber met with the newly appointed imperial German ambassador, Botho von Wedel, at the beginning of December, his strong identification with the Austrian state collided head on with the pro-German image he had received in Berlin. During this meeting, Wedel spoke out for a coup d'état that should give the Germans of Austria a leading position in the empire; in effect much of what Heinrich Friedjung had argued about with Koerber a few weeks earlier. Wedel declared that "Germany views it as the duty of the Austrian government to act decisively against the Slavic threat." Koerber replied emphatically that he simply could not let the new young Emperor Karl commit unconstitutional acts of the type demanded by the German national parties in Austria. This would only damage the trust of a large part of the population in the crown and in the young monarch, Koerber maintained. Koerber also said that he sincerely hoped the German government would understand his position and not support the German nationalists in Austria in regard to this question.[140]

After his resignation Koerber wrote to Wedel: "I part with the conviction that I have fully done my duty toward the new ruler. I will not take part in any immature experiments."[141] From Koerber's perspective, the coup d'état plans primarily meant jeopardizing the legitimacy of the supranational Josephist Austrian state; this state was, as usual with Koerber, the first priority. In his decidedly inopportune actions during these turbulent weeks in the fall of 1916, Koerber demonstrated his unbending loyalty to the Liberal Josephist legacy. Nevertheless, his failure exposed the crucial weak point in Liberal Josephism when confronted with the pressures of nationalism: the built-in dependence on a Germandom that was at this time increasingly attracted to a much more chauvinistic, imperialistic German nationalism.

4. Heinrich Friedjung: History and Politics

From his historical studies on the struggle for supremacy in Germany, Heinrich Friedjung had drawn the conclusion that individuals played an important role in shaping historical developments. In the long run, structural conditions were dominant, but in the short run, Friedjung concluded that individuals could play a decisive role in shaping and redirecting historical developments.[142] There is little doubt that the important role Bismarck had played in the unification of Germany markedly influenced Friedjung in this regard.[143] The only problem for Friedjung here was that Bismarck had played his historical role in a way detrimental to Austria, and especially to the Austrian Germans. Around the turn of the century, Friedjung was increasingly devoting himself to historical studies betraying a more directly affirmative stance on Austrian history than only a few years earlier. At the German historians' congress in Halle in the spring of 1900, Friedjung gave a lecture dealing with that moment of German history in 1813 when Napoleon had been defeated and the political order of Europe would again be newly shaped. In his lecture, Friedjung viewed this moment as a window of opportunity for restoring the Holy Roman Empire in some shape, giving its crown back to the Austrian emperor, Franz I, and laying the tracks for a different, Austrian-led development of Germany in the nineteenth century.[144] After the lecture, Friedjung wrote to his acquaintance, the high-ranking Austro-Hungarian diplomat Alois Lexa von Aehrenthal, declaring himself to be rather content with the response he had received. However, "certain northern German historians were of the opinion that I had overestimated the chances for an Austrian-German empire in 1813. It is the same old story. Prussia's greatness was meant to be from the beginning, and no wisdom could help her rival to turn things around."[145] It was no coincidence that Friedjung was so eager to hear Aehrenthal's opinion of this Weichensteller in German history. In Friedjung's eyes, in fact, the powerful figure of Aehrenthal was the potential carrier of historical change that could, perhaps, even redress the balance between Austria and Prussia.

Friedjung had become acquainted with Aehrenthal in 1898 while doing research on the recently deceased former Austro-Hungarian foreign minister, Gustav Kálnoky. During his research, he had come into close contact with Aehrenthal, who had been Kálnoky's chef de cabinet and right-hand man. Aehrenthal gave Friedjung access to parts of Kálnoky's political papers and correspondence, and to himself in a series of conversations on his former superior. Aehrenthal also supplied Friedjung with a political biographical sketch of Kálnoky. Friedjung told Aehrenthal that the biographical article on Kálnoky he worked on would be built around this sketch, and later he even described his finished article as the product of a joint effort.[146] As it seems, the sketch Aehrenthal had given Friedjung was the outline for a political biographical article on Kálnoky that Aehrenthal had been working on since shortly after his superior's resignation in 1895. Apparently Aehrenthal had been thinking of publishing something in defense of Kálnoky, who had been brought down in the internal political struggles within the empire.[147]

Kálnoky had fallen over a conflict with the Hungarian minister president, Desző Bánffy, which might be said to have revolved around the constitutional question of the jurisdiction and function of the common foreign minister. As it seems, Friedjung's article on Kálnoky is to a rather great extent colored by Aehrenthal's view of Kálnoky, and perhaps even to more of Aehrenthal's own political convictions. Contextually, Friedjung's article can be read as a critique of the policies of Kálnoky's successor, Agenor Gołuchowski. Gołuchowski worked with a minimal definition of the common role of the foreign minister. In Friedjung's article, Kálnoky is presented as viewing this common role as essential, even as striving to expand it into functioning as an Austro-Hungarian Reichskanzler.[148] On exactly this question, Aehrenthal would repeatedly come into conflict with Goluchowski during the following years, maintaining that the foreign minister was the constitutional guarantor of the internal as well as the external unity of the empire, of its international political identity. When he himself was appointed foreign minister in 1906, Aehrenthal also had a series of conflicts with the Austrian and Hungarian minister presidents over this constitutional role of the common foreign minister, trying to enforce a stronger unity in the political system of the empire.[149]

As discussed in the previous chapter, Aehrenthal and Koerber had practically been involved in a concerted action on this very question. Since Friedjung had supported Aehrenthal journalistically on this question, it seems logical that he would lobby very actively for Koerber's return to the Austrian minister presidency after Aehrenthal had been appointed foreign minister in late 1906. Friedjung had a good opportunity because of Aehrenthal's hostility to the current minister president, Max Vladimir von Beck. Nevertheless, in the end it seems as if Koerber was still too controversial after the many conflicts of his own recent minister presidency, and Aehrenthal chose to support another candidate.[150] Heinrich Friedjung had nurtured great hopes for the combination Aehrenthal-Koerber, but he had his doubts concerning Aehrenthal. Whether Koerber shared Friedjung's vision of a German-led empire perhaps did not matter much in the final analysis, as long as Koerber's centralism in practice supported an imperial state whose center and administrative apparatus was de facto dominated by the Austrian Germans. Moreover, Koerber also helped to stabilize the Dual Alliance, also an important goal in Friedjung's eyes. However, whether the "strong hand" at the top of the political system that should realize a more unified empire supported this goal was of overriding concern. If *Aehrenthal* did not further the creation of a German-led empire that expanded in the Balkans, then Friedjung's whole project would capsize.

Friedjung was reasonably certain that his man had the right qualities; Aehrenthal seemed to promote a German-led empire, and he was known to carefully weigh expansive plans for the Balkans. However, the Dual Alliance was a more problematic matter. Friedjung's high estimation of Aehrenthal had been grounded during their conversations on Kálnoky in the last years of the old century. During these contacts, Friedjung became privy to Aehrenthal's important role in the system shift of 1899, when Aehrenthal had thrown his weight in the balance against the conservative, Slavic-oriented government of Bohemian aristocrat Franz Thun, and for a "German" orientation.[151] As discussed above, Aehrenthal at this time wanted to return to basing the empire on its Germans and Hungarians. This helped to influence Friedjung into repeatedly vouching for Aehrenthal's "German identity" during the following years against allegations, not least from the Reich-German foreign ministry, that Aehrenthal belonged to the Slavic-conservative camp in Austria and thus was an enemy both of the German orientation in Austria and of Imperial Germany.[152]

However, Aehrenthal's policies here were not based on a German national view. They were based on instrumental considerations for strengthening the empire; giving the Germans their hegemonic role back was simply a way of stabilizing the structure of domination. All the while that he was actively supporting Aehrenthal and vouching for his loyalty to the German cause, Friedjung probably sensed Aehrenthal's political instrumentalism; Friedjung remained deeply uncertain as to Aehrenthal's true loyalties.[153] Aehrenthal's Russian orientation in international relations made Friedjung uneasy. For Friedjung, the German alliance was primary; it was a question of identity.[154] As recounted above, Aehrenthal's diplomatic game had quite different aims, which included organizing a reactionary international, and in this quest national loyalties were secondary. Friedjung might have done well to follow his instinct here. Instead, he staked his whole project on a charismatic leader, on whose qualities he, in the end, was deeply uncertain. It might very well have been Friedjung's historical studies into the Austrian political regeneration of the 1850s that made him support this new Schwarzenberg in his apparent quest to restore Austrian power and glory.

In any case, in the fall of 1908 Friedjung was swept along by the strong political currents released by Aehrenthal. Since Aehrenthal's appointment as foreign minister in late 1906, Friedjung's contacts with him had intensified once again. In early 1908, Friedjung experienced that Aehrenthal was taking him into his confidence as an informal adviser.[155] Furthermore, literally on the eve of the annexation of Bosnia and Hercegovina, on 6 October Friedjung was called to Aehrenthal's office at the Ballhausplatz and taken into confidence on the grand political action that was just unfolding. After a long discussion, Aehrenthal encouraged Friedjung to give his opinion on the action as a historian in the *Neues Wiener Tageblatt*. Friedjung reacted to this request with a eulogy on "the Great-Power Austria-Hungary" a few days later.[156] At the beginning of 1909, Friedjung's relationship to Aehrenthal had been so intensified that he had begun to be recognized as an important informal adviser to the foreign minister. At least Friedjung was led to believe as much by Aehrenthal's subordinates in the ministry.[157]

In February 1909, Aehrenthal invited Friedjung to a meeting in the foreign ministry, which initiated a coordinated press campaign to prepare the ground for a planned military attack against Serbia. Aehrenthal stated to Friedjung that the crisis would be resolved in March and that war against Serbia was a distinct possibility.

Friedjung was given the mission within this campaign to write an article about the subversive activities of Serbia in the South-Slav provinces of Austria-Hungary. Aehrenthal gave him some documentation on these activities, which allegedly had been collected by the embassy in Belgrade. Friedjung also took the opportunity to quiz Aehrenthal on the aims of the war, trying to make the foreign minister consider the possibility of tying a defeated Serbia close to Austria-Hungary after the war through some sort of customs union.[158] Friedjung thus expected the Austro-Hungarian campaign against Serbia in 1909 to constitute the next step on that imperial expansion in the Balkans he saw as the historical role of the Austrian Germans. At the end of March, the conflict with Serbia reached its climax, and while it still seemed probable that it might come to a military confrontation, Friedjung's officially sanctioned article "Österreich-Ungarn und Serbien" was published in the *Neue Freie Presse*.[159]

Almost simultaneously with the publication of Friedjung's provocative article, Serbia folded and open conflict was avoided. With hindsight we can say that Friedjung was, perhaps, a bit too detailed in his accusations against political circles within Austria-Hungary, and within a short time a lawsuit against him was filed.[160] Friedjung initially tried to use the trial to justify the annexation. However, when the documents he based his case on turned out to be forgeries, and when he subsequently lost all support of the Austro-Hungarian foreign ministry in late 1909, Friedjung's whole undertaking collapsed.[161] Only days after the beginning of the process, it was settled through mediation, and Friedjung's campaign against Serbia dissolved into nothing. In the end phase of the affair, Aehrenthal had abandoned Friedjung, and the affair ended the relationship between them.[162] Notwithstanding this, Friedjung continued to support Aehrenthal. In his late historical work, *Das Zeitalter des Imperialismus 1884–1914* (3 vols., 1919–1922), Friedjung maintained that Aehrenthal's policies had been right for Austria, and he continued to defend Aehrenthal's annexation of Bosnia-Hercegovina until the last.[163]

◆

During the Friedjung affair, Heinrich Friedjung had finally dissolved the last remnants of the line of demarcation between historical scholarship and political engagement. Because Friedjung, at the start of the legal proceedings, had already staked his reputation in a rather reckless fashion as a historian on the authenticity of the documents he used as evidence, the nebulous resolution to the process significantly affected his prestige as a historian.[164] Despite the catastrophic results, Friedjung did not draw the expected lesson from this experience; after these events, he only fused his historical scholarship closer with his political engagement. The next large-scale work Friedjung undertook, *Das Zeitalter des Imperialismus 1884–1914*, was a true work of contemporary history, focusing on the competition of the European Great

Powers for global power during Friedjung's own lifetime. Here he disappeared into the vortex of current events; this work is the most journalistic and least successful of his three main historical works.

However, Friedjung's very choice to throw himself into the Great Power politics of his own day most certainly reflects his recent personal involvement in Austro-Hungarian power politics. Moreover, as his political engagement for Austria-Hungary was fundamentally existential, this move into writing the history of his own time could only accentuate the quality of existential work, of identity therapy, in Friedjung's work. However, the move from narrating the traumatic events of the mid-nineteenth century, to narrating the unfolding history of Europe of his own day would also alter this existential quality; it shifted Friedjung's narration from a retrospective and reflective mode to a prospective and constructive one. During World War I, Friedjung apparently planned a new work on the history of Europe. As it seems, he did not get much beyond collecting material for this study, the narrative structure of which seems to have been built around the rise of Mitteleuropa. It is interesting that most of the material collected consists of memoranda, protocols to meetings, letters, speeches, and so on in connection with the political movement during the World War for realizing Mitteleuropa as a union built around Germany and Austria-Hungary.[165] Of course one of the most prominent participants of this political movement was Heinrich Friedjung himself.

◆

The outbreak of war in 1914 drew Heinrich Friedjung into renewed political activity for realizing that program of closer ties to Germany and expansion in the Balkans and the Orient that he had been propagating since 1880. Already in the fall of 1914, his articles in newspapers in Imperial Germany announced this program, so in December 1914, for example, in the *Vossische Zeitung* of Berlin, Friedjung maintained that the war was making an age-old dream of the Germans come true, that of economically uniting Germany, Austria-Hungary, the Balkans, and Asia Minor.[166] Simultaneously, in the late fall of 1914 the most influential of those political networks mentioned earlier as working to bring about a union between Austria-Hungary and Germany was forming in Vienna around Gustav Marchet and Joseph Baernreither. Friedjung was soon channeling his engagement through this group; he was made responsible for the question of a military union with Germany in the work of the group.[167]

Friedjung later expanded his memorandum to dealing also with the economic integration between the two empires and with internal reform in Austria-Hungary, and it thus stood on its own. When the expanded version of the memorandum was finished in August 1915, it was presented as a group effort with a clear reference to the Marchet-Baernreither group. The authors, or rather editors, who presented this *Denkschrift aus Deutsch-Österreich* were Friedjung, the economist Eugen Philippovich,

Heinrich Friedjung during World War I; Nachlass Josef Redlich, courtesy of Fritz Fellner, Vienna

the historian Hans Uebersberger, and the politician and later president of the First Austrian Republic, Michael Hainisch, all active members of the Marchet-Baernreither group.[168] Friedjung was identified as the leading member of the group of editors, and the *Denkschrift* was distributed privately.[169] During the fall of 1915, Friedjung accompanied the targeted distribution of the *Denkschrift* with a press campaign in German newspapers. For example, he published several articles in the influential *Vossische Zeitung* of Berlin on the coming order in the Balkans, and especially on the future of Serbia. Regarding the latter, Friedjung connected with his own campaign against Serbia of 1909, asserting that now the time had come to "unite the South-Slav lands under Habsburg rule."[170] A little later Friedjung would celebrate the military campaign in the Balkans as a reinvigoration of Austria, raising her from a "spiritual-political decline" from which she had suffered since the defeats of 1859 and 1866.[171]

The *Denkschrift* itself deals primarily with a military and economic union built on a deepened political alliance between the two Central European empires. The military aspect is especially prominent, and this was apparently the part Friedjung himself was responsible for.[172] The military union, it seems, was the ultimate bond that would ensure the Austrian Germans their backing from Imperial Germany. Because of this it is interesting to note what this backing should facilitate. The last section of the *Denkschrift*, "Innerpolitische Reformen," contains a program for the restructuring of Austria and Austria-Hungary, and this part Friedjung had also been involved in.[173]

On the larger scene of Austria-Hungary, the military union was expected to strengthen the Gesamtstaat to such a degree that Hungary could be kept down and be embedded in the larger structure. At the same time Croatia was to be severed from Hungary, and Hungary's non-Magyar nationalities, no doubt primarily the Hungarian Germans, should be given expanded rights. Bosnia-Hercegovina and the eventually annexed territories in Serbia should be put under military government for an unspecified length of time. So also should the likewise "treacherous" Ruthene (Ukrainian) lands northeast of Austria. This whole Polish-Ukrainian land complex of Galicia and Bukovina should also be severed from "Western Austria" and would together with the newly annexed territories in Russian-Poland be tied directly to Vienna through the internal Verwaltung, but only indirectly through parliamentary delegations. This latter measure would ensure German hegemony in West-Österreich. Through the military union, an indirect hegemony would be maintained over the whole Austrian-Hungarian-Polish-South Slav empire that was taking shape before Friedjung's eyes. The German hegemony within Western Austria should be even more accentuated by the German state language in this state, which should also be reshaped into a unitary state, thus putting the Czechs in a permanent minority position.[174]

Friedjung partly distributed the *Denkschrift aus Deutsch-Österreich* personally to a great many officials in Austria and Germany, sometimes sending a long letter to accompany it. The first edition was out of print by mid-September, and by the end of the year 500 copies had been distributed.[175] In his accompanying letter to German chancellor Bethmann Hollweg, Friedjung was asking for "a powerful initiative from the imperial German government," because it was not to be expected that the fragmented Austro-Hungarian state institutions and leadership would be able to act decisively. Friedjung concluded this letter by depicting the creation of Mitteleuropa as the crown of his lifelong preoccupation with the history of Austria and Germany: "Because I dedicated years of my life to writing the history of the Bruderkrieg of 1866 with the intention of portraying this struggle as the precondition for the true reconciliation that should follow upon it, my works and efforts are therefore now directed at serving the goal of the unification of Mitteleuropa and portraying it as a product of the glorious war of 1915."[176]

During his campaign in distributing the *Denkschrift,* Friedjung targeted not only high civil officials, but, true to his own emphasis on a military union, also high military officials.[177] Friedjung's interest in generals at this time should also be seen in the context of the military victories of the allied imperial armies. The front moved eastward during the spring and summer of 1915, and Warsaw had fallen in early August. Shortly afterward, German troops were transferred to the Serbian front, where in October a united army under Field Marshal August von Mackensen swept victoriously over Serbia. Mackensen was one of the generals Friedjung had sent the *Denkschrift* to, and to Friedjung's joy, Mackensen replied early in October from the headquarters of his army in Temesvár in Southern Hungary, where it was preparing for its upcoming offensive. Mackensen was enthusiastic over the idea of a military union supported by an economic union between the two empires and commended Friedjung on his expert knowledge in military questions. Friedjung's ideas would find only supporters in the imperial German army. "I hope that the idea expressed in the *Denkschrift* will be realized," Mackensen concluded.[178]

Friedjung was enraptured by this support and became positively intoxicated as Mackensen's army swept over Serbia during the following weeks. On 18 October he wrote to the German economist Gustav Schmoller about Mackensen's potential role in realizing Mitteleuropa. Friedjung maintained that the Imperial German government should have demanded a union between the two empires as a precondition for even sending Mackensen's army to the south, and to at least use Serbia and Poland as objects of exchange for the same purpose: "Mackensen, who was in Vienna, is quite the man to deliver this message," Friedjung asserted.[179] Only a few days later, Friedjung wrote Mackensen directly in this purpose: "The right man must be chosen to present these proposals to the Emperor of Austria! . . . Who, may I ask, could achieve a stronger effect in this matter than the conqueror of Belgrade, the general who has followed in the footsteps of Prince Eugene of Savoy? I beg your pardon, Excellence, for being so presumptuous . . . I am moved . . . by the patriotic hope to see my fatherland being moved to decisions that will open up a glowing future."[180] The Prussian General Mackensen as the savior of the Austrian Germans? The bare idea generates the fear of Austria-Hungary being turned into a German protectorate.[181] And this was, of course, somewhat more than Friedjung was hoping for.

In the meantime, there had been new developments in the Reichskanzlei in Berlin. From the internal, official correspondence, it is evident that Bethmann Hollweg had been very inspired by the *Denkschrift aus Deutsch-Österreich*; it seems even to have been important for setting off the diplomatic offensive Berlin launched on the Mitteleuropa question in the period September to November 1915 and that culminated in the intergovernmental conferences in Berlin on 10–11 November.[182] Friedjung had unwavering support from the German ambassador in Vienna, Heinrich von Tschirschky, who had relayed Friedjung's *Denkschrift* with the diplomatic courier to Bethmann Hollweg in Berlin.[183] The result had been that Bethmann Hollweg had invited Friedjung to a personal meeting in Berlin. Friedjung asked for the meeting in late October , writing to Bethmann Hollweg: "I feel obliged to act as an interpreter for your Excellency of a world view, which I have repeatedly given expression to in my historical works and not only since the beginning of the war."[184] The meeting took place on 1 November, during which Friedjung argued for an enlargement of Austria(-Hungary), both in the Russian parts of Poland and in the Balkans, and for sharp measures internally in Austria. All this would be possible, Friedjung maintained, with imperial decrees and a strong hand supported by Berlin, ultimately by the new structures of Mitteleuropa.[185]

Disappointingly, Bethmann Hollweg did not respond to Friedjung's presentation in even remotely the way Friedjung was hoping for.[186] Moreover, two weeks later Mackensen replied and explained that although he was full of appreciation for Friedjung's strivings, he could not play the role Friedjung had devised for him.[187] In the late fall of 1915, it seemed like Friedjung's campaign of propaganda and lobbying for Mitteleuropa, which in itself was very successful, had lost its decisive political momentum. In retrospect, we can wonder what made Friedjung go to these extremes of trying to enlist the full force of Imperial Germany to drag Austria-Hungary into a union. Of course just as Friedjung had repeatedly stated, this was an old struggle of his. Notwithstanding this, Friedjung's staunch German-Austrian world view, with its skepticism toward Prussia's leading role in Germany, makes it difficult to fully understand the lengths he went to here. However, from the private notes he made, commenting on the *Denkschrift aus Deutsch-Österreich* and his role in it, we find it evident that Friedjung also deeply feared subordination to Imperial Germany. That which Friedjung viewed as the basic problem of the *Denkschrift* is clear in these notes: going far enough to awaken the interest of Imperial Germany in a union with Austria-Hungary (something in which it eminently succeeded), but without losing its independence and sovereignty in the process (something that soon became an irreversible process in the Dual Alliance).[188]

Friedjung and his associates had set themselves a very difficult task: to mobilize Imperial Germany for the historical rise of the Austrian Germans. In the end, perhaps it was just as well that Prussian General Mackensen did not present Reich-German demands to Franz Joseph in Vienna as an overture to Mitteleuropa. Such a historical narration of the creation of Mitteleuropa also seems peculiarly unsuited to the German-Austrian world view Friedjung had exhibited throughout his life. Nevertheless, Friedjung's historical narration of the rise of the German-Austrians ended in the wreckage of the Mitteleuropa project. Consequently, this narration was never set down in the planned book on the history of Europe. It is, however discernible in Friedjung's failed life project.

5. Conclusion

After the defeat in war and the dissolution of Austria-Hungary in 1918, Heinrich Friedjung modified his view on the role of human agency in history. The historian must acknowledge, Friedjung now stated, that the role of individuals in history "was in no age of so little import . . . as in the age between the resignation of Bismarck and the outbreak of the world war."[189] Friedjung's own political experience in the decades after Bismarck's resignation in 1890 here directly shaped his pessimistic view on the role of human agency in history. However, as recounted above, twenty years earlier Friedjung had come to other conclusions, which from around 1900 led him into a new sort of political engagement as he tried to influence and support key political decision makers that he judged to be leading Austria in the right direction. This new political engagement should be counted along with his party political activities in the 1870s and 1880s, especially because they had many of the same intentions, and that was to solve the identity crisis of the German-Austrians and to promote the historical rise of this group. Therefore William McGrath's conclusion about Friedjung's political career might need some modification; McGrath asserted that the anti-Semitism of the German nationals in the 1880s "completely destroyed Heinrich Friedjung's political career."[190]

As discussed in the introduction to this book, the type of political behavior Friedjung engaged in from around 1900 was actually an integrated part of the political culture of late Imperial Austria; the stable structures and far-reaching powers of the Rechtsstaat made it possible for individuals to interact directly with the Verwaltung to influence things in civil society. Friedjung's way of interacting with key decision makers to bring about change of a more fundamental political nature only brought this type of politics to an unusually high level. His shift of political mode during the 1890s can only too easily be explained by pointing to his personal marginalization in German-Liberal party politics. However, because his shift of mode took place in the period of ascending mass parties and a general loss of influence of the old Liberal elites, it can also be viewed as part of a more general pattern that, as suggested by James Shedel,[191] from this time led the old (now disenfranchised) Liberal elite to rely directly on the Verwaltung for its political influence. As we will see in the following parts of this book, this kind of "politics through the bureaucracy" seems to have been a present option and a normal part of Austrian political life of the period.

However, the problem of anti-Semitism in the German-Liberal camp and Friedjung's Jewish identity cannot be entirely avoided. I tend to view it partly as a pseudo-problem, created because we cannot regard Friedjung's time today without letting the fact of the Holocaust influence our view. It is partly this that makes the Jew Friedjung's way of stubbornly maintaining his German identity in an age of accelerating anti-Semitism so difficult to understand, or even to accept. However, I would like to ask what difference it would have made if Friedjung had not been a Jew. The disintegration of the German Liberals as the major political force in Austria in the 1880s and 1890s was so complete that even their old leader, Ernst von Plener, around 1900 found himself completely isolated and thrown out of politics. Like Plener and many other Liberals, Friedjung from this time sought other ways of making politics.

Nevertheless, Robert Wistrich went so far as to conclude from his analysis of Friedjung's radical German nationalism of the 1870s and 1880s that Friedjung must also have been a cultural anti-Semite.[192] As far as I know, however, Friedjung never did or said anything to confirm such a reading; he did not even attempt to shed his Jewish identity. Quite to the contrary, he seems to have effortlessly fused his Jewish identity with his German identity. Thus I find Marsha Rozenblit's conclusions about the tripartite identity constructed by the Austrian Jews during the late nineteenth century more useful than Wistrich's in understanding Friedjung. Rozenblit has identified a pattern in which many Austrian Jews in the last phase of the Habsburg Monarchy were Austrian in a political sense, German (or Czech, or Polish) in a cultural sense, and members of the Jewish people (in an ethnic and/or religious sense). According to Rozenblit, this was a peculiarly Austrian matrix, possible only at this time in multinational Austria.[193] This political and cultural matrix may have served to make possible Friedjung's peculiar mix of a strong German (cultural) identity closely tied to an Austrian (political) loyalty together with the maintenance of his Jewish identity.

Indeed, Friedjung's public identification with the German nation was so strong as to seemingly make his exclusion from the German national camp the crucial event in his life. However, as discussed in the first chapter of this section, there is a strong continuity in Friedjung's development; the essence of his life's project was his struggle to work out the identity of the Austrian Germans. The development that is discernible in this central trajectory in Friedjung's life, as I would argue, is that it went from an acute and desperate identity crisis in the 1870s, when Friedjung found himself threatened in his personal identity by the events of 1866 (the exclusion from Germany) and 1867 (the exclusion from Hungary); through a phase of intense critical examination of the weaknesses of Austria (resulting in the major work *Der Kampf um die Vorherrschaft in Deutschland* in 1897); and on to the affirmative stance on Austria which expressed itself in his new political engagement from around 1900.

Through this development Friedjung's German identity remained at the core of his life-project; the development of the identity trajectory described above only made it change its expressions gradually. During the nadir of Friedjung's identity crisis in the 1870s, he sought salvation in a pure German nationalism idealizing the individualist, Protestant Prussian culture, a stance that I believe has so far colored the image of Friedjung much too strongly. When Friedjung later found new stability in his identifications, he also shifted his emphasis over to the problems of (German-) Austrian culture, finally ending up on an affirmative stance on Austria that he maintained up to the dissolution of the empire in 1918 and beyond.

In the foreword to his *Historische Aufsätze* (1919), Friedjung wrote this: "We old Austrians have been defeated, but we have not been shaken in our conviction that our empire played its remarkably difficult role with honor." Friedjung's argument here developed into a pleading for the historical viability of the recently dissolved Habsburg Monarchy. Admittedly, he then also addressed the problem of the Germans of Austria, maintaining that large parts of them had identified primarily with the empire, but that others "repressed their longing for the German motherland so that they could serve her better in her largest colony."[194] However, in consideration of his own long engagement for Austria, it is not completely clear that Friedjung would have viewed himself as one of the "colonizers." I believe that his identification with Austria at this late stage had brought him at least a step closer to the other group, to those who primarily identified with the old empire.

◆

Ernest von Koerber was not so fortunate as to have an identity to fall back on. Indeed, one could say that those who were primarily identified with the imperial Austrian state lost their Heimat in 1918. Ernest von Koerber was closely identified with the Austrian state, and to a certain degree his personalized political project was a direct outgrowth of the old Liberal-Josephist state tradition that came to an end in November 1918.

Furthermore, Koerber virtually personified the Weberian concept of the bureaucrat, which in the final analysis must also be seen as a factor in his project. Although we can see Koerber's project as political, as I have here, we could also shift perspective and see his interpretation of the role of the Austrian minister president as one of bureaucratizing this function, as reducing the Austrian government to a bureaucratic instrument. Constitutionally speaking, the will controlling this instrument was, of course, the emperor's. However, because Franz Joseph also faded more and more into a strictly bureaucratic role, the question of the purpose of the Austrian state became acute. As I see it, Koerber's answer to it was clear: to reconstruct and reassert the Austrian Rechtsstaat as the framework for a modern multinational society, a truly Liberal aim. But Koerber's project of modernizing the Josephist state had a crucial weakness.The German-speaking centralism of the Josephist state limited its capacity to function as a framework for a multinational democratic state in an age when democracy was increasingly assuming a national shape. Koerber grappled with this problem throughout his career; his response was that of attempting to meticulously *separate* the German-speaking state (which *needed* to be German-speaking to function) from multinational society, trying to make them *cooperate* in the modernization of Austria. Nevertheless, its basic German character in combination with the built-in dependence on its German core group made it difficult to sustain the illusion that the Josephist state was nationally neutral. This illusion was finally shattered under the pressures of the World War, when external as well as internal German nationalism came very close to converting the Josephist state into an instrument of German domination over Central and southeastern Europe. Koerber's brief appearance at the head of this power structure in the fall of 1916 revealed the impotence of Liberal Josephism in the face of rampant German nationalism. In a more general way, his project was similar to Alexander Bach's attempt to modernize Austria through her Verwaltung fifty years earlier; this parallel can also be drawn with regard to the ultimate fragility of Liberalism and progressiveness in both these projects embedded in an old imperial structure of domination.

Just as with Friedjung, Koerber's life project was propelled by the personally felt need to find a way out of the Austrian identity crisis created by the events of 1866–67. He was born not long after the revolutionary upheavals of 1848–49, and he grew up during the extended period of crisis that ended with defeat in the war against Prussia in 1866 and the creation of the Dual Monarchy in the following year. Koerber's whole career as an imperial Beamte, which began in 1874, was marked by the balancing act enforced on Austria under the dual pressure from Berlin and Budapest. Eventually this pressure multiplied, and in the end Koerber's Josephist state simply disintegrated. Often a sharp observer, Friedjung understood that these political conditions caused the deep pessimism that he and many others had observed in Koerber's personality. He realized that Koerber's pessimism was in fact a structural phenomenon in someone whose identity was closely tied to the crisis-ridden Austrian Josephist state.[195] Therefore it seems only natural that Koerber's terminal illness was initiated by a stroke in the fall of 1918, shortly after the dissolution of the empire.

Notes

1. See Beilage I (Furniture and household goods) and Beilage II (Books) to no. 19 of the *Mitteilungen des "Dorotheum" Wien I, Dorotheergasse 17,* from 10 May 1919. The furniture and household goods were shown from 15 to 17 May, and the auction took place during three days, 19–21 May. The books were shown during the same days the furniture and household goods were auctioned, and they were auctioned on 22 May. A copy of the auction catalog lies in the Nachlass Friedjung (WStLB) K.3, Umschlag (U.) "Unterlagen und Studiennotizen zur europäischen Geschichte."
2. Friedjung's obituary in the *Neues Wiener Tageblatt* on 11 March 1919, 2–4, and an article about the funeral on 8 March in the same newspaper, *Neues Wiener Tageblatt,* 9 March, 10–11. The latter contains a long list of the people paying their respects at the funeral. Regarding the funeral, see also the diary of Josef Redlich, who was there: "Das ganze ministerielle Altösterreich war noch einmal versammelt da. . . ." (Entry for 10 March 1919, in Redlich, *Schicksaalsjahre,* 2:2:335f).
3. See, for example, the conversation with Friedrich Stadler von Wolffersgrün on 25 April 1919, Franz Adlgasser & Margret Friedrich, eds. *Heinrich Friedjung. Geschichte in Gesprächen. Aufzeichnungen 1898–1919,* 2 vols. (Vienna: Böhlau Verlag, 1997) (henceforth quoted as Friedjung, *Geschichte in Gesprächen* 1/2), here 2:441–44. There is also material of this type in the Nachlass Friedjung. See foremost Nachlass Friedjung (WStLB), K.2, U.2, which contains the greater part of the material on Koerber. The notes on the abovementioned conversation with Friedrich Stadler lies here (Folio F. 285–286), together with a sketch of Koerber's familial and close private relations (F. 297–298) and two rough copies of biographical articles on Koerber (F. 287–296, F. 300–323). For a sketch of Koerber's familial and close private relations, Friedjung has, among others, interviewed Koerber's nephew, a Baron Jacobs, who allegedly together with a cousin of Koerber's, Béla Szillay, had sifted Koerber's papers, destroyed most of them, and turned the rest over to a notary public. Just as Friedjung did, Jacobs heard the rumor that Koerber had given his most important papers (his "politischer Nachlass") to "a friend abroad," but knows nothing further

about this. Compare Friedjung's questioning of Friedrich Stadler on this issue (Friedjung, *Geschichte in Gesprächen*, 2:444, note a). No Koerber *Nachlass* has ever surfaced, and it is probable that the process here described by Friedjung constituted its dissolution and partial destruction.

4. The notes on the conversations with Koerber are published in Friedjung, *Geschichte in Gesprächen*. Together with the notes on conversations with Alois Lexa von Aehrenthal, the Koerber notes constitute the most voluminous material on a single person in the Friedjung papers. In published form, the Koerber notes are spread out chronologically, but in the Nachlass Friedjung, almost all the Koerber notes lie together in (WStLB) K.2, U.2, which also contains other material in connection with Koerber (for example, the material mentioned in note 3 above and several notes on conversations with other people *about* Koerber).
5. See Friedjung, "Ernest von Koerber." Except for the material in connection with this article mentioned in the previous notes, there is a rather late rough copy, almost identical with the published version, in the Nachlass Friedjung (HHStA) K.1.
6. As Fritz Fellner has emphasized, the three components of historical scholarship, journalism, and politics can hardly be separated in Friedjung's life career. See Fellner, "Heinrich Friedjung," 644.
7. On Friedjung's early involvement in politics, see Alfred Dechel, *Das 'Linzer Programm' und seine Autoren. Seine Vorgeschichte unter besonderer Berücksichtigung der Rolle des Historikers Heinrich Friedjung* (Unpublished dissertation, University of Salzburg, 1975); William J. McGrath, *Dionysian Art and Populist Politics in Austria* (New Haven: Yale University Press, 1974); and Erich Zailer, *Heinrich Friedjung. Unter besonderer Berücksichtigung seiner politischen Entwicklung* (Unpublished dissertation, University of Vienna, 1949). See also Robert S. Wistrich, *The Jews of Vienna in the Age of Franz Joseph* (Oxford: Oxford University Press, 1990), and Heinrich Friedjung, *Ein Stück Zeitungsgeschichte* (Vienna: Genossenschafts-Buchdruckerei, 1887).
8. Two of Friedjung's three grand historical works, *Der Kampf um die Vorherrschaft in Deutschland 1859–1866*, 2 vols. (Stuttgart: J.G. Cotta, 1897) and *Österreich von 1848 bis 1860*, 2 vols. (Stuttgart: J.G. Cotta, 1908/12), deal with the crucial period 1848–67 in Austrian history. Friedjung's notes on the above-mentioned conversations have been published in Friedjung, *Geschichte in Gesprächen*. The fusion with his political journalism is particularly evident in his third large-scale historical work, Heinrich Friedjung, *Das Zeitalter des Imperialismus 1884–1914*, 3 vols. (Berlin: Neufeld & Henius, 1919–22; partly posthumously), and also in several historical essays on persons and events during the last decades of the Habsburg monarchy. Most of the latter were collected in Heinrich Friedjung, *Historische Aufsätze* (Stuttgart: J.G. Cotta, 1919). The fusion of historical scholarship and journalism and Friedjung's use of the interview method are examined by Fellner, "Heinrich Friedjung," and by Adlgasser & Friedrich, "Einleitung."
9. It was published in ten editions from 1897 to 1918.
10. Friedjung's preoccupation with "partisanship" and "truthfulness" can be found in many instances in his letters and historical writings (see, for example, the case quoted in the text below). For another interesting example, see the letter Friedjung wrote to Masaryk during the Friedjung affair. (See the concept of a letter to Tomas G. Masaryk, dated 20 May 1909, Nachlass Friedjung [WStLB], K.2, U.6.)
11. Friedjung, *Österreich von 1848 bis 1860*, 1:VIII.
12. See Friedjung, *Das Zeitalter des Imperialismus*, 2:12–16. In the category of philosophical history Friedjung placed "[die] Formeln der Hegelschen Philosophie oder der Rassentheorie Gobineaus oder . . . des marxistischen Systems. . . ." (13).

13. Friedjung, *Das Zeitalter des Imperialismus,* 2:15.
14. Heinrich Friedjung, *Der Ausgleich mit Ungarn. Politische Studie über das Verhältnis Österreichs zu Ungarns und Deutschland* (Leipzig: Otto Wiegand, 1877), 14ff. (quotation on p. 18).
15. Concept of an undated letter, judging from its contents to Engelbert Pernerstorfer, and written in the winter of 1913–14, Nachlass Friedjung (HHStA), K.5.
16. There is a tendency to view Friedjung's political development as going from an Anschluss-oriented German nationalism in the 1870s to a more and more pronounced Great Austrian, imperialist stance, fully developed around 1900. It also involved a shift that entailed going from opposition to the state to support for it, and from social radicalism to a form of socially rather conservative old Liberalism. See Harry Ritter, "Progressive Historians and the Historical Imagination in Austria: Heinrich Friedjung and Richard Charmatz," in the *Austrian History Yearbook* 19/20 (1983–84): 45–90; Dechel, *Das 'Linzer Programm' und seine Autoren*; and Zailer, *Heinrich Friedjung* for this tendency. But some also emphasize the remarkable continuity in Friedjung's political thinking; see Fellner, "Heinrich Friedjung," and Adlgasser & Friedrich, "Einleitung."
17. See the program of the planned new Deutsche Volkspartei authored by Friedjung (the so-called Friedjung-Programm). The program is reproduced in Klaus Berchtold, ed. *Österreichische Parteiprogramme 1868–1966* (Munich: Oldenbourg Verlag, 1967), 189–92.
18. Berchtold, ed. *Österreichische Parteiprogramme,* 191.
19. The above-described stance is visible already in the "Friedjung-Programm" of 1880 (see Berchtold ed. (*Osterreichische Parteiprogramme,* 191f.) See also the conclusion in Friedjung, *Der Kampf um die Vorherrschaft in Deutschland,* 2:572, and the interview with Bismarck (ibid., 2:575–80). In the political tract, Heinrich Friedjung, *Denkschrift aus Deutsch-Österreich* (Leipzig: S. Hirzel, 1915), 3–17, Friedjung celebrated the Dual Alliance as the first step to the closer union of Mitteleuropa that should be realized during the war. For his notes on the meeting with Bethmann Hollweg in early November 1915, see Friedjung, *Geschichte in Gesprächen,* 2:406–13. As late as autumn 1918, Friedjung retained this connection between the Dual Alliance and the main goal of the Great War of extending the alliance into a union between Austria-Hungary and the German Empire (see Friedjung, *Das Zeitalter des Imperialismus,* 1:35). The Dual Alliance played a certain role at this time as a substitute for the "lost" Great-German solution, both in Germany and Austria. See, for example, the reflections on this in Pantenburg, *Im Schatten des Zweibundes,* 9ff., 53ff., 466ff.
20. See Friedjung, *Der Kampf um die Vorherrschaft in Deutschland,* for example, 1:340 and 2:6–7, 333, 373–74, 553–56.
21. See Heinrich Friedjung, *Benedeks nachgelassene Papiere. Herausgegeben und zu einer Biographie verarbeitet von Heinrich Friedjung* (Leipzig: Grübel & Sommerlatte, 1901).
22. See Friedjung, *Der Kampf um die Vorherrschaft in Deutschland,* 2:574.
23. Ibid., 2:556.
24. This view is particularly clear in the unpublished late manuscript on the internal history of Austria-Hungary 1867–1914, in Nachlass Friedjung (WStLB), K.3, U. "Studiennotizen, Aktenabschriften und Briefe zur österreichischen Reichsgeschichte." Friedjung highlights the simultaneity of divergent tendencies in 1879: "Man hat es auffallend gefunden, daß sich zwischen der innern und der äussern Politik der Hofburg ein derartiger Widerspruch klaffte: wurde doch im Jahre der Berufung Taaffes das Bündnis mit Deutschland geschlossen, trotzdem aber im Innern durch zwanzig Jahren mit kurzen Unterbrechungen gegen die Deutschen regiert."(F.11). Later (F.51) he highlights the shift of 1899 in a positive way when he describes the beneficial rule of the central bureaucracy, led by Koerber, Beck,

Gautsch, and Bienerth, i.e., 1900–1911, which according to Friedjung was a result of the insight that no one could rule Austria against its Germans.

25. The work was never finished mainly, it seems, because the offer to write *Das Zeitalter des Imperialismus* came in between.
26. Friedjung, *Österreich von 1848 bis 1860,* passim and especially the programmatic statement in 1:IX. On the rehabilitation of Austrian Vormärz culture, see 2:297–508 and especially the conclusions on 2:509f.
27. Schwarzenberg is treated extensively throughout the work. See, for example, Friedjung, *Österreich von 1848 bis 1860,* 1:96ff. and 2:135–70.
28. On Bach, see Friedjung, *Österreich von 1848 bis 1860,* 1:27–35, 308–32, 477–84, and 2:171–209. See also Heinrich Friedjung, "Alexander Bach's Jugend und Bildungsjahre" (1907), reprinted in Friedjung, *Historische Aufsätze,* 24–39.
29. On Bruck, see Friedjung, *Österreich von 1848 bis 1860,* 1:292–307. See also Heinrich Friedjung, "Mitteleuropäische Zollunionspläne 1849–1853" (1910), reprinted in Friedjung, *Historische Aufsätze,* 64–89. There is a clear parallel between the way Friedjung treats Bruck and the way he relates to the Mitteleuropa question in his own time, especially during the war years. Compare here Friedjung, *Denkschrift aus Deutsch-Österreich* (1915).
30. On Schmerling, see Friedjung, *Österreich von 1848 bis 1860,* 1:166–95.
31. Letter from Eisenmann to Friedjung, 4 September 1904, Nachlass Friedjung (HHStA), K.5. The background to this discussion was Eisenmann's book on the Austro-Hungarian Ausgleich of 1867 (*Le Compromis Austro-Hongrois de 1867,* 1904). See also Friedjung's review article on Eisenmann's book, "Ein französischer Historiker über das moderne Österreich" from 1904, reprinted in Friedjung, *Historische Aufsätze,* 463–73. The impression of Friedjung's very strong identification with the German-centralistic imperial rule in Austria is strengthened by the further contents of Eisenmann's long, above-quoted letter. Despite Friedjung's accusations of partisanship for the Hungarians and the Czechs, Eisenmann here exhibits a very strong identification with the Habsburg Empire. He repeats that he does not share French hostility toward Germany and Austria, but on the contrary considers the Habsburg Empire as fulfilling an important role in Central and Eastern Europe. Compare also Eisenmann's in retrospect almost ridiculously positive reading of the prospects of internal change and development in the Habsburg Empire in his article on Austria-Hungary in the *Cambridge Modern History.* See Louis Eisenmann, "Austria-Hungary," *The Cambridge Modern History,* vol. 12: *The Latest Age* (Cambridge: Cambridge University Press, 1910), 174–212.
32. On the second day of his minister presidency, Koerber invited Friedjung to an "exchange of opinions." This invitation fits the general picture of Koerber's personal relations with the press, since Friedjung was a very influential political journalist. This was the first time they had met, though. Friedjung recounted the conversation in a letter to Alois Lexa von Aehrenthal from 23 January 1900 (published in *Aus dem Nachlass Aehrenthal. Briefe und Dokumente zur oesterreichisch-ungarischen Innen- und Aussenpolitik 1885–1912),* 2 vols., Salomon Wank, ed. (Graz: Wolfgang Neugebauer Verlag, 1994), here 1:193–95. Friedjung relayed a relatively negative picture of Koerber to Aehrenthal. This impression might have something to do with Koerber's open statement, that he saw a restoration of the dominating position of the German parties in Austria, "as before 1879," as impossible, a statement that touched directly on the high expectations Friedjung had for the shift of political systems. As late as September 1900, Friedjung seems to be expecting Koerber to resign at any time. See notes on a conversation with Koerber, 23 September 1900, Freidjung, *Geschichte in Gesprächen,* 1:346f.

33. Notes on a conversation with Aehrenthal on 31 January 1909, in Friedjung, *Geschichte in Gesprächen*, 2:191–93. See also a conversation of 8 November 1908 (*Geschichte in Gesprächen*, 2:120–28) and a letter from Friedjung to Aehrenthal on 4 November 1908, published in *Aus dem Nachlass Aehrenthal*, 2:634f.
34. See, for example, Friedjung, *Geschichte in Gesprächen*, 2:8, notes on a conversation with Koerber on 17 January 1904, and ibid., 2:23, 14 February 1905.
35. The many-layered relationship between Friedjung and Aehrenthal can be followed well in the many notes on conversations with Aehrenthal from1898 to 1909, which are published in Friedjung, *Geschichte in Gesprächen* and in their correspondence, which in its main part is published in *Aus dem Nachlass Aehrenthal*, and in a smaller part of this correspondence, which has not been published. See HHStA, Nachlass Aehrenthal, K.2 and Nachlass Friedjung (HHStA), K.5. It is interesting that only with the assistance of Aehrenthal did Friedjung receive access to the official archives in his research on Schwarzenberg. See Adlgasser & Friedrich, "Einleitung," 15.
36. Partly, of course, the second volume of Friedjung, *Österreich von 1848 bis 1860* (1912), which contains the main part of Friedjung's writing on Schwarzenberg, but also in Heinrich Friedjung, "Fürst Felix Schwarzenberg und Graf Albrecht Bernstorff" (1912), reprinted in Friedjung, *Historische Aufsätze*, 90–125.
37. Heinrich Friedjung, "Kaiser Franz Josef I. Ein Charakterbild" (1919), reprinted in Friedjung, *Historische Aufsätze*, 493–541.
38. The discussion of Friedjung's image of Koerber departs from his biographical article on Koerber; see Friedjung, "Ernest von Koerber." However, it also draws heavily on Friedjung's notes on conversations with Koerber (and on Koerber with others) from 1900 to 1919, published in Friedjung, *Geschichte in Gesprächen*, and of unpublished material (including rough drafts and notes) in the Nachlass Friedjung (in both WStLB and HHStA). The quotation above is the first line of the published version of the biographical article.
39. See particularly the sketch of Koerber's familial and close private relations, in Nachlass Friedjung (WStLB), K.2, U.2 (F.297–98), and the rough draft of the biographical article (ibid., F.300–323), which elaborates more on Koerber's family background than the published version does. The quotation above is from this rough draft. See also the notes on a conversation with Koerber's friend Friedrich Stadler von Wolffersgrün on 25 April 1919, Friedjung, *Geschichte in Gesprächen*, 2:441–44. On Koerber's Hungarian relations, the families Nagy von Galantha, Szillay, and Szvéteray are especially mentioned in Friedjung's papers. It seems that Koerber had a particularly close relationship with his cousin Béla Szillay, with whom he traveled extensively in the years after his retirement in 1904 (on this, see especially Koerber's letters to Jakob Herzog, ÖNB/HS 276/45).
40. Notes on a conversation with Friedrich Stadler von Wolffersgrün on 25 April 1919, in Friedjung, *Geschichte in Gesprächen*, 2:441–44.
41. We can follow how Friedjung gradually formed his picture of Koerber through his many conversations with him and others from 1900 to 1919, Friedjung, *Geschichte in Gesprächen*.
42. Friedjung, "Ernest von Koerber," 41.
43. Ibid., 35.
44. Already in September 1900, Friedjung found Koerber exhibiting this focus on the constitutional relationship between the two parts of the empire, and this despite the strong political focus on the Czech-German question during this year. See Friedjung's notes on a conversation with Koerber on 23 September 1900, Friedjung, *Geschichte in Gesprächen*, 1:346–48.
45. Friedjung, "Ernest von Koerber," 33.
46. See ibid., 29.

47. Ibid., 27.
48. Notes on a conversation with Koerber in November 1916, Friedjung, *Geschichte in Gesprächen*, 2:414–418.
49. Friedjung, "Ernest von Koerber," 24.
50. Ibid., 37.
51. Wolfgang Mommsen, "Max Weber on Bureaucracy and Bureaucratization: Threat to Liberty and Instrument of Creative Action," idem, *The Political and Social Theory of Max Weber, Collected Essays* (Cambridge: Polity Press, 1989), 114.
52. Letter from Koerber to Friedjung on 1 August 1912, Nachlass Friedjung (HHStA), K.2. The second volume of Friedjung's *Österreich von 1848 bis 1860* had just been published.
53. On the Koerber Nachlass, see note 3 above. However, the result of a rather intensive search for private letters from Koerber in other private Nachlässe in Vienna yielded not much beyond single letters and two more extended exchanges of letters (the latter are Koerber's letters to Jakob Herzog, ÖNB/HS: 276/45, and to Oskar Lasser von Zollheim, HHStA, Nachlass Lasser von Zollheim, K.11). The most voluminous of these correspondences is the one with Herzog, which mainly took place after 1904 when Koerber in retirement traveled extensively and thus needed to write letters to stay in touch. Before 1904, Koerber probably either had very little time to write letters (he worked continuously) or he needed not to write them because he met friends and acquaintances regularly.
54. On Max Weber's ideal type of bureaucrat, see Bendix, *Max Weber*, 321–47, and Reinhard, *Geschichte der Staatsgewalt*, 126–32. On Joseph's II Hirtenbrief as a model for Weber, see Reinhard, *Geschichte der Staatsgewalt*, 409. The Hirtenbrief has been reproduced in Walter, *die österreichische Zentralverwaltung*, Abt. II, vol. 4:123–32.
55. Josef Redlich's diary testifies to this; see Redlich, *Schicksaalsjahre*, where the entries on Koerber are numerous.
56. Friedjung often met Koerber in the salon of Frau Helene Schneeberger, wife of Viennese lawyer Wilhelm Schneeberger and Koerber's mistress (see the entries on Koerber in Friedjung, *Geschichte in Gesprächen*). The correspondence with Jakob Herzog indicates a personal relationship where the exchange most often took place within the families, in Koerber's case with his mother, who lived with him until her death in 1905 (see note 53). Oskar Lasser's friendship seems to have gone back to Koerber's student years (see note 53). The diary of Josef Redlich also contains many entries where Redlich meets personally or in a smaller circle with Koerber in the home of either one; see Redlich, *Schicksaalsjahre*.
57. Koerber's letters to Herzog, ÖNB/HS: 276/45, are a good source of these travels.
58. The most comprehensive attempt to analyze and explain the Koerber era has been made by the American economic historian Alexander Gerschenkron in his book entitled *An Economic Spurt That Failed: Four Lectures on Austrian History* (Princeton: Princeton University Press, 1977). The second important work on Koerber is by the Austrian historian, Alfred Ableitinger, entitled *Ernest von Koerber und das Verfassungsproblem im Jahre 1900. Österreichische Nationalitäten- und Innenpolitik zwischen Konstitutionalismus, Parlamentarismus und oktroyiertem allgemeinen Wahlrecht* (Vienna: Böhlau Verlag, 1973). These books will be dealt with below. A third work that can be mentioned in passing is Herwig Leitgeb's unpublished doctoral dissertation, *Die Ministerpräsidentschaften Dr. Ernst v. Körber in den Jahren 1900–1904 und Oktober-Dezember 1916* (University of Vienna, 1951). Another unpublished dissertation is by Eibe Hinrichs, *Die Wirtschaftspolitik Ernest von Koerbers als Integrationsfaktor für die Nationalitäten des Habsburgerreiches (1900–1904)* (University of Vienna, 1998). Hinrichs makes an interesting attempt to put Gerschenkron's economic perspective in a political context. Besides these works there are several biographical articles,

not counting Friedjung's (see note 5): by Koerber's junior colleague in the Austrian civil service, Rudolf Sieghart, "Ernest von Körber," in *Deutsches Biographisches Jahrbuch*, vol. 2: 1917–20 (Stuttgart: Deutsche Verlags-Anstalt, 1928); by Koerber's younger contemporary, the historian and journalist Richard Charmatz, "Ein moderner Ministerpräsident"; by Erich Kielmannsegg, *Kaiserhaus, Staatsmänner, Politiker. Aufzeichnungen des k.k. Statthalters Erich Graf Kielmannsegg*, Walter Goldinger, ed. (Vienna: Oldenbourg Verlag, 1966), who was also a colleague of Koerber's in the civil service; and one by the Austrian historian Alexander Novotny, "Ministerpräsident Ernest von Koerber." See also Richard Charmatz's contemporary history of Austria, where the image of Koerber as "a modern minister president" was first presented, and Richard Charmatz, *Österreichs innere Geschichte, 1848–1907*, 2 vols. (Leipzig: Teubner, 1909/11), here 2:139–59.

59. Gerschenkron, *An Economic Spurt*, 23–26 (quotation on 25–26). Gerschenkron's frame of reference is economic historical, and his theoretical point of departure is modernization theory, more specifically the question of how different societies/states tackled the problem of economic modernization. The key phrase is "Great Spurt." The economic modernization theory, which was especially popular in the 1960s and 1970s, maintains that societies go through different phases, the modern one being characterized by a "Takeoff" into sustained growth. The notion of "Great Spurt," however, has more to do with the specific case where a society lagged behind the general (in effect the European) development in this regard and thus needed some help and guidance to achieve the "Takeoff." This role could be played by the banks, which was the case in Italy, or the state, which Gerschenkron tries to demonstrate was the "true" meaning of the Koerber plan in Austria (on modernization theory and the Koerber plan; see especially Gerschenkron, *An Economic Spurt*, 45–62).

60. The constitutional reform plan is analyzed in Ableitinger, *Ernest von Koerber*, 176–213. The document itself has later been published in *Briefe und Dokumente zur Geschichte der österreichisch-ungarische Monarchie. Der Verfassungstreue Großgrundbesitz 1880–1899/1900–1904,* 2 vols., Ernst Rutkowski, ed. (Munich: Oldenbourg Verlag, 1983–91), here 2:371–442. This constitutional reform plan will be reexamined below.

61. See Ableitinger, *Ernest von Koerber*, passim. See especially the introduction (11–22) and the conclusion (213–25) for the general argument.

62. See Boyer, "The End of an Old Regime." Boyer particularly reviews the Social Democratic and Christian Social movements (model of popular sovereignty) and the plans of the shadow cabinet of Arch-Duke Franz Ferdinand (the dynastic-corporate model). On the administrative reform commission, see especially 176–83. See also Gernot D. Hasiba, "Die Kommission zur Förderung der Verwaltungsreform (1911–1914)," in *Recht und Geschichte. Festschrift Hermann Baltl zum 70. Geburtstag*, Helfried Valentinitsch, ed. (Graz: Leyka Verlag, 1988), 237–62, and part three below.

63. On Joseph II, see, for example, T.C.W. Blanning, *Joseph II* (London & New York: Longman, 1994). On his state reforms, see Helene Liebel-Weckowicz, "Auf der Suche nach neuer Autorität: Raison d'Etat in den Verwaltungs- und Rechtsreformen Maria Theresias und Joseph II," *Österreich im Europa der Aufklärung*, Plaschka et al., eds., 339–364, and Werner Ogris, "Zwischen Absolutismus und Rechtsstaat", in ibid., 365–376. On Koerber's administrative measures trying to reconstruct the lost modes of operation, we can mention especially his creation of a *Verordnungsblatt* for the interior ministry, accompanied by strict regulations on the operation of this periodical of administrative ordinances as a way of ensuring the implementation of new instructions and regulations. See Anton Pace, ed., *Ernst Mayerhofers Handbuch für den politischen Verwaltungsdienst*, 8 vols. (fifth edition, Vienna: Manz, 1895–1913) here 1:434ff., on the original eighteenth-century mode

of operation, which Koerber's measure here seems to reconnect with. On the place of the *Verordnungsblatt* in Koerber's program, see Fredrik Lindström, "Ernest von Koerber and the Austrian State Idea: A Reinterpretation of the Koerber Plan (1900–1904)," *Austrian History Yearbook* 35 (2004): 174.

64. Alexander Bach has been sadly neglected in scholarship. See Hans Loew, *Alexander Freiherr von Bach* (unpublished dissertation, University of Vienna, 1947), 91ff., on his administrative reforms. On this, see also Harm-Hinrich Brandt, *Der österreichische Neoabsolutismus: Staatsfinanzen und Politik 1848–1860* (Göttingen: Vandenhoeck & Ruprecht, 1978), 248–51, 254–60.
65. On similarities between Koerber's and Bach's administrative reforms, see Pace, *Ernst Mayerhofers Handbuch*, 1:12ff., and below (in the section on Koerber's administrative reform). Koerber handpicked Pace in July 1900 from the vice presidency of the Oberster Rechnungshof. Before that, Pace had served as Landespräsident in Bukowina, in the Statthalterei in Graz, and in the interior ministry. Koerber described Pace as someone who could ". . . sich bei dem Beamtenkörper des Ministerium des Innern die nötige Autorität zu verschaffen. . . ." See AVA, Ministerium des Innern, Präsidium, K.1363, Z.4457/1900 (25 July). Pace served as editor of *Ernest Mayerhofers Handbuch für den politischen Verwaltungsdienst* from 1895 to 1913 and was thus a sort of guardian of the Josephist and Bach legacy of the Austrian Verwaltung. Ernest Mayerhofer's *Handbuch* was originally written as a part of Bach's project of constructing a new Austrian Verwaltung in the 1850s and was first issued in 1856. It was then turned into an institution and continuously updated. The job of editor was taken over by Anton Pace in 1895.
66. See Reinhard, *Geschichte der Staatsgewalt*, 409.
67. On Bach's instruction of August 1849, see Loew, *Alexander Freiherr von Bach*, 91ff. The instruction has been reproduced in Walter, *Österreichische Zentralverwaltung*, Abt. III, vol. 2:105–10.
68. See Stefan Malfér, "Der Konstitutionalismus in der Habsburgermonarchie—Siebzig Jahre Verfassungsdiskussion in 'Cisleithanien,'" in *Die Habsburgermonarchie*, Rumpler & Urbanitsch, eds., 7:43–66, for contemporary views of the crisis of the Austrian state around 1900. Koerber's administrative instruction of January 1900 has been reproduced in Gustav Kolmer, *Parlament und Verfassung in Österreich*, 8 vols. (Graz: Akademische Druck- und Verlagsanstalt, 1972–80; reprint of first edition from 1902–14), here 8:3f. The second instruction of 1916 has been reproduced in Alois Czedik, *Zur Geschichte der k.k. österreichischen Ministerien 1861–1916*, 4 vols. (Vienna: Prochaska, 1917–20), here 4:529f.
69. The chairman of the commission, Erwin von Schwartzenau, its permanent secretary, Anton Pace, the head of the administrative office of the commission, Robert Davy, and the very active and prominent member of the commission, Guido von Haerdtl, had all held important posts under Koerber in the interior ministry in 1900–1904. Haerdtl and Davy had been key persons in the internal work on administrative reform, and Pace and Schwartzenau held important executive functions under Koerber. On all this see Lindström, "Ernest von Koerber and the Austrian State Idea."
70. Alfred Ableitinger touches superficially on the subject (see Ableitinger, *Ernest von Koerber*, 80, 153, 188f., 221f.), and Alexander Gerschenkron hardly does that. Gerschenkron, though, makes the noteworthy admission that his analysis of Koerber is "incomplete inasmuch as nothing has been said on Koerber's actions as an administrator during his years in office when he tried to 'modernize' the administration of the country" (see Gerschenkron, *An Economic Spurt*, 44), after which he mentions Koerber's numerous initiatives in the field of Verwaltungsreform.

71. Koerber's reform plan is treated in Lindström, "Ernest von Koerber and the Austrian State Idea." In the main, the following three sections build on this article and the references therein.
72. On the problem of the constitutional monarchy, see Böckenförde, "Der Verfassungstyp der deutschen konstitutionellen Monarchie im 19. Jahrhundert," 146–70; on the argument on historical legitimacy, see ibid., 160–61. See further on the problem of constitutional monarchy the different contributions in Ernst Wolfgang Böckenförde, ed. *Probleme des Konstitutionalismus im 19. Jahrhundert* (Berlin: Duncker & Humblot, 1975). With the focus on Austria, see Brauneder, *Österreichische Verfassungsgeschichte*, 154–75; idem, "Die Verfassungsentwicklung in Österreich 1848–1918," in Urbanitsch and Rumpler, eds. *Die Habsburgermonarchie* 7: 69–237; Malfèr, "Der Konstitutionalismus in der Habsburgermonarchie," 11–67. For the larger European context to the constitutional monarchy, see also Lothar Gall, *Europa auf dem Weg in die Moderne 1850–1890* (Munich: Oldenbourg Verlag, 1997), 11–20, and Reinhard, *Geschichte der Staatsgewalt*, 406–40.
73. However, as most observers note, Koerber, after restricting the sphere of operation of §14 added a potentially dangerous formulation about "the special Austrian conditions," making it necessary for the government to be allowed to employ the §14 (and rule without parliament) when not even the most basic needs of the state could be secured; he thus expanded the sphere of "state emergencies" into the sphere of the normal business of government. Even though he closely circumscribed this extended sphere of state emergencies (such as raising taxes according to the latest parliamentary sanction and paying salaries to civil servants etc. in case the parliament was hindered because of obstructions from dealing with this legislation), Koerber's proposed constitutional regulation here could potentially lessen the government's motivation to cooperate with parliament and lead to a renewed abuse of §14. This regulation is problematic, but I think we should not view it as an example of authoritarian behavior. I believe it should be read as a symptom of how serious Koerber judged the state crisis to be in 1900; he simply did not dare to completely disarm the government. Compare here Ableitinger, *Ernest von Koerber*, 211–13, and Gernot D. Hasiba, *Das Notverordnungsrecht in Österreich (1848–1917). Notwendigkeit und Mißbrauch eines 'staatserhaltenden Instrumentes'* (Vienna: Verlag der österreichischen Akademie der Wissenschaften, 1985), here 118 (note 134).
74. See *Briefe und Dokumente* 2:396.
75. Koerber maintained that the unconstitutional way in which he intended to implement the reform "did not disturb constitutional life or even the essence of the existing constitution, but it meant only to buttress them." (*Briefe und Dokumente*, 2:396). Later, in 1916 Koerber commented on this problem retrospectively: "When the old emperor had granted the constitution, but never taken an oath on it, he should, in a generous interpretation, really be able to suspend it again." PEA, Österreich 86, no. 2/22, report by Ambassador Wedel dated Sylvester (New Year's Eve) 1916.
76. The speech is reproduced in *Kolmer, Parlament und Verfassung*, 8:17–20. In presenting his legislative program, Koerber spoke a great deal about economic reform measures, something that was duly noted by Gerschenkron.
77. For an interpretation of Koerber focusing on his "domestication" of the parliament, see Höbelt, *Kornblume und Kaiseradler*, 180–99. On the detail of Koerber's parliamentary politics, see Kolmer, *Parlament und Verfassung*, 8, passim.
78. Koerber made a special point of emphasizing this in his meeting with Friedjung on 20 January 1900. See Friedjung's letter to Aehrenthal, 23 January 1900, in *Aus dem Nachlass Aehrenthal*, 1:193–95.

79. On the Verständigungskonferenzen, see Ableitinger, *Ernest von Koerber*, 82–157. The protocols have been published in *Briefe und Dokumente*, 2:38–216. On the Czech parties during the Koerber era, see Křen, *Die Konfliktgemeinschaft*, 225–54. On the German-Liberals and Koerber, see Höbelt, *Kornblume und Kaiseradler*, 180–199. Luboš Velek has dealt closely with the problem of the Czech parties and Koerber. See, for example, his articles "Koerberovy Česko-Německé smiřovací konference 1900" [Koerbers Czech-German conciliation conferences in 1900], in *Časopis Národního muzea—řada historická* 168/1–2 (1999): 28–54, and "Sestavení Vlády Ernesta von Koerbera a obnovení Úřadu Českeho ministra krajana roku 1900" [Koerber's formation of government and restoration of a Czech *Landesmann* ministry], *Paginae historiae* 6 (1998): 38–63. Through Koerber's correspondence with leading Czechs, such as the head of the Young Czech parliamentary club, Bedřich Pacák, the minister (Landesmannminister) in his own government, Antonín Rezek, and the prominent Young Czech politician and former minister in the Thun government, Josef Kaizl, it is evident that he kept in close touch with and made a real effort to enlist the moderate Czech parties in his parliamentary support. I especially find Koerber's letters to Pacák revealing. Koerber's letters to Pacák and Kaizl lie in their respective Nachlässe in the Archive of the National Museum in Prague [Archiv Národního Musea]; those to Rezek lie in the Czech Literary Archive in Prague [Literárni Archiv Památníku Národního Písemnictví]. My sincere thanks to Luboš Velek for locating and copying these letters for me.
80. See John W. Boyer's observation on the Social Democrats attitude toward the central ministries, in Boyer, *Culture and Political Crisis*, 121. See also Alexander Gerschenkron's reflections on Koerber and the Social Democrats, in Gerschenkron, *An Economic Spurt*, 64–70. However, compare Mommsen, *Die Sozialdemokratie und die Nationalitätenfrage*, 341–61. Karl Renner's relationship with Koerber is treated in part three below. See also the correspondence between Koerber's right-hand man, Rudolf Sieghart, and Engelbert Pernerstorfer in the files of the Ministerratspräsidium (Bohemica-Akten), PMR/R: K.1, in the Czech State Archives in Prague.
81. On the Christian Socials and Koerber, see Boyer, *Culture and Political Crisis* (quotation on 40). On Koerber and the municipal franchise reform, see ibid., 24f.
82. On the Verfassungstreue Grossgrundbesitz, see *Briefe und Dokumente* 2, where the strong support of this grouping for Koerber, as well as their close contact, comes across clearly. For one good example, see the letter from Oswald Thun-Salm (head of the party) to Max Egon Fürstenberg on 10 December 1903, in *Briefe und Dokumente* 2:808–09.
83. See Höbelt, *Kornblume und Kaiseradler*, 199.
84. The administrative instruction of 20 January 1900 has been reproduced in Kolmer, *Parlament und Verfassung*, 8:3f. The second Hirtenbrief, the administrative instruction of 18 November 1916, has been published in Czedik, *Zur Geschichte der k.k. österreichischen Ministerien*, 4:529f.
85. See Lindström, "Ernest von Koerber and the Austrian State Idea," 168–81.
86. John W. Boyer focuses on one such instance, the hostility of the Christian Social regime in Vienna to Koerber's reform project. See Boyer, *Culture and Political Crisis*, 33ff. and 41. Koerber's reform was also criticized by the association of provincial "governments"; see the protocol of the Wiener Konferenz der Landesauschüsse 16–18 May 1905, a copy of which can be found in AVA, Nachlass Davy, K.2.
87. Koerber expressed this reservation in an internal memorandum in the interior ministry. See Z.8580/MI/1904, in AVA, Nachlass Davy, K.2. (This document has a file number issued by the interior ministry, but it cannot be located in the archive there; I found it in the Nachlass of one of Koerber's interior ministry subordinates, Robert Davy.)

88. This memorandum of late January 1905 is described rather comprehensively by Koerber in a conversation with Friedjung on 28 June 1905; see Friedjung, *Geschichte in Gesprächen*, 2:25–27. My attempt to find the memorandum itself in the relevant archives in Vienna was unsuccessful. On Koerber's view that the 1867 constitution was no longer sustainable, see his conversation with Friedjung at the very time Koerber is supposed to have written the memorandum (on 31 January 1905, in Friedjung, *Geschichte in Gesprächen*, 2:18).
89. On this problem, see Somogyi, for example, *Der gemeinsame Ministerrat*; on Koerber's role, ibid., 191–95, and Stourzh, "Der Dualismus," 1201–08.
90. I have discussed these constitutional politics of Koerber's in more detail in Lindström, "Ernest von Koerber and the Austrian State Idea," 156–68 (see also the references therein).
91. Conversation with Koerber on 23 September 1900, in Friedjung, *Geschichte in Gesprächen*, 1:346–48.
92. See Friedjung, *Geschichte in Gesprächen*, 2:25–27.
93. The imperial Austrian bureaucracy has received scant attention in Austrian historiography. For two social-historical studies, see Heindl, *Gehorsame Rebellen*, and Megner, *Beamte*. For an outline of its organizational history after 1848, see Walter Goldinger, "Die Zentralverwaltung in Cisleithanien—Die Zivile gemeinsame Zentralverwaltung," in *Die Habsburgermonarchie 1848–1918*, vol. 2: *Verwaltung und Rechtswesen*, Adam Wandruszka & Peter Urbanitsch, eds. (Vienna: Verlag der österreichischen Akademie der Wissenschaften, 1975), 100–89. The Austrian civil service can be viewed as shaped by the different historical phases of imperial Austria. The Josephist bureaucracy was founded and decisively shaped by the Enlightenment centralization and modernization project under Maria Theresia and Joseph II (1740–90), but received a more conservative and clerical tendency under the era of Franz I and Metternich (1792–1835–1848). Arguably, both these tendencies were restated under the simultaneously conservative and modernizing neoabsolutism of the 1850s. This might account for its distinct dual character in the age of the Dual Monarchy (1867–1918), where one can identify two main wings of the Josephist bureaucracy, the Liberal and the Conservative (or clerical) wing. On this, for example, see Alois Czedik's insistence on categorizing those imperial bureaucrats he was treating in his chronicle of the imperial Austrian governments as either Liberal or Conservative Beamte (see Czedik, *Zur Geschichte der k.k. Ministerien*). For an interesting perspective on the bureaucracy during the period that concerns us here, see Josef Redlich, *Austrian War Government* (New Haven: Yale University Press, 1929), especially 34–40.
94. See Redlich, *Austrian War Government*, 37f. Redlich pointed out the finance minister in the Taaffe government, Emil Steinbach, as the most prominent representative of the conservative wing of the Josephist bureaucracy during its last decades.
95. See Redlich, *Schicksaalsjahre*, 1:145 (entry on 25 August 1912).
96. Koerber had made a deep impression both on his superiors in the trade ministry and on the organization, and also on the functionings of the ministry itself during the late 1880s and early 1890s (see here, for example, the documentation on Koerber in AVA, Handelsministerium, Präsidiales, Z. 2870–1893, Z.3228, 3306/1893, and Z.2790/1895). The praise Koerber received from his superiors was almost certain to have attracted the attention of Franz Joseph, who was the first Beamte of his own state. At the latest, though, Franz Joseph would have noted Koerber in 1893, when his attention was drawn to the important role Koerber was playing in the Ministry of Trade. Franz Joseph has made his characteristic double lines in the margins of the report, where Koerber's prominent role in the ministry is discussed. See AVA, Handelsministerium, Präsidiales, Z. 1870–93. See further, Ableitinger, *Ernest von Koerber*, 80f., where Ableitinger recounts how Koerber had a supporter in Adolf von Braun, who was then head of the imperial chancellery.

97. On Aehrenthal's relationship to Kálnoky, see below in chapter three.
98. See the correspondence between Aehrenthal and Goluchowski from January to April 1904 in *Aus dem Nachlass Aehrenthal,* 1:317–36. On this whole exchange, see Salomon Wank, "Varieties of Political Despair: Three Exchanges between Aehrenthal and Goluchowski 1898–1906," in *Intellectual and Social Developments in the Habsburg Empire from Maria Theresia to World War I,* Stanley Winters & Joseph Held, eds. (New York: Columbia University Press, 1975), 214–21. For later important examples of Aehrenthal's constitutional politics, see Aehrenthal's memorandum of 23 October 1906 in *Aus dem Nachlass Aehrenthal,* 1:411, and for his actions during the Ausgleich negotiations in 1906–07, see Éva Somogyi, "Aehrenthals Reformbestrebungen 1906–1907," *Österreichische Osthefte* 30 (1988): 71–73.
99. On Koerber's view of Aehrenthal, see the letter from Friedjung to Aehrenthal of 23 January 1902 in *Aus dem Nachlass Aehrenthal,* 1:260–263, and Friedjung's notes on a conversation with Koerber on 30 October 1903 in Friedjung, *Geschichte in Gesprächen,* 1:496–98. On Aehrenthal's appreciation of Koerber, see Aehrenthal's family correspondence in *Die Aehrenthals. Eine Familie in ihrer Korrespondenz 1872–1911,* 2 vols., Franz Adlgasser, ed. (Vienna: Böhlau Verlag, 2002), here 2:779 (note 1614), 792, 800, 834, 854, 873. See also the letter from Aehrenthal to Koerber dated 5 January 1905, *Aus dem Nachlass Aehrenthal,* 1:352f.
100. On these politics of Aehrenthal, see the documentation in *Die Grosse Politik der Europäischen Kabinette 1871–1914. Sammlung der diplomatischen Akten des Auswärtigen Amtes,* Johannes Lepsius, Albrecht Mendelssohn-Bartholdy & Friedrich Thimme, eds., 40 vols. (Berlin: Deutsche Verlags Gesellschaft für Politik und Geschichte, 1922–27), here vol. 22, chapter CLX. See also the most recent treatment of this issue in Pantenburg, *Im Schatten des Zweibundes,* 364–401 (and the references therein). In October 1908, these plans lost their viability because of the intense Russian hostility toward Austria-Hungary after the annexation of Bosnia-Hercegovina.
101. Aehrenthal presented these proposals in a seemingly agitated state in the two following semiofficial letters (so-called *Privatschreiben*) sent one after the other to Goluchowski on 20 and 25 July 1906; see *Aus dem Nachlass Aehrenthal,* 1:385–91. There then followed two more letters in August (see ibid. 1:393f., 399ff.). Goluchowski took his time and answered only in mid-September (see ibid. 1:403ff.).
102. See Friedjung's notes on a conversation with Aehrenthal on 11 June 1900 in Friedjung, *Geschichte in Gesprächen,* 1:344f.
103. Koerber cooperated with the former German-Liberal leader Ernst von Plener in preparations for the conference of the Inter-Parliamentarian Union in Vienna in 1903, both with government funds and personnel from the interior ministry. Koerber also held the welcoming speech at the conference. On Koerber and the Inter-Parliamentarian Union, see Ernst von Plener, *Erinnerungen,* 3 vols. (Stuttgart: Deutsche Verlagsanstalt, 1911–21), here 3:335; Koerber's letters in HHStA, Nachlass Plener, K.19; and the material in connection with the conference in AVA, Ministerratspräsidium, especially K.43 (Z.1530/1901) and several documents from 1903 in K.50–52. For Aehrenthal's view of the Inter-Parliamentarian Union as even more dangerous than the communist forces of the Russian revolution, see the letters cited in note 101 above.
104. On Aehrenthal's proposals in 1898–99, see Ernst Rutkowski, "Aehrenthal über die innenpolitische Lage Österreich-Ungarns im Sommer 1899," *Südost-Forschungen* 23 (1964), and Salomon Wank, "Zwei Dokumente Aehrenthals aus den Jahren 1898–99 zur Lösung der inneren Krise in Österreich-Ungarn," *Mitteilungen des Österreichischen Staatsarchivs* 19 (1966). Aehrenthal's two memorandums of 1898–99 are reproduced in the latter article,

but they can also be found in *Briefe und Dokumente*, 1:581–90 and 1:631–38. On Aehrenthal's constitutional politics as foreign minister, see Somogyi, "Aehrenthals Reformbestrebungen," passim; idem, *Der gemeinsame Ministerrat*, 237–44; and Salomon Wank, "Aehrenthal's Programme for the Constitutional Transformation of the Habsburg Monarchy: Three Secret Mémoires," *Slavonic and East European Review* 41, no. 97 (June 1963).

105. On this whole phase (1897–99) in the relations between Imperial Germany and Austria-Hungary, see Pantenburg, *Im Schatten des Zweibundes*, 57–139. See also the documentation in *Die Grosse Politik*, 13, chapter LXXXVII (among which is a selection of the correspondence between the foreign ministry in Berlin and the embassy in Vienna in the years 1898–99). Bülow and Eulenburg simply tried to force the resignation of the Thun government, arguing that it was undermining the Dual Alliance, but according to Pantenburg, the official imperial German attempt to influence things in Austria was in the main counterproductive. However, she admits that there was an amorphous influence from Imperial Germany, not least from its very active press, which probably affected decisions in Vienna to some degree. On this, see Pantenburg, *Im Schatten des Zweibundes*, 127–137 and 466ff.

106. This special identity-based character of the Dual Alliance is the gist of Pantenburg's argument in *Im Schatten des Zweibundes*; see especially ibid., 9, 53ff. and 466ff. It is visible, for example, in Foreign Secretary Bülow's instructions to Eulenburg shortly after Thun's speech: "Außerdem läßt der Geist, welche die Rede des Grafen Thun atmet—falls dieser maßgebend für die Leitung der österreichischen Politik bleiben sollte—, es zweifelhaft erscheinen, ob die unter solchen Umständen erfolgende Fortsetzung des deutsch-österreichischen Bündnisses mehr als eine Form bedeuten würde. Das deutsche Volk hat sich aber daran gewöhnt, mit diesem Bündnis wie einem effekten Bestandteil des nationalen Inventariums zu rechnen." (GP 13:125; Bülow to Eulenburg on 5 December 1898).

107. So, for example, in the report of an audience with Franz Joseph, dated 11 December 1900, in PAAA, Österreich 70/38: "Ich wagte seine Majestät an die Wirkung des Ministeriums Thun auf Deutschland zu erinnern." And in the summer of 1901, Eulenburg is telling Franz Joseph about the changes in the tone of the German press since Koerber came to power: "Die leicht erregbare deutsche Presse, . . . habe . . . eine wesentlich andere und ruhigere Haltung gezeigt als 'früher.' Der Kaiser verstand sehr wohl, wen ich mit diesem 'früher' meinte." (Report from 21 June 1901, in PAAA, Österreich 86 no. 1/13). And thus it goes on.

108. On the Badeni conflict, see Sutter, *Die Badenischen Sprachenverordnungen*, passim. On the German parties in this conflict and its aftermath, see Höbelt, *Kornblume und Kaiseradler*, 150–80. The Badeni ordinances made the whole of the Bohemian administration bilingual. What the German nationalists reacted against was that now Czech was made an administrative language also in compact German-speaking areas. For a vivid description of the eruption of physical violence between German and Czech parliamentarians in the Austrian Parliament in late November 1897, see Gerschenkron, *An Economic Spurt*, 16ff.

109. See Lichnowsky's report to Chancellor Hohenlohe-Schillingsfürst, dated 21 October 1899, in PAAA, Österreich 70/36.

110. Friedjung recounted the conversation with Koerber in a letter to Alois Lexa von Aehrenthal on 23 January 1900, *Aus dem Nachlass Aehrenthal*, 1:193–95.

111. Eulenburg's report to Chancellor Hohenlohe-Schillingsfürst, 21 November 1899, *Die Grosse Politik* 13:175f.

112. See Eulenburg's reports from 16 March, in PAAA, Österreich 70/36, and from 27 April 1900, PAAA, Österreich 70/37, and those of Legationsrat Pürkler from 9 and 19 June and from 29 August 1900, PAAA, Österreich 70/37–38.

113. See Eulenburg's reports from 4 and 11 December 1900, PAAA, Österreich 86 no. 2/12 and Österreich 70/38.
114. See Ambassador Wedel's report to Chancellor Bülow from 8 February 1903, in PAAA, Österreich 86, no. 2/13.
115. See the concept of Bülow's letter to Wedel from 13 June 1904, PAAA, Österreich 86, no. 2/13.
116. On the state-level Mitteleuropa question during the war, see Henry Cord Meyer, *Mitteleuropa in German Thought and Action, 1815–1945*, (The Hague: Nijhoff, 1955), and Gary W. Shanafelt, *The Secret Enemy: Austria-Hungary and the German Alliance, 1914–1918* (Boulder & New York: Columbia University Press, 1985). The recent work by Achim Müller, *Zwischen Annäherung und Abgrenzung. Österreich-Ungarn und die Diskussion um Mitteleuropa im Ersten Weltkrieg* (Marburg: Tectum-Verlag, 2001), covers the Austrian side of it well and also provides good insight into the official Reich-German side. See further, Richard W. Kapp, "Bethmann Hollweg, Austria-Hungary, and Mitteleuropa, 1914–1915," *Austrian History Yearbook* 19–20 (1983–84): 215–236. Gustav Gratz & Richard Schüller, *Die Äussere Wirtschaftspolitik Österreich-Ungarns. Mitteleuropäische Pläne* (New Haven: Yale University Press, 1925), give a close documentation of the official Austro-Hungarian actions in this field. Heinrich von Tschirschky's important role comes out in Müller, *Zwischen Annäherung und Abgrenzung*. For a few examples of the German national activism of von Tschirschky, see Tschirschky's report in early September 1914 [A 20240], in PAAA, Österreich 83/1, and his report to Jagow of 29 October 1915, in André Scherer & Jacques Grunewald, eds. *L'Allemagne et les problèmes de la paix pendant la première guerre mondiale. Documents extraits des archiv de l'Office allemand des Affaires étrangères*, vol. 1: *Des origines la déclaration de la guerre sous-marine a outrance (août 1914–31 janvier 1917)*, publiés et annotés par André Scherer et Jacques Grunewald (Paris: Presses universitaire de France, 1962), 192ff.: ". . . Ich habe mir wiederholt erlaubt, darauf hinzuweisen, dass nur durch militärischen und wirtschaftlichen engsten Anschluss eine dauernde Kettung der Monarchie an uns und zugleich eine Stärkung des deutschen Elementes in Österreich zu erreichen sein werden."
117. On Naumann's Mitteleuropa activism, see Peter Theiner, *Sozialer Liberalismus und deutsche Weltpolitik. Friedrich Naumann im Wilhelminischen Deutschland (1860–1919)* (Baden-Baden: Nomos Verlagsgesellschaft, 1983), 236–258, and Theodor Heuss, *Friedrich Naumann: Der mann, das Werk, die Ziet* (Stuttgart: Rainer Wunderlich, 1949), 333–43, 369–81. See also Müller, *Zwischen Annäherung und Abgrenzung*, 142–253. See also most of Naumann's writings in connection with *Mitteleuropa*, in Friedrich Naumann's *Werke*, 6 vols., Thomas Nipperdey & Wolfgang Schieder, eds. (Opladen: Westdeutscher Verlag 1964–66), here 4:374–977. See also the rich material in BArch, Nachlass Naumann (N 3001); Naumann's notes on his Viennese trip, entry of 18 February 1915 (the day of return to Berlin), BArch, Nachlass Naumann, N 3001/217. During the weeks and months following the trip to Austria-Hungary, Naumann published a great many articles on Mitteleuropa, also focusing strongly on the special conditions of Austria-Hungary. Several were published in *Werke*, 4:459–84. See especially "Kriegschronik" of 19 February 1915, in *Die Hilfe* no. 8/1915 (25 February), published in Naumann, *Werke*, 4:459ff.: "Auf der Heimfahrt werden die Eindrücke aus Österreich und Ungarn gesammelt und geordnet. Es ist doch etwas großes, daß von der Nordsee bis nach Siebenbürgen ein gemeinsamer Herzschlag vorhanden ist! Jetzt oder nie gelingt der Völkerverband oder Wirtschaftsverband Mitteleuropa. . . . [D]as Deutschtum für sich allein reicht zu dieser geschichtlichen Aufgabe nicht aus und läßt sich geographisch gar nicht aus den ihm benachbarten Bestandteilen herauslösen." Also interesting is a letter that seems to date Naumann's discovery of

the concept of Mitteleuropa exactly during his trip to Austria-Hungary. See the copy of a letter from Naumann to Wilhelm Kestranek dated 29 December 1915, in BArch, Nachlass Naumann, N 3001/16 (F.133): "[I]ch [habe] meinen ersten Vortrag über Mitteleuropa etwa Mitte Februar 1915 gehalten . . . nach dem ich von Kriegsanfang an die Entwicklung unter diesem Gesichtspunkt betrachtet habe."

118. See Koerber's letter to the leader of this group, Gustav Marchet, 15 February 1915, in HHStA, Nachlass Marchet, K.19 (F.756). There are a great many membership lists in ibid. K.8, 9, and 19, where Koerber's name figures on some. Koerber seems also to have been a candidate for a leading position in Austria in the plans of this network. However, on the list Naumann brought home with him after his visit in Vienna in mid-February 1915, Koerber's name has already been crossed out (BArch, Nachlass Naumann, N 3001/15).

119. See the letter to Naumann from Richard Charmatz, dated 12 April 1915, BArch, Nachlass Naumann, N 3001/15 (F.257), and Naumann's notes on a conversation with Koerber on 4 June 1915, Nachlass Naumann, N 3001/217 (F.33).

120. Letter from Koerber to Naumann of 15 October 1915, BArch, Nachlass Naumann, N 3001/38 (F.54).

121. See the protocol to the meetings on 8 March and 18 June 1915 in *Protokolle des Gemeinsamen Ministerrates der Österreichisch-Ungarischen Monarchie (1914–1918),* 215–65. In the latter of these meetings, István Tisza angrily attacked Koerber and asserted that those high-ranking German-Austrian bureaucrats who engaged themselves openly for Mitteleuropa should be forbidden to do so (see 259).

122. See the protocols to the common ministerial councils on 6 October 1915 and 7 January 1916, in *Protokolle des Gemeinsamen Ministerrates der Österreichisch-Ungarischen Monarchie (1914–1918),* 285–314, 352–81 (quotation on 304).

123. See Heuss, *Friedrich Naumann,* 342, 378.

124. On this phase in the Reich-German official Mitteleuropa policy, see Müller, *Zwischen Annäherung und Abgrenzung,* 164–76. The conference took place on 10–11 November 1915.

125. The German memorandum on the conference of 10–11 November 1915 and the following note of 14 November can be found in Scherer & Grunewald *L'Allemagne:* 211–15, 218–21 (quote from the memorandum, 212).

126. On this whole problem see Müller, *Zwischen Annäherung und Abgrenzung,* passim, and the references given in note 116 above.

127. See Ambassador Tschirschky's reports of 20 February 1915, in PAAA, Österreich 86 no. 2/20. Koerber was also favorably reviewed in the Reich-German press; see the *Vossische Zeitung* of 12 February 1915, 1–2 (Morgenausgabe).

128. See Tschirschky's report of 29 October 1915, 8 September 1916, and 9 October 1916, PAAA, Österreich 86, no. 2/21. See also Bethmann Hollweg to Emperor Wilhelm on 30 September 1916, Scherer & Grunewald 1:486, and Bethmann Hollweg to Hindenburg on 29 September 1916, in Scherer & Grunewald 1:482ff. See further, Tschirschky's report to Bethmann Hollweg from 28 September 1916, in Scherer & Grunewald *L'Allemagne:* 477–81. Tschirschky here states, "Ich glaube, dass von uns aus der Versuch gemacht werden müsste, eine Sanierung der hiesigen Verhältnisse herbeizuführen."

129. See Jagow's note to German Interior Minister Delbrück dated 13 November 1916. See also his memorandum of "November 1916," both in BArch, Reichskanzlei, R43/406. The memorandum contains this passage: "[Es] ist mit Sicherheit anzunehmen, dass das neue Ministerium Koerber der wirtschaftlichen Annäherung an Deutschland eher noch freundlicher gegenübersteht als das frühere Ministerium Stürgkh, und dass deshalb mit einem gedeihlichen Fortgang der Angelegenheit in nicht zu langer Zeit gerechnet werden darf."

130. Koerber sent the correspondence on to the different Austrian ministries. A copy of Hohenlohe's report with summaries of Burían's and Koerber's letters lies in AVA, Finanzministerium, Z.2006/1916. The relevant documentation in the Ministerratspräsidium has not survived.
131. See the material in connection with this in AVA, Ministerratspräsidium, K.346 and K.347 ("Ausgleich 1916"). See also the very enlightening entries in Josef Redlich's diary from the weeks of Koerber's second minister presidency, Redlich, *Schicksaalsjahre*, 2:150–69 (entries from 28 October—16 December).
132. Friedjung's notes on a conversation with Koerber in November 1916, in Friedjung, *Geschichte in Gesprächen*, 2:414–18.
133. Already on the day of his appointment, Koerber had also tried to enlist Josef Redlich, the former initiator and prominent member of the commission, to lead an administrative reform unit in the interior ministry. See Redlich, *Schicksaalsjahre*, 2:150–52 (entry of 28 October 1916). Only slightly later, the whole personnel of the old administrative bureau of the commission, including its head Robert Davy, was transferred from the bureau of the minister president, where they had led a shadow existence for two years, to the interior ministry. See the administrative instruction of 11 November 1916, in AVA, Ministerratspräsidium, K. 290, Zl.5852/1916.
134. See Schwartzenau's report to Minister President Stürgkh from 14 January 1915 (Zl. 465/1915), attached to Zl. 5302/1916, AVA, Ministerratspräsidium, K.289.
135. See AVA, Ministerratspräsidium, K.291, Z.5977/1916, containing the original documents on this question and several reports from different administrative branches and organs. These documents are partly burned, but Koerber's instruction of 18 November 1916 has been published in Czedik, *Zur Geschichte der k.k. Ministerien*, 4:529f. It can also be found in the archives of several of the other Austrian ministries.
136. See Ambassador Wedel's report of 5 December 1916, PAAA, Österreich, 86, no. 2/21.
137. See Koerber's request to Karl, AVA, Ministerratspräsidium, K.291, Z.6042/1916. From the files it actually looks like Koerber was lecturing the new emperor on correct administrative practice in this exchange. If this is so, they could not have received a worse start on their relationship, especially since the content of Koerber's request that Karl should immediately take the oath on the Austrian constitution was an attempt to restrict the new emperor's freedom of action.
138. Koerber wanted to hold a purely formal parliamentary session where Karl should swear the oath on the constitution. However, the parliament had been closed since the beginning of the war and the parliamentary building had been used as a military hospital. Beginning on 23 November, Koerber took measures to clear out the hospital and set the plenary hall in order. See the relevant documentation in AVA, Ministerratspräsidium, K.291 and K.292: for example, Zl.6045/1916 and Zl.6431/1916. Apparently the parliamentary building was emptied by 5 December and was expected to be ready for use on 18 December, but at this time Koerber had already resigned. Compare also German Ambassador Wedel's report on Koerber's reflections on this question on New Year's Eve 1916: "Je mehr die Zeit bis zur Eidesleistung verstreicht, die Koerber in einer lediglich formellen und Huldigungs-Tagung des Parlaments bald vornehmen wollte, umso ungewisser wird das Gefühl im Lande. . . ." See the report dated Sylvester [New Year's Eve] 1916, PAAA, Österreich 86, no. 2/22. To Koerber this oath on the constitution was crucial in securing the unity of the "Gesamtheit" of the Austrian state and people.
139. On Emperor Karl I, see Peter Broucek, *Karl I. (IV.). Der politische Weg des letzten Herrschers der Donaumonarchie* (Vienna: Böhlau Verlag, 1997).

140. See Wedel's report to Bethmann Hollweg of 5 December 1916, PAAA, Österreich 86, no. 2/21.
141. See the report from Wedel on 22 December 1916, PAAA, Österreich 86, no. 2/21. See also Heinrich Friedjung's notes on a conversation with Koerber on 16 December 1916, Friedjung, *Geschichte in Gesprächen,* 2:418–21.
142. See Friedjung, *Der Kampf um die Vorherrschaft in Deutschland,* 2:1–7.
143. For an analysis of the image of Bismarck in Friedjung's historical works, see Karl Glaubauf, *Bismarck und der Aufstieg des Deutschen Reiches in der Darstellung Heinrich Friedjungs* (Unpublished dissertation, University of Vienna, 1979).
144. See especially the correspondence between Friedjung and Aehrenthal on this lecture, partly in *Aus dem Nachlass Aehrenthal,* 1:207, 211, but primarily in the HHStA, Nachlass Aehrenthal, K.1, K.2, and the Nachlass Friedjung (HHStA), K.5. Aehrenthal had helped Friedjung with research in the Haus-, Hof-, und Staatsarchiv in Vienna and with contacts regarding Russian sources in St. Petersburg. (Aehrenthal was then the newly appointed ambassador to Russia.) Friedjung also wrote to the Prussian State Archives on this matter; see the concept of a letter dated 25 March 1900, Nachlass Friedjung (WStLB), K.2.
145. See letter to Aehrenthal dated 10 April 1900, *Aus dem Nachlass Aehrenthal,* 1:211.
146. There is much material in connection with this "cooperation" between Friedjung and Aehrenthal, in *Aus dem Nachlass Aehrenthal,* 1:130–53 (several letters from March through October 1898), and in Friedjung, *Geschichte in Gesprächen,* see especially 1:53–71, 206–10. Aehrenthal's political biographical sketch on Kálnoky has not been found, but after having seen Friedjung's finished article, Aehrenthal made this comment: "Ich habe . . . mich an der außerordentlich klaren, die Bedeutung Kálnoky's in das richtige Licht stellenden Darstellung erfreut." Letter to Friedjung, 29 September 1899, *Aus dem Nachlass Aehrenthal,* 1:171f. Regarding this cooperation, see also Adlgasser & Friedrich, "Einleitung," and Fellner, "Heinrich Friedjung."
147. See letter from Jettel to Aehrenthal, 24 March 1896, in *Aus dem Nachlass Aehrenthal,* 1:103f.
148. See Heinrich Friedjung, "Graf Gustav von Kalnoky," Friedjung, *Historische Aufsätze,* 327–61, especially 330ff. The article was first published in 1900. At about the same time, Friedjung published a widely noted article in the German daily *Allgemeine Zeitung* ("Graf Goluchowski und die österreichische Verfassungskrisis," 12 May 1900) attacking Goluchowski's "weak" conception of the internal role of the Austro-Hungarian foreign minister. There is a newspaper cutting of this article in the Nachlass Aehrenthal (HHStA), K.1, Konvolut "Friedjung."
149. On Aehrenthal's constitutional politics, see Rutkowski, "Aehrenthal über die Innenpolitische Lage"; Somogyi, "Aehrenthals Reformbestrebungen"; idem, *Der gemeinsame Ministerrat;* Wank, "Aehrenthal's Programme"; idem, "Zwei Dokumente Aehrenthals," and idem, "Varieties of Political Despair." See also above, previous chapter.
150. See Friedjung's notes on a conversation with Aehrenthal on 29 November 1907 (Friedjung, *Geschichte in Gesprächen,* 2:68ff.), where Aehrenthal expresses his hostility to the current Beck government and Friedjung enters Koerber's name into the discussion. On the decision against Koerber, see the conversation with Aehrenthal on 8 November 1908, in Friedjung, *Geschichte in Gesprächen,* 2:120–28, quotation on 125. At about the same time, Koerber had evidently let a colleague of Aehrenthal's know that he was interested in returning to office (ibid). See also the letter from Friedjung to Aehrenthal dated 4 November 1908, *Aus dem Nachlass Aehrenthal,* 2:634f. See further Aehrenthal's interview with Koerber and the chosen candidate, Richard von Bienerth (interior minister in the Beck government), where the two of them are judged by Aehrenthal to have a similar political profile. Note on con-

versations with the retired minister president, Dr. von Koerber, and the interior minister, Baron Bienerth, dated 20 April 1908, HHStA, Kabinettsarchiv, Direktionsakten, K.17, no. 28/1908.

151. See especially the letter from Friedjung to Aehrenthal on 21 April 1900, *Aus dem Nachlass Aehrenthal,* 1:214–20. See also Rutkowski, "Aehrenthal über die Innenpolitische Lage."

152. See especially the material surrounding an attack on Aehrenthal in the German daily, the *Allgemeine Zeitung,* in early 1902 (11.1.1902, "Antideutsche Einflüsse in der russischen Hauptstadt"). Here Aehrenthal, who was then ambassador to Russia, was pictured as a threat to the Dual Alliance between Germany and Austria-Hungary because of his friendliness to Russia. See the correspondence in *Aus dem Nachlass Aehrenthal,* 1:260–75 and Friedjung's notes on conversations with Jettel, Eulenburg, and Max Egon Fürstenberg in January 1902, Friedjung, *Geschichte in Gesprächen,* 1:435–44. See also the material on Aehrenthal's uncertain political identity in the eyes of the German foreign ministry, primarily in PAAA, Österreich 86 no. 2/11–12.

153. See Friedjung's note on a conversation with Aehrenthal and diplomat Emil Jettel in late November 1901, in Friedjung, *Geschichte in Gesprächen,* 1:420f.: "Ich fange an zu begreifen, ja eigentlich als selbstverständlich zu finden, daß man in Berlin solches Mißtrauen gegen [Aehrenthal] hegt."

154. For an excellent concise discussion on the political relationship between Friedjung and Aehrenthal, see Adlgasser & Friedrich, "Einleitung," 18–25 (and the Friedjung notes referred to here).

155. See notes on conversations with Aehrenthal in January-February 1908, in Friedjung, *Geschichte in Gesprächen,* 2:72–77.

156. See notes on conversations with Aehrenthal on 6 October 1908, Friedjung, *Geschichte in Gesprächen,* 2:99–103 (quotation on 103). See also Friedjung's article "Die Großmacht Österreich-Ungarn," *Neues Wiener Tageblatt,* 10.10.1908, 1–2.

157. See notes on a conversation with Kálmán Kánia, head of the press department of the foreign ministry (Literarisches Bureau), on 28 January 1909, Friedjung, *Geschichte in Gesprächen,* 2:188ff. Kánia said: "Es gebe jetzt einen einzigen Weg, um an Aehrenthal eine abweichende Meinung gelangen zu lassen, und das sei Dr. Friedjung." (189). The view of Friedjung's important role had wider currency, though. The British foreign minister, Grey, intimated as much to Austro-Hungarian Ambassador Mensdorff later in 1909; see *Österreich-Ungarns Außenpolitik von der bosnischen Krise 1908 bis zum Kriegsausbruch 1914.* Ludwig Bittner, Heinrich von Srbik & Hans Uebersberger, eds. 9 vols. (Vienna: Österreichischer Bundesverlag, 1930), here 2:448f.

158. See notes on a conversation with Aehrenthal on 12 February 1909, Friedjung, *Geschichte in Gesprächen,* 2:205f.

159. See *Neue Freie Presse,* 25.3.1909, 2–4 (Morgenblatt). The article had a distinct official character. It was brought directly from the foreign ministry to the editor's office of the *Neue Freie Presse.* Friedjung was no longer involved after dropping the article off at the Ballhausplatz. See Friedjung's diary entry on 3 April 1909, Friedjung, *Geschichte in Gesprächen,* 2:225ff.

160. On the day after Friedjung's article had been published, some Croatian politicians called on the editor of the *Neue Freie Presse,* members of the Serbo-Croat coalition in the provincial assembly in Zagreb, one of the political groups accused by Friedjung of having members in the service of the Serbian foreign ministry. They demanded that Friedjung should name his sources and the Croatian politicians he accused. Friedjung replied that he had based the article on "unanfechtbaren Aktenmaterial" that he had controlled just as rigorously as he always controlled historical sources. See Friedjung's diary entry from 3 April, Friedjung,

Geschichte in Gesprächen, 2:225–29 (see especially the editor's notes on 228). This exchange of notes between Friedjung and his soon-to-be accusers took place in the *Neue Freie Presse* 27–28.3.1909.

161. See notes on a conversation with Aehrenthal on 12 April 1909, in Friedjung *Geschichte in Gesprächen*, 2:231ff. See also Friedjung's letters to Aehrenthal on 20 and 29 April 1909, *Aus dem Nachlass Aehrenthal*, 2:673–77.
162. There is a wealth of documents from the foreign ministry on this last phase of the Friedjung process published in *Österreich-Ungarns Aussenpolitik*; see especially 2:549–624.
163. On Friedjung's late view of Aehrenthal, see Friedjung, *Das Zeitalter des Imperialismus*, 2:236–42.
164. On Friedjung's staking his reputation as a historian on the authenticity of the documents he had used, see Friedjung, *Geschichte in Gesprächen*, editor's note on 2:228, and Friedjung's article in the *Neue Freie Presse* on 28 March 1909.
165. See the folder marked "Unterlagen und Studiennotizen zur europäischen Geschichte," WStLB, Nachlass Friedjung, K.3.
166. Heinrich Friedjung, "Von Hamburg bis Bagdad," *Vossische Zeitung*, 17 December 1914, 1–2.
167. On this activism, see the references in notes 116–118 above. It seems that Friedjung had already shown an early version of his memorandum on a military union with Germany to a few members in March 1915, and in late April it was on the agenda of the Marchet-Baernreither group for later in the spring. See letter from Baernreither to Friedjung, 29 March 1915, WStLB, Briefsammlung Friedjung, and Marchet's "Schema der Beratungen" on 30 April 1915, HHStA, Nachlass Marchet, K.9 (F.533).
168. See Friedjung, *Denkschrift aus Deutsch-Österreich*, "Vorbemerkung."
169. See Marchet's letter to Friedjung from 25 August 1915, WStLB, Briefsammlung Friedjung. The *Denkschrift* was distributed privately so that it could circumvent the prohibition in Germany on discussing war aims publicly. Friedrich Naumann later tried to help Friedjung launch a "popular" version of the *Denkschrift* in Germany; see the letter from the publisher Hirzel to Friedrich Naumann, 22 December 1915, BArch, Nachlass Naumann, N 3001/310.
170. See, for example, Friedjung's articles in the *Vossische Zeitung*: "Ein Friedensbund auf dem Balkan" (30 September 1915, 1–2), "Die Stellung Bulgariens" (2 November 1915, 1–2), and "Die Zukunft Serbiens" (5 December 1915, 1–2).
171. See "Oesterreich-Ungarn im Aufstieg," *Vossische Zeitung*, 5.3.1916, 1–2.
172. For a thorough analysis of the *Denkschrift aus Deutsch-Österreich*, see Günther Ramhardter, *Geschichtswissenschaft und Patriotismus. Österreichische Historiker im Weltkriege 1914–1918* (Vienna: Verlag für Geschichte und Politik, 1973), 73–99. On Friedjung's role in it, see Friedrich Naumann's notes on a conversation with Eugen Philippovich on 12 February 1915, BArch, Nachlass Naumann, N 3001/217: "Friedjung arbeitet mit alten Generälen eine Militärkonvention [aus]."
173. In his "Randbemerkungen zur Denkschrift," Friedjung commented on his contribution to the *Denkschrift* and noted this: "Mir persönlich stehen von dem in der Denkschrift behandelten Materien die militärischen natürlich am nähesten, dann aber aus persönliche Neigung die innenpolitische." See WStLB, Nachlass Friedjung, K.3, U. "Unterlagen und Studiennotizen zur europäsichen Geschichte." Thus the combination of military union and internal restructuring in Austria and Austria-Hungary might be said to have stemmed the most directly from Friedjung's mind.
174. See chapter "IV. Innerpolitische Reformen," in Friedjung, *Denkschrift aus Deutsch-Österreich*, 77–97.

175. See letter from Friedjung to Marchet, 21 September 1915, HHStA, Nachlass Marchet, K.11 (F.2), and the letter from the publisher Hirzel to Friedrich Naumann, 22 December 1915, BArch, Nachlass Naumann, N 3001/310.
176. See the concept to Friedjung's letter to Bethmann Hollweg, 31 August 1915, WStLB, Nachlass Friedjung, K.3, U. "Unterlagen und Studiennotizen zur europäsichen Geschichte."
177. Letter from Friedjung to Marchet on 30 September 1915, quoted in Ramhardter, *Geschichtswissenschaft und Patriotismus*, 93f. Friedjung wrote: "Es ist fast noch wichtiger, daß die Vorschläge von hoher militärischer als von bürgerlicher-amtlicher Stelle gekannt und gewürdigt werden. Denn die Zukunft wird dadurch bestimmt werden, ob sich unter unseren siegreichen Generälen auch zur Staatsleitung berufene politische Köpfe befinden. Die Anregungen mögen von wem immer herrühren, die Anstöße müssen von hohen Militärs ausgehen."
178. Letter from Mackensen to Friedjung, 1 October 1915, WStLB, Briefsammlung Friedjung.
179. Letter from Friedjung to Schmoller, 18 October 1915, BArch, Reichskanzlei, R43/405. Schmoller sent this copy on to the Reichskanzlei to let the German government use the information in their dealings with Vienna, probably with Friedjung's approval. See Schmoller's accompanying letter to Undersecretary Wahnschaffe dated 22 October 1915 (ibid.).
180. Concept of a letter from Friedjung to Mackensen. 21 October 1915.WStLB, Nachlass Friedjung, K.2 (Umschlag A).
181. A few weeks earlier, Friedjung had received another letter in connection with the *Denkschrift* that, with hindsight, could make a person think more deeply about the situation. Erich Ludendorff, at the time chief of staff of Hindenburg's eastern army, had replied very concisely to Friedjung's *Denkschrift*: "Auch ich bin der Ansicht, daß das Bündnis zu einem Wehrverband werden muß." See letter from Ludendorff, 30 September 1915. WStLB, *Briefsammlung Friedjung*. A couple of years later Ludendorff would be the driving force behind reducing the Austro-Hungarian army to an annex of the imperial German army.
182. See the correspondence in Scherer & Grunewald, *L'Allemagne:* 165–223, 31 August until November. See especially the correspondence between Bethmann Hollweg and General Falkenhayn, the German commander in chief. On 31 August, Falkenhayn launched a plan for a Mitteleuropäischer Staatenbund (ibid. 1:163ff.), which just might be another inspiration from the *Denkschrift*. Falkenhayn also received it, but it is not clear when. On 11 September Bethmann Hollweg wrote that "he had heard" that Falkenhayn had also received this *Denkschrift* (173f). Falkenhayn thanked Friedjung only in a much later letter, dated 28 October 1915. WStLB, Nachlass Friedjung, K.1, U.5. See also Kapp, "Bethmann Hollweg, Austria-Hungary and Mitteleuropa," and Fritz Fellner, "Denkschriften aus Österreich. Die österreichische Mitteleuropa-Diskussion in Wissenschaft und Politik 1915/16," idem, *Vom Dreibund zum Völkerbund*, Heidrun Maschl und Brigitte Mazohl-Wallnig, eds. (Vienna: Verlag für Geschichte und Politik, 1994), on this problem.
183. See letter from Tschirschky to Friedjung, 8 September 1915, WStLB, Nachlass Friedjung, K.1, U.5: "Sie wissen, daß ich aus Überzeugung und mit aller mich zu Gebote stehenden Kräfte mich in den Dienst dieser Sache stelle."
184. See letter from Bethmann Hollweg to Friedjung. 25 September 1915. WStLB, Briefsammlung Friedjung. Bethmann Hollweg at this time confirms that just as Friedjung asked, he has given a copy of the *Denkschrift* to Emperor Wilhelm. Friedjung asked for the meeting in late October. See the concept of a letter to Bethmann Hollweg. 25 October 1915. WStLB, Nachlass Friedjung, K.2 (Umschlag A).
185. See Friedjung's notes on a conversation with Bethmann Hollweg, 1 November 1915, Friedjung, *Geschichte in Gesprächen*, 2:406–13.

186. See Friedjung's notes on his meeting with Bethmann Hollweg. 1 November 1915 (ibid.). Also, see Joseph Maria Baernreither's note on a conversation with Friedjung, 17 November 1915, in HHStA, Nachlass Baernreither, K.6 (Tagebuch XV).
187. See Mackensen's letter from 13 November 1915, WStLB, Briefsammlung Friedjung.
188. See "Randbemerkungen zur Denkschrift." WStLB, Nachlass Friedjung, K.3, U. "Unterlagen und Studiennotizen zur europäischen Geschichte."
189. Friedjung, *Das Zeitalter des Imperialismus*, 2:5.
190. See McGrath, *Dionysian Art and Populist Politics*, 241.
191. On this argument, see Shedel, *Art and Society*, 48–50. Shedel has expanded the argument to deal with the Rechtstaat as such, Shedel, "Fin de Siècle or Jahrhundertwende."
192. See Robert Wistrich, *The Jews of Vienna in the Age of Franz Joseph* (Oxford: Oxford University Press, 1990), 161–63.
193. See Marsha Rozenblit, *Reconstructing a National Identity* (Oxford: Oxford University Press, 2001), 14–38. Although I judge Rozenblit's theory about the tripartite identity of Austrian Jews as having sizable explanatory force, I am more doubtful about her Steven Beller-like essentialist assumptions that clear and absolute social boundaries existed between Jews and Gentiles in late Imperial Austria.
194. Friedjung, *Historische Aufsätze*, foreword (XIII).
195. Friedjung, "Ernest von Koerber," 38, 41.

PART TWO

Hugo von Hofmannsthal (Leopold von Andrian)

◈ The Problem of the Austrian Culture ◈

> The fire is rampant, red alert in Mauer, the Russians are plundering Mauer and Liesing. Although we were ill, Resi and I had to get out of bed, in a great hurry, get a little bread and jewellery, and some more things were packed into bags. The valuable things had already been taken away or hidden, and off we went into the street. Marie stayed on to lock the house. Papa carried his manuscripts in his hand, and all in all the scene must have looked rather comical, and I think the villagers of Rodaun were laughing at us. The whole thing was exaggerated; a couple of Russians had attempted to break into a railway wagon. That was it.[1]

On one of the first days of November 1918, Hugo von Hofmannsthal and his family, in panic, as it seems, left the house in Rodaun, outside of Vienna, in which they had lived since the early years of the 1900s. The perceived threat from escaped Russian prisoners of war during these confused last days of the Austro-Hungarian Empire was exaggerated, as Hugo's daughter Christiane noted in her diary on the day after the hurried family evacuation. Hofmannsthal's reaction seems more in tune with the expected arrival of a hostile army than with the petty plundering of a few escaped prisoners of war. A couple of days after this evacuation, the family was back in Rodaun, where Hofmannsthal was engaging intensely in the organization of a militia defense force for the small country communities on the southeastern outskirts of Vienna. Needing assistance in his endeavors, he writes about the incident a few days before to his friend Robert Ehrhart, a high-ranking civil servant and right-hand man to the imperial Austrian minister president in close-by Vienna. Now he feels more secure, Hofmannsthal states to Ehrhart, since he and his household have armed themselves with rifles. The house in Rodaun, and the whole village as such, seems to

The Fuchs Schlössl, Hugo von Hofmannsthal's house in Rodaun: Street view; Freies Deutsches Hochstift, Frankfurter Goethe-Museum

assume the appearance of a fortress as Hofmannsthal expands on his plans to organize a militia self-defense force consisting of 4 to 6 lorries armed with machine guns to defend the countryside surrounding his home.[2]

The house in Rodaun was very important to Hofmannsthal. One could say that it constituted the locus of his identity. Here his artistic life and the lives of his family and friends had their centers of gravity. At the time he and his wife, Gertrud, as a newly married couple moved into the house in summer 1901, Hofmannsthal wrote rapturously to all his friends about this new center of his life.[3] Here their three children Christiane, Franz, and Raimund would be born and grow up. And Hofmannsthal would always treat the visits of his artistic colleagues and foreign friends to the house as a sort of ritual, or perhaps rite of initiation, into his personal and creative lives.[4] About a year before finding the house during a trip to France in the spring of 1900, Hofmannsthal had ruminated about his "continued longing for a house." He pondered the stabilizing effects on the personality, on one's identity, of owning a house, and he expressed his wish "to enclose a written note with a few of Gerty's pearls in the foundation stone of our little house."[5] Hofmannsthal had suffered a prolonged personal crisis, to a great extent a crisis of identity, during the years preceding his marriage in 1901. He had unsuccessfully tried to find a passable route into adult life and to establish himself socially and economically in the Viennese Grossbürgerliche society. Shortly after moving into the house in Rodaun with his wife, Hofmannsthal indicated to his father that he had now found the basic stability he needed in order to move on in life. Among the fundamental factors that made him feel this way, he enumerated to his father, were his parents, his wife Gerty, his many good friends, and "my dear house."[6]

Placed in the middle of that Lower Austrian landscape Hofmannsthal repeatedly praised in his letters at the time,[7] the house also seems to have been the center of gravity for his cultural identity. In his descriptions of the house, he usually emphasized that it was from the period of Empress Maria Theresia, which was a key period in Austrian history for Hofmannsthal's understanding of the Austrian identity; the house in Rodaun had actually been built for Maria Theresia's governess, Countess Fuchs, something that Hofmannsthal also liked to recount.[8] In a letter to Christiane Thun-Salm a few months after moving into the house, Hofmannsthal complained about the difficult political situation in Austria, which also personally affected him deeply, he wrote. But he gathered strength from the house in Rodaun, that locus of his identity: "I rejoiced at imagining you in my little country house, in a fall evening at dusk, and to think: This is Austria."[9]

The image of the house in Lower Austria would reappear a few years later in a literary context. In Hofmannsthal's key work of cultural criticism, *Die Briefe des Zurückgekehrten* (1907), this house might be said to have symbolized the potentiality of German cultural regeneration through the special qualities of Austrian culture. It is interesting that these fictitious letters of a German-Austrian returning home to Germany after several years in other parts of the world and finding a disintegrating German culture, which makes him increasingly depressed, are dated during the spring of 1901. The last of the letters, where his childhood memory of his family's house in (Upper) Austria at least offers the possibility of finding, after all, living, whole culture somewhere in this Germany, is dated 9 May 1901.[10]

The Fuchs Schlössl, Hugo von Hofmannsthal's house in Rodaun: Court view with stairs to main entrance; Freies Deutsches Hochstift, Frankfurter Goethe-Museum

The Salon of the house in Rodaun with Hugo von Hofmannsthal and his wife Gertrud in the background, early 1900s; Freies Deutsches Hochstift, Frankfurter Goethe-Museum

A month later, on 8 June, Hofmannsthal married Gertrud Schlesinger, and shortly afterward they moved into that house in (Lower) Austria.[11]

To Hofmannsthal, Austria was condensed into that piece of land surrounding Vienna, which carried also the name of the old Central European empire, and into that house in the midst of this landscape that he had turned into the center of his world, the center of gravity of his identity, one dimension of which was his Austrian cultural identity. Several years later, during the extraordinary conditions of the World War, Hofmannsthal embarked on a proper mission to regenerate this Austrian identity. There is an interesting, existential tension in this preoccupation of his during the war. On the one hand, Hofmannsthal exhibited a very strongly expressed belief in the Austrian idea and developed an intense activity and engagement in furthering it, and on the other hand he exhibited a deep, constantly present fear of its complete destruction in the catastrophe of the Great War. For instance, the notion of the Austrian mission of defending Europe from the "hordes of the east" was strongly present in Hofmannsthal's Austrian idea as propagated during the early war years, and its corollary, the destruction of Austria under pressure from the armies of the east, also marked Hofmannsthal's behavior during this same time. Already during the war euphoria of the fall of 1914, Hofmannsthal exhibited this tension fully developed because he feared that the Russian advance on the eastern front in these early months of the war might overrun Vienna, and Rodaun, and he made preparations for evacuating the house, and Austria, with his family and fleeing to Germany.[12] The appearance of plundering Russians near his home in Rodaun in early November 1918 probably resonated strongly with these fears of breakdown under the onslaught of the "hordes of the east." The image of the Hofmannsthals leaving Rodaun in November 1918, in panic, carrying their belongings, might have seemed amusing to the villagers of Rodaun, but Hofmannsthal at this time simply saw his very worst pent-up fears become reality.[13]

In this part I will study Hofmannsthal's political engagement in general, and more specifically his lifelong concern with his Austrian identity. The preoccupation with Austria expressed itself prominently in Hofmannsthal's literary production, parts of which are indeed best understood in terms of identity. The present investigation will therefore lead more directly into the problem of the Austrian identity, the "soft" side of the Austrian state problem, which is at the center of the present work. The secondary character of this part, Leopold von Andrian, was a close friend of Hofmannsthal's and a sometime partner in the project of furthering an Austrian identity.[14] Andrian chose to channel his engagement for Austria more directly through the institutions of the Austrian state, but Hofmannstal in his political engagement moved between the institutions of this state and a freer engagement for Austria in civil society.

1. Understanding Hofmannsthal

In previous scholarship on Hofmannsthal, his preoccupation with the Austrian identity is generally viewed as exclusively tied up to his propaganda work during World War I. Furthermore, Hofmannsthal's activities during the war as such are generally viewed as somehow isolated from Hofmannsthal's literary production and from his personal development in general. Hermann Rudolph criticized this latter tendency in his important study on Hofmannsthal's political thinking. Rudolph convincingly demonstrated that Hofmannsthal's activities during the war years should be seen as an outflow of a deep, identity-related need to engage with society, an outflow that can be traced far back in Hofmannsthal's personal development and followed in his literary production. However, Rudolph failed to make the connection between this lifelong preoccupation of Hofmannsthal's and the actual content of his engagement during the war years, the Austrian idea, or identity. Rudolph rather viewed this latter engagement as wholly contingent on the peculiar conditions of the war and asserted, "It is quite obvious, that Austria played no role for [Hofmannsthal's] thinking in the prewar period."[15] This tendency is reinforced in one of the latest large works on Hofmannsthal. In this work, Jacques Le Rider maintained that "With Hofmannsthal the question of national identity does not arise before the outbreak of the First World War."[16] This view on Hofmannsthal's relationship to Austria will be modified in the present study. I will argue that an affirmative stance on Habsburg Austria and a will to engage himself for this polity was a constant, albeit problematic part of Hofmannsthal's development from early on. In the process of this argument, Hofmannsthal's political engagement during the period 1914–18 will be integrated more fully into his biography.

An important undertow in the crucial parts of the scholarship on Hofmannsthal is the observed need for engagement with society.[17] Hermann Broch began by charting Hofmannsthal's life career as a "second assimilation," an attempt to follow up on the first assimilation, that of his Jewish forefathers to the German-Catholic Grossbürgertum of Vienna, with a second assimilation, to the Austrian aristocracy. Broch highlighted Hofmannsthal's strong attraction to the way of life of the Austrian aristocracy and observes how he cultivated friendships with its members, and as far as he could, how he also cultivated a personal lifestyle of an aristocratic type. Moreover, Broch views this attempted assimilation to the Austrian aristocracy as part of Hofmannsthal's wider political and social engagement, which he judges as a misdirected attempt by Hofmannsthal to make his art serve the cultural regeneration of a defunct political and social order; in Broch's view the failure had catastrophic results for Hofmannsthal personally and for his art.[18]

The basic pattern behind the essays in Carl Schorske's book on Fin-de-Siècle Vienna (of which only two deal with Hofmannsthal) is that of the failure of Austrian Liberalism, the ideology of Hofmannsthal's Viennese Grossbürgerliche class. According to Schorske, this failure was to a great extent the failure of rational politics as such. It resulted in political alienation, and it evoked several different "irrational," artistic, and other responses, which Schorske investigates in his book. Just like Hermann Rudolph, Schorske identifies the strong will to connect with society as determining Hofmannsthal's development. Schorske focuses on Hofmannsthal's dramatic works during the early years of the new century as an attempt at a new politics of ritual aiming at a cultural regeneration of society. At this time Hofmannsthal began experimenting with the theater as a medium for a cultural-political "ceremony of the whole," of creating wholeness in a culture fragmented by modernization, a project that Schorske then examines in Hofmannsthal's late works of the 1920s as ultimately failing. In these late works Hofmannsthal, according to Schorske, ended up alienated from society.[19]

However, Schorske's influential approach to fin-de-siècle Vienna has later been heavily criticized.[20] One of the more interesting parts of this criticism is the fundamental questioning of the central category in Schorske's work, that of the crisis resulting from the failure of Liberalism. John W. Boyer and Pieter Judson, to mention the two most central works, have here empirically qualified the notion of its failure.[21] However, James Shedel has given this criticism a most interesting twist by arguing that there was no real crisis of Liberalism at all. Shedel turns Schorske on his head, arguing that there was in Imperial Austria a very robust political framework, the Rechtsstaat, that artists and intellectuals in Vienna could realize their projects within (and not against).[22] Following Shedel, Hofmannsthal's project of cultural regeneration was not alienated from the social and political order; it was an affirmation of it, which took place in close rapport with the state. Significantly, Schorske skips over exactly that period in Hofmannsthal's life (1906–20), which saw his most intense affirmative engagement for Habsburg Austria. Viewing Hofmannsthal's life-career in its entirety, Shedel's perspective looks more accurate; Hofmannsthal began with a strong attachment to and idealization of Habsburg Austria in the 1890s, which gradually matured into an affirmative political project for the cultural regeneration of this polity and society.

In its later stages, Hofmannsthal's political engagement became more overtly political. Hermann Rudolph traced its development up to its last phase, when it connected up to radical conservatism. Not least, Hofmannsthal's use of the term "conservative revolution" in the nebulous speech *Das Schrifttum als geistiger Raum der Nation*, given in Munich in 1927, has connected him with ideologies such as Fascism and Nazism. Rudolph identifies an accelerating, in certain regards radical, conservatism in Hofmannsthal after 1918, but in his final analysis he dissociated him from the political movements of this type. Rather, Rudolph judges Hofmannsthal's "radicalism" at this late stage in his life as a utopian response to his own marginalization.[23]

Michael P. Steinberg took Hofmannsthal's role as a sort of ideologue for the Salzburg festival, starting in 1918–19, as the point of departure for a sharper judgment. Steinberg uses, as he sees it, the totalizing Baroque ideology of the "World as Theater," strongly present in the Salzburg festival, but also an important strand in Hofmannsthal's longer artistic development, as the prism through which he sees Hofmannsthal's career as a whole. Through this prism, Steinberg sees a German-national cultural imperialism, which he calls "nationalist cosmopolitanism," that is not a direct precursor of Nazism and Fascism, but related to them and prone to reduction to such an ideological turn. However, Steinberg tends in the direction of a kind of culturalistic Sonderweg argument, since he indicts nearly the whole of German intellectual history as "nationalist cosmopolitanist" (the line goes from Goethe via Hofmannsthal to Hitler, one might say).[24] Steinberg's analysis suffers somewhat from a totalizing and reductionist view of Hofmannsthal's post-1918 version of the Austrian identity: he simply sets out to describe it as a Pan-German cultural imperialism barely concealed under a false "Austrian" (or Habsburg) surface of federalist ideas and Central European Völkerverbrüderung.[25] Such a tension between Germanism and Austrianism is certainly present in Hofmannsthal's view of the Austrian identity, but in the present approach it will be viewed as substantial, rather than as an ideological falsity. What is problematic with Steinberg for the present concern of approaching the problem of the Austrian identity is that his own German-national interpretation of the Austrian identity tends to conceal all ambiguity. However, the view of Hofmannsthal's development in a conservative direction is firmly established to have run parallel to his engagement with society from around the turn of the century and to have accelerated from around the time of World War I. Steinberg's view here is in substance not too different from Rudolph's, and it is confirmed also in other works.[26]

In the 1980's debate on the Austrian identity,[27] Hofmannsthal became the object of a sort of tug-of-war between the adherents of the Austrianist and Germanist views of Austrian history. Normally, Hofmannsthal falls rather naturally into the former category. He has even become a sort of Austrian national icon, a problem that will be looked into below. In his works, the Austrian cultural historian Friedrich Heer, for instance, habitually refers to Hofmannsthal as an exponent of the essence of Austrianess. In the debate, however, the German historian Karl Dietrich Erdmann concluded that the use of Hofmannsthal to support an Austrianist position was completely misdirected, since Hofmannsthal had unequivocally exhibited his German consciousness and confessed his Germandom in his writings on the Austrian idea during the First World War.[28] This paradox that Hofmannsthal was used as a prominent example by both sides in the debate on the Austrian identity might serve as a point of departure for a closer scrutiny of the directions Hofmannsthal's political engagement took in the following chapters. However, I will first delineate the general problem of Hofmannsthal's political engagement.

Hofmannsthal's Political Engagement

I believe Hermann Rudolph rightly noted Hofmannsthal's need for political engagement as a crucial key for understanding his development. However, like James Shedel, I think we must see this need as one anchored in a fundamental attachment to the political order of Habsburg Austria, and not, like Carl Schorske, as a result of political alienation resulting from the failure of Liberalism. As Shedel has emphasized, the Austrian Liberal elite was hardly alienated; after it had been defeated in the arena of mass politics, it continued to wield massive influence through its strong position in the administrative, judicial, educational, and cultural institutions of the Austrian state. Like many from his class, Hofmannsthal naturally leaned on the structures of the Rechtsstaat in his attempt to shape his life, rather than relying on the political influence of the Liberal party in parliament and other representative bodies. However, I believe Shedel underestimates the political crisis shaking the Austrian state around the turn of the century, at a time when Hofmannsthal was trying to find a stable basis for his adult life. The sense of crisis in Hofmannsthal's development at this time is at least partly due to the crisis shaking that framework he was relying on. This political crisis, I would argue, gave Hofmannsthal's project of the cultural regeneration of Habsburg Austria its shape and direction.

Consequently, I would like to modify the view of a shift in Hofmannsthal's development, as put forward by Hermann Rudolph—who talks about Hofmannsthal's move from cultural criticism to cultural synthesis, and Carl Schorske—who identifies a similar shift in Hofmannsthal from social alienation to social engagement. Instead I would say that *Hofmannsthal's affirmation of Habsburg Austria was constant; it was only the form it took that differed over time.* In the 1890s (up to 1901), Hofmannsthal moved close to the state structures in his search for a place in this order, and a few years later—1906 can be identified as an important shift—he moved out into civil society and developed his widely noted ideas on cultural political leadership. As I will sketch out below, Hofmannsthal in both these phases was concerned with harnessing culture for the political regeneration of Austria and with finding a role for himself in this project. His actual cultural political activities, which later again brought him into more direct contact with state institutions, will then be traced in the following chapters.

Leopold von Andrian, who will be presented more closely in the next chapter, is a good comparison here. Andrian began his development in a position very close to Hofmannsthal's—with a strong affirmation of Habsburg Austria and a will to engage himself for this order in some way—but Andrian already in the late 1890s firmly shifted in on the more bureaucratic route and very consciously chose to seek expression for his affirmation of Austria through a career in the diplomatic service.

When tracing Hofmannsthal's development back to the 1890s, the focus is usually squarely on his membership in the Jung-Wien circle around Hermann Bahr.[29] Although, as we will see, the Jung-Wien group and particularly Hermann Bahr are also relevant to Hofmannsthal's political development, there are other aspects of this early period in his life that are often ignored. Knowing that Hofmannsthal became a great author tends to make us see his artistic development as the important aspect of his development to trace. However, up to around 1900 it was by no means certain that Hofmannsthal would become the professional and immensely successful author that he became in the event. This should make us take a broader look at this early period; other aspects of it are important when judging his political development in a wide sense.

Simultaneously with his participation in the Jung-Wien circle, Hofmannsthal finished one of the elite schools of the Viennese Bürgertum, the Akademisches Gymnasium, and enrolled at the university. His choice of studying law at the University of Vienna in 1892 was typical of his class and would have led him to either a job in the private sector, like his father the banker Hugo von Hofmannsthal Sr., or to one in the state bureaucracy. However, Hofmannsthal apparently felt constricted and stifled by the prospect of becoming a Beamte: many times in these years, and also later, he critically noted the constrictions of the civil service, not least when it came to outlook and intellectual horizons. After two years of studies, Hofmannsthal took a break to do his year as a reserve officer (1894–95 as Einjährig Freiwilliger); after this he did not return to law studies. At this time, Hofmannsthal declared in a letter to a friend that he could not follow through on the intended career path in the civil service and now instead aimed for a university career. From 1895 to 1901, Hofmannsthal pursued this ambition. He studied Romanistik and finished his dissertation in 1897 (in philology). After this time he worked on his Habilitationsschrift, which he presented to the faculty in the spring of 1901, and he applied to become a Privat-Dozent.[30]

Parallel to these academic studies, Hofmannsthal continued working on his artistic career, which would, however, take off only in 1903. Also during these years he did a series of terms in the military. Hofmannsthal's military service in the latter half of the 1890s was the first instance when he seems to have found a relatively unproblematic way of affirming Habsburg Austria. As Colin Fewster has convincingly argued, the established view of Hofmannsthal as finding military service tedious and morally degrading (as a sensitive poet should, of course) is hardly sustainable in the face of the evidence: ". . . Hofmannsthal's cavalry service brought considerable satisfaction both to the military authorities and to himself. . . . he viewed it rather as a school for physical and moral improvement and . . . as a very practical way of demonstrating his belonging to society. . . ."[31] In military service, Hofmannsthal found a very concrete way of affirming and integrating himself into the political and social order of Habsburg Austria. However, it was hardly a career choice; in the early 1900s he remained in an uncertain position concerning his future.

It was at this time that Hermann Bahr approached him with a proposition. Bahr more or less offered Hofmannsthal a civil service job in cultural politics, an offer that, I would say, with hindsight looks like hitting the core of Hofmannsthal's needs and expectations of engaging himself socially and politically on his own terms. This offer has a dual background. First, it was part of Hermann Bahr's ongoing project of cultural entrepreneurship, which in the late 1890s had linked up with the Secession. In the Secession, Bahr found a project conceiving society as a Gesamtkunstwerk, a modern art movement that had social and cultural political ambitions.[32] Second, this movement was in 1899 tied into the newly created Art Council

(Kunstrat) in the Austrian ministry of culture and education, where the Secession for a few years had a direct line into the Austrian government. From early 1900 the new and dynamic Koerber government tried to harness culture as part of its wider project of regenerating the Austrian state. In the spirit of his superior, Koerber's minister of culture and education, Wilhelm von Hartel, presented a very ambitious program of centralizing state sponsorship of art into an Art Authority (Kunstamt), with the aim to use art as a social political instrument and to harness it for patriotic purposes. Like so many initiatives of the Koerber government, the Art Council did not survive this administration. Moreover, the Art Council and adjoining plans were severely damaged already in the conflict over Gustav Klimt's faculty pictures for the university building in Vienna starting in 1901. Consequently, the cultural political arm of the Koerber government was never really developed as planned.[33] Nevertheless, this was not yet clear in 1900 when Bahr approached Hofmannsthal and it was apparently a position in the planned Art Authority that Bahr wanted Hofmannsthal to apply for. Considering his long-standing aversion to the constrictions of the Austrian civil service, Hofmannsthal's response was enthusiastic: "I feel attracted to the proposition, and I am in any case ready to negotiate with Hartel," he replied to Bahr.[34] The relative importance for Hofmannsthal of the chance to work in this projected authority can be seen in the way his own expectations for it lie well in line with his culture-political thinking and actions in a longer perspective—this will be returned to below.

The civil service job in culture-politics, arguably Hofmannsthal's ideal job, if he were ever to have one, came to nothing, and in the following year he followed through on his plans for a university career. In the spring of 1901, he handed in his Habilitationsschrift during the same time period as he married and moved into his new house in Rodaun with his wife, Gertrude. In the summer of 1901, Hofmannsthal looked as if he were settling in with a traditional Viennese bourgeoisie life style. A job at the university would only have rounded off the picture. However, at exactly this time a crisis occurred that led him to

Hofmannsthal during his military service in 1895; Freies Deutsches Hochstift, Frankfurter Goethe-Museum

withdraw his Habilitationsschrift in December 1901 before the faculty had reached a decision. In the following summer of 1902, Hofmannsthal wrote the generally recognized paradigmatic work of his creative crisis, the prose narrative *The Letter of Lord Chandos*, which I feel is autobiographical in a much more concrete way than is usually recognized; we could say that in it Hofmannsthal distanced himself from the institutions of the Rechtsstaat with its traditions of rational science and bureaucracy and turned to the "real life" of civil society with which he now wanted to engage through his art.[35]

As several scholars have pointed out, Hofmannsthal formulated his culture-political program in 1906 in the programmatic speech *Der Dichter und diese Zeit*. However, he had been trying out these ideas for some time. There are interesting parallels between Hofmannsthal's Habilitationsschrift, a sort of political biographical work on Victor Hugo (1900–01), and the memorandum he wrote during the same time (late 1900) to the minister of culture and education, Wilhelm von Hartel, in response to Hermann Bahr's offer. The Victor Hugo study ties in the French nineteenth-century author to the political and social upheavals of his time.[36] Hofmannsthal follows Hugo from his childhood, in the context of the rise and fall of French hegemony in Europe, and through the political upheavals and the strong currents of social change during the first half of the nineteenth century. Victor Hugo is described as living in a period when greatness has been lost and strong currents of change are at work. Hofmannsthal views him as treading in a productive relationship with these changes, which finally brings him into direct political engagement. Hofmannsthal depicts Victor Hugo, both in his political engagement and in his artistic work, as attempting to create unity and wholeness in an age of disruptions, to shape his world and age.

Hofmannsthal's narrative of the life-career of the French author in many ways appears as a self-reflection of his own attempt to shape and direct his life at this time; both on the personal level and on the level of society, Hofmannsthal seems to have his own time and its problems in mind when writing about Hugo and his time. In fact, Hofmannsthal's depiction of Victor Hugo's life is in certain ways peculiarly like Hofmannsthal's own subsequent life-career.[37] The depiction of the ultimate failure of Victor Hugo's political engagement, which led to withdrawal from the world after the political reaction in France of 1851, creates an almost eerie impression because of its similarities to Hofmannsthal's own reactions at the dissolution of Imperial Austria in 1918:

> The deeper the spirit gets engaged in the affairs of worldly life, the stronger it is affected by that which really takes place in this world; by making the affairs of an era to one's own personal affairs, one can then not withdraw again from the bitter results of events. . . . There is no more terrible experience for the defeated party, because it means the complete breakdown of both inner and outer life.[38]

The existential language Hofmannsthal already at this time uses to reflect on the deeply personal dimension of political and social engagement signals the fundamental importance of such engagement to him, and this should be kept in mind when pondering his later culture-political activities.

The memorandum Hofmannsthal wrote to Wilhelm von Hartel in late 1900 is interesting here in several ways. It contains Hofmannsthal's reflections on the planned Art Authority; the memorandum contains the descriptions of the problems of the present age that the authority should deal with. These reflections on the need for the government to work actively on re-creating lost cultural wholeness in society strongly echo Hofmannsthal's simultaneous study on Victor Hugo. They are also very similar to his cultural political writings during the following years. In the memorandum, Hofmannsthal contemplates the dawning new age of the twentieth century: "It seems like we stand at the beginning of a new era, an era that will leave no form untouched. . . . The individuals feel their form of life being shaken in its foundation by the upheavals of the whole."[39] Hofmannsthal's recipe to counter this destabilization of culture and society is built on the creation of a government authority (or a group of authorities) that should coordinate and channel the attempt to harness art and high culture in general and put them in the service of (re)creating cultural wholeness in a modernizing, fragmenting society.

Der Dichter und diese Zeit (1906) is widely regarded as a key text for understanding Hofmannsthal's development. For Carl Schorske, it is an important document in understanding Hofmannsthal's "political turn," and for Hermann Rudolph it is the document that most directly signals Hofmannsthal's turn from cultural criticism to cultural synthesis, that is, to an affirmative stance to society and culture. As I see it, there is no shift of this type. *Der Dichter und diese Zeit* is an expression of Hofmannsthal's longer affirmation of Habsburg Austria. However, it signals Hofmannsthal's attempt to formulate a program for actively affirming his belonging to society *wholly outside of the structures of the state. Der Dichter und diese Zeit* was written as a speech, which Hofmannsthal delivered in several German cities in December 1906, and then in January 1907 in Vienna. The speech is strongly culture critical, but it revolves around the antidote to this condition, around the need for harmonization of the conflicting elements of modern culture. It describes the important role, indeed the duty, of the modern poet to serve as a vessel for the meaning of the age and to transmit this meaning to the people, to the unhappy creatures of a society that has lost its wholeness: "In [the poet] everything must be brought together. It is he who connects the elements of the age within himself."[40]

In the year before he wrote *Der Dichter und diese Zeit,* Hofmannsthal had developed some plans with Harry Kessler, the German cultural entrepreneur, that fit the general picture of Hofmannsthal's preoccupations at this time. In 1905, he presented to Kessler a scheme for a private elite school to educate young men in the spirit of cultural wholeness.[41] Hofmannsthal attempted to engage his and Kessler's mutual friend, the art historian and civil servant Eberhard von Bodenhausen, as headmaster and driving force of this planned new elite school and sent him an outline of his ideas about it. Hofmannsthal's school should shape young people (in effect young men) into strong, responsible individuals with love for nature and art, with respect for the past, and with tolerance for the coming "balanced and focused individuals who could as well become good civil servants or officers as colonizers or politicians."[42] In short, an elite fitting the blueprint that was soon to be systematically set down in *Der Dichter und diese Zeit*; an elite group filling about the same function as that culture political authority Hofmannsthal had sketched a few years earlier. The import of these Hofmannsthal ideas of cultured whole people who could harmonize fragmenting culture by creating wholeness out of the elements of their time is not least shown in his recurring use in the early 1900s of a formulation from the English poet Addison: "The whole man must move together." This formula, which Hofmannsthal almost made into a slogan for his personal development,[43] as well as for his will to imbue modern society with cultural wholeness, seems, in fact, to sum up his preoccupations at this time.

Hofmannsthal's early political engagement also set the tracks for the way he in practical terms shaped his culture-political engagement from now on. Harry Kessler's biographer, Peter Grupp, has noted about the view of politics in the circles Kessler moved in: "They testify to a belief in the possibility to wield decisive influence over political affairs through individual engagement or the engagement of an elite group wholly outside the established bureaucratic and political structures."[44] Such a view of politics would not only guide Hofmannsthal's culture-political activities for the rest of his life, not least during their peak in the Great War; it also seems to delineate his view of politics as such. Hofmannsthal's ostensibly Weberian turn from bureaucratic engagement for Habsburg Austria to political engagement thus had a strongly elitist character and in practice remained closely dependent on the bureaucratic structures he had seemingly left behind; the wielding of influence almost always assumed the shape of personally involving or directly influencing highly placed decision makers.

In Hofmannsthal's concrete culture-political initiatives as well as in his programmatic statements, we can discern a view of the strong individual or elite group as moving and changing society. One of those persons whom Hofmannsthal most evidently held such expectations for was the projected headmaster of that school he and Kessler had planned in 1905, Eberhard von Bodenhausen. When Hofmannsthal twenty years later, after his friend's death, made notes for a biographic essay on Bodenhausen, the echoes of *Der Dichter und diese Zeit* were strong. Bodenhausen had made a career change from the German civil service to industry (Krupp) in 1906, leaving the cultural activities of his youth behind, and as time passed he became a very influential person in late Wilhelmine Germany. For a moment in the summer of 1917, he was even a candidate to replace Theobald von Bethmann Hollweg as chancellor and would thus have reached a position where he could have strongly influenced events. Hofmannsthal described Bodenhausen as the type for a culturally whole leader with the ability to create unity and to shape his times.[45] As it seems, Hofmannsthal's view of Bodenhausen in the late 1920s was not merely a retrospective construction. It might even be that Bodenhausen, the art historian and literary publicist, the civil servant and captain of industry, was an important inspiration for the needed culturally whole (political) leadership described in *Der Dichter und diese Zeit.* In a letter to Bodenhausen, shortly after Bodenhausen's move to Krupp and shortly before writing *Der Dichter und diese Zeit*, Hofmannsthal elaborated on his hopes that Bodenhausen in his new career in the world of power would retain the "internal breadth" he had acquired in activities in the arts and literature. Significantly, Hofmannsthal has quoted Addison at the top of the letter as a motto for Bodenhausen's new career at Krupp: "The whole man must move at once."[46]

In the spring of 1907, in the same period that Hofmannsthal delivered his speech *Der Dichter und diese Zeit* in Vienna and started to work on its twin work, *Die Briefe des Zurückgekehrten*, there was actually a feeling of hope in the lately so conflict-ridden and paralyzed political culture of Austria. The franchise reform of 1906–07 unleashed a multitude of hopes and expectations on new departures in the political life of Austria. Hofmannsthal did not remain unaffected. This is not least evident from his rejoicing over the beginning political career of his acquaintance, the Austrian constitutional lawyer and historian, Josef Redlich. At the end of 1906, Redlich had left his scholarly career and been elected on a German-Liberal program (Deutsche Fortschrittspartei) to the provincial assembly of his home province, Moravia. After Redlich had presented his candidature to the Austrian parliament in the first election of the new system with general male franchise in the spring of 1907, in which he was subsequently also elected, setting off a most successful parliamentary career, Hofmannsthal wrote to tell Redlich that he followed his political career with the greatest of interest. Hofmannsthal also described himself as indirectly partaking in developments as a part of that truly political class of "independent people" that had been absent in Austria, but which was the essential basis for any truly political life and which might just be reestablished through the political changes that were taking place.[47]

As it seems, Hofmannsthal was here again thinking in terms of that (elite) class of culturally whole political leaders that had preoccupied him lately. This time his interest is also directed at a versatile personality, a potential carrier of change. Josef Redlich, the scholar with a background in publishing, who now took the step into politics, would become an influential person in late Imperial Austria. In the summer of 1917, he would even appear before the young Emperor Karl I as a candidate for the Austrian minister presidency, carrying a program of peace and constitutional and national reform of the ailing imperial state of the Habsburgs. At least Hofmannsthal had a keen sense of whom he should invest his political hopes in.

After 1906 Hofmannsthal would continue to experiment with different forms of culture-politics. To an increasing degree he would also start to direct these activities with the aim of furthering an Austrian cultural identity as the shape of the wholeness he was searching for in his affirmation of the old order of Habsburg Austria. In fact, Hofmannsthal's political project would be decisively shaped by his search for an Austrian identity, his search for the meaning of that culture he so strongly felt himself to be a part of. In this search, Leopold von Andrian would be a constant companion, and his influence over Hofmannsthal would extend beyond the latter's death; in the 1930s, Andrian actively shaped the memory of Hofmannsthal as an Austrian cultural icon.

2. Guardians of Austrian Culture: Hofmannsthal and Andrian

In the spring of 1894, the diary of Hugo von Hofmannsthal and the one of his close friend Leopold von Andrian both showed a marked preoccupation with Austrian culture in general and in particular with the "soul," the "character," or, perhaps, the identity of the city of Vienna, their hometown. They walked around in the city and made excursions in its surroundings, taking down their impressions of places and landscapes and of the city as such in their diaries. In both diaries there appear descriptions of themselves as the "last Austrian poets" and as a sort of guardians of Austrian culture.[48] When writing a commemorative article about his friend Hofmannsthal in 1948, Andrian especially recalled these early years of their friendship in the 1890s, which he characterized as circling around the problem of Austrian culture.[49] The importance of the notion of an Austrian culture to both Andrian and Hofmannsthal is actually a strain that can be traced over time in their relationship. It was probably most intense in their youth, but it reappeared recurrently and received a new immediacy during World War I.[50] However, Hofmannsthal would not follow the clean-cut Austrian "national" route taken by Andrian; he went through a much more complex development with regard to his view of the Austrian identity. Their parallel, sometimes intersecting trajectories will be traced in this and the following chapters.

Andrian, Hofmannsthal, and the Austrian Identity

With Andrian, the Austrian identity became a lifelong concern that peaked in his active struggle in the 1930s and 1940s for an independent Austrian nation against what he saw as the German national imperialism of the Nazis.[51] In the 1890s, it was also Andrian who gave the fullest artistic expression to this preoccupation of the two friends with the Austrian identity. Andrian himself viewed his short novel *Der Garten der Erkenntnis* (1895) as particularly successful in its rendering of an intensely subjective experience of the "soul of the (Austrian) people" and of the "soul of Vienna."[52] In the narrative of a young prince "whose lands bordered on Germany," long passages appear depicting Vienna, the imperial, multinational city, echoing the entries in both Andrian's and Hofmannsthal's diaries from the year before the book was published.[53] Furthermore, when Andrian in 1919 reissued *Der Garten der Erkenntnis,* he did it as a sort of patriotic statement. In the new preface he emphasized his "peculiar, betrayed, painfully loved Austrian fatherland" as the most important ambience in this book about friendship and youth.[54] Later, in the preface to his *Österreich im Prisma der Idee* (1937), Andrian even more unequivocally cultivated the image of "that most Austrian Garten der Erkenntnis"[55] as an expression of his lifelong struggle for the Austrian identity.

The self-therapy contained in both the original *Der Garten der Erkenntnis* and in the act of its reissue in 1919 originated in a personal identity crisis of the same general type that Hofmannsthal had experienced around the turn of the century. In regard to Andrian, though, the crisis went much deeper and was more disruptive, and, as one effect, it ended his literary career. After a nervous breakdown in the late 1890s, Andrian would suffer recurring nervous problems throughout his life. Andrian's identity crisis was not least one of his sexual identity. The social and cultural milieu of his upbringing in fin-de-siécle Vienna was strongly condemning of homosexuality, and this seems to have been an important reason for his drawn-out identity crisis. During his career in the diplomatic service, Andrian also felt compelled to hide his homosexuality, something that must have contributed to sustaining his identity crisis.[56]

Perhaps this wider crisis of identity made Andrian depend much more directly than Hofmannsthal on that Austrian cultural identity he nurtured and fought for throughout his life. This also explains his very active, almost relentless engagement for the political vessel of this identity up to 1918, the Austro-Hungarian Empire. Much like Hofmannsthal, Andrian sought to give purpose to and stabilize his identity through political engagement. However, to Andrian this engagement became a monolithic, all-encompassing identification with Austria, which expressed itself very directly through his service to the empire as a diplomat. At the start of his diplomatic career in 1901, Andrian confided in Hofmannsthal that his engagement for "Austria and her development" could be counted among the most important things in his life, and it was intimately tied up to his own personal development and family background.[57] Over time, this political engagement of Andrian's intensified and received an ever more accentuated identity character. It expressed itself comparatively early as an idolization of Alois Lexa von Aehrenthal, who was Andrian's superior first at the embassy in St. Petersburg and then, of course, as foreign minister. To Andrian, as to a

Leopold von Andrian; Austrian National Library, ÖNB/Sign. KOS5319D

whole generation of younger Austro-Hungarian diplomats, Aehrenthal was the almost mythic restorer of Austro-Hungarian power and glory. As consul general in Warsaw in Russian Poland in the years preceding the outbreak of World War I, Andrian viewed himself as Aehrenthal's personal representative on this frontier of the empire, as carrying a mission within the larger plan of Austro-Hungarian political regeneration. Aehrenthal's premature death in 1912 was a severe blow to Andrian and his young colleagues in the Austro-Hungarian foreign ministry, apparently depriving them of the meaning of their service.[58] However, during the war he returned to Poland on a special mission, and the way he handled this mission makes it appear almost as a personal crusade for Austria(-Hungary) against both Russia and Prussia (i.e., Imperial Germany). In fact, it is not difficult to see it as a struggle for his own personal identity, which by this time was closely tied up to the destiny of Austria.

This accounts for the breakdown Andrian suffered at the dissolution of Austria-Hungary in 1918. In his late commemorative article on Hofmannsthal, Andrian asserted that neither he nor Hofmannsthal ever really recovered from this event.[59] It seems significant that Andrian took Hofmannsthal's premature death in 1929 as another blow on the same scale as the one he had received in 1918.[60] Apparently, Andrian lost more than a personal friend at the death of Hofmannsthal. He lost a comrade in arms in the struggle for the Austrian identity. This is at least the impression one receives from Andrian's continuing shaping of the memory of Hofmannsthal during the decades following the latter's death.[61] An important contribution to Andrian's continued preoccupation with Hofmannsthal is the political tract *Österreich im Prisma der Idee* (1937), written with the aim to "scientifically prove" the separate existence (from Germany) of an Austrian nation. The book was not only dedicated to Hofmannsthal; under a thin disguise, Andrian here also lets Hofmannsthal give expression to his (alleged) Austrianness.[62] The combined impression of Andrian's representation of Hofmannsthal here and in his commemorative article of 1949 is that Hofmannsthal should be understood as an essential expression of Austrian culture. Indeed, Andrian went further and co-opted Hofmannsthal into the camp of political Austrianism; Andrian even asserted that Hofmannsthal's "uniquely beautiful life work" by itself justified the now (in 1949) "almost universally accepted concept of the Austrian nation."[63]

One might say that the unequivocal judgment on Hofmannsthal's Austrianness that is contained in Andrian's late publications reviewed above constitute the end point of his lifelong attempt at controlling and determining Hofmannsthal's cultural identity. At this later time, of course, Andrian encountered no opposition, but during the greater part of their friendship, he and Hofmannsthal intermittently discussed and debated the problem of Austrian identity in a much more lively way. In fact, within a certain common frame of reference, their differences often seemed quite considerable. An early instance of this running debate occurred in 1898 when Hofmannsthal together with Harry Kessler had hatched the idea of producing an issue of the literary periodical *PAN* on the theme of young Austrian literature. Hofmannsthal contacted Andrian for a contribution, but found the latter in his most difficult, patriotic mood. Andrian started making far-reaching demands on the shape of the coming presentation, wanting to write a programmatic article for presentation to the youths of the German Empire, "a manifest" in which he would emphasize the separateness of culture and art in Austria from culture and art in Germany. The reason for these difficulties was that Andrian had learned that Kessler planned several issues dealing with different "centers of German culture." When the debate heated up, Andrian only the more stubbornly stuck to "my principle, not to let Vienna be treated as a German provincial center, not to view Austria as an annex to Germany."[64] A couple of years later, when Hofmannsthal writes to Andrian from Paris telling him about how he finds the Belgian poets of "Germanic extraction" the most interesting, he is again reprimanded by Andrian: "I truly hope that in your feelings of Germanic solidarity vis-à-vis France, you will not forget that you are Austrian, not German."[65]

In these and similar exchanges with Andrian during the early years of the new century, Hofmannsthal exhibits a relaxed attitude on the problem of the Austrian identity and its relationship to Germany, which only makes Andrian the more eager to return his friend to the Austrian fold. A similar stance can be found in Hofmannsthal's simultaneous exchanges with his Reich-German friend Harry Kessler. In 1901, Hofmannsthal tries to impress Kessler with the peculiarities of the Austrian audience, since it is both socially and nationally so heterogeneous, lacking all kinds of centers and common arenas. He also intimates the possibility of viewing the Austrian culture as separate from the German culture, much, as he says, as one could see American culture as separate from the British.[66] In 1907, Hofmannsthal received Kessler in the temple of his cultural identity, in the house in Rodaun, and they evidently discussed these questions during his stay. Upon the return to his home in Weimar, Kessler elaborates on how the visit deeply impressed on him the importance of Austria in German history; not least, their walks through Vienna, "through the baroque palaces," were a strong experience in this regard, as he writes. To Kessler's outpouring, Hofmannsthal replied that he was happy that his friend now had received an understanding of Austrian culture and history: "Now you have an idea of what Austria is, and therefore you can also understand why I stay here."[67] In these early exchanges with Andrian and Kessler, the overall impression is that Hofmannsthal is rather stable in his identification with Austria, but that this identification does not exclude a simultaneous identification with Germany, indeed as viewing Austrian culture as in some ways a part of German culture. The recurring conflicts with Andrian are due to the latter's insistence on viewing Austrian culture as wholly separate from the German. One can discern certain shifts in Hofmannsthal's attitude during the following period, but the (apparent) ambivalence remains.

The changes are visible, for example, during the Bosnian annexation crisis in 1908–09, when Hofmannsthal exhibited a stronger Austrian self-assertion than previously. Immediately after the annexation in October 1908, he had a very lively exchange with Kessler, who took a critical view of the actions of Hofmannsthal's newly found hero, Austro-Hungarian Foreign Minister Aehrenthal. Hofmannsthal countered: "In this question we are of diametrically opposed opinion. . . . I admire Aehrenthal greatly, and I find what he has done the most skillful thing done on this continent for at least the last twenty years. . . . You are *not* seeing these things in a proper way."[68] And in March the following year, Hofmannsthal is positively intoxicated in his Austrian patriotism when the Austro-Hungarian armies are amassing on the southeastern borders of the empire in preparation for the planned campaign against Serbia. The climax of the Bosnian crisis came during those same days that Hofmannsthal's and Richard Strauss's first opera, *Elektra,* had its successful Viennese premiere, and to Hofmannsthal this artistic success seems to go up into a larger experience of Austrian revitalization:

> [The final rehearsals and the premiere] fell within exactly those forty-eight hours when the war was imminent and trains with our brave people unceasingly departed for the south. It was also for that reason beautiful days. The silent determination and elevatedness of all the people, the sudden end of all conflicts—there was something very beautiful about it. It was almost as if we had regretted the turn that events had taken, and also that we had not acted against Russia and, if necessary, against both Russia and Italy.[69]

This time of high patriotic sentiment is also the time of the beginning of work on Hofmannsthal's perhaps greatest contribution to his and Andrian's celebration of Austrian culture, *Der Rosenkavalier*, which will be returned to presently. And a couple of years later, Hofmannsthal even seems to have abandoned his relative consensus with Harry Kessler on Austrian culture as being part of German culture. In 1911, for instance, he is reprimanding Kessler for his lacking an understanding of Austrian society and culture. Kessler's German frames of reference, Hofmannsthal maintains, are completely inadequate in this "completely differently oriented culture," which is geared not toward Germany, but toward its "enormous only half-civilized" hinterland.[70]

Nevertheless, the evident and rising affirmation of Austria discernible in Hofmannsthal during these years was fragile. In 1913 he seems to have hit a low point when almost in desperation he wrote to Andrian about his complete loss of faith in Austria as a result of the never-ending internal conflicts: "We must admit to ourselves, Poldy, we have a Heimat, but no fatherland—in place of it we have just got a ghost."[71] Andrian reacted very strongly, not least since he evidently interpreted Hofmannsthal's distinction as one between a German-Austrian Heimat and a (truly) Austrian fatherland:

> I was always proud that you are an Austrian and that you could have become what you are only in Austria. . . . He who is conscious enough to scrutinize his feelings and who concludes that he is a 'German,' he cannot be an Austrian. . . . To simultaneously be a German and an Austrian seems impossible to me.[72]

Andrian's and Hofmannsthal's running, but in the main an amicable polemic, the beginning of which has been recounted above, appears to be summed up and brought to a conclusion according to Andrian's view of it in his late work *Österreich im Prisma der Idee* (1937). This work contains several sections that are discussions on the problem of the Austrian identity, of the Austrian nation, between "the nobleman" Heinrich Phillip (Andrian) and "the poet" Erwin (Hofmannsthal). In these fictitious discussions, Andrian actually seems to work out the problem of Hofmannsthal's cultural identity, not least for himself.

In the first passage, which is readily readable as an exchange between Andrian and Hofmannsthal, Andrian lets Erwin (Hofmannsthal) take a position similar to that discernible in their recounted debates, above, a position that unites affinity to the larger sphere of German culture and language with a political adherence to the Austrian Vaterland.[73] Andrian later lets Erwin (Hofmannsthal) modify his position somewhat, insofar as he now more strongly emphasizes that the Austrian variety of the German language, in certain respects, should be seen as a language of its own, a language especially cultivated by Austrian nobility, but also found in a natural, less articulated, and less refined form in the German-Austrian peasant population, and notably among the Viennese. It was the great historical crime of the German-Austrian middle classes, Erwin (Hofmannsthal) maintains, and particularly of their intellectuals, not to cultivate the Austrian variety of German as their scholarly and professional language, but instead to choose an essentially Prussian variety of the common language.[74] It is exactly here where Andrian sets in the main thrust of his historical argument, in apparent unison with Hofmannsthal, insofar as he develops a historical discourse on the failure of the German-Austrian middle classes in the late nineteenth century to fulfill the historical development of a separate Austrian nation. Andrian traces the Austrian Sonderentwicklung (from Germany) all the way back to the late Middle Ages, but it was during the Baroque period that the special Austrian aristocratic culture blossomed, a culture that embodied both "the multiplicity and unity of the empire." Together with the Austrian people (meaning the lower classes), and especially the Viennese "people," this Austrian nobility developed and cultivated a special culture not least expressed in manners, ceremonies, and celebrations "in which a German element could just be discerned, not more." It constituted an Austrian nationality that prefigured "an Austrian nation encompassing all the classes," including all the peoples except the Poles and Ruthenians, who had come too late to the Austrian union of peoples, and the Hungarians, who were only partly integrated in the Austrian nationality at the beginning of the nineteenth century. It was now the light of history falling on the middle classes, who sadly failed to rise to the occasion and bring a long historical development to full fruition.[75]

Andrian here continues that the German-Austrian Bürgerlichkeit was, even in the late nineteenth century, not unpatriotic. "It remained in its heart devoted both to its narrower little-Austrian fatherland, as well as to the projection of this fatherland onto the other peoples of the Habsburg Empire according to the Great-Austrian idea." But because of its linguistic and cultural dependence on Germany, captivity in which it had entered on its own volition, this class was less Austrian and more German than the other classes of Austria. With time, this tendency developed into an inner division ("ein innerer Zwiespalt"), but the Austrian Bürgertum was for a long time successful in uniting two patriotisms, two mutually excluding value systems "in one soul," as Andrian expresses it. To sustain this unsustainable state, the Austrian middle classes developed a dreamlike dual ideology that united their two fatherlands within a historical vision of a German Weltreich, where the Austrian Germans would function as leaders in an empire encompassing both Germany and the eastern dominions of the Habsburg Empire. The war of 1866 with the following political exclusion of the Austrian Germans from Germany constituted the actual bankruptcy of this ideology, but despite this, the German-Austrian political parties desperately tried to sustain their position, paying a high price of increasing dependence on Imperial Germany and intensifying conflicts with the other nationalities within the Habsburg Empire. The final price was paid in the Great War, when the

German-Austrian Bürgertum staked its whole future on a German victory and its accompanying rise of a Great-German empire in Mitteleuropa. Instead, of course, this class lost everything, and after 1918, to paraphrase Andrian's image, it purified its soul and opted for a German Anschluss nationalism.[76]

Taken together, Andrian's late view of Hofmannsthal as presented in *Österreich im Prisma der Idee* retained a certain ambivalence as to his cultural identity, though he here finished by explicitly proclaiming Hofmannsthal an arch-Austrian. The sin Andrian suspects Hofmannsthal of, and here posthumously purifies him from, is the above-recounted sin of the German-Austrian Bürgertum, that of trying to unite two conflicting value systems in his "soul." The question is, of course, to what degree Andrian was justified in cleansing Hofmannsthal's memory from this cultural, even existential ambivalence, as Andrian perceived it. This problem will be again returned to below, but first some space will be devoted to scrutinizing Hofmannsthal's main contribution to the Austrian identity project at this time.

Der Rosenkavalier

The traces of Hofmannsthal's adherence to that Austrian culture described in Andrian's historical discourse are multifarious. Among the most important instances of this identification was, as Hermann Broch rightly observed, the strong idealization of the Austrian high aristocracy that Hofmannsthal gave expression to throughout his life. During his military service in the late 1890s, Hofmannsthal was especially thrilled about serving in a regiment whose officers were the offspring of old aristocratic families, carrying names that were intimately bound up to a long and glorious Austrian history.[77] Andrian had certain difficulties with Hofmannsthal's aristocratic snobbery, and he later noted critically that Hofmannsthal had actually divided his friends into different circles, one of which was the "aristocratic" circle of friends. Andrian characterized this circle as "people with Austrian-aristocratic manners," a type of person to which Hofmannsthal was naturally drawn and to which he gave literary expression.[78] Hofmannsthal's relationship to Christiane Thun-Salm, a member of the Bohemian high aristocracy,[79] was a special relationship of this sort. In Countess Thun-Salm, Hofmannsthal had a direct line into that Habsburg court aristocracy, which was the main historical carrier of the special Austrian culture Hofmannsthal (and Andrian) identified with. Their relationship was markedly asymmetric, though, insofar as Christiane Thun-Salm never invited Hofmannsthal into the actual social life of her class. Hofmannsthal received only a whiff of the life of this class at the small luncheons she invited him and a few other artistic friends to in her winter residence, the Palais Esterhazy in central Vienna.[80] But this seems actually to have been quite enough for Hofmannsthal. He seems to have consciously and willingly subordinated himself socially to the countess, such as when he entertained the idea in his letters to her of spending the summer at work on his literary projects in the forester's cabin on the lands of the Thun-Salm castle at Sehuchitz in Bohemia, being allowed to come to dinner at the castle once in a while.[81]

Christiane Thun-Salm was a poet, author, and dramatist in her own right, and Hofmannsthal was probably part of *her* "artistic" circle of friends, albeit a very important friend of this type, confirming her in a role that was not exactly appreciated in her social class. Although her literary work was hardly part of the avant-garde of literary developments, it rather seems like Hofmannsthal genuinely appreciated her work. This appreciation probably stemmed from her stories often taking place in the environment of her social class, the Austrian high aristocracy, and giving expression to its culture by its descriptions of, for instance, its manners and ways of speaking. The actual aristocratic milieu and the prominent appearance of both social dialects and the linguistic coloring of the different cultures and regions of the multinational empire all belonged to those traits of the Der Rosenkavalier that Hofmannsthal found inspiration for in Christiane Thun-Salm's literary work.[82] Their correspondence is full of references to their mutual love and admiration for Austrian culture, in a way that no other of Hofmannsthal's correspondences are. The most interesting of their exchanges is perhaps the one surrounding the 2 December 1908 performance in the Court Opera in Vienna of Christiane Thun-Salm's festival drama *Des Kaisers Traum* as part of the celebrations of Franz Joseph's 60th jubilee as emperor, the so-called Kaiserhuldigungsfest. Thun-Salm had written this festive play for the 50th jubilee in 1898, the celebration of which had been canceled because of the murder of Empress Elisabeth in the summer of that year. Thun-Salm's festival drama is a rather conventional celebration of Austrian imperial history through a series of historical tableaus, which are presented as the dream of the brilliant imperial future of the thirteenth-century emperor, Rudolf of Habsburg, ending with a tableau celebrating the benevolent Emperor Franz Joseph, who was present at the performance at the Court Opera and seemed to enjoy it greatly. Hofmannsthal engaged himself strongly in the project, wanting to rework the play and give it a more powerful dramatic focus. Instead of the pageant-like string of scenes Thun-Salm had written, Hofmannsthal wanted to divide the play into two main parts. The first should be a dialogue between Emperor Rudolf and the "Future," which focuses squarely on the present Austria (and its glorious living history), letting its different qualities and characteristics emerge gradually in the dialogue's questions and answers. It should end, Hofmannsthal maintains, with Emperor Rudolf's eager wish to see a vision of this magnificent future, a wish that is fulfilled by the presentation of a mass chorus scene where all the peoples of the realm pay homage to Rudolf's descendant, Emperor Franz Joseph.[83] The end of the play in Hofmannsthal's proposed version is modeled on the Kaiserhuldigungsfestzug, which had been arranged in Vienna on 12 June 1908, two days before Hofmannsthal wrote down his ideas of a reworking of Christiane Thun-Salm's festive play. The Kaiserhuldigungsfestzug was a pageant where the different peoples of the Habsburg realm had been represented in historical and traditional costumes, paying homage to their emperor, Franz Joseph, which quite apparently had struck a chord in Hofmannsthal.

This preoccupation of Hofmannsthal with the undisguised Austrian patriotism of *Des Kaisers Traum* in 1908 coincides in time with his patriotic rejoicing over Aehrenthal's powerful diplomatic action in 1908–09. However, Hofmannsthal's interest in *Des Kaisers Traum* also has a direct bearing on the shape of *Der Rosenkavalier* (1909–10), a work that should be seen as an expression of Hofmannsthal's celebration of Austrian culture. In a very general way, these two works must be seen to be related to each other, but the celebration of Austrian culture and history in *Der Rosenkavalier* is much more complex and subtle than in Christiane Thun-Salm's explicitly festive and patriotic play. *Der Rosenkavalier* was the first work expressly written by Hofmannsthal as a libretto for an opera by Richard Strauss. The work originated during a few days in early 1909, which Hofmannsthal spent with Harry Kessler in Weimar. Kessler's involvement in the creation of *Der Rosenkavalier* became a source of conflict when Hofmannsthal did not acknowledge Kessler as a collaborator. But Kessler's own version of the collaboration seems rather plausible, insofar as he maintained that he had supplied most of the ideas for the dramatic and comical situations, and Hofmannsthal had supplied the lyrical dressing needed to give life to Kessler's "situations."[84] Part of Hofmannsthal's lyrical, or perhaps rather "pictorial" talent, was also the matter contained in the sheer mass of details constituting the Austrian cultural and historical ambience of *Der Rosenkavalier*. In its detail, this ambience was influenced by the Austrian culture pictured in Christiane Thun-Salm's literary works, but the overall structure of the deployment of Austrian cultural forms and historical references is rather related to that historical discourse on the Austrian nation later written by Andrian in his *Österreich im Prisma der Idee*.

Der Rosenkavalier is set in mid-eighteenth-century Vienna during the reign of Maria Theresia. This era was also a sort of historical intersection between that great Baroque era of blossoming aristocratic culture, focused by Andrian as a crucial time in the Austrian nation building, and a period of beginning an integration of the Habsburg dominions into a modern (imperial) Austrian state. Empress Maria Theresia was later to play a role in Hofmannsthal's creation of an Austrian national mythology in his writings on the Austrian idea during World War I. In the opera libretto of 1910, this is not yet explicit, but she might nevertheless be identified in the leading female character, the princess Werdenberg, whose Christian name aptly is Marie Therése.[85] In the plot, the princess's fear of growing old, of change, is put to the test when her younger lover, Octavian Rofrano, falls in love with Sophie Faninal, the daughter of a rich Viennese burgher. At the beginning of the action, a cousin of Marie Therése's, a baron, Lord Ochs of Lerchenau, a somewhat uncouth country gentleman, approaches her to acquire help in his marriage plans. He needs a "Rose Cavalier"—someone to represent him and to present a silver rose to the bride to be in the Viennese tradition of the marriage proposal as invented by Hofmannsthal. The intended bride turns out to be Sophie Faninal, and the princess chooses Octavian to represent the groom. In the scene where the rose is presented, Octavian and Sophie fall in love, after which the bridegroom arrives and makes a very tactless and rude entrance, treating Sophie as something he has just bought. This behavior does not deter Sophie's father, who is positively exalted at the prospect of becoming related to the Austrian high aristocracy of the Rofranos and Werdenbergs. The rest of the opera circles around Octavian's plot to discredit Ochs in the eyes of Sophie's father and to win her hand in marriage. Toward the end of the last act, when Ochs desperately tries to repair the damage done to his reputation by Octavian's successful scheme, Marie Therése arrives and takes control of matters. She overcomes her fears of change and takes charge of developments by using her social status to stop Ochs from using his standing to win the day. Octavian and Sophie can thus be united, but at a heavy cost to herself.

Hofmannsthal's Austria is represented at several levels of the drama. Austrian culture in the meaning given to it by Andrian, a culture shared by the aristocracy and the lower classes, especially the Viennese, is represented by the very active use of different Austrian provincial and social dialects. Hofmannsthal has even invented a special way for the Austrian aristocracy to speak, a mix between older Austrian court usage and chancellery German and freely invented forms to make this ancient language more easily understandable. But he also deploys different Austrian dialects, especially Viennese and Bohemian-German, colored differently depending on their social origins. As Alan Jefferson has noted, Hofmannsthal also used elements from both a Bohemian village wedding and an old aristocratic tradition of estate weddings when he composed that central ceremonial scene of the opera, the presentation of the silver rose, thus strengthening this impression of a culture common to the upper and lower classes.[86] Significantly, the main representative of the Austrian Bürgertum in the drama, Sophie's father, Herr von Faninal, seems to have great difficulties in understanding both the aristocrats and the members of the lower orders, and his desperate attempt at social integration with the aristocracy, which is also an attempt at *cultural* integration, serves as a generator of comical points in the drama.[87]

The Austrian nobility is thus contrasted with the bürgerliche element of the Faninals, who are rising socially through their successful merchant activities, but appear less than integrated both socially and culturally. The Faninals also represent an important element for the future of Austria, an element with a special role in that Austrian nation building Andrian described as entering a crucial stage with the rise of the bürgerliche classes. *Der Rosenkavalier* can be read as a clash between two possible responses from the Austrian aristocracy toward the crucial question of the social integration of these new elements. Marie Therése might be said to represent the "good" and future-oriented side of the old system, carrying a capacity for change and adaptation in this system, a capacity to integrate the new and the old. Baron Ochs, however, represents the reverse tendency of the old system, to defend the powers and privileges and to refuse to acknowledge any social changes that may imperil these privileges. The defeat of Ochs at the hands of the princess and her subsequent active contribution to ensure the union between Octavian (the aristocracy) and Sophie (the Bürgertum) thus holds a symbolism of social renewal. Read against Andrian's historical narrative of the development of the Austrian nation, Hofmannsthal here seems to have gone back to when the Austrian nation-building process went astray and to have rewritten the history of this crucial juncture, creating a symbolic narrative of the (re)integration of the "less Austrian and more German" bürgerliche element into the Austrian nationality.

Hofmannsthal's play also mirrors the cultural and national composition of the multinational empire. Vienna is pictured as the center of an "Austrian" cultural sphere, which appears as a synthesis between the south and the north, the east and the west. The spatial (geographic) pattern of this cultural sphere is that of a German-Austrian core, which in different ways has integrated the cultural and national elements of the imperial realm. The most important meeting here is that between South-German and Italian cultures, the elements of which positively permeate the setting. This meeting between the south and the north seems to be the essence of Austrianness. Hungary appears more like an eastern partner of Austria, represented at the highest level of society. This Austria obviously also contains Slav-speaking provinces, but they receive a much more cursory treatment. They appear mainly as the hinterlands of the great empire. Bohemia is represented as an integrated part of the German-Austrian core of the empire, thus at the most giving Czech culture a subordinate part in this Austrian cultural sphere. Croatia is allotted a more important role of a distant and mystical country of forests and mountains, where Prince Werdenberg, Marie Therése's husband, is on a hunting expedition during the action of the drama. The threat of his return to upset things in Vienna even seems extra ominous because of the mystical aura of the Croatian forests. Croatia symbolizes the magic and romanticism of a Slav world that actually appears as a contrast to the civilized Austrian culture at the center of Hofmannsthal's concerns. In some ways Croatia appears as an internal colony, or, perhaps, the Other within.

As a result of the combination of such a cultural hierarchy and a very strong sense of social hierarchy, centered on the Austrian aristocracy, the broader image of political order distinguishable in *Der Rosenkavalier* is strongly imperial. Vienna is the center of German-Austrian aristocratic culture, which rules over a large nationally heterogeneous empire. Such a mental structure can actually be discerned in Hofmannsthal rather early, around the time of his turn-of-the-century crisis. Already in 1896, in a letter to Andrian from his military posting in Tlumacz, Galicia, Hofmannsthal indirectly placed himself at the center of a similar political and social universe as that discernible in *Der Rosenkavalier.* In this letter he starts out by expressing his admiration for the officers of his regiment as "true Austrian soldiers" who seem imbued with that wholeness that would preoccupy Hofmannsthal for the next ten years, and with that ideal Austrianness that was essential to him throughout his life. But after this he shifts into a critical analysis of practically all the other categories among the soldiers. Members of his own category, those gentlemen (junge Herren) doing their military service, do not find his approval. Their deficiency is that most of them are not at all real gentlemen, "*not* out of Society . . . practically all from the provinces." In short, they belong further down on that social and cultural hierarchy whose imprint *Der Rosenkavalier* bears. When Hofmannsthal turns to the lower orders, his description of the Ruthenian private soldiers of the regiment makes it exceedingly clear that we have here reached the base of the social hierarchy and the outermost circle of the Austrian cultural sphere. In fact, his following description of the local Jewish population in Tlumacz, Galicia, makes us wonder if we have not moved beyond the outermost boundaries of that imperial realm that was Hofmannsthal's Austria.[88]

Der Rosenkavalier is indubitably the work in both Strauss's and Hofmannsthal's productions that has attained the most popularity. I would argue that this is not least due to the very strong Austrian ambience in the work, which must be seen as essential for achieving that status of the Austrian national opera that *Der Rosenkavalier* in effect has. This is not only because the rose ceremony invented by Hofmannsthal has become a very real Austrian tradition, or at least a Viennese one with sustained longevity. There is a special Austrian dimension also in the musical and theatrical *forms* used in *Der Rosenkavalier*, which has probably contributed to its status as one of the last great popular operas. Hofmannsthal from early on referred to *Der Rosenkavalier* as Strauss's and his *Figaro*, much like he would later refer to their later magical opera *Die Frau ohne Schatten* as their *Zauberflöte.* There are in *Der Rosenkavalier*, in fact, many conscious parallels to Mozart's *Le Nozze di Figaro* (1786),[89] which strengthened the Austrian ambience of the work further. But the most powerful element of all is the use of Viennese waltz tunes throughout the opera. The introduction of the waltz was Hofmannsthal's idea, though Strauss is responsible for its ubiquitous presence in the work. It is arguably this (widely noted) anachronism that was the crucial element in the strong appeal of the opera. But this is not least because the Viennese waltz draws together the large web of historical and cultural allusions to Austria in a form that was a living Viennese musical form with wide popularity.

There seems to have been no record of contemporary reaction to the *Rosenkavalier* by Leopold von Andrian. But there were several reactions that noted its patriotic Austrian qualities. The historian Heinrich Friedjung was enthralled that Hofmannsthal had breathed life into the historical period of Maria Theresia by giving the traditional Austrian Volksstück a historic-romantic dressing. Hofmannsthal had thus even contributed to expanding his "historical knowledge," as Friedjung wrote.[90] Another Austrian patriot and acquaintance of Hofmannsthal's who was overwhelmed by this supple celebration of their common fatherland was Josef Redlich. On 18 March 1911 he wrote to Hofmannsthal in a euphoric tone about *Der Rosenkavalier*:

> How beautifully does the great Theresian Age speak to us through your verses! So many powers were at that time given free rein . . . in Vienna, in the whole of German Austria! It is good for us to remind ourselves of this age: we—who must accomplish the mission of imbuing the new great Austria with new powers and to make her conscious of her own worth. The great empress created our state, and still everything that is alive and well in this state goes back to her, and, as I believe, our present Austrian culture also originates in that age. Only when we again possess a strong Austrian state—though on another basis than the state of Maria Theresia—will we also experience a powerful renaissance of Austrian culture.[91]

Redlich's high patriotic sentiment was probably enhanced because he was approaching what seemed to be the zenith of his political career. A few months after writing to Hofmannsthal, in June 1911, that administrative reform commission Redlich had taken the initiative to a few years earlier was actually going to initiate its work, with Redlich himself as one of its members. Redlich was thus just about to embark on a reform of that Austrian state founded by Maria Theresia and her advisers in the 1740s, which he experienced as brought to life in Hofmannsthal's supreme celebration of Austrian culture and history.

As recounted above, Hofmannsthal himself was more ambivalent in his affirmative stance toward Austria during these years. A couple of years after the première of *Der Rosenkavalier*, Hofmannsthal despaired over the state of things in his fatherland. He wrote to Andrian: "Not that I would like to, or even could bear to see this ancient empire crumble. But you cannot engage your soul merely for its continued existence, with no guiding idea whatsoever, without suffering severe damage to your soul. Although reactionary, the Metternichian era at least served an idea. What idea do we serve?"[92] Hofmannsthal recounted how he especially had lost his faith in the class that he so spectacularly celebrated in *Der Rosenkavalier*, the Austrian high aristocracy, as the carriers of Austrian renewal. Andrian replied with a long defense of Austria, countering Hofmannsthal's doubts and criticisms one by one. Andrian especially tried to impress on Hofmannsthal that that truly Austrian class Hofmannsthal himself had confessed to wanting to belong to a few years earlier, but now despairs over, is not simply there. It must be mobilized through the activation of the "Austrian idea," which Andrian emphasized was "an ideal that goes far beyond the simple nation-state, namely, that of the cooperation and partial integration of the spirits of all the different peoples, whose existence is possible only within a great empire, whose existence therefore is directly dependent on the existence of Austria." This is the great political mission of the immediate future, Andrian concluded.[93] When Hofmannsthal picked up the thread from this heated discussion one year later, the Great War was on and his patriotic sentiment soared again. Now Hofmannsthal and Andrian are discussing a culture-political venture, the publication of a series of books focusing on the Austrian identity.

3. Hofmannsthal in the Great War

The breakout of war in August 1914 set Hofmannsthal off on his widely observed patriotic action for the Austrian idea. In much of the scholarship on Hofmannsthal, these activities are viewed as a temporary deviation, which is embarrassing enough, but comprehensible in view of the strong patriotism that swept through intellectual circles in the whole of Europe at that time. With the background drawn in the previous chapters, however, Hofmannsthal's sustained propaganda action during World War I looks more like the maturing of long-held sentiments. Hofmannsthal's opportunity during the war to openly engage himself politically for Habsburg Austria was used fully, and it was sustained with a force that conveyed its existential, identity-related foundations. However, more difficult to understand in view of the above is his active avoidance of military service during the entire war. After having joined his regiment in Istria for a short time—Hofmannsthal was now forty years old and served in a Landsturm regiment—he uses his connections in high places in Vienna for a transfer to the War Relief Authority (Kriegsfürsorgeamt) there. Then in the spring of 1915, Hofmannsthal again used his connections to attain a freer position.[94]

This position, which Hofmannsthal in the main upheld until the end of the war, was built on a sort of illusionary trick, where the bureau of the Austrian minister president (Ministerratspräsidium) instructed the Austrian home defense ministry (Landesverteidigungsministerium) that Hofmannsthal was needed for special service in the foreign ministry. But the foreign ministry never recognized him as working for it in the way intimated by the Austrian minister president, Karl Stürgkh, in this instruction. In fact, some people in official positions had the distinct impression that Hofmannsthal was working for the bureau of the Austrian minister president.[95] In effect, this meant that Hofmannsthal could expect to be called into service as soon as the bluff was called. The diplomat Georg von Franckenstein, a youth friend of Hofmannsthal, aptly characterized the situation when he suggested that Hofmannsthal should arrange a private intelligence network in the ministries in Vienna that could forewarn and forestall unwanted developments of this kind.[96] He did, and this service worked well. The last time (as far as I know) Hofmannsthal was called up for military service, in the spring of 1917, the first Sektions-Chef in the bureau of the Austrian minister president, Robert Ehrhart, and the Chef de Cabinet in the foreign ministry, Ferdinand Colloredo, both personal friends of Hofmannsthal, quickly and efficiently responded to Hofmannsthal's call for help and averted the danger.[97]

Because of his simultaneous patriotic engagement for Austria, this behavior looks peculiar. However, it should be noted that Hofmannsthal did not use his free position to return to his private concerns. On the contrary, until at least 1917 propaganda work for Austria dominated his life. After the summer of 1915, he admittedly wrote fewer propaganda articles, but he activated himself more strongly in other ways. He had several patriotic publishing projects going; the Austrian Library, which will be looked at later, was the most ambitious and successful. Moreover, he went on several lecture trips making a sort of more indirect cultural political propaganda in Germany, Poland, Sweden, Norway, and Switzerland. Only toward the end of the war did he resume artistic work, and—as will also be discussed below—his major work of this period, the play *Der Schwierige* (The Difficult One), was actually a sort of summing up of his culture-political concerns during the World War. This type of strong identification with Austria, the same as that observed in his earlier periods, was part of his engagement for Austria during the war. It even seems like this identification matured during the war. In the summer of 1917 he wrote to Max Mell, his editorial assistant in the ongoing large-scale publishing venture of the Austrian Library: "The tremendous gain for me . . . is that in the present crisis I have learned to understand the Austrian element in myself and my own part in Austrian culture, and I have learned to understand both as necessary."[98]

Hofmannsthal's avoidance of military service during the war may be difficult to comprehend, but because of the strong current of continuity in Hofmannsthal's political engagement for Habsburg Austria, both before and after 1914, it is also difficult to condemn it. During the war, Hofmannsthal was engaging in the type of culture-political leadership that he had projected on Victor Hugo in 1900 and that he had developed as a program in *Der Dichter und diese Zeit* in 1906. The subject of his propaganda echoes his youthful identification with Austrian culture back in the 1890s as well as his major artistic work on this theme, *Der Rosenkavalier*: the Austrian cultural identity and the role and function of Austria in Europe and in the world. Although during the war Hofmannsthal apparently did not want to channel his energy through military service, he did move closer again to the state structures; he worked closely with institutions and persistently strove for official recognition from the state for his propaganda work. During the war his lately more distanced relationship to Leopold von Andrian was intensified once more as they more or less embarked on a common crusade for Austria.

The Poet in These Times of War

An overview of Hofmannsthal's wartime activities shows the strong consistency in his engagement for Austria. However, it also demonstrates a development, a gradually deeper and more profound understanding, of the Austrian identity. In the fall of 1914, Hofmannsthal approached his friend Alexander Hoyos, then Chef de Cabinet in the foreign ministry, and Foreign Minister Leopold von Berchtold's right-hand man, trying to convince Hoyos to take him on in the press department (the Literarisches Büro) of the foreign ministry. Hofmannsthal argued that this department should view it as a crucial task to create a "guiding idea" for the war effort, and it was for this venture that Hofmannsthal volunteered to undertake at the foreign office. Hoyos declined Hofmannsthal's offer.[99] Instead, Hofmannsthal used his position at the press department of the War Relief Authority to do something very similar; in the first year of the war, Hofmannsthal published about fifteen war-propaganda articles in Austrian and German newspapers.[100]

At the time he approached the foreign ministry, Hofmannsthal was actively partaking in one of those political clubs that sprang up in Vienna in 1914, the so-called Dienstagsverein (Tuesday Club), formed around a core of junior diplomats and meeting in the office of the director of the imperial archives (the Haus-, Hof-, und Staatsarchiv), the historian Hanns Schlitter. In these early meetings of the Dienstagsverein, Leopold von Andrian was apparently a driving force behind a project aimed at bolstering the Austrian identity. However, when the so-called Austrian Library (Österreichische Bibliothek) took shape in the spring and summer of 1915, Andrian had been posted as a diplomatic representative to the occupied territories in Poland, and it was Hofmannsthal who ran the project.[101] In the summer of 1915, Hofmannsthal made a determined attempt to have the Austrian Library accepted as an official Austrian government project. He approached his friend Robert Ehrhart at the bureau of the minister president, asking for meetings with Minister President Stürgkh and Minister of Culture and Education Max Hussarek.[102] Although Hofmannsthal never received this official stamp of approval, the Austrian Library became a very successful scheme. Between 1915 and 1917, all in all twenty-six small and inexpensive volumes on Austrian patriotic themes were published, which were sold in Austria and Germany and issued free to soldiers and other service personnel.[103]

In 1915, Hofmannsthal made trips to occupied Poland and Belgium, collecting impressions that he made use of in his war propaganda. In the fall of 1915 and spring of 1916, Hofmannsthal made extended trips to Berlin. He made contact with the Austro-Hungarian embassy there, meeting with both Ambassador Gottfried Hohenlohe and junior diplomats he was acquainted with, and he attempted to establish himself as some sort of culture-political agent for the Austro-Hungarian Empire in Germany.[104] In July 1916 he accepted an invitation from Andrian to hold a speech in

Warsaw as part of Andrian's propagandistic effort to win the Poles for a union with Austria. This job was only semiofficial; when Andrian attempted to make Foreign Minister Stephan Burian give some sort of official recognition to Hofmannsthal for, as Andrian maintained, his crucial propagandistic effort for the Austrian cause in Warsaw, Burian declined.[105]

In the fall of 1916, Hofmannsthal undertook a lecture tour to Scandinavia, where he held speeches in Kristiania (Oslo), Gothenburg, Lund, and Stockholm. The following lecture tour Hofmannsthal made to Switzerland in the spring of 1917 actually earned him his first direct recognition from the Austro-Hungarian foreign ministry, insofar as Hofmannsthal's lectures were part of the officially sanctioned cultural propaganda in neutral Switzerland. This recognition also gave Hofmannsthal renewed hopes for an official role in the Austro-Hungarian war effort. The new foreign minister, Ottokar Czernin, reinvigorated the cultural politics of the Austro-Hungarian foreign ministry, and in the spring of 1917, Hofmannsthal began collaborating with the new head of the press department in the ministry, Friedrich von Wiesner.[106] After the trip to Switzerland, which had been done in collaboration with Wiesner, he wrote to Robert Ehrhart about his plans for expanding and deepening this collaboration because he felt himself able to contribute substantially to the propaganda work of the foreign ministry.[107] However, the contact with Wiesner did not develop into sustained employment by the foreign ministry.

In June 1917, Hofmannsthal made a trip to Prague to retie the bonds to some Czech intellectuals he had involved in his patriotic Austrian publishing projects in 1914 and 1915. Instead of finding supporters for his cause in Prague, Hofmannsthal became a first-hand witness to the intensified Czech nationalism, which had exploded after the reopening of the Austrian parliament on 30 May 1917. Hofmannsthal's strong reactions to his experience in Prague have been recorded in all too many of his published correspondences to need repetition here. In his substantial work on Hofmannsthal's political activities during World War I, Heinz Lunzer even highlighted this trip as the end point of Hofmannsthal's wartime political engagement as such.[108] As I see it, this is going too far. The experience in Prague significantly affected Hofmannsthal's political engagement for Austria, but it did not lead him to turn away from politics; instead it deepened his engagement. A couple of weeks after returning from Prague to Vienna, Hofmannsthal wrote to Robert Ehrhart:

> My impressions in Prague were very strong (perhaps the strongest that I have received from any external phenomenon since the fall of 1914).... All in all, despite the difficulties I retain the hope of being able to achieve something and to do some good in that cultural sphere I have access to.[109]

Neither was Hofmannstal's most immediate reaction to the impressions in Prague hardly defeatist. On the contrary, the summer of 1917 looks more like an injection of new energy into Hofmannsthal's activities. At this time he took up the slumbering idea of a second dramatic work on the problem of Austrian culture and identity, *Der Schwierige*, which demanded an intense bout of work in the summer and fall of 1917. Moreover, Hofmannsthal in the fall of 1917 attempted to launch a very ambitious publishing project called the Czech Library (Tschechische Bibliothek), aiming at making Czech culture more known to the German-Austrians as well as to the Reich-Germans.[110]

After the summer of 1917, Hofmannsthal practically ended his propagandistic lecture trips and transferred his focus to the Austrian and Czech libraries, to his Austrian drama *Der Schwierige*, and to theater politics around the Burgtheater and the planned new culture-political institution of the Salzburg Festival, projects of a more indirect culture-political type, but with more fundamental cultural aims. Hofmannsthal's engagement in the summer and fall of 1918 in Leopold von Andrian's work as director (General-Intendant) of the court theaters in Vienna effectively became the end point of Hofmannsthal's political trajectory during the war.

The Austrian Library

The Austrian Library was probably the most successful of a whole range of propaganda activities Hofmannsthal engaged in during the World War.[111] It also seems like Hofmannsthal thought so himself. In November 1917 he wrote to Ehrhart that he wanted to keep up the work on this project because he had recently had his aims with the Austrian Library confirmed in a review of it in a German paper. The review stated that "the special quality of the publication consists in its expressing many things behind the mask of history, things that otherwise cannot be said directly in the same efficient and suggestive way." This is exactly my aim and I will stick to it, Hofmannsthal concluded.[112]

Like most of Hofmannsthal's wartime activities, the Austrian Library had a twofold purpose. First, it aimed at producing an integrative Austrian ideology, around which the different political groupings and nationalities in Austria could rally. Second, it aimed at presenting Austria in Imperial Germany, making the meaning and role of Germany's ally in this great conflict better known and thus supporting its place in the future organization of Europe. During the war there was a gradual shift from a clear emphasis on the first function toward the latter.

As is evident from his letter to Alexander Hoyos in November 1914, where he recommended himself for a position in the press department of the foreign ministry, Hofmannsthal had a rather good sense of the internal political fragmentation in Austria at the outset. He concluded that this fragmentation was due to the uncertainty regarding the aims of the war. What was needed was "a higher political idea" that could succinctly explain the war and give a sense of direction to the common war effort.[113] Hofmannsthal would gradually mold such an idea throughout the war, but at the outset to a greater extent he conceived his war propaganda projects as politically integrating, both through their concrete historical and cultural content and through their sociological dimension. It is evident from Hofmannsthal's correspondence with Leopold von Andrian and also Anton Kippenberg, director of the Insel publishing house in Leipzig, which published the Austrian Library, that the political integration of a wide portion of the German-Austrian party spectrum was a fundamental idea supporting the Austrian Library project as such.[114]

This aim to contribute to shaping a broad political base within the German nationality in Austria was complemented by Hofmannsthal's strong emphasis on tying in elements from the other Austrian nationalities also. In the first sketch for a presentation of the Austrian Library, composed sometime in the fall of 1914, Hofmannsthal placed special emphasis on integrating the Hungarian historical experience and also integrating the Slavic culture and history in the empire "in cooperation with Slavic Austrians."[115] The Hungarian element was later deemphasized, but at least the Slavic element retained its place in the project. However, the attempt to enlist Slavic Austrians as contributors ran into difficulties. This is perhaps illustrated best by the destiny of another project in the early phase of the war, that of the Ehrenstätten Österreichs. This was conceived as a picture book with short comments, depicting places and landscapes with important historical connotations in Austrian history. In this project the supranational, or multinational aim of Hofmannsthal's project was perhaps the clearest, since it aimed at integrating a much broader historical experience than the Austrian Library's *German-language* publications ever could. As would become a pattern in Hofmannsthal's wartime propaganda, the Czech historical experience was given a special place in this never-realized work focusing on Austrian historical sites capable of generating a broad consensus.[116]

From his exchange in late 1914 and early 1915 with Jaroslav Kvapil, Czech dramatist and director (Intendant) of the Bohemian National Theater in Prague at the time, Hofmannsthal learned of the full width of the internal differences in multinational Austria and that it was not possible to simply ignore them. Kvapil was very helpful and supportive of the project as such, but he steadfastly maintained his own position on the question of the Czechs in Austrian history, that "that which we Czechs have become in the last hundred years, we have become without the help of Austria—sometimes even against the will of Austria. . . ."[117] Despite this rather clear message, Hofmannsthal retained his aim to integrate the Slavic-Austrian and especially the Czech historical experience in his Austrian ideology throughout the war.[118] During the summer and fall of 1915, when he was intensifying his attempts to turn the Austrian Library into a political instrument through contacts with the Austrian government and with the embassy in Berlin, Hofmannsthal simultaneously intensified his attempts to engage Czech intellectuals in the work on integrating the Czech culture and historical experience in the upcoming series of the Austrian Library.[119] Hofmannsthal's continued interest in tying in the Slavic experience to his conception of Austria can be traced throughout the war. It received a new impetus only from the experience in Prague in June 1917, after which Hofmannsthal further intensified his attempts to approach the Czechs as a crucial key to the whole problem of the Austrian identity. However, it also seems that his newly acquired insights into the Czech relationship with Austria, as well as his difficulties in engaging Czech intellectuals for his project, led him to partly rethink his position as early as 1915.

Hofmannsthal's success in mobilizing support within the German nationality in Austria was also limited. The crucial conservative contributor Richard von Kralik responded in a positive fashion and contributed a volume of excerpts from the sermons of the seventeenth-century Jesuit preacher Abraham a Sancta Clara, an important representative of the Austrian Baroque. But Kralik retained a certain distance to the project as such.[120] The Catholic-conservative historian Hanns Schlitter responded negatively when he heard that the German-national and Liberal historian Heinrich Friedjung was also involved in the project, which highlights the problem of even housing competing German-Austrian views of history within such a consensual frame as Hofmannsthal attempted to create.[121] With the poet Anton Wildgans, Hofmannsthal had a more decisive experience in late 1914, an experience similar to the one he had at the same time with Jaroslav Kvapil. Wildgans had published several patriotic Austrian poems shortly after the outbreak of war, which Hofmannsthal judged as fitting well into the program for the Austrian Library. He suggested to Wildgans that he should complement the already existing set with another poem, one that focused on the multitude of peoples in Austria and how they lived together and shared the same landscapes: Hofmannsthal asked, "Would it be too much to ask for such an Austrian poem?"[122] Apparently it was, since Wildgans replied to Hofmannsthal's request with a long excursion on the problem of the Austrian identity. Wildgans professed to love the Austria that Hofmannsthal had described in his letter, and his admission that Austria as a descendant of the universal Holy Roman Empire probably embodied a higher idea than the mere national state. Despite all this, Wildgans professed to believe in the multinational state only as an entity led by a hegemonic nationality: "And thus I must wish that this leading role in our fatherland will be given to the German people." Only in this way could Austria become great again, Wildgans concluded his argument. Regrettably, he was also forced to admit, "I cannot write such a poem as you are asking for."[123]

Hofmannsthal probably had a great many experiences of the type he had had with Wildgans and Kvapil in the early months of his culture-political project, and they probably made him wary of the difficulties in his undertaking. However, it also seems like Hofmannsthal found essential inspiration for the "higher political idea" he was searching for in a short text that was issued in early 1915, called *Österreichs*

Kriegsziel, by the constitutional and administrative expert Karl Brockhausen. Toward the end of his most intense period of war propaganda, in August 1915, Hofmannsthal wrote an enthusiastic review of this work, which he deemed had found that critical balance with regard to the war that so many other attempts to understand the war had missed: "The development in it of the Austrian idea, the Austrian problem, the concept of symbiosis in which the argument peaks: all this makes this publication into one of those that can improve our spiritual atmosphere."[124] The Austrian war aims Brockhausen discussed in his work have nothing to do with the general war-aims discussion at the time in Austria and Germany. Rather, he transports the whole problem to the level of the higher cultural meaning of the struggle. Brockhausen departs from Austria's historical mission, that of functioning as a cultural link between east and west in Europe, between Slavic Eastern Europe and Latin and Germanic Western Europe, asserting that this role has received a renewed importance in the great struggle. The deeper meaning of the war is that of "the struggle for the culture of all those Slavs who can be included in Western culture," i.e., to secure that cultural sphere in eastern Europe and the Balkans, which has received Western culture through Austria's historical mission against the influence of the eastern Slavic empire of Russia. This deeper meaning is also linked to the problem of peace in Europe. The coming peace will be stable only if the Austrian union of nationalities can stand the test of the war because Austria is a microcosm of Europe as such, Brockhausen asserted. If the Austrian solution does not survive, neither will stable peace in Europe.[125]

Taken together, impressions like those from Kvapil, Wildgans, and Brockhausen most probably gave Hofmannsthal the momentum to move on from the attempt to create a common Austrian ideology, which was actually anchored in the different political groupings and nationalities of Austria, into the realm of the Austrian idea and its role in Europe. The echoes of Brockhausen are found in much of Hofmannsthal's later wartime writings, but they can also be traced in the last group of war propaganda articles from the late spring and summer of 1915.[126] This tendency, moving from concrete political mobilization to more fundamental political and social regeneration, is reflected also in the last scheme of Hofmannsthal during the war with a directly political aim. In a memorandum probably composed together (or at least discussed) with Andrian in Warsaw in July 1916, Hofmannsthal proposed to create "centers," or political clubs, in all major Austrian cities, which should collect all that willpower, courage, and moral power that had been generated by the war and channel it into support for the state. The first step in the process of creating a unified Austrian political will, Hofmannsthal suggests, must be to build a rudimentary organization, a center to which a great many individuals will be tied, individuals who have in common "the affirmation of the Austrian state idea and the need for political engagement."[127]

In fact, the group described in the memorandum is similar to that Austrian "political class," the mobilization of which Andrian a few years earlier had proclaimed to Hofmannsthal as the great political goal of the immediate future.[128] The basic ideas in it are also very close to Hofmannsthal's prewar ideas on the need for a culturally whole politics, which for instance expressed itself in his and Harry Kessler's school project in Weimar, and which he gave its most succinct expression in *Der Dichter und diese Zeit*. Moreover, these ideas were clearly developed in a more strongly state-oriented direction during the war. In a speech Hofmannsthal presented in Scandinavia, one of several, in the fall of 1916, *Freiheit und Gesetz*, we can see how the prewar ideas formulated in *Der Dichter und diese Zeit* are theoretically transformed into something resembling the so-called Deutsche Freiheit: the individual becomes one with the state through the internalization of the law.[129] In Hofmannsthal's reformulation of his basic political program at this time, political leadership is institutionalized in the state. This is Hofmannsthal's most direct response to the "Ideas of 1914," and it points forward to *Das Schrifttum als geistiger Raum der Nation* ten years later.

Andrian at War (Preusse und Österreicher I)

At the outbreak of war, Leopold von Andrian returned to Vienna from his diplomatic posting in Warsaw, in the Russian part of Poland. From August 1914 until February 1915, when he was sent back as the Austrian diplomatic representative in occupied Poland, Hofmannsthal and Andrian met regularly, not least in the meetings of the Dienstagsverein, and began planning the patriotic project that would become the Austrian Library. During this same time, Andrian was employed in the work on war-aims planning in the foreign ministry, and in this work he relaunched the Austrian idea he had defended so heatedly against Hofmannsthal's doubts only a year earlier. The likeness was striking between the Austrian idea he presented to Hofmannsthal in 1913 and the "Austro-Hungarian idea" he presented as fundamental to the whole war effort in a memorandum to Foreign Minister Berchtold in August 1914.[130] This memorandum, which deals with the question of territorial expansion of the empire in the northeast, is just the same as Andrian's other memoranda and reports during the war years, characterized by an inner tension.

There is a gap in his political conception during this time between what could be called the Austrian cultural identity and the Austrian political identity; or, expressed differently, between the Austrian identity and the mission of the Habsburg Empire. In his memorandum, Andrian emphasizes the need for "spiritual foundations" for any territorial acquisitions to the empire. He uses the catastrophic consequences of Metternich's Italian acquisitions in 1815 as an example, which lacked such a foundation and which were also lost in a very costly and demoralizing process during the nineteenth century. However, the Austro-Hungarian idea, that Andrian views as capable of constituting the spiritual foundation of the empire, turns out to be smaller than the territorial and national composition of the empire. Rather, it turns out to be layered, with an inner core composed of the Germans, the Hungarians (Magyars), the Czechs, the Slovaks, the Slovenes, the Croats, and the Bosnian Muslims, and then outer layers, tied more loosely to the empire (with less "Zusammenhangs-notwendigkeit" with the empire, as Andrian expresses it).[131] Nevertheless, in this memorandum as well as in his later wartime activities Andrian engaged himself in territorial acquisitions. In 1915 and 1916 he will even work hard to bring about the Austro-Polish solution, i.e., annexing the whole of Russian Poland to the Habsburg Empire. It might be that Andrian's deeply felt Austrian identity stood in a field of tension to the Aehrenthalean component in his political education, which was supported by a likewise deeply felt veneration for Aehrenthal.[132]

In his second war-aims memorandum in December 1914,[133] Andrian tries to bring these two poles together, insofar as he maintains that the only true war aim of the empire is the struggle "in a higher sense of ensuring the continued existence of the monarchy,"[134] a struggle for the continued independence and for the moral and material reinforcement of the empire. Insofar as this necessitates territorial changes, they may have to be made. But in this case their consequences must be carefully considered because

> For an empire like the Austro-Hungarian Monarchy, which is not built on a unitary national foundation, the principle of continuity in the historical community and other state-building and state-supporting factors are, in the absence of a community of language, an invaluable good, which should be tampered with only in the gravest of emergencies.[135]

In a reflection during the last years of his life, Andrian seems to supply the key to what during the war years looked like a tension between the type of importance he attached to the continuity of the historical community, on the one hand, and his active engagement for territorial expansion of the Habsburg Empire practically until the end of the war, on the other. Much like Hofmannsthal, Andrian viewed the war as potentially reinvigorating Austria and the Austrian idea. Through the sheer fact of withstanding the type of intense external pressure that war brought with it, Andrian was hoping for a temporary subjective experience in the Austrian peoples of belonging together, which then could be utilized for a far-reaching internal reform that would be experienced as legitimate and that would ensure the continued existence of the Habsburg Monarchy for a long time to come. Therefore, as Andrian concluded retrospectively, "Our external war aim is territorial change that makes possible a constructive internal politics. It does not matter whether the result is territorial expansion or contraction; our war aim is therefore very elastic, which is good."[136]

The "invaluable goods" Andrian talked about in the above-quoted memorandum from 1914, as a result of the long historical integration process of several Central European peoples, is the content of what Andrian during World War I called the Austrian idea, which he would later discuss in terms of the Austrian nationality. Andrian had a consistent conception of this Austrian nationality over time. However, during the momentous historical events that took place from 1914 to 1945, this conception also went through definite changes, the greatest being the gradual acceptance after 1945 of the Austrian nation (as he called it then) as having shrunken into the costume of that little Austrian state that was founded anew in 1945. Beginning with Andrian's first articulated characterization of the Austrian idea in the letter to Hofmannsthal in 1913, it is notable that he mentions merely the Poles and the Rumanians as not culturally belonging to Austria. The memorandum of August 1914 has left out also the Italians, the Ruthenians (Ukrainians), and the Serbs, and it more directly proclaims the Germans and Hungarians as first among equals. In the historical discourse on the Austrian identity in his late work, *Österreich im Prisma der Idee* (1937), Andrian also accords the Hungarians a special, only semi-integrated position more closely associated with little Austria focused around the version of the Austrian idea that he refers to as Austrian nationality.

As discussed previously, the same general type of spatial and cultural patterns and hierarchies in the conception of Austria can be identified in Hofmannsthal's work already during the prewar era. During the war years, and especially in the early war propaganda, it appears most prominently in the notion that the innermost core of this Austria is constituted by the Hereditary Lands and the lands of the Bohemian crown.[137] Later, when Hofmannsthal discussed the concept of the nation with regard to Austria in his more deep-probing speech *Österreich im Spiegel seiner Dichtung*, his conception of Austria seems also to have shrunk, all the way down to this cultural core. Here he openly declares that this Austrian nation he speaks of does not only consist of German Austria, but at least of "the solid core of the Hereditary Lands with Bohemia."[138] The rest is left open in the nebulous outer layers of the Austrian cultural sphere. The cultural-geographic "core" of the Austrian idea is similar in the views of Andrian and Hofmannsthal, and Hofmannsthal's Austrian nation is more concentrated around the German element. For Andrian, the political idea of the empire was much more in the fore. In Hofmannsthal's case, the focus is squarely on the cultural question of the role and the identity of Austria in the field of tension between Germany and the East and the South.

Shortly after being released from duty in the War Relief Authority, Hofmannsthal made the first of his wartime trips. In June 1915 he visited Andrian in Krakow, and they also made trips together into the occupied territories of Russian Poland. After his return, Hofmannsthal wrote a propaganda article about the civilizing mission fulfilled by the Austrians in these occupied territories. The tenor of the article rhymes well with that of Andrian's diplomatic reports from Krakow and later from Warsaw.[139] Andrian would continue to hold the Austrian banner high in Poland, propagating the Austro-Polish solution vehemently in the local Polish society, all the way up to the beginning of 1917 when he was more or less sent packing by the very annoyed Imperial German occupation authorities in Warsaw. However, Hofmannsthal's most important lesson during this same time was his sharpened perception of the relationship between Austria and Germany. During the winter of 1915–16, he also visited Berlin twice, the second time staying for about three months, taking part in the intense political activity in this city. Through his membership in the political club the Deutsche Gesellschaft 1914, Hofmannsthal received a firsthand view of political developments in Germany.[140] In Berlin he also became acquainted with Kurt Riezler, an official in the Reichskanzlei and an important adviser to Chancellor Bethmann Hollweg.[141]

Already as a general-consul to Warsaw in the prewar years Andrian had viewed his mission as that of a struggle for the sympathies of the Polish population. At this time the struggle stood mainly between Austria(-Hungary) and Russia.[142] After the outbreak of war, Germany sailed up as a second opponent and, as it seems, the most important opponent of Austria on this cultural field of battle. Toward the end of his spell as Austrian diplomatic representative to the German-administrated part of occupied Poland, Andrian summed up the events of the foregoing two years. In this report he viewed the problem of Poland almost exclusively as that of a struggle between Austria-Hungary and Germany. This struggle began with a basic consensus that Russian Poland should be integrated into the Habsburg Empire; it then moved through a phase of competition between local German and Austro-Hungarian representatives for the sympathies of the Polish population, and into a phase of open confrontation between Vienna and Berlin over the fate of Poland. In late 1916, a compromise was reached, and a "sovereign" Poland was proclaimed, with a not-closer specified tie to both of the united empires.[143] Andrian's retrospective view here coolly sums up what (after a closer look at his reports from the period reveals) seems like an intense struggle with existential overtones against *German* expansionism, an expansionism that Andrian in part seems to have perceived as having been directed against *Austria*. Already from Krakow during the spring of 1915, Andrian argued that a stronger political orientation was needed in the Austrian military government in Poland. Attempts must be made to win certain elements in Polish society for "the Austrian idea."[144] In the summer, he reports on the fundamental differences in the Austrian and German occupation authorities. The latter are conducting a very blunt, aggressive occupation policy, which repels the Poles, but the Austrians, who were much more sensitive to Polish feelings, are winning the hearts of the Poles. This stark contrast in the behavior of the two occupation forces has brought that good with it, Andrian muses, that the Poles of all classes increasingly prefer that the whole of Poland should be integrated with Austria-Hungary.[145]

Upon arriving in the newly conquered Warsaw in August 1915, Andrian immediately started his culture-political offensive also there. One day after his arrival, on Emperor Franz Joseph's birthday, 18 August, he arranged a celebration in cooperation with the local Catholic clergy, immediately sharply marking the Austrian presence in Warsaw.[146] During the following time, Andrian's reports to Vienna received an increased edginess, resulting from what he perceives as the more or less openly anti-Austrian campaigns organized by the German press officer in Warsaw.[147] However, soon thereafter in late October 1915, a much more sinister threat against Andrian's designs on Poland appeared in Warsaw in the person of Kurt Riezler, adviser to the German chancellor Bethmann Hollweg. During this visit to Warsaw, when he also met and discussed Polish matters with Andrian, Riezler noted thoughtfully in his diary: "No matter what we actually do, in the feelings and thoughts of the people [of Poland] our mere presence here is interpreted as a struggle between Germany and Austria for the soul of Poland."[148]

After having met with Riezler in late October, Andrian went back to Vienna for a few days. On his return to Warsaw, he received the information that Riezler in his absence had been conducting serious political discussions with leading Polish representatives. Apparently, Riezler had put forward plans for a German-Polish solution, that of integrating Poland in the German empire as a kingdom with the same semisovereign status as Bavaria. Since the official German policy at this time was still the Austro-Polish solution, and since Riezler was a well-known close adviser to Bethmann Hollweg, Andrian reacted very strongly to this behavior.[149] His accusations from this time on, that the Germans were making foul diplomatic play and creating intrigue in the "Russian fashion,"[150] further strengthens the already strong feeling in these reports that Andrian is making a sort of low-intensive, diplomatic war on Imperial Germany. At this time, Austro-Hungarian Ambassador Gottfried Hohenlohe in Berlin felt compelled to question and counter the strong hostility toward Germany, Austria-Hungary's ally (!), which he found in Andrian's reports. During a conversation with the Reich-German foreign secretary, Gottlieb von Jagow, Hohenlohe intimated Andrian's criticism against Riezler's behavior and also raised the "rumor" of the German-Polish solution. After this conversation, Hohenlohe found himself assured, as he reported home to Foreign Minister Burian, that Andrian's reports about the German policies in Poland were exaggerated.[151]

At around the same time Riezler visited Warsaw, an intergovernmental conference took place in Berlin on the newly proposed concept of Mitteleuropa as the solution to the problems Germany and Austria-Hungary were having in reorganizing Central Europe (and Europe at large) in the wake of their military successes. The idea of Mitteleuropa had been discussed in different guises since the fall of 1914, but in October 1915 Friedrich Naumann had popularized a special variety of this concept, one building primarily on the close integration of the core of Mitteleuropa, which was Germany and Austria-Hungary.[152] During the following time, this concept received wide currency and for many actually became that "higher political idea" that guided the understanding of the aims and reasons for the war in the two allied empires, which Hofmannsthal had been searching for since the fall of 1914. It is possible that Riezler's unofficial political foray in Warsaw should be understood as part of the reorientation that was going on in the Reichskanzlei in Berlin at this time.

Only in the late spring of 1916 did Andrian comment comprehensively on the Mitteleuropa policy that Germany was then ever more eagerly presenting as the solution to the Polish problem, as well as the solution to the current problems of the Central Powers at large. Here his whole mental makeup of deep hostility toward Germany is exhibited. Andrian had come to the conclusion,

> that since a decisive victory over Germany's enemies has become improbable, important political thinkers and decision makers in Imperial Germany have set up another war aim as compensation for the losses made in the war: to chain their ally, the Austro-Hungarian monarchy, so closely to the German Empire that a different economic and political orientation than the one pursued in Berlin will for eternity become impossible in Austria-Hungary.[153]

In the report, Andrian openly expresses the conviction that suffuses his reports from the preceding year and, indeed, seems to constitute the raison d'étre of his whole mission to Warsaw: that Imperial Germany, in practical terms, is waging a hidden war on Austria-Hungary, with the aim to subordinate it to Germany.[154]

Viewed from the opposite side, Andrian's fear does not appear unfounded. Kurt Riezler did not belong to the Pan-German (Alldeutsche) annexationist fraction in Imperial Germany, but to the liberal, moderate imperialist fraction that supported Bethmann Hollweg's attempt to sustain a political Burgfrieden during the war through a "politics of the diagonal" (Politik der Diagonale). He was, though, enough impressed by his times, and not least by the Weltpolitik of the Wilhelmine empire, to be an imperialist and a social Darwinist with high expectations for the future German role in Europe and in the world. In his criticism of Fritz Fischer, German historian Karl Dietrich Erdmann has pointed out that the so-called September Program of 1914 (containing Reich-German war aims encompassing annexations in Europe) was according to all evidence written by Kurt Riezler, and that it is difficult to tie it directly to Bethmann Hollweg.[155] What is clear from Riezler's diaries, though, is that at least *his* wartime thinking followed such general patterns as was laid out in the September Program. On the questions of Poland and Mitteleuropa, Riezler belonged to those who rather consequently tried to influence

Bethmann Hollweg in the direction of using the war to create a large German empire in Central Europe that could dominate the whole of the Continent, much what Andrian feared. Riezler foresaw territorial annexations only to a very limited extent. He mainly envisaged an empire built on military conventions, economic domination, and indirect political domination through some form of federative or confederative structure that encompassed rather large parts of Europe, from Scandinavia in the north to the Balkans in the south and from Belgium and the Netherlands in the west to Poland and farther in the east.[156] Riezler was working to realize what he in a succinct formulation described to Bethmann Hollweg as "my new Europe, i.e., the European ramifications of our will to power."[157]

Part of this solution was, indubitably, the need to tie Austria-Hungary closer to Germany in much the way Andrian had feared.[158] Perhaps Andrian got a feeling for Riezler's way of thinking when they met in Warsaw at the end of October 1915. During this meeting, Riezler had openly stated that the Austro-Polish solution was very problematic because every time it was aired in Germany, it summoned up a strong opposition in public opinion. What Germany had conquered in war could not simply be given away, Riezler had concluded.[159] In an official memorandum, Riezler divulged the underlying fear that drove this argumentation of his, the fear of the encirclement of Germany. If Austria-Hungary received Poland, then it would become stronger and experience a decisive change in its identity, becoming more Slavic; thus it would also potentially become hostile to Germany and ally with other powers against Germany. Riezler laconically summed up his historically informed Austrophobia: "That could lead to a new Kaunitz coalition."[160]

In his contacts with Andrian and Riezler during 1915–16, Hugo von Hofmannsthal was exposed to the problem that from about this time preoccupied him strongly: the relationship between the Prussian and the Austrian identities and the import of this relationship for the future of Europe. While in Berlin, he found that his contacts with other Reich-Germans most certainly filled out that German or Prussian picture drawn of Kurt Riezler. In these arguments about Poland, we can discern a strongly existential strain in the German relationship to Austria, and it can be found high up in the political structure.[161] Perhaps it was a trace of a Prussian inferiority complex, remaining from the time of Austrian hegemony in the German League and the Holy Roman Empire?

The sharply divergent Austrian and German perceptions of the Polish problem, and the mutual fears and hostility they unleashed, which Hofmannsthal became privy to in these contacts, were probably very important for his subsequent understanding of the Austrian idea. Despite the apparent differences between the German and Austrian perception of things among those close to Hofmannsthal, it seems that he was able to strike a chord in both the Austrian and the German camp from early on. *Österreich im Spiegel seiner Dichtung*, the speech that grew out of Hofmannsthal's

Berlin stay in 1916, first presented in Leipzig in March 1916,[162] made Andrian delirious with Austrian patriotism when Hofmannsthal repeated it in Warsaw at the beginning of July. It seems that Andrian was most impressed with Hofmannsthal's capacity to win both the German and the Polish parts of the audience in Warsaw with his exploration of the Austrian Wesen. Andrian also encouraged Hofmannsthal to hold the same speech on a following propaganda tour in Germany, obviously experiencing it as supporting the Austrian cause.[163] Hofmannsthal's speech in Warsaw was part of a culture-political offensive Andrian tried to set in motion to counter a corresponding German offensive, which had been launched after the official change of course in Berlin with regard to the Polish question. Now, in the late spring of 1916, the Germans openly wanted to win the sympathies of the Poles. This had been shown, for example, in the very successful patriotic celebration in Warsaw of the Polish constitution of 1791 on 3 May 1916. Andrian now wanted to retake the initiative, and Hofmannsthal's speech two months later was a very important part of this attempt.[164] Afterward, Andrian also seems to have experienced the speech as a great victory in his culture-political war against the Germans. In his report to Foreign Minister Burian, he described it as a significant propagandistic success that had "overshadowed everything so far undertaken by the Germans."[165] Andrian also took Hofmannsthal's speech as the point of departure for attempting to launch a series of Austrian lectures in Warsaw.[166]

On his part, Hofmannsthal seems to have shared the feeling of success, despite previous doubts.[167] On the day he was leaving Warsaw, he wrote to Robert Ehrhart: "Despite everything, I have now held a speech here in Warsaw, not least because Andrian insistently wanted me to, and I have got the impression that this difficult balancing act actually succeeded beyond all expectations. . . . It really makes me happy that it worked so well in such unfavorable circumstances."[168] However, at this time Hofmannsthal had already moved on from his more narrow Austrian patriotic propaganda and had begun to focus more on the problem of the relationship between Germany and Austria, one guise of which was Mitteleuropa.

Hofmannsthal and Mitteleuropa (Preusse und Österreicher II)

At the beginning of January 1915, Hofmannsthal made his first serious attempt at creating a formula, "eine leitende Idee," for understanding the relationship between Austria and Germany. On 10 January the result was published in the *Vossische Zeitung* of Berlin under the title *Wir Österreicher und Deutschland.* Hofmannsthal here described Austria as carrying in its present self the whole of German history, especially the living experience of the old Holy Roman Empire with its unbounded character, also encompassing within its limits other nationalities mixed in with the German element: "If one views Austria thus, as one part of the old German Empire, in which all the powers of German history are alive and effective, then this means for the Germans that Austria is not a closed chapter, but an unsolved mission. . . . Austria must again and again be recognized as the German mission in Europe."[169] Hofmannsthal set his article off by emphasizing how unknown Austria was in Germany, indeed, how it was one of the least known countries in the world to the Germans. He even concluded that since Bismarck's death, Germany had been unable to muster one single authority on Austrian history and society. France had Louis Eisenmann and England had both Wickham-Steed and Seton-Watson, but Germany had no one. The Berliner Friedrich Naumann most probably read Hofmannsthal's article, and it might even have inspired him in his strong orientation toward Austria-Hungary from about this time on. Naumann would later formulate his Mitteleuropa vision more or less as the (re)union of the two halves of the old Holy Roman Empire. He also saw the old empire, which he described in Hofmannsthal-like terms of tying in the Germans to the other nationalities of Central Europe, as the relevant historical experience for his own vision. Only a month later, in the beginning of February, Naumann would make his first trip to Austria-Hungary and this trip became the igniting spark for his engagement in the political project of Mitteleuropa.[170] We could say that during the course of the war, Naumann became that German specialist on Austria, whose absence Hofmannsthal had deplored in his article.

Before taking this role upon himself, Naumann had put the question of how the relationship between Germany and Austria-Hungary should be understood to several prominent German scholars. But as he complained to his friend Max Weber, no one had an inkling of "how the relationship between Berlin and Vienna should be conceptualized."[171] In his contacts with the overwhelmingly kleindeutsche-oriented German historians, Naumann had, perhaps, blocked his own way by formulating the problem mainly in terms of Great-German and Little-German solutions, where the former was clearly presented as the constructive view during the present conditions. "Both our government and the whole German people need a guiding idea in this question," Naumann concluded his appeal to the scholars to engage with the problem of the relationship between the two allied empires.[172] After having failed to find the expertise on Austria-Hungary needed in Germany, Naumann threw himself into the work, and only weeks later he returned from Vienna with the Mitteleuropa concept in his pocket. The concept that he would work with from now on was to a great extent built around the closer union between Austria-Hungary and Germany, something he had found overwhelming support for, especially in Vienna. During the following months, Naumann studied and wrote articles about Austria-Hungary, attempting to enlighten the Germans about this state and its peculiarities. During the summer he isolated himself and then came out with the book in which he had focused that needed vision, that "leitende Idee," which he had named Mitteleuropa.[173]

Hugo von Hofmannsthal had received a copy of *Mitteleuropa* from Josef Redlich in November 1915, and in January 1916 he met Naumann twice in Berlin.[174] And Hofmannsthal should have been interested. What Naumann presented was more or less a conception worked out in detail of that German mission in Europe that Hofmannsthal himself had talked about in his January 1915 article, *Wir Österreicher und Deutschland*. And Naumann's conception was informed; he had learned a lot about Austria-Hungary and integrated this knowledge into his conception of Mitteleuropa. Hofmannsthal is even reputed to have thanked Naumann for the way he presented Austria in his book.[175] To an extent, the similarities between the two are also striking and obvious. However, the place Hofmannsthal had reserved for Austria, that of constituting a bridge between Germany and the Slavic world, Naumann has filled with Mitteleuropa. Despite this obvious closeness, Hofmannsthal only touched on the subject of Mitteleuropa a handful of times in his subsequent wartime writings, and he then dealt with the concept in a carefully distanced manner. It seems to me that Hofmannsthal's somewhat strange reaction to this perhaps most important of all political ideas in Germany and Austria during the World War should not be regarded as indifference or hostility, but rather as a too-close *similarity in conception* that became difficult to deal with because it was joined to a *decisive difference*. This difference was the soul of Mitteleuropa, Naumann's variety of which had a strongly Prussian emphasis. Naumann's Mitteleuropa identity constituted the diametrical opposite of that self-understanding Hofmannsthal focused on in his Austrian identity. The process Naumann describes seems to be that of the gradual demise and subordination of Austrian culture to the Prusso-German "neudeutsche Wesen" of that "mitteleuropäische Wirtschaftsvolk," which should result from the union. The cultural relationship between Berlin and Vienna he describes is, at the very least, strongly asymmetrical.

This could also explain the apparent loss of direction Hofmannsthal experienced in his political project during his prolonged stay in Berlin in the spring of 1916. The trip was undertaken with primarily political purposes, but for long stretches of time Hofmannsthal redirected his attention from politics to his artistic work for the first time since the outbreak of the war. Furthermore, his political writings after the Berlin stay assumed a much more profound character than before. Something happened during this time. The first time Hofmannsthal used the concept of Mitteleuropa was in the presentation of volumes 14–19 of the Austrian Library, published on 16 April 1916 in the Viennese daily the *Neue Freie Presse*. Here Hofmannsthal tries to take over the concept of Mitteleuropa, turning it rather into an essentially Austrian concept, when he discusses Prince Eugene of Savoy as the true inventor of the political idea of Mitteleuropa.[176] The next time he returns to the concept is in his speech, *Österreich im Spiegel seiner Dichtung*, in the version held in the Urania in Vienna on 21 October 1916. Here with great circumspection Hofmannsthal places himself in opposition to Naumann and the concept of Mitteleuropa, not even mentioning his opponent's name, intimating that the problem of Austria and Germany must be handled with great care, more care, perhaps, he seems to say, than Naumann can muster.[177] The third, and as far as I know the last time he used the concept, in his article *Die österreichische Idee* from November/December 1917, Hofmannsthal has distanced himself completely from the concept. Here he concludes that "Mitteleuropa is a practical and topical concept," a concept lacking those transcendent and spiritual values that infuses Austria and makes Austria crucial for the future of Europe.[178] This roundabout way of dealing with Naumann probably originated in Hofmannsthal's response to that core of the concept of Mitteleuropa. What Hofmannsthal propagated during the war (and before it) was in the main the antithesis of that hypermodern Protestant Prusso-German identity Naumann presented as the future identity of Mitteleuropa. The soul of Hofmannsthal's Mitteleuropa was old German or Austrian.

The substitution of Mitteleuropa for Austria that Naumann undertook also meant that the function was changed. The boundary (Austria) between Germany and the East that Hofmannsthal wanted to see as open and communicative was turned into a new homogenous entity (Mitteleuropa) straddling this old boundary and presumably also erecting a new one somewhere farther east (presumably a more definite, Prussian type of border). Perhaps this recognition was what from this time on propelled Hofmannsthal ever deeper into the boundary function as Austria's crucial function in Europe. In the November 1917 article *Die österreichische Idee,* Hofmannsthal formulated the Austrian mission as that of functioning as a communicative boundary between "Old-Europe" (Latin-Germanic Europe) and "New Europe" (Slavic Europe): "This Europe, which wants to form itself anew, needs Austria: an elastic form, a true organism . . . It needs her to grasp the polymorphic East."[179]

In the work that grew most directly out of the Berlin experience, the speech *Österreich im Spiegel seiner Dichtung*, Hofmannsthal delved deep into the particularistic character of Austria, only to then undertake a foray into Germany, asserting that also the basic character of Germany is particularistic. Therefore, he seems to say, the union between Germany and Austria should rather proceed from this common quality. Instead of the uniform concept of Mitteleuropa, Hofmannsthal here emphasizes the fundamental dualism, as he sees it, of the Central European political sensibility, always having a province, a nationality, or (in Germany) a state as its base, and then on the second level the empire (Austria-Hungary or Germany).[180] One could suggest that what Hofmannsthal does in this, perhaps, most direct response to *Mitteleuropa*, is to substitute Austrian multiplicity and heterogeneity for the unity and homogeneity of (Prussian) Mitteleuropa.

The difference between Naumann and Hofmannsthal is most evident in their very different views of the role of Bohemia in that coming new Central Europe. Naumann liked to enliven his visionary political writing in the manner of the preacher that he was with stories and images of the coming new world. When sketching a future image of Mitteleuropa toward the end of his book, Naumann also touched on the nationality question, in effect describing the Czechs as politically, economically, and culturally subordinated to Germany in the new Mitteleuropa of 1925.[181] Hofmannsthal's approach to Bohemia was diametrically different. He took the German-Czech relationship as a crucial test for the German culture. In the sketches for a "Memorandum on the Czech question," probably written down in Prague or shortly after the Prague trip in June 1917, Hofmannsthal started out this way: "Here Germans confront the concrete problem of relating to a small nation in such a way that their culture is recognized as the higher and more effective."[182] One of Hofmannsthal's two main political preoccupations during the last phase of the war was exactly this German-Czech relationship. His last large-scale publishing project during the war, the Czech Library, was part of a broad attempt to grasp "Böhmisches Wesen,"[183] to bring Czech culture into touch with German culture and to enlighten the Germans about this "small nation."[184] This relationship was, of course, a vital boundary question for the future of German culture in Europe. The other side of this boundary question constituted Hofmannsthal's second main political preoccupation during this time: the relationship between that old German, or Austrian, culture that had the capacity for synthesis and the bridging of differences, and the new German, or Prussian culture, that lacked this capacity, but which through the sheer force of its modern industrial Wesen was reshaping Central Europe, and perhaps even Europe as a whole, according to its image.

Der Schwierige (Preusse und Österreicher III)

> You say in your letter that I am involved in many things; however, for me there is a unity of meaning to all these things; if I write a comedy about a no longer existing aristocracy, or if I go to Prague and make wholly inopportune politics (or nonpolitics)—it is all merely the attempt to become one with myself.[185]

Hofmannsthal had a disjoined conception about the relationship between the Austrian and the German identity during the prewar period. He housed his Austrian and German identities apparently without feeling the need to clarify their interrelationship. This disjoined character was reproduced throughout the first war years. Parallel to his profuse writing on Austrian culture and history during 1914 and 1915, we can trace a continued interest, but from these Austrian writings a wholly separate one, in German culture and history.[186] The Berlin experience in Berlin in 1916 seems to have brought about a qualitative change in this regard. From now on, Hofmannsthal tried to conceptualize his Austrian identity and its relationship to German culture comprehensively. Fundamentally, the result was a view of the Austrian identity as a *boundary identity* that Hofmannsthal gave its most distinct expression to in the article *Die österreichische Idee* (November-December 1917).[187] But toward the end of the war, the Austrian identity came under increasing pressure, both from within German-Austria and from Germany, to conform and to subordinate itself to a larger German identity with basically Prussian qualities. Hofmannsthal had been able to inform himself of this tendency firsthand, not least during his Berlin stay, and this might have sharpened his perception for the need to defend the Austrian boundary identity against being integrated into a unified German identity.

Hofmannsthal's last wartime political text, if we can call it that, was *Preusse und Österreicher. Ein Schema.*[188] It contains two juxtaposed catalogues of Prussian and Austrian qualities, neither of which are explained or commented on. We can sense Naumann's neudeutsche Wesen as one inspiration behind the Prussian qualities, just as Hofmannsthal's and Andrian's lifelong preoccupation with Austrian culture can be recognized behind the enumerated Austrian qualities. It has been read both as an absolute contrast between two separate and incompatible national cultures, and as two complementing elements of one larger German culture. I would suggest that neither view is correct. The latter comes the closest to grasping the relationship, but with the important qualification that Hofmannsthal viewed the Austrian identity as a boundary identity to link German culture to other European cultures, and thus he viewed the Austrian identity not as part of a larger German identity, but rather as being *another German identity*, separate from the Prusso-German culture of the empire, and housing those culturally unbounded old-German qualities that had been lost in the culturally sharply bounded national German empire.[189]

In his work on the comedy *Der Schwierige*, which saw an intense period of work exactly in the summer of 1917, but which was only finished in 1920, Hofmannsthal developed the theme of *Preusse und Österreicher* in a most profound, existential way.[190] Just like Hofmannsthal's previous attempt in this Austrian identity genre, *Der Rosenkavalier*, *Der Schwierige* belongs to that handful of Hofmannsthal's work that remains in the theater repertoire. I would argue that this has something to do with its existential dimension. In this work Hofmannsthal might be said to be engaged in a sort of Austrian self-therapy, pondering his own cultural identity, working out the Austrian national character and contrasting it to the increasingly dominant Prussian national character. *Der Schwierige* shines with an Austrian ambience that Hofmannsthal had not least learned from Christiane Thun-Salm during the early years of the century. As he said himself, *Der Schwierige* plays in "a no longer existing aristocracy," which was, of course, that same aristocracy that he and Andrian had always identified as the historical carrier of Austrian culture. Unlike the *Rosenkavalier*, Hofmannsthal now deals with the present, his own time, and this Austrian aristocracy has by now exhibited its historical failure. The treatment of Austrian culture and mentality is therefore much more complex here. It is still affirmative, but also self-critical and self-ironical. The Austrian mentality is still fundamentally superior to its Prussian counterpart, but its time seems somehow to be running out in a world that seems much more congenial with the Prussian world view than with the Austrian.

The main character in the play, Count Hans Karl Bühl (The Difficult One himself), is trying to readjust to social life in Vienna after his war experiences. Kari, as he is called, has been profoundly changed by his front experience in a way similar to how Hofmannsthal in his early war writings was hoping the whole of Austrian society would be affected by the war. Kari Bühl has had his Austrian qualities reinforced by this experience, one might say. But the change he has gone through also receives an ironic turn, since Kari Bühl seems overwrought by hesitation and indecisiveness and is characterized by a complete lack of determination: these are strains in his personality that constitute a caricature of the Austrian national character. His adversary, the north German baron Neuhoff, describes him as "absolute, presumptuous nothingness."[191] At the same time, there is no doubt that Kari Bühl somehow dominates the whole scene, though he does not control developments actively. The "Prussian" of the story, Baron Theophil Neuhoff, on the other hand, acts very forcefully, maneuvering actively to get his way. But again and again he runs his head into the wall, completely failing to get anywhere. Neuhoff tries to win the hand of Countess Helene Altenwyl in a rather clumsy and forceful manner, asserting that he should have his way simply because he is driven "by the strongest willpower . . . in the feeblest of all worlds," thus pitting Prussian willpower against the weak Austrian culture. However, Helene Altenwyl merely replies, "I am of this world, and I am not feeble," which also shows itself to be absolutely true when Neuhoff slightly later admits his complete defeat at her hands.[192] And Neuhoff later is rebutted a second time, by another Austrian woman, Countess Antoinette Hechingen, whom he also attempts to win by demonstrating his Prussian forcefulness and determination.[193]

A second character of mainly negative valence in *Der Schwierige* is the German-Austrian scholar, Professor Brücke, second chairman of the Austrian Academy of Sciences, described ironically as "a famous man." Brücke can be said to represent that Prussian-German culture of the book that has infiltrated Austria through its German-speaking Bürgertum, a dear subject to Leopold von Andrian. Brücke has similar character traits to Neuhoff. In an Austrian social world, where the harboring of ulterior intentions in social intercourse is regarded as utterly uncultured, Neuhoff and Brücke run around trying to further their own social and respective scholarly careers. In fact, Brücke appears as wholly foreign to the social and cultural milieu the play acts in, making himself more or less impossible in every situation he gets into. He even appears as more foreign than Neuhoff, and then Neuhoff's North-German origins make him an utter stranger in this Vienna. After having been told that Neuhoff is not at all from some Baltic province far away, "where the wolves are howling," but from Holstein, Kari Bühl's sister Cresence maintains her point about Neuhoff: "What's the difference? Either way he is a complete stranger."[194]

In the story, Austrian culture wins out over Prussian (un)culture, but simultaneously Hofmannsthal presents an Austrian culture that is definitely losing out against the rather unsympathetic modernity represented by the new Germany. In its rich texture, this work also contains a comment from Hofmannsthal on his own wartime activities. *Der Schwierige* is usually seen as a descendant from *The Letter of Lord Chandos* in its language criticism. Several of the reflections on this question also seem autobiographical. For example, Kari Bühl is a member of the Austrian Herrenhaus (upper house of parliament) and is under pressure to go there and hold a speech for the political grouping he belongs to. However, he has been evading these expectations, and toward the end of the action he explains why to his (after long hesitation and many an evasive action) newly found love, Helene Altenwyl, the daughter of his political associate Count Poldo Altenwyl:

> I should rise and hold a speech about conciliation and the peaceful coexistence of nations—I, a man who is utterly convinced of one thing: that it is impossible to open your mouth without creating the deepest of confusion! . . . I should take a host of words in my mouth, of which every single one appears directly indecent to me![195]

Here Hofmannsthal seems to make a rather harsh judgment on his own wartime attempt to create syntheses and to bridge differences between cultures through the printed and spoken word. However, when making this judgment, he had, of course, already shifted over into the medium of the theater, which stood at the center of his concerns during the last months of Austria-Hungary.

The Burgtheater was a central, perhaps the central, cultural institution in Vienna, at least for the Viennese Grossbürgertum that Hofmannsthal grew up within.[196] This accounts for much of his problematic relationship with this institution, which, to make things worse, largely and for a long time ignored him as a dramatist. However, in the final months of the monarchy, Hofmannsthal was given an unparalleled opportunity not only to get his own works into the repertory of this theater, but also to partake in the work of recasting this institution into a cultural political instrument for furthering the spread of the Austrian idea. On 18 July 1918, Leopold von Andrian was appointed new director of the court theaters (General-Intendant der Hoftheatern). This was a big step for Andrian, who had to resign from the diplomatic service to accept this post. It seems that he did not take this step as a form of recognition of and retreat after the defeat of his personalized campaign against Germany in Poland, but rather as a shift to a new internal "front" in his struggle for the Austrian idea. In view of his judgment that the only true war aim for Austria-Hungary was internal regeneration and reorganization, the timing of this shift also seems to make Andrian's choice a positive, offensive one: In the summer of 1918, the question of reconstruction after the end of the war was becoming a crucial question. The opportunity to partake in the running of the Burgtheater did not fall into Hofmannsthal's lap; he had been very active behind the scenes in furthering Andrian's candidature.[197]

At the beginning of his directorship, Andrian set out his aims in a proper program. First of all, he demanded and got wide-ranging prerogatives for directly intervening in the work of the Burgtheater and the Court Opera. The memorandum laying out his aims begins by describing the difficult balancing act of making the arts serve political aims. Andrian here points out architecture and drama as two arts with a special political potential. However, he continues, in the latter it is extremely important to give artistic quality the highest priority; only when this has been ensured can dramatic works be made to serve political aims. In the case of the Burgtheater, which was clearly at the center of Andrian's program, the fundamental problem is the history of this theater as the first of *German* stages. According to Andrian, the Burgtheater had already lost this position during the last third of the nineteenth century, after the Austrian exclusion from Germany in 1866, without, however, any serious attempt being made since this time to refashion the Burgtheater as a truly *Austrian* stage. The major problem with the Burgtheater, as Andrian saw it at the time of his takeover, was that it completely failed to reflect the multiplicity and heterogeneity of Austrian culture: Its program could as well have been that of any provincial center in the German Empire. Here Andrian's program proper sets in, as he draws the outline of a plan to turn the Burgtheater into a truly Great-Austrian stage, to function as a prism between German culture and the cultures of the non-German peoples of the Habsburg Empire. This reform should be carried out on several levels and would need sustained control to work properly. First, the core repertory should be shifted to works of a type that previously were hardly represented at all; that would include modern Austrian bürgerliche plays as well as Austrian Volksschauspiele, and modern Hungarian bürgerliche plays and the dramas of the Slavic peoples. Second, these plays must be acted in an idiomatic way, conforming in style of acting, manners portrayed, and ways of speaking with Austrian sensibilities. Andrian gives as an example here the tendency to picture a lieutenant of the imperial guards in a play by Schnitzler, Bahr, or Molnar as a Prussian officer, a practice that should be absolutely unthinkable in the future. Third, this whole reform will necessitate a thorough reform of the staff of actors. Some with a marked Prussian way of speaking and acting must be dropped, and an effort must be made to shape a new truly Austrian corps, which might also necessitate influencing the education of actors to ensure continuity in actors who can work in the new Austrian theater. Last, the reformed Burgtheater should function as a power source also for the provincial theaters, for example, by making regular guest appearances in the province, relaying truly Austrian theater both directly and by functioning as an example for provincial theaters and by schooling provincial audiences.[198]

Hofmannsthal was closely involved in the activities surrounding this reform of the Burgtheater and would have underwritten much of Andrian's program, though some of its eccentricities are most certainly Andrian's own; its strong anti-Prussian element, for example, is clearly recognizable from Andrian's foregoing "warfare" against Imperial Germany in Poland. However, we should not underestimate Hofmannsthal's role behind this program, because the entire effort most of all looks like a focal point for the whole of Hofmannsthal's longer history of trying to work culture politically. On the one hand, in terms of form, the reform of the Burgtheater follows in a tradition from his memorandum to Minister of Education Wilhelm von Hartel in 1900, via *Der Dichter und diese Zeit* in 1906, to the proposal for political clubs probably drawn up in cooperation with Andrian in 1916. On the other hand, in terms of content the Burgtheater was not just any culture-political institution; it was the media for that which made up Hofmannsthal's main body of artistic works, his dramatic production, much of which had also been written within the general culture-political program of *Der Dichter und diese Zeit*. In this indirect way, Hofmannsthal's mark is realized throughout Andrian's directorship of the Burghteater.

Hofmannsthal's mark was more directly present in that broadening of the culture-political offensive around the Austrian idea that gradually built up during the time following Andrian's appointment in mid-July. It was Hofmannsthal who wrote the memorandum on the planned new festival at Salzburg signed by Max Reinhardt and sent to Andrian in his official capacity as head of the court theaters.[199] The Salzburg Festival project bears the mark of broader theatrical concerns, but it also falls in well with the planned reform of the Burgtheater as the new festival is defined against the North-German cultural center at Bayreuth. Its aim is to function as a center for the much more complex and multifaceted Austrian Art. The general program for the reform of the Burgtheater is also recognizable in the fundamental aim of the planned festival of functioning as a culture-political power source for the regeneration of the monarchy after the soon-to-be-ended war. In view of this, it was also important to win the support of Emperor Karl, who apparently agreed to function as a protector of the new festival, and the festival was tied to the court theaters and to Andrian in Vienna and thus received official recognition for its culture-political aims. Hofmannsthal was soaring high in his expectations at this time, seeing the developments at the Burgtheater and in Salzburg as fulfilling his whole destiny as a dramatist and as a passionate Austrian: "Here everything comes together, all my hopes for a renaissance of the Austrian theater," he wrote euphorically to Andrian.[200] Looking back ten years later, Andrian noted that in the early fall of 1918 this whole culture-political project was in principle clinched. However, only a few weeks later Emperor Karl abdicated, pulling Andrian down with him. Simultaneously, the whole institutional framework for this last of Hofmannsthal's and Andrian's joint culture-political projects, as well as the whole object of their concerns, Greater Austria, was swept away.

4. Austrian Identity after the Empire

The Salzburg Festival was realized after 1918 outside the type of official institutional framework for which it had originally been planned. Still today, though, it makes certain culture political noises in the right places in its program, for example, concerning its European role. But this cannot be compared to the very concrete culture-political program that was devised in the last months of the Austro-Hungarian Empire. In the early years of this cultural institution, however, the culture-political ambition was much more to the fore, retaining much of the ambition laid out in the programs from the summer of 1918, now merely transposed to the new conditions of the Republic of Austria. For one of its founders and key persons in the interwar era, Max Reinhardt, the change in 1918 was probably of lesser importance. For Reinhardt, the theatrical ambition was to be in a position of prominence, and the notion of a cosmopolitan Austrian culture could still be used to define the Salzburg Festival against its main competitor in Germany, the Bayreuth Festival.[201] However, for Leopold von Andrian the essence of this culture-political institution had been lost with the destruction of the Austro-Hungarian Monarchy, and when he was asked to play a leading role also in the republican version of the festival, he declined.[202] One could have expected a similar reaction from Hofmannsthal. However, he quite on the contrary engaged himself strongly in the Salzburg Festival, functioning as one of its leading triumvirate with Reinhardt and Richard Strauss. Hofmannsthal in effect became the ideologue of the festival, drawing up its programmatic statements, writing articles, and, perhaps most important, supplying or at least attempting to supply its core repertoire with older works, such as *Jedermann*, *Der Rosenkavalier*, and *Cristinas Heimreise*, and also by writing new ones such as *Das Salzburger Grosse Weltheater*.[203]

However, his engagement for the Salzburg Festival also after 1918 is explicable in the light of his mature understanding of the Austrian identity, which he reached in the last years of the war. This view of the Austrian identity saw it as a boundary identity with the mission to link German culture to the Latin, Slavic, and Hungarian cultures, thus filling a key function in European culture at large. Hofmannsthal's understanding of the Austrian identity therefore entailed a cultural role that

Hofmannsthal in the 1920s; Freies Deutsches Hochstift, Frankfurter Goethe-Museum

could be played also by a republican little Austria. There is in fact a strong sense of continuity in Hofmannsthal's view of the Austrian identity from the last years of the war and into the 1920s. In his first programmatic text, *Deutsche Festspiele zu Salzburg* (1919), he has merely withdrawn into that geographic core of his Austrian idea that was identifiable already during the war.[204] In a second programmatic article, Hofmannsthal described Salzburg's location in Europe as "the heart of Europe. Halfway between Switzerland and the Slavic lands, halfway between Northern Germany and Lombard Italy, in the middle between North and South."[205] It looks most of all as if Hofmannsthal has merely somewhat contracted that cultural sphere he immediately identified with the Austrian boundary identity, now, for example, leaving Czech culture outside, but that this identity has retained the same function as before the dissolution of the empire. This supposition is confirmed by one of the few directly political statements Hofmannsthal made about the dissolution of the empire and the consequences.

In a letter during summer 1919, Hofmannsthal felt compelled to relate to the idea of Anschluss, which now had sailed up as the major political idea for German-Austria, and that was finally decided in the negative only a few months later. Here Hofmannsthal distanced himself from the idea of the unitary German nation-state and argued for the importance of "mediating forms" (Zwischenformen) that could reproduce the qualities of the old, culturally unbounded empire in the present,

> For me the question is this: Would it do more good to the whole of German culture and society if we were integrated into its present [political] form, or would it do more good if we stayed outside? . . . Would it not facilitate Bohemia's finding a better, less definite situation if we stayed outside? Is not the whole question that of creating new fields of tension, and are not the problems created by leaving Austria outside of Germany a productive field of tension of exactly the type needed?[206]

As it seems, the Austrian idea he had developed during the last phase of the war had already to some extent discounted the political failure of Austria-Hungary.

The shift at this time in Hofmannsthal's orientations was more marked in another way. The collapse of the empire reoriented Hofmannsthal toward the past. This is quite evident in the character of his three main dramatic works on the subject of the Austrian identity. In *Der Rosenkavalier,* Hofmannsthal self-confidently projects the future of Austria on some of its most glorious history. The Austria he draws here has an inner cultural strength and capacity for change. In *Der Schwierige,* history has caught up with Hofmannsthal. The image of Austria in this work is complex, but the Austrian culture here seems ailing, disoriented, lacking a future. Significantly, *Der Schwierige* plays in "the present" (that is, around 1918). In his last work on the Austrian identity, the opera *Arabella* (1929), in cooperation with Richard Strauss, history has raced past Hofmannsthal, leaving him looking back, examining the possibilities for a cultural regeneration of Austria in the period before his own birth (the 1860s).

This reorientation toward the past after an extremely active participation in the present during the war years can also be seen in the complex development of Hofmannsthal's project of a novel, *Andreas*, which preoccupied him off and on from 1907 to 1927. This novel was from early on a treatment of the problem of identity, of the problem of "becoming one with oneself" (das Eins-werden mit sich selber),[207] as Hofmannsthal expressed it in a sketch in 1913. With time, and especially after the dissolution of Austria-Hungary, the increasingly fragmented sketches for this novel became more and more historically oriented. They expanded in the direction of a historical novel of an Austrian family, stretching from the time of Maria Theresia and the following hundred years up to the revolution of 1848. An important point of focus is the patriotic regeneration in the Austrian defensive struggle against Napoleon in 1808–09.[208]

As it seems, Hofmannsthal was here turning his novel into a self-therapeutic project, where he wanted to trace the historical roots to that Central European cultural and political complex that was Austria. In a review from 1931 of the posthumously published fragment of *Andreas*, the historian of literature Walter Brecht recounted what he had learned firsthand from Hofmannsthal about his plans to turn this novel into a grand attempt at grasping the Austrian historical experience:

> In this way [Hofmannsthal wanted to] picture Austria as a whole, more culturally than politically, in its nowadays even by the German's almost forgotten important influence toward the east, the south, the west, the north, its inner greatness and power, and its peculiar way of life.[209]

Because this grand treatment of the Austrian identity only kept spinning out in different directions, never finding its true form, might be seen as symptomatic for

Hofmannsthal's problems to come to terms with the loss of that political and social order within which he had built his life and his literary accomplishments.[210] However, he did engage once more in a successful self-therapeutic treatment of the Austrian identity: his cooperation with Richard Strauss on the opera *Arabella.*

Arabella, or the Reconciliation of Austria with the Slavic East

In *Arabella*,[211] the last of Hofmannsthal's librettos for Richard Strauss, Hofmannsthal returns to the 1860s, the last period of a unitary Austrian empire, which was also the very last period of Austrian hegemony in Germany. To Hofmannsthal this was probably a time when the old-German cultural and political configuration of Central Europe could still potentially be saved. Among other things, this would require a wholly different German-Austrian attitude to the other nationalities of the empire, and this is exactly the subject of *Arabella.* The Arabella of the story is the daughter of Count Waldner, a retired colonel in the Austrian army and an incurable gambler. At the start of the action, it is quite clear that the Waldner family is broke. Waldner's interest in the question of his daughter's planned marriage is, thus, primarily motivated by financial concerns. However, Arabella's motives are much more idealistic: she is on the lookout for *Der Richtige*, Mr. Right, which has endlessly dragged out the choice from among suitors. The rather shabby state of the Waldner family is mirrored in the dubious qualities of the Austrian, Viennese society that frames the action. Michael Hamburger has suggested that Hofmannsthal drew a picture of the socially and economically troubled Austria of the 1920s,[212] but I would prefer viewing it as an element in Hofmannsthal's allegory of the historical regeneration of Austrian culture.

The new suitor who appears on the stage at this point of the drama represents the second main element of this allegory. The young Croatian nobleman Mandryka has opened a letter that Count Waldner had sent to his deceased father, a colleague of Waldner's from the army. There was a picture of Arabella in the letter, and Mandryka junior fell madly in love with her. As it turns out, this young Slav is the answer to both Count Waldner's dream (Mandryka is wealthy) and to Arabella's (who falls in love with him), as well as to Hofmannsthal's own call for a cultural regeneration of Austria that comes from its vast Slavic hinterland. Most of the action, if one can call it that, takes place after all this is quite clear. The drama evaporates already early in act two, and the rest of this act and the final one does not really move the action much forward. But this part of the opera contains a mass of symbolism collected in several scenes apparently composed just to relay and fill out the allegory. So, for example, Hofmannsthal has written a large-scale ensemble scene in the Viennese tradition of operetta, which plays in the cabby's ball (Fiakerball), presenting a scene of social and cultural interaction between the different classes of Austrian society. Richard Strauss composed waltz tunes for it, again creating a strong image of Austrian culture in the manner of *Der Rosenkavalier*. More important is the way Hofmannsthal reconnects to his wartime preoccupation with the Slavic culture of Austria, and especially with Czech culture. Hofmannsthal presented several Slavic folk songs to Strauss to be used to give the whole work a Slavic air, and these songs actually came from the aborted wartime project of the Czech Library. When developing this Slavic aspect of the work in a letter to Strauss, Hofmannsthal also elaborates on Mandryka's character. He contrasts these qualities, developed in the unspoiled environment of the Croatian villages and oak forests, to the vulgarity and frivolity of Vienna. With Mandryka, Hofmannsthal writes, "appears the vast half-Slavic Austria in a Viennese comedy and thus lets a completely different air rush into it. . . ."[213]

The themes of social change so very much to the fore in *Der Rosenkavalier* are absent in *Arabella*. But this latter work contains a different theme of change. The union between a young Maria Theresia figure, representing the good qualities of Vienna, and a young Slavic nobleman, representing the unspoiled energies and qualities of the Slavic hinterland of Austria, symbolizes a change that was wholly absent in *Der Rosenkavalier*: the cultural regeneration of Austria through the fusion of the old German-Austrian culture with the young Slavic culture. In *Der Rosenkavalier*, the regeneration came wholly from within the German-Austrian culture, a culture that was also at the top of an imperial, cultural, and political hierarchy that integrated Slavic culture on a subordinated position. This can be seen, for instance, by comparing with the image of Croatia in *Der Rosenkavalier*, where the Croatian forests are invoked as a mystical, underdeveloped country of colonial character. The change is also detectable in the central symbols of the two works. The presentation of the silver rose in the earlier work, a historical tradition invented by Hofmannsthal, functions as a symbol for the union of the Austrian aristocratic and bürgerliche classes. The Slavic custom, also invented by Hofmannsthal, where the bride-to-be should accept the proposal of marriage by presenting a glass of water to the suitor is the symbol of the union between the German-Austrian and Slavic cultures. Because Arabella accepts Mandryka by enacting a Slavic ritual, this also reinforces the symbolism of conciliation. In this image, Hofmannsthal focuses on the impressions he made during 1917, that the German culture must meet the Slavic culture on equal terms, and in *Arabella* he gave shape to his final conclusion about the Austrian historical experience.

Andrian and the Creation of an Austrian Nation

After 1918, Andrian would gradually develop his legitimist dynasticism into an Austrian nationalism that could, if necessary, do without the Habsburg dynasty. More precisely, Andrian developed his premodern monarchic stance into a philosophically and metaphysically grounded authoritarian ideology that has been judged as protofascist; this stance also made Andrian into an early and eager member of the Vaterlandsfront, the government-created party of the authoritarian Catholic one-party state (the Ständestaat) that was created in Austria in 1934.[214] However, the overriding goal of any Austrian regime, as Andrian saw it, would be to create an Austrian nation. Already around 1925 Andrian had been hoping for a strong statesman to appear who could firmly guide developments and direct the whole institutional capacity of the Austrian state toward the one goal of the "Austrianization of Austria, to create a population that first and foremost feels itself to be Austrian . . . whether we with time are going to be blessed with an Austrian language is an open question . . . we must strive to create an Austrian nation."[215] From the time of the Nazi takeover of power in Germany until the Anschluss in 1938, Andrian would activate himself for the Austrian nation in a way reminiscent of his engagement for the Austrian idea during World War I.

The Catholic-authoritarian Ständestaat of the years 1934–38, with its Austrian ideology and its increasing self-perception as anti-Prussian and anti-Nazi, was the necessary framework for Andrian's political work to realize this program.[216] Andrian published political articles in several periodicals close to the regime, such as *Christlicher Ständestaat* and *Vaterland. Blätter für katholisches Österreichertum*, where he fit in well with the general anti-Prussian tenor. One of his main preoccupations at this time was to extend his definition of the Austrian nation beyond the markers of a more general cultural and historical character, which had already been his focus when propagating the multinational Austrian idea before 1918, into the field of a separate Austrian language. In the early 1930s he campaigned for an Austrian language academy, which should take as its primary missions the production of a dictionary of the Austrian language and the propagation of the proper use of this language.[217] This notion of a separate Austrian language was central also to that bible for Austrian patriots, Andrian's *Österreich im Prisma der Idee*, which was discussed above in chapter two. Andrian argued that the Austrian language was important for the self-esteem of the Austrians and that it was vital to further this language to raise the Austrians out of their feeling of inferiority vis-à-vis the Germans.

The most central instance of Andrian's activities was his partaking in the foundation of the Austrian Society of Art and Sciences, which in different ways was intended to further the perception of the uniqueness of the Austrian people through artistic and scientific work. Once a year the society planned to hold an Austrian academy to focus on efforts to spread an Austrian consciousness and to make itself and its work known within Austria and elsewhere. The first academy was held in Salzburg in July 1936 on the subject of "the Austrian idea," and it had 400 participants. The most important component of the society was probably the publishing house (Österreichischer Verlag für Kunst und Wissenschaft). Andrian also had contacts with other publishers in the Austrian patriotic field, one of which was Filip

Schmidt-Dengler, who had wide-ranging plans to publish an Austrian "mirror of the past" (Vergangenheitsspiegel), a series containing biographies, autobiographies, and cultural historical works of high quality that should demonstrate the important historical role played by old Austria. Schmidt-Dengler published Andrian's *Österreich im Prisma der Idee* in 1937, and a year later the publishing house of the Austrian Society, in cooperation with the Austrian government, gave Andrian the commission to prepare a short popular version of this Austrian bible, titled *Die Grundlehren des österreichischen Glaubens*, which should be printed in a large edition and spread as part of the Austrian defense struggle against Nazi Germany.[218]

It has been judged that Andrian during the mid-1930s achieved a sort of position as an important representative of political Austrianism, and his main work of this period, *Österreich im Prisma der Idee*, has been judged an important example of the attempt to establish the separate existence of an Austrian nation through literary means.[219] This central role of Andrian's was once again played out in the midst of world historical upheavals, as the process of printing and distributing his *Grundlehren des österreichischen Glaubens* was intensified in early March 1938 in order to be part of the propaganda offensive initiated by the Austrian government with respect to the planned plebiscite on the question of Austrian independence. The issue was marketed by a sticker on the dust jacket of every copy, which carried these words: "On the final struggle for Austrian freedom" ("Vom Entscheidungskampf um Österreichs Dasein und Freiheit"). But the entire edition remained in the printer's shop because the pro-Austrian campaign it was part of was interrupted by the arrival of Nazi German troops.[220]

Andrian was in France at the time of the Anschluss and initially seems to have taken the German invasion as the final blow to the Austrian nation as a German aggression against Austria with the intention to permanently Germanize this land.[221] Andrian subsequently fled to South America and spent most of the 1940s there. When he returned to Europe a few years before his death in 1951, he had difficulties actually reconnecting to the political and cultural movement for the Austrianization of Austria at this time, but he joyfully registered the realization of that Austrian nation for which he had struggled for so long.[222]

5. Conclusion

The question of whether Hofmannsthal, had he lived, in the 1930s would have engaged himself for the Austrian Ständestaat as Andrian did is difficult to answer. His artistic work for the Salzburg Festival as well as his late political writings were appreciated in circles that were closely involved with this regime in the years 1934–38.[223] Hofmannsthal might have become involved with this regime out of Austrian patriotic reasons. However, this is not at all such a clear-cut matter as it looks today, when Hofmannsthal has been turned into an Austrian national icon. In fact, one of Andrian's major contributions to the construction of an Austrian national mythology was, arguably, his sustained effort to ensure that Hofmannsthal and his artistic work was integrated into the core of this mythology.

Already in the early 1930s, shortly after Hofmannsthal's death, Andrian began propagating Hofmannsthal's artistic works as central to Austrian culture and literature, as part of "the Austrian soul," and tied him to the Austrian literary tradition of Raimund, Nestroy, Grillparzer, and Stifter. Furthermore, Andrian viewed Hofmannsthal as crucial to the creation of an Austrian nation because in the 1930s he was still very much part of the living memory of Austrian youth. In 1935, Andrian even proposed to create a government authority that should begin with publishing Hofmannsthal's culture-political writings related to the Austrian idea in a special edition that should be made widely available for teachers as well as for students, because "there should be no educated Austrian who does not know his Hofmannsthal." Andrian then proposed as a second important mission for this authority to pick up and carry on Hofmannsthal's work from World War I on an Austrian Library. Moreover, Andrian projected his own feelings on Hofmannsthal, asserting that the dissolution of Austria-Hungary was the greatest, most disruptive catastrophe for this Austrian poet, and that Hofmannsthal's premature death in 1929 was an effect of that fundamental cause.[224] Both during the 1930s and then again after 1945, Andrian furthered such a view of his friend, not least in his many contacts with publishers and historians of literature, such as Filip Schmidt-Dengler, Herbert Steiner, and Richard Alewyn. The first major edition of Hofmannsthal's collected works that was undertaken by Herbert Steiner in the 1950s might to some degree have been influenced by Steiner's contacts with Andrian, and most definitely it was influenced by that general view of Hofmannsthal that Andrian was party to creating in the strongly Austrian national atmosphere of the Ständestaat.[225]

Although we should be careful about accepting at face value such a view of Hofmannsthal as canonized in this Austrian national tradition, neither should we simply sweep it aside as an ideological construction. Toward the end of World War I, Hofmannsthal had worked out a view of the Austrian identity that had certain elements in common with that tradition, but which was much more profound and complex than the corresponding view within the Austrian nationalist camp. In this perspective one could point out *Arabella* (1929) as Hofmannsthal's political testament. Here Hofmannsthal presented the crucial lesson about the boundary identity that he came to view the Austrian identity as: the need to free the German-Austrian mentality of its imperial experience and to meet Slavic culture on equal terms. In the midst of the interwar era, Hofmannsthal's conclusion was arrived at in a distinctly inopportune moment, in a cultural and political climate permeated by imperial Phantomschmerz.

It was also much more farsighted than both the German-national Gesamtdeutsche view and its opponents, the still vaguely imperialist adherents of the Austrian idea.

Notes

1. Entry on 5 November 1918 in the diary of Christiane von Hofmannsthal. See Christiane von Hofmannsthal, *Tagebücher und Briefe des Vaters an die Tochter* (Frankfurt am Main: S. Fischer Verlag, 1991), 22f.
2. Letter from Hofmannsthal to Robert Ehrhart dated 6 November 1918, HHStA, Nachlass Sperl-Ehrhart, K.16. Hofmannsthal then wanted to expand this militia: ". . . zunächst für die weitere Umgebung Wiens, weiterhin womöglich für ganz Niederösterreich fliegende Colonnen aufzustellen . . ."
3. See especially the descriptions of the house in the letter to Eberhard von Bodenhausen on 16 March 1901, in *Briefe der Freundschaft. Hugo von Hofmannsthal. Eberhard von Bodenhausen* (Berlin: Eugen Diedrich, 1953), 15–17, and in the letters to Christiane Thun-Salm of 23 July and 11 October 1901, in *Hugo von Hofmannsthal—Christiane Gräfin Thun-Salm. Briefwechsel. Mit Briefen Hofmannsthals an Paul Graf Thun-Hohenstein*, Renate Moering, ed. (Frankfurt am Main: S. Fischer Verlag, 1999), 10ff., 19f. The house in Rodaun and the Lower Austrian landscape surrounding it is a recurring theme in Hofmannsthal's letters during 1901.
4. See especially the four letters to the German poet Rudolf Alexander Schröder, May-July 1901, *Briefe 1890–1909. Hugo von Hofmannsthal*, 2 vols. (Berlin: S. Fischer Verlag, 1935–37), 2:44–49, whom Hofmannsthal nearly hounded into visiting him in the house in Rodaun (Schröder finally came for a prolonged stay). See also the letters surrounding Harry Kessler's much later first visit to Rodaun in 1907, in *Hugo von Hofmannsthal—Harry Graf Kessler. Briefwechsel 1898–1929*, Hilde Burger, ed. (Frankfurt am Main: Insel Verlag, 1968), 153–56.
5. Entry in Hofmannsthal's diary for 2 May 1900, see Hugo von Hofmannsthal, *Reden und Aufsätze III (1925–1929), Aufzeichnungen*, in *Gesammelte Werke in zehn Einzelbänden* (Frankfurt am Main: Fischer Taschenbuchverlag, 1980), 432. On this, compare also Hofmannsthal's long letter from Paris to Richard Beer-Hofmann on 2 April 1900, in *Hugo von Hofmannsthal—Richard Beer-Hofmann. Briefwechsel*, Eugene Weber, ed. (Frankfurt am Main: S. Fischer Verlag, 1972), 96–99, on what is taking up his mind during this trip: ". . . wie ein kleines Landhaus in Grinzing oder Döbling aussehen müßte, das ich haben möchte und um welchen Preis es zu erwerben wäre. . . ."
6. See Hofmannsthal's letter to his father, 4 [September] 1901, in *Briefe 1890–1909*, 2:56f.
7. For two examples of this idolization of the Lower Austrian landscape close in time to moving into the house in Rodaun, see the letter to Arthur Schnitzler,12 August 1901, *Hugo von Hofmannsthal—Arthur Schnitzler. Briefwechsel*, Therese Nickl & Heinrich Schnitzler, eds. (Frankfurt am Main: S. Fischer Verlag, 1964), here 151f., and the letter to Christiane Thun-Salm, 23 July 1901, in *Hugo von Hofmannsthal—Christiane Gräfin Thun-Salm. Briefwechsel*, 10ff.
8. See, for instance, the letters to Eberhard von Bodenhausen (16 March 1901, *Briefe der Freundschaft*, 15–17), to Harry Kessler (4 April 1901, *Hugo von Hofmannsthal—Harry Graf Kessler. Briefwechsel*, 31f.), and to Richard Dehmel (1 December 1901, in *Briefe 1890–1909*, 2:60f.).

9. See Hofmannsthal's letter to Christiane Thun-Salm, 11 October 1901, in *Hugo von Hofmannsthal—Christiane Gräfin Thun-Salm. Briefwechsel,* 19f.
10. *Die Briefe des Zurückgekehrten* was written in 1907, and the first three were published in the German weekly *Morgen* in the summer of 1907. Two more were later added and published in the following year. It is the third and originally last letter that contains the reference to the house in (Upper) Austria. This work will be further discussed below. See Hugo von Hofmannsthal, *Erzählungen, Erfundene Gespräche und Briefe, Reisen,* in *Gesammelte Werke in zehn Einzelbänden* (Frankfurt am Main: Fischer Taschenbuchverlag, 1979), here 544–71. The memory of the *Zurückgekehrte* of his childhood home is fashioned along the lines of Hofmannsthal's descriptions of his house in Rodaun and its surroundings. It should be noted that in the two last letters and thus in the final version of the work as such, the full weight of possible cultural redemption of Germany is relocated to an artistic experience, to the strong regenerative experience of colors that the *Zurückgekehrte* has at an art exhibition of paintings of Vincent van Gogh. In the third and originally last letter, the tone is much more pessimistic, but the house in (Upper) Austria here carries at least the hope of cultural wholeness.
11. It is interesting that Hofmannsthal seems to have had plans to continue the series of letters from the *Zurückgekehrte.* See Ellen Ritter, "Hugo von Hofmannsthal: 'Die Briefe des Zurückgekehrten'," *Jahrbuch des Freien Deutschen Hochstifts* (Tübingen: Max Niemeyer Verlag, 1988), 226–52, for a documentation of these plans. Ritter also emphasizes the autobiographical and political undertext in this project.
12. See Heinz Lunzer, *Hofmannsthals politische Tätigkeit in den Jahren 1914–1917* (Frankfurt am Main: Verlag Peter D. Lang, 1981), 77. The escape would be made to the castle Neubeuern in Bavaria, which belonged to Hofmannsthal's friend Ottonie Degenfeld. The escape route was confirmed, but never used.
13. On Hofmannsthal's immediate experience of the end of the war and the breakup of Austria-Hungary, see his letter to Yella Oppenheimer on 17 November 1918, "Hugo von Hofmannsthal—Yella, Felix, und Mysa Oppenheimer. Briefwechsel. Teil II: 1906–1929," Nicoletta Giacon, ed. *Hofmannsthal-Jahrbuch* 8 (2000): 75–78.
14. On Andrian, see Schumacher, *Leopold von Andrian,* Renner, *Leopold Andrians 'Garten der Erkenntnis',* and Dorowin, *Retter des Abendlandes,* 91–139. See also the source publication (with biographical essays interwoven) Ursula Prutsch & Klaus Zeyringer, eds. *Leopold von Andrian (1875–1951). Korrespondenzen. Notizen, Essays, Berichte* (Vienna: Böhlau Verlag, 2003). See also further below.
15. See Hermann Rudolph, *Kulturkritik und konservative Revolution: Zum kulturell-politischen Denken Hofmannsthals und seinem problem-geschichtlichen Kontext* (Tübingen: Niemeyer, 1971), 81–109 (quotation on 95). Rudolph notes that the neglect of Hofmannsthal's wartime writing in the literature historical scholarship on him is not caused by any lesser importance of these writings to Hofmannsthal's thinking, "sondern einer gewissen Scham darüber, daß Hofmannsthal sich vor allem zu Kriegsanfang allzusehr und jedenfalls in einer Weise, die dem Hofmannsthal-Bild vieler Interpreten nicht angemessen erscheint, mit dem Zeitgeschehen und dem Zeitgeiste eingelassen habe." (See 81f.)
16. Jacques Le Rider, *Hugo von Hofmannsthal. Historismus und Moderne in der Literatur der Jahrhundertwende* (Vienna: Böhlau Verlag, 1997), 40.
17. The research on Hofmannsthal has with time assumed enormous proportions, and I will not pretend to have mastered it, especially not the large specialized scholarship on his literary production. It will be consulted in special cases only. The main frame of reference in the present work is the narrower field of cultural and political historical research on Hofmannsthal, most prominently represented by Hermann Broch, *Hugo von Hofmann-*

sthal and his Time. The European Imagination 1860–1920, translated, edited, and with an introduction by Michael P. Steinberg (Chicago: The University of Chicago Press, 1984) [Originally published in German in 1955], Le Rider; *Hugo von Hofmannsthal*, Rudolph *Kulturkritik und konservative Revolution*, Carl Schorske, *Fin-de-Siècle Vienna. Politics and Culture* (London: Weidenfeld & Nicolson, 1980); Michael P. Steinberg, *The Meaning of the Salzburg Festival. Austria as Theater and Ideology, 1890–1938* (Ithaca: Cornell University Press, 1990); and Lunzer, *Hofmannsthals politische Tätigkeit*, closely charts Hofmannsthal's activities during the years 1914–17. See also the more specialized works with bearing on the present study by Paula Sutter Fichtner, "Schorske's Garden Transformed Again: War Propaganda, Aesthethics, and the Conservative Revolution," in *Essays on World War I: Origins and Prisoners of War*, Samuel Williamson Jr. & Peter Pastors, eds. (New York: Columbia University Press, 1983), 83–102; J. Colin Fewster, "Hugo von Hofmannsthal and the Cavalry," *Seminar. A Journal in Germanic Studies*, vol. 32:2 (May 1996), 115–28; Karl Müller, "Hugo von Hofmannsthal's Zeit- und Kulturkritik seit dem Ersten Weltkrieg," *Austriaca* 18/37 (1993), 193–214; Gerald Stieg, "Hofmannsthal und die Salzburger Festspiele," *Austriaca* 18/37 (1993), 287–98; Jens Rieckmann, *Aufbruch in die Moderne. Die Anfänge des Jungen Wiens. Österreichische Literatur und Kritik im Fin de Siècle* (Königstein/Ts: Athenäum, 1985); idem, "Zwischen Bewusstsein und Verdrängung. Hofmannsthals jüdisches Erbe," *DVjs* 67 (1993): 466–83; and Judith Beniston, *"Welttheater." Hofmannsthal, Richard von Kralik, and the Revival of Catholic Drama in Austria, 1890–1934* (London: Maney, 1998). Although mainly literature historically oriented, Richard Alewyn, *Über Hugo von Hofmannsthal* (Göttingen: Vandenhoeck & Ruprecht, 1958), and Michael Hamburger, *Hugo von Hofmannsthal. Zwei Studien* (Göttingen: Sachse & Pohl Verlag, 1964), are indispensable. In view of the immense interest in Hofmannsthal, it is peculiar that there has been no proper biography on him, except, of course, for the condensed biographical overview by Werner Volke, *Hofmannsthal*. However, see Weinzierl, *Hofmannsthal*.

18. On the "second assimilation" of Hofmannsthal, see Broch, *Hugo von Hofmannsthal and his Time*, 102–08. On his broader judgment, see passim. Compare also Fewster, "Hofmannshal and the Cavalry," 122ff., on Hofmannsthal's admiration for the aristocracy and his cultivation of an aristocratic appearance.
19. See Schorske, *Fin-de-Siècle Vienna*, particularly 15–22, 279f, 302–19. Schorske does not comment on the intervening period encompassing the war years.
20. For an overview of the recent reevaluation of the research on fin-de-siécle Austria, including the criticism of Schorske, see Steven Beller, ed. *Rethinking Vienna 1900* (New York: Berghahn Books, 2001). In this criticism there was a specific part dealing with Schorske's apparent blindness to the Jewish dimension in society and culture of fin-de-siècle Vienna; on this, see also Steven Beller, *Vienna and the Jews 1867–1938. A Cultural History* (Cambridge: Cambridge University Press, 1989).
21. See Boyer, *Political Radicalism in Late Imperial Vienna*, and idem, *Culture and Political Crisis in Vienna*. See also Judson, *Exclusive Revolutionaries*.
22. See Shedel, "*Fin de Siècle* or *Jahrhundertwende*," and Shedel, *Art and Society*.
23. Heinz Lunzer (*Hofmannsthals politische Tätigkeit*) has minutely documented Hofmannsthal's activities during the war years (up to 1917), but refrained from analyzing them comprehensively in their larger context. On the 1920s, see Rudolph, *Kulturkritik und konservative Revolution*, especially 211–34.
24. Steinberg, *The Meaning of the Salzburg Festival*. See especially the biographical study on Hofmannsthal couched within Steinberg's larger work (142–63), and the chapter on "Nationalist cosmopolitanism" (84–116). See also the final discussion on the relatedness between Hofmannsthal's "totalizing ideology of the Baroque" and Nazism/Fascism on 223ff.

25. See especially ibid., 21–36. Steinberg here compares Hofmannsthal/Salzburg to Wagner/Bayreuth, seeing the two as closely related in ideology. I would rather see the Salzburg festival, as in important regards, defined *against* Bayreuth.
26. Fichtner, "Schorske's Garden Transformed Again," views Hofmannsthal and his associates in the cultural political project of the *Österreichische Bibliothek* during the war years as forerunners of the radical conservatism of the 1920s (also known as the movement of the conservative revolution). She thus joins Steinberg in a sharper judgment than Rudolph of Hofmannsthal's late political activities. Müller, "Hugo von Hofmannsthal's Zeit- und Kulturkritik," and Stieg, "Hofmannsthal und die Salzburger Festspiele," basically support this sharper judgment, although both qualify their judgment by questioning Hofmannsthal's true engagement in such political movements as radical conservatism, Austrian Catholic authoritarianism, and Fascism. All in all, it seems difficult to go beyond a characterization of Hofmannsthal in his late period as generally strongly conservative and with a somewhat sloppy relationship to certain dubious political movements of the interwar era. But the debate on Hofmannsthal and the "conservative revolution" goes on. Lately Jacques Le Rider has analyzed Hofmannsthal's Austrian idea and the late speech on the conservative revolution (*Das Schrifttum als geistiger Raum der Nation*) as an expression of the idealization of the old supranational role of the Habsburg empire inherited from the universal Holy Roman Empire. See Le Rider, *Hugo von Hofmannsthal*, 229–286, and "Hugo von Hofmannsthal and the Austrian Idea of Central Europe," in *The Habsburg Legacy. National Identity in Historical Perspective. Austrian Studies 5,* Robert Robertson & Edward Timms, eds. (Edinburgh: Edinburgh University Press, 1994). Le Rider's is a view that focuses on Hofmannsthal's own evolving conservatism rather than on its political context of the interwar era, and as such it is an important corrective to the above views.
27. References to the debate on the Austrian identity in the 1980s and 1990s are given above in note 16 in the Introduction.
28. See Erdmann, *Die Spur Österreichs*, 73f., 93, 100. Erdmann actually closes his whole argument by quoting Hofmannsthal (100). The cover of this Manesse Bücherei edition, containing Erdmann's two main contributions to the debate (*Die Spur Österreichs in der deutschen Geschichte* and *Drei Staaten, zwei Nationen, ein Volk*), is a facsimile of Hofmannsthal's handwritten manuscript of his article "Wir Österreicher und Deutschland" from the *Vossische Zeitung* (Berlin) of January 10, 1915. This image reinforces Erdmann's view of Hofmannsthal as "a trace of Austria in German history."
29. On Hofmannsthal and the Jung-Wien circle, see Rieckmann, *Aufbruch in die Moderne.*
30. The basic biographical information on Hofmannsthal's studies and the problematic choice of a career can be found in Volke, *Hofmannsthal.* See the letter to Harry (Heinrich) Gomperz, 25 July 1895, in *Briefe 1890–1909*, 1:153ff. (it is quoted extensively in Volke, *Hofmannsthal*, 51f.). See also the letter to Theodor Gomperz, 15 December 1901, in *Briefe 1890–1909*, 1:337f. Hofmannsthal wrote of his attempt to be both an artist and a scholar/teacher as splitting his soul in two halves, resulting in "eine innere Doppelexistenz." There was at this time also most certainly a general crisis in Hofmannsthal's personal development, which had different sources. Hofmannsthal's creative crisis around 1900 has been widely observed in the scholarship, tied up to the language crisis of *The Letter of Lord Chandos*, and needs no presentation here (for a fairly recent treatment of this problem, see Le Rider, *Hugo von Hofmannsthal*, 101–28). However, as fundamental to this artistic crisis, I would sooner emphasize Hofmannsthal's problems in the 1890s in navigating between his need for creative expression and the demands of his class and his father on having a proper profession and income. This tension between internal and external pressures resulted, I would say, in Hofmannsthal's gradual shift starting in 1895 from studies in law, favored by

his father, to those in philology, which was a sort of compromise, which in turn gave way to an all-out attempt to support himself as an author (starting in late 1901). But it was only from around 1903 that Hofmannsthal was sufficiently successful as an author to support himself and his family. For an overview of his development in these years, see Volke, *Hofmannsthal*, 52ff. Hofmannsthal's letters to the university professor, Theodor Gomperz, and his son Heinrich, Hofmannsthal's friend, in *Briefe 1891–1900*, also gives important insight into Hofmannsthal's attempts to find a career path. Another strand in his crisis around 1900 might, as Jens Rieckmann has argued, have been a sexual identity crisis, which Hofmannsthal very consciously solved in 1901 through his marriage to Gertrude Schlesinger (on this, see Jens Rieckmann *Hugo von Hofmannsthal und Stefan George. Signifikanz einer 'Episode' aus der Jahrhundertwende* (Tübingen: Franke, 1997). For a recent and well-balanced treatment of the matter of Hofmannsthal's sexual orientations, see Weinzierl, *Hofmannsthal*, 103ff.

31. Fewster, "Hugo von Hofmannsthal and the Cavalry," 126. Fewster has evaluated the large mass of letters Hofmannsthal wrote while in service. The most important of these can be found in *Briefe 1890–1909*, particularly 1:118–210, 240–55.
32. On the Secession and Hermann Bahr's involvement in this movement, see Shedel, *Art and Society*, 5–43. On Bahr, see also Donald G. Daviau, *Der Mann von Übermorgen. Hermann Bahr 1863–1934* (Vienna: Österreichischer Bundesverlag, 1984).
33. On the Art Council and the Secession, see Jeroen Bastiaan van Heerde, *Staat und Kunst. Staatliche Kunstförderung 1895–1918* (Vienna: Böuhlau Verlag, 1993), especially 49–58, 87–92. Carl Schorske also treats the larger context, the cultural policies of the Koerber administration, the heart of which was Wilhelm von Hartel's creation of an Arts Council (Kunstrat) that supported the modernistic artistic currents in, for example, the Secession movement. See Schorske, *Fin-de-Siécle Vienna*, 231–44. As Schorske notes, "Thus it came about that while other European governments still shied away from modern art, the ancient Habsburg monarchy actively fostered it." (237).
34. Letter from Hofmannsthal to Hermann Bahr, 9 October 1900, *Briefe 1890–1909*, 1:319f. Hugo von Hofmannsthal Sr. most certainly played a role here, trying to help young Hugo into a "proper" job. The outlines of this affair can be discerned in several sources. Most important here are Hofmannsthal's memorandum and a letter of his to Hermann Bahr (in *Briefe 1890–1909*, 1:319–23). A few more letters from Hofmannsthal Sr. to Hermann Bahr, Österreichische Theatermuseum (ÖTM), Nachlass Hermann Bahr, written at roughly the same time, fill in the picture of the senior's role in this affair. See also the letters quoted in Franz Hadamowsky, *Hugo von Hofmannsthal. Katalog der Ausstellung im Prunksaal der Österreichischen Nationalbibliothek (11. Juni bis 16. Oktober 1971). Bearbeitet von Franz Hadamowsky* (Vienna: Österreichische Nationalbibliothek, 1972), 18–19.
35. I believe that Carl Schorske, "Grace and the Word: Austria's Two Cultures and Their Modern Fate," *Austrian History Yearbook* 22 (1991): 31, comes close to this conclusion: "Hofmannsthal accepted the breakdown of language itself. Like a baroque man, he affirmed polylingual reality." However, Hofmannsthal was not paralyzed by this crisis of rational language; rather he accepted its limitations as an instrument of communication and moved on to his cultural political experiments with the theater and other ways of reaching out into society. On *The Letter of Lord Chandos*, see also Le Rider, *Hugo von Hofmannsthal*, 101–28.
36. *Studie über die Entwicklung des Dichters Victor Hugo* (1901), reprinted in Hofmannsthal, *Reden und Aufsätze I (1891–1913)*, in *Gesammelte Werke in zehn Einzelbänden* (Frankfurt am Main: Fischer Taschenbuchverlag, 1979), 247–320. The Victor Hugo study contains four chapters, the last two of which deal with a more technical literature analysis. The

first two chapters ("Lebenslauf als Entwicklung geistiger Form" and "Das Weltbild in den Werken"), constituting much more than half the text, deal with Victor Hugo's personal development and political engagement in a biographical mode.

37. The description of social and political engagement in the Victor Hugo study is reflected in an interesting way in Hofmannsthal's much later attempt to interpret his own personal and artistic development through a phase model in his "Ad me ipsum" (1916), see Hofmannsthal, *Reden und Aufsätze III*, 597–627. The interpretation of his own personal development here follows the basic matrix of his own description of Victor Hugo's development from fifteen years earlier.
38. Hofmannsthal, *Reden und Aufsätze I*, 272, 288.
39. Memorandum to Wilhelm von Hartel, reprinted in *Briefe 1890–1909*, 1:320–23 (quotation on 321). The published memorandum is abridged; see also the handwritten original in ÖTM/AM 25 844 Ba (Nachlass Hermann Bahr).
40. Hofmannsthal, *Reden und Aufsätze I*, 68.
41. On Kessler, see Peter Grupp, *Harry Graf Kessler. Eine Biographie* (Frankfurt am Main: Insel Verlag, 1999). Hofmannsthal became acquainted with Kessler in 1898. Already at this time, Kessler nurtured ideas on the type of culture political engagement that both he and Hofmannsthal would develop during the coming years. On this, see also *Hugo von Hofmannsthal—Harry Graf Kessler. Briefwechsel*. However, it must be said that Hofmannsthal had pondered these problems for a long time. Already in 1895 he jotted down an idea in his diary, "Dialog über die Funktion des Dichters in der Ökonomie des Ganzen," which sounds peculiarly like that speech of his eleven years later (see Hofmannsthal, *Reden und Aufsätze III*, 408).
42. Letter from Hofmannsthal to Bodenhausen, 25 April 1905, in *Briefe der Freundschaft*, 64–68.
43. For instance, it appears repeatedly in Hofmannsthal's diary during the years 1902–06; see Hofmannsthal, *Reden und Aufsätze III*, 435, 451, 475, as well as in his prose works of the period. Mary F. Gilbert, "Hofmannsthal's essays, 1900–1908: A poet in transition," in *Hofmannsthal. Studies in Commemoration*, F. Norman, ed. (London: Publications of the Institute of Germanic Studies, University of London, 1963), 46, notes that Hofmannsthal loved this formulation of Addison's and also that it is the central statement of the first two letters of the *Zurückgekehrte*. Hofmannsthal often used a variety of the quote interchangeably with the original: "The whole man must move at once."
44. Grupp, *Harry Graf Kessler*, 15.
45. See the sketches for "Andenken Eberhard von Bodenhausen" (1926–28), in Hofmannsthal, *Reden und Aufsätze III*, 155–69.
46. See Hofmannsthal's letter to Bodenhausen from 7 June 1906, in *Briefe der Freundschaft*, 78ff.
47. See letter to Josef Redlich, 22 February 1907, in *Hugo von Hofmannsthal—Josef Redlich. Briefwechsel.* Helga Ebner-Fußgänger, ed. (Frankfurt am Main: S. Fischer Verlag, 1971), 7f.
48. See, for instance, the entry in Andrian's diary on 26 April 1894, in "Leopold Andrian über Hugo von Hofmannsthal. Auszüge aus seinen Tagebüchern," Ursula Renner, ed. *Hofmannsthalblätter* 35/36 (1987): 10. Compare Hofmannsthal's entry in his diary on 23 April 1894, in Hofmannsthal, *Reden und Aufsätze III*, 381f.
49. See Leopold von Andrian, "Erinnerungen an meinen Freund," in *Hugo von Hofmannsthal. Die Gestalt des Dichters im Spiegel der Freunde,* Helmut Fiechtner, ed. (Vienna: Humboldt Verlag, 1949), 53.

50. On this compare H.R. Klieneberger, "Hofmannsthal and Leopold Andrian," *The Modern Language Review* 80 (1985), who characterizes Andrian's preoccupations of this type as paralleling Hofmannsthal's and as significantly influencing the latter's wartime conception of the Austrian idea. On this, see further below.
51. On this, see the last chapter below.
52. See the notes in Andrian's diary from 1902, in "Leopold Andrian über Hugo von Hofmannsthal," 34f.
53. See especially the passage in Leopold Andrian, *Der Garten der Erkenntnis. Mit Dokumenten und Zeitgenössischen Stimmen*, Walter H. Perl, ed. (Frankfurt am Main: S. Fischer Verlag, 1970), 27–31. See Klieneberger, "Hofmannsthal and Leopold Andrian," 622–26, for an analysis of *Der Garten der Erkenntnis,* focusing also its strong "Austrian" content. *Der Garten der Erkenntnis* also contains another important layer of meaning: it is a veiled autobiographical treatment of Andrian's homosexuality. On this, see Jens Rieckmann, "Knowing the Other. Leopold von Andrian's *Garten der Erkenntnis* and the Homoerotic Discourse of the Fin de Siécle," in *Gender and Politics in Austrian Fiction, Austrian Studies 7,* Ritchie Robertson and Edward Timms, eds. (Edinburgh: Edinburgh University Press, 1996). Karl Kraus's critical rendering of the title as *Der Kindergarten der Unkenntnis* must also be cited here.
54. See Andrian, *Der Garten der Erkenntnis*, 59. In this preface, Andrian also writes of: "Die bezaubernde Gestalt seines österreichischen Vaterlandes, dem seine Jugend zujubelte. . . ." (61).
55. See Leopold von Andrian, *Österreich im Prisma der Idee. Katechismus der Führenden* (Graz: Schmidt-Dengler, 1937), 8.
56. On the problem of Andrian's sexual identity, see Renner, *Leopold Andrians 'Garten der Erkenntnis,'* 30ff., Rieckmann, "Knowing the Other," and Prutsch & Zeyringer, eds. *Leopold von Andrian*, 19–28. Klieneberger, "Hofmannsthal and Leopold Andrian," 633, also raises the issue of Hofmannsthal's ambivalent sexual orientations in his youth as an important point of reference for Andrian, who without success sought a balance in his sexual identity similar to that which Hofmannsthal had achieved. See here also Andrian's commemorative article on Hofmannsthal (Andrian, "Erinnerungen an meinen Freund"), 61f., and his notes for this article, in "Leopold Andrian über Hugo von Hofmannsthal," 38. On the import of Jewish ancestry for Andrian and Hofmannsthal, see Klieneberger, ibid. 619ff., and compare Rieckmann, "Zwischen Bewusstsein und Verdrängung."
57. See Andrian's letter to Hofmannsthal, 18 February 1901, in *Hugo von Hofmannsthal—Leopold von Andrian. Briefwechsel*, Walter H. Perl, ed. (Frankfurt am Main: S. Fischer Verlag, 1968), 146–51.
58. On the general question of the younger generation of diplomats and their idolization of Aehrenthal, see Fritz Fellner, "Die Mission Hoyos," in idem, *Vom Dreibund zum Völkerbund. Studien zur Geschichte der internationalen Beziehungen 1882–1919*, Heidrun Maschl & Brigitte Mazohl-Wallning, eds. (Vienna: Verlag für Geschichte und Politik, 1994), and John Leslie, "Österreich-Ungarn vor dem Kriegsausbruch. Der Ballhausplatz in Wien im Juli 1914 aus der Sicht eines österreichisch-ungarischen Diplomaten," in *Deutschland und Europa in der Neuzeit, Festschrift für Karl Otmar Freiherr von Aretin zum 65. Geburtstag*, 2 vols. (Stuttgart: Steiner Verlag Wiesbaden, 1988), 2:661–84. On Andrian's diplomatic career, see Prutsch & Zeyringer, eds. *Leopold von Andrian*, 91–105. On Andrian and Aehrenthal, see Andrian's letter to Aehrenthal, 27 October 1906, in *Aus dem Nachlass Aehrenthal*, 1:415. See also the letter from Andrian, 7 November 1911, in Nachlass Friedjung (HHStA), K.4. This letter does not seem to be addressed to Friedjung; instead it appears to

be one of those many documents Friedjung collected during his historical studies (it contains a staunch defense of Aehrenthal against someone who has exhibited a critical attitude toward the foreign minister). On Andrian's perception of himself as Aehrenthal's spearhead in Russian Poland, see especially his letter to Friedrich Szápary from 4 April 1913, Prutsch & Zeyringer, *Leopold von Andrian*, 204–06. See also his notes on conversations with his superior Aehrenthal in St. Petersburg in 1906–07, in ibid, 155–57.

59. See Andrian, "Erinnerungen an meinen Freund," 53.

60. See Andrian's letter to Gerty von Hofmannsthal, 29 August 1929, in *Hugo von Hofmannsthal—Leopold von Andrian. Briefwechsel*, 439f: "So geht mir's manchmal bei schweren Unglücksfällen, auch beim Zusammenbruch [von Österreich-Ungarn] war es so."

61. Except for Andrian, *Österreich im Prisma der Idee*, and Andrian, "Erinnerungen an meinen Freund," discussed here; see also Leopold von Andrian, "Hofmannsthal und die österreichische Jugend," *Vaterland. Blätter für katholisches Österreichertum* 8, no. 9 (1934–35): 130–36. See also below.

62. The purpose of the book is presented in its preface; see especially 12: "Die österreichische Nation zu sichern ist der gegenwärtigen Generationen erste Pflicht, sie ihnen einzuprägen, ist dieses Buch geschrieben worden." The book is constructed as a running conversation ("Wechselrede") between four Austrian patriots. In this discussion, the Jesuit, Father Gabriel, represents the Catholic world view, and the young Heimwehr officer, Franz, the Austrian youth. The "nobleman" Heinrich Philipp is in his diplomatic background and old-Austrian, dynastic convictions most closely modeled on Andrian himself (he is also presented as of that same age that Andrian was at on the date of the fictitious debate). Erwin, the poet, in many ways a representation of Hofmannsthal, is a representative of Austrian art and culture (Erwin is aged 55, the age Hofmannsthal was when he died. On this, see Klieneberger, "Hofmannsthal and Leopold Andrian," 634f.). In the debates between Heinrich Philipp and Erwin it seems almost like Andrian is continuing his and Hofmannsthal's discussions on the Austrian identity. One can discern a serious attempt by Andrian here to come to terms also with their mutual differences, although the resolution turns Hofmannsthal unequivocally into an Austrian patriot.

63. See Andrian, "Erinnerungen an meinen Freund," 54.

64. See the letters from July through August 1898, *Hugo von Hofmannsthal—Leopold von Andrian. Briefwechsel*, 104–15 (quotation on 110). The planned Austrian issue of *PAN* never materialized.

65. See Hofmannsthal's letter, 7 March 1900, and Andrian's reply of 10 March, *Hugo von Hofmannsthal—Leopold von Andrian. Briefwechsel*, 141–44.

66. See letter to Kessler, 16 August 1901, *Hugo von Hofmannsthal—Harry Graf Kessler. Briefwechsel*, 33–37.

67. See Kessler's letter, 28 March 1907, and Hofmannsthal's reply, 5 April, *Hugo von Hofmannsthal—Harry Graf Kessler. Briefwechsel*, 153–56.

68. See Hofmannsthal's letter, 13/15 October 1908, ibid., 196–200 (quotation on 198).

69. See Hofmannsthal's letter, 26 March 1909, ibid., 215f.

70. See Hofmannsthal's letter 25 April 1911, ibid., 326f.

71. See Hofmannsthal's letter from 24 August 1913, *Hugo von Hofmannsthal—Leopold von Andrian. Briefwechsel*, 198–201.

72. Letter from Andrian to Hofmannsthal from 18 September 1913, ibid., 201–205.

73. See Andrian, *Österreich im Prisma der Idee*, 252–62.

74. See particularly ibid., 340–55 (Erwin).

75. Ibid., 332–39 (quotations on 336–38).

76. Ibid., 355–66 (quotation on 359).

77. See Fewster, "Hugo von Hofmannsthal and the Cavalry," 122ff.
78. See "Leopold Andrian über Hugo von Hofmannsthal," 37. Andrian was something of an exception to this rule, whereas he was included in both the "aristocratic" and the "artistic" circles of friends.
79. Christiane Thun-Salm (1859–1935) was married to Oswald Thun-Salm, member of one of the most prominent Bohemian aristocratic families and leader of the Verfassungstreue Grossgrundbesitz, the German-Liberal fraction of the great-landowners curia in the Austrian parliamentary system (up to the abolition of this curia in 1907). She was born Waldstein zu Wartenberg, another prominent Bohemian family. Her ancestry might, in fact, have held extra fascination for Hofmannsthal, since she came from the family of the great seventeenth-century general, Albrecht von Wallenstein. While commenting on his illustrious aristocratic company in his regiment, Hofmannsthal summed up: "und, wenn man nur will, so riechen die nach Wallenstein und nach . . . sehr stilvollen Gobelins des Heiligen Römischen Reiches. . . ." (*Briefe 1890–1909*, 1:119.)
80. On their relationship, see the biographical note in the appendix of *Hugo von Hofmannsthal—Christiane Gräfin Thun-Salm. Briefwechsel*, 231–43.
81. See Hofmannsthal's letters to Christiane Thun-Salm, 30 September, 6 November, and 9 December 1902, *Hugo von Hofmannsthal—Christiane Gräfin Thun-Salm. Briefwechsel*, 54f., 59–62.
82. About Christiane Thun-Salm's literary works, see the appendix in ibid., 233ff.
83. See Hofmannsthal's letter to Christiane Thun-Salm,14 June 1908, ibid., 173–75. See also the commentary on the writing, staging, and performance of *Des Kaisers Traum*, ibid., 335–43, and Christiane Thun-Salm's detailed description of the inception of the work in the letter to Hofmannsthal from 28 June 1908 (ibid., 175–79), where she declined to rework the play according to Hofmannsthal's ideas because she did not want to give up the original music written for it in 1898 by composer Anton Rückauf, who had since died. This experience in 1908 can also be seen as having had a bearing on Hofmannsthal's plans in 1914–15 to write a patriotic Austrian festival drama (*Oesterreichisches Festspiel*); see the commentary notes and fragments in Hofmannsthal, *Sämtliche Werke* 19:7–11 and 297–98. See Daniel Unowsky, *The Pomp and Politics of Patriotism: Imperial Celebrations in Habsburg Austria, 1848–1916* (West Lafayette, Indiana: Purdue University Press, 2005), 82–88, for the official character of Thun-Salm's commission for a play.
84. On this collaboration, see Grupp, *Harry Graf Kessler*, 188ff., and the relevant letters in *Hugo von Hofmannsthal—Harry Graf Kessler. Briefwechsel.* See further Kessler's letter to Eberhard von Bodenhausen, dated 24 March 1912, in *Eberhard von Bodenhausen—Harry Graf Kessler. Ein Briefwechsel 1894–1918*, Hans-Ulrich Simon, ed., (Stuttgart: Klett, 1978), 92–94. On the inception of *Der Rosenkavalier*, see also Alan Jefferson, *Richard Strauss. Der Rosenkavalier* (Cambridge: Cambridge University Press, 1985), 1–20. The text of *Der Rosenkavalier* is published in Hugo von Hofmannsthal, *Dramen V (Operndichtungen)*, in *Gesammelte Werke in zehn Einzelbänden* (Frankfurt am Main: Fischer Taschenbuchverlag, 1979), 9–104.
85. The identification between Marie Therése Princess Werdenberg with Empress Maria Theresia is made, for instance, by Jefferson, *Richard Strauss. Der Rosenkavalier*, 13, and Hamburger, *Hugo von Hofmannsthal*, 110.
86. On Hofmannsthal's invented language, see Jefferson, *Richard Strauss. Der Rosenkavalier*, 120ff. On the inspiration for the presentation-of-the-rose scene, see ibid., 19f.
87. I am at loss to judge to what degree this lack of integration into Austrian culture shows in Faninal's way of speaking. If he spoke with more German, or even Prussian inflections and vocabulary, the image of the Austrian Bürgertum according to Andrian's historical

discourse would be complete. In his later work on the theme of Austrianness, *Der Schwierige*, Hofmannsthal would deploy an Austrian bürgerliche scholar as an impossible character in a story where Austrian aristocrats *and* their servants are represented as carriers of Austrian culture.

88. See Hofmannsthal's letter, 20 May 1896, *Hugo von Hofmannsthal—Leopold von Andrian. Briefwechsel*, 68f. In the memorandum Hofmannsthal wrote to Minister of Culture Wilhelm von Hartel in 1900, we can find a similar mental structure, but this time with the Austrian Verwaltung at its center. The culture political authority Hofmannsthal sketched in this document should be strongly centralized, focusing the cultural politics of the whole of Austria at the center of the imperial political system. See *Briefe 1890–1909*, 1:320–23.
89. See Jefferson, *Richard Strauss. Der Rosenkavalier*, 12ff. A parallel to *Le Nozze di Figaro* can be mentioned as the formal designation of *Der Rosenkavalier, Komödie für Musik*, which echos the *Comedia per Musica* of its 1786 predecessor by Mozart. Another is the role of Octavian, a soprano *Hosenrolle*, which is modeled on that of *Figaro's* Cherubino, and the princess, Marie Therése, bears similarities to *Figaro's* Countess Rosina. More general characteristics collected from eighteenth-century opera abound. Baron Ochs' catalogue aria can be mentioned, just as the Italian aria sung in the levee scene of the first act, which is to a text of Metastasio, court poet to Maria Theresia.
90. See Friedjung's letter to Hofmannsthal, 30 April 1911, FDH, Hofmannsthal-Archiv.
91. See *Hugo von Hofmannsthal—Josef Redlich. Briefwechsel*, 10ff.
92. See Hofmannsthal's letter, 24 August 1913, *Hugo von Hofmannsthal—Leopold von Andrian. Briefwechsel*, 198–201. This letter has recently been reprinted in Prutsch & Zeyringer, eds. *Leopold von Andrian*, 214–16.
93. See Andrian's letter, 18 September 1913, *Hugo von Hofmannsthal—Leopold von Andrian. Briefwechsel*, 201–05. It is worth quoting at some length here: "Im Speciellen möchte ich erwähnen, daß ich nie Deine Auffassung über den hohen Adel, als den die Reichs-Idee tragenden Stand, geteilt habe . . . . Ich erwarte überhaupt von keinem Stand als solchen die Regeneration Österreichs, wohl aber von den vielen Gutgesinnten in allen Ständen, welche zu gruppieren und zu sammeln, eine der großen politischen Aufgaben der nächsten Zukunft sein wird. Eng zusammenhängt mit dieser Frage die der 'österreichischen Idee'. . . . Sie lautet etwa so. Ein Ideal, welches das des einfachen Nationalstaates weit übersteigt, ist die Cooperation und teilweise Verschmelzung der Genien all der Völker, deren Existenz nur innerhalb eines großen Reiches überhaupt möglich ist, deren Existenz also direkt von der Existenz Österreichs abhängig ist. . . ." This letter has recently been reprinted in Prutsch & Zeyringer, eds. *Leopold von Andrian*, 216–19.
94. On this spell of active military duty and its termination, see Lunzer, *Hofmannsthals politische Tätigkeit*, 25–41. On Hofmannsthal's release from military service, see also the documents in the appendix of *Hugo von Hofmannsthal—Josef Redlich. Briefwechsel* (a selection of official documents surrounding Hofmannsthal's release from military duty). See also the circumspect and informative discussion on Hofmannsthal's actions at the outbreak of war, Weinzierl, *Hofmannsthal*, 60–69.
95. See especially the correspondence between Minister President Stürgkh and the home defense ministry, in the appendix to *Hugo von Hofmannsthal—Josef Redlich. Briefwechsel*, 129f. See also the letter from Colonel Paic (representative of the Austrian Armeeoberkommando in Warsaw). Paic had been present at Hofmannsthal's speech in Warsaw in July 1916 and reported to Austrian army headquarters in Teschen about him: "Wenn ich richtig orientiert bin, war er anfänglich bei der Kriegsfürsorge in Wien eingeteilt und steht nunmehr dem k.k. Ministerratspräsidium für besondere Verwendung zur Verfügung." (ibid., 147).

96. See Georg von Franckenstein's letter to Hofmannsthal, 6 July 1915, FDH, Hofmannsthal-Archiv. See also Franckenstein's letters to Robert Ehrhart (at the bureau of the Austrian minister president) and to Albert Nemes (at the foreign ministry) in the appendix to *Hugo von Hofmannsthal—Josef Redlich. Briefwechsel*, 131–34.
97. See Hofmannsthal's call for help to Robert Ehrhart, dated 14 April [1917], HHStA, Nachlass Sperl-Ehrhart, K.16. See also the following correspondence between the foreign ministry, the bureau of the Austrian minister president, and the Lower Austrian Statthalterei in the appendix to *Hugo von Hofmannsthal—Josef Redlich. Briefwechsel*, 153f., in which the order for Hofmannsthal to report to military service was recalled.
98. Hofmannsthal, in a letter to Max Mell, 5 August 1917, *Hugo von Hofmannsthal—Max Mell. Briefwechsel.* Margret Dietrich & Heinz Kindermann, eds. (Heidelberg: Lambert Schneider, 1982), 130f.
99. The concept of Hofmannsthal's letter to Hoyos (dated 13 November 1914) is reprinted in Lunzer, *Hofmannsthals politische Tätigkeit*, 124–27. See also Hoyos's declining reply (ibid., 127f.).
100. Most of them have been published in Hugo von Hofmannsthal, *Reden und Aufsätze II (1914–1924), Gesammelte Werke in zehn Einzelbänden* (Frankfurt am Main: Fischer Taschenbuchverlag, 1979).
101. On Hofmannsthal's involvement in the Dienstagsverein, see Lunzer, *Hofmannsthals politische Tätigkeit*, 57–72. Compare also the correspondence between Hofmannsthal and Andrian on the project of the Austrian Library in 1914–15, *Hugo von Hofmannsthal—Leopold von Andrian. Briefwechsel*, 208–18. Hofmannsthal was assisted in the work on the Austrian Library by two editors, Felix Braun and Max Mell. Regarding this work, see *Hugo von Hofmannsthal—Max Mell. Briefwechsel*, for the relevant period.
102. See Lunzer, *Hofmannsthals politische Tätigkeit*, 150–53, regarding the contacts with Stürgkh. See also Hofmannsthal's letters to Robert Ehrhart, primarily the series of letters from August–September 1915, HHStA, Nachlass Sperl-Ehrhart, K.16. See also Ehrhart's letter to Hofmannsthal, 21 August 1915, FDH, Hofmannsthal-Archiv, and the letters concerning these contacts in the appendix to *Hugo von Hofmannsthal—Josef Redlich. Briefwechsel.*
103. An overview of the whole series can be found in Hofmannsthal, *Reden und Aufsätze II*, 528f.
104. These plans of Hofmannsthal are primarily known through his mentioning of them in letters to Andrian during the winter of 1915–16. Here he also repeatedly mentions a "memorandum" in which he delineates his scheme for culture-political activities in Germany during the war and which he passed around to the relevant people. The memorandum has seemingly been lost. See *Hugo von Hofmannsthal—Leopold von Andrian. Briefwechsel*, especially 219–26.
105. See Andrian's letter to Burian, 11 July 1916, in the appendix to *Hugo von Hofmannsthal—Josef Redlich. Briefwechsel*, 145f.
106. See Lunzer, *Hofmannsthals politische Tätigkeit*, 221–25 (and note 23 on 381).
107. See Hofmannsthal's letter to Ehrhart, from 9 May [1917], HHStA, Nachlass Sperl-Ehrhart, K.16.
108. Regarding the trip to Prague, see Lunzer, *Hofmannsthals politische Tätigkeit*, 240–54 (and the references to correspondences given there). See also Martin Stern, "Hofmannsthal und Böhmen (2). Die Rolle der Tschechen und Slowaken in Hofmannsthals Österreich-Bild der Kriegszeit und seiner Prager Erfahrung im Juni 1917," *Hofmannsthalsblätter* 2 (1969).
109. See Hofmannsthal's letter to Robert Ehrhart, 6 July [1917], HHStA, Nachlass Sperl-Ehrhart, K.16.

110. On the Czech Library, see Martin Stern, "Hofmannsthal und Böhmen (3). Hofmannsthals Plan einer 'Tschechischen Bibliothek' (1918). Ein Aufklärungswerk für die Deutschen," *Hofmannsthalsblätter* 3 (1969), and below. This project failed, just as the planned fourth series of the Austrian Library did at about the same time, mainly because of the difficulties in running a large publishing operation in the conditions of chronic shortages (of paper, for example) that characterized the Central Powers in the last year of the war. For an idea about these problems, see Hofmannsthal's correspondence in the last phase of the war with the Insel publishing house in Leipzig, which published the Austrian Library; *Hugo von Hofmannsthal. Briefwechsel mit dem Insel-Verlag, 1901–1929*, Gerhard Schuster, ed. (Frankfurt am Main: Buchhändler-Vereinigung, 1985).

111. The Austrian Library has not yet received a closer scholarly scrutiny. Sutter Fichtner, "Schorske's Garden Transformed Again," deals with this culture-political project, albeit from a special perspective. Heinz Lunzer, *Hofmannsthals politische Tätigkeit*, seems to have planned a study exclusively dealing with the Austrian Library, which, as far as I know, has not yet materialized (see 91 and note 2).

112. See the letter to Robert Ehrhart, 13 November 1917, HHStA, Nachlass Sperl-Ehrhart, K.16.

113. See the concept of Hofmannsthal's letter to Hoyos, 13 November 1914, reprinted in Lunzer, *Hofmannsthals politische Tätigkeit*, 124–27.

114. See Hofmannsthal's letter from the fall of 1914, *Hugo von Hofmannsthal—Leopold von Andrian. Briefwechsel*, 208f. See further, Hofmannsthal's letters, 19 February and 2 March 1915, in *Hugo von Hofmannsthal. Briefwechsel mit dem Insel-Verlag*, 525–27, 529–33. There are several lists of members of the editorial committee and of contributors in the letters to the Insel-Verlag and in the editorial comments in this publication. See ibid., 524–58.

115. See "Ankündigung A.E.O.V.—Bücher aus Österreich," in Hofmannsthal, *Reden und Aufsätze II*, 430. It was never published at the time, but was replaced with a different presentation when the first series of the Austrian Library was launched in the spring of 1915.

116. On the project of Ehrenstätten Österreichs, see Martin Stern, "Hofmannsthal und Böhmen (1). Der Briefwechsel mit Jaroslav Kvapil und das Projekt der 'Ehrenstätten Österreichs,'" *Hofmannsthalblätter* 1 (1968). See especially the presentation dated 2 November 1914, circulated to potential contributors throughout Austria (reprinted on ibid., 5–7). See also Lunzer, *Hofmannsthals politische Tätigkeit*, 94–97.

117. The exchange of letters between Hofmannsthal and Kvapil from December-January 1914–15 is reprinted in Stern, "Hofmannsthal und Böhmen (1)," 14–21.

118. On this sustained effort, see Stern, "Hofmannsthal und Böhmen (2)," passim.

119. See Hofmannsthal's letter to Bedrich Hlavác from 29 July 1915, reprinted in ibid., 107f: "Jede Anregung, was in dieser Bibliothek an tschechischem Kulturgut älterer und neuerer Zeit zu bringen wäre, wird von mir aufs dankbarste angenommen werden . . . .Ich wäre Ihnen . . . aufrichtig dankbar, wenn Sie mein Unternehmen im tschechischen Publikum gelegentlich im Sinne unseres Briefwechsels einführen würden, denn aus dem engeren Kreise des deutschen Oesterreich herauszutreten ist in dieser Sache mein dringendster Wunsch."

120. See vol. 8 of the *Österreichische Bibliothek, Abraham a Sancta Clara*. On the relationship between Hofmannsthal and Kralik, see Bernhard Doppler, "Konkurrenz um das katholisch-österreichische. Hofmannsthal, Richard von Kralik und das Haus Habsburg. Eine Dokumentation," *Hofmannsthalblätter* 40 (1990). See also Beniston, "*Welttheater*."

121. Andrian approached Schlitter on the question of winning Friedrich Funder, the editor of the largest Christian-Social newspaper, *Der Reichspost*, for the cause of the Austrian Library and reported to Hofmannsthal about the negative response to Friedjung's participation, which seems to have had anti-Semitic overtones. Schlitter promised to try, but as far as I

know, the *Reichspost* never partook in furthering the project. See Andrian's letter to Hofmannsthal, 7 December 1914, *Hugo von Hofmannsthal—Leopold von Andrian. Briefwechsel*, 210f. Heinrich Friedjung was represented in the Austrian Library with an excerpt from his large-scale historical work, *Der Kampf um die Vorherrschaft in Deutschland*, which was strongly critical of that conservative Catholic-Austrian tradition that Schlitter, Funder, and Kralik subscribed to. The excerpts used in the Austrian Library did not reflect this critical stance, though. Used were the chapters on the two battles in which the Austrian forces had actually been victorious during the war of 1866, the land battle at Custozza and the sea battle at Lissa, both against the Italians. Excellent material for raising the morale in the present war, of course. See Friedjung, *Custoza und Lissa*, vol. 3 of the *Österreichische Bibliothek*.

122. See Hofmannsthal's letter to Wildgans, 5 December 1914, *Hugo von Hofmannsthal. Anton Wildgans. Briefwechsel.* Norbert Altenhofer, ed. (Heidelberg: Lothar Stiehm Verlag, 1971), 5–7.
123. See Wildgans's letter, 7 December 1914, *Hugo von Hofmannsthal. Anton Wildgans. Briefwechsel*, 7–10. However, Wildgans later did partake in the Austrian Library, vol. 12, *Anton Wildgans: Österreichische Gedichte 1914–15*.
124. See "'Österreichs Kriegsziel' von Professor Carl Brockhausen," in Hofmannsthal, *Reden und Aufsätze II*, 503. Brockhausen's text was originally a lecture held in Vienna in the fall of 1914; see Carl Brockhausen, *Österreichs Kriegsziel* (Vienna: Hölzel, 1915). At around the same time, Hofmannsthal mentioned Brockhausen as one of several prominent political thinkers he wanted to engage in another of his publishing projects, an Austrian issue in the important German political periodical, *Süddeutsche Monatshefte*. See the letter to Robert Ehrhart, 21 September 1915, HHStA, Nachlass Sperl-Ehrhart, K.16.
125. See Brockhausen, *Österreichs Kriegsziel.* In fact, Brockhausen's analysis seems to foretell the development of much of the rest of the twentieth century, that of World War II and of Soviet hegemony in Eastern Europe, as a result of the breakdown of the Austrian solution.
126. See Hofmannsthal, *Reden und Aufsätze II*, 397–420 (especially the article "Krieg und Kultur").
127. See the memorandum "Gedanken über eine österreichische Vereinigung zur Erwerbung politischer Bildung," reprinted in the appendix to *Hugo von Hofmannsthal—Josef Redlich. Briefwechsel*, 142–45.
128. See above at the end of chapter two and in *Hugo von Hofmannsthal—Leopold von Andrian. Briefwechsel*, 198–205.
129. See "Aufzeichnungen zu Reden in Skandinavien," in Hofmannsthal, *Reden und Aufsätze II*, 28–42.
130. Andrian's memorandum "Die Frage österreichischen Gebietserwerbes im Nordosten im Falle eines glücklichen Krieges der Zentralmächte gegen Rußland" has been reprinted in Wolfdieter Bihl, "Zu den österreichisch-ungarischen Kriegszielen 1914," *Jahrbücher für Geschichte Osteuropas* (Wiesbaden: Verlag Otto Harrassowitz, 1968), 512–30. Compare with Andrian's letter to Hofmannsthal, 18 September 1913, *Hugo von Hofmannsthal—Leopold von Andrian. Briefwechsel*, 201–05.
131. See Bihl, "Zu den österreichisch-ungarischen Kriegszielen 1914," 512f.
132. Such a supposition would seem to be supported by the way Andrian employs the Bosnian annexation as a significant event in raising the esteem of Austria-Hungary in Poland and increasing the support for an expanded Austro-Slavic solution. See Andrian's letter to Friedrich Szápary, the Chef de Cabinet in the foreign ministry, 4 April 1913, Prutsch & Zeyringer, eds. *Leopold von Andrian*, 204–06. On Andrian's veneration for Aehrenthal, see the references given above in note 58.

133. See Andrian's memorandum, "Übersicht der für den Friedensschlusz in Erwägung zu ziehenden Lösungsmodalitäten der gegenwärtigen Krise," HHStA, PA I, K.496.
134. Ibid., 1.
135. Ibid., 31f.
136. Andrian expresses this in a late fragment of a strongly autobiographically colored historical novel, which was the last instance of his self-therapy with regard to the Austrian identity. See Prutsch & Zeyringer, eds. *Leopold von Andrian*, 836–50 (here 847f.). Quotation on 848.
137. See, for instance, "Grillparzer's politisches Vermächtnis" and "Ankündigung A.E.I.O.V—Bücher aus Österreich," in Hofmannsthal, *Reden und Aufsätze II*, 410, 430. In the former work, which was the foreword to vol. 1 of the *Österreichische Bibliothek*, this notion is presented as a political inheritance from the arch-Austrian poet and dramatist (and civil servant) Franz Grillparzer: "Daß Böhmen zu uns gehört, die hohe, unzerstörbare Einheit: Böhmen und die Erblande."
138. See Hofmannsthal, *Reden und Aufsätze II*, 21.
139. On this trip, see Lunzer, *Hofmannsthals politische Tätigkeit*, 141f. See also "Unsere Militärverwaltung in Polen," in Hofmannsthal, *Reden und Aufsätze II*, 421–28. See also Andrian's report, 23 June 1915, two days after Hofmannsthal's return to Vienna, which speaks of the "erfreuliche Eindrücke" of his last inspection trip into the occupied territories and sounds, even in its detail, much like Hofmannsthal's article. See HHStA, PA I, K.918. The source publication Prutsch & Zeyringer, eds. *Leopold von Andrian*, 250–484, contains many such reports (though not the one cited here) that Andrian made from Poland during his mission there.
140. On this prolonged stay in Berlin and Hofmannsthal's membership in the Deutsche Gesellschaft 1914, see Lunzer, *Hofmannsthals politische Tätigkeit*, 168–78.
141. Hofmannsthal's acquaintance with Kurt Riezler is mentioned in several of his letters to Eberhard von Bodenhausen at this time. See *Briefe der Freundschaft*, 214, 220. Hofmannsthal does not, though, appear in Kurt Riezler's diary; see Kurt Riezler, *Tagebücher—Aufsätze—Dokumente*. Karl Dietrich Erdmann ed. (Göttingen: Vandenhoeck & Ruprecht, 1972). See also *Dichter und Gelehrter*, 242, and Lunzer, *Hofmannsthals politische Tätigkeit*, 171.
142. On Andrian's stance during the prewar years, see, for instance, his letter to Friedrich Szápary, 4 April 1913, in Prutsch & Zeyringer, eds. *Leopold von Andrian*, 204–06. See further those reports of Andrian's from 1912–14 that are published in *Österreich-Ungarns Außenpolitik*, vols. 4–8.
143. Andrian's report of 30 December 1916 has been reprinted in Heinz Lemke, "Die deutsche Polenpolitik 1914 bis 1916 in der Sicht eines österreichisch-ungarischen Diplomaten. Der Bericht Baron Andrians vom 30. Dezember 1916," *Jahrbuch für Geschichte der UdSSR und der volksdemokratischen Länder Europas*, vol. 7 (Berlin: Rütten & Loening, 1963).
144. See Andrian's report, 31 March 1915, Prutsch & Zeyringer, eds. *Leopold von Andrian*, 254–58.
145. See Andrian's report, 23 June 1915, HHStA, PA I, K. 918.
146. See Werner Conze, *Polnische Nation und deutsche Politik im ersten Weltkrieg* (Cologne: Böhlau Verlag, 1958), 86. Conze notes that Andrian immediately aroused hostility in the German officers corps in Warsaw through his behavior, a hostility that was reinforced because Andrian had both the Austrian anthem and, until this time, the banned Polish national anthem sung at this church service.
147. See, for instance, the reports of 24 August (HHStA, PA I, K. 927) and 8 September 1915 (ibid., K.926). The name of the German press officer was Georg von Cleinow.
148. See the entry for 27 October 1915, Riezler, *Tagebücher—Aufsätze—Dokumente*, 311.

149. See Andrian's report of 11 November 1915, in Prutsch & Zeyringer, *Leopold von Andrian*, 294–95.
150. Ibid., 295.
151. See Hohenlohe's report, 23 November 1915, HHStA, PA I, K.926.
152. On Friedrich Naumann and the governmental negotiations on Mitteleuropa, see part one of this book and the references given there.
153. See Andrian's report, 24 April 1916, Prutsch & Zeyringer, eds. *Leopold von Andrian*, 317–23 (here 321).
154. Also see on this notion Gary W. Shanafelt, *The Secret Enemy: Austria-Hungary and the German Alliance, 1914–1918* (Boulder & New York: Columbia University Press, 1985), which is a comprehensive attempt to interpret the whole war period in similar terms. At this point, Ambassador Hohenlohe in Berlin again protested strongly against the anti-German tone in Andrian's reports. See Hohenlohe's report to Burian, 8 May 1916, Prutsch & Zeyringer, eds. *Leopold von Andrian*, 329–37.
155. On Riezler and this problem, see Karl-Dietrich Erdmann, "Kurt Riezler—ein politisches Profil (1882–1955)," introduction to Kurt Riezler, *Tagebücher—Aufsätze—Dokumente.* On Riezler and the Fischer controversy, see especially ibid., 56ff.
156. This Mitteleuropa vision permeates Riezler's diary during the early years of the war. See, for instance, Riezler, *Tagebücher—Aufsätze—Dokumente*, 225, 231, 253, 265, 268, 272, 300, 307, 325, 327, 329, 333, and others.
157. See entry for 18 April 1915, Riezler, *Tagebücher—Aufsätze—Dokumente*, 268.
158. See, for example, the entries in ibid., 304, 313, 325, and others.
159. See Andrian's report from 30 October 1915, HHStA, PA I, K.927.
160. See Riezler's memorandum on the Polish question, 20 August 1915, Riezler, *Tagebücher—Aufsätze—Dokumente*, 680–82. "Kaunitz coalition:" The European coalition of powers collected by the Austrian chancellor, Wenzel von Kaunitz, against Frederick the Great's Prussia in the Seven Years' War (1756–63), which almost lead to the annihilation of Prussia.
161. Foreign Secretary Gottlieb von Jagow argued against the Austro-Polish solution in much the same terms that Riezler did. See Jagow's letter to the ambassador to Vienna, Heinrich von Tschirschky, 16 February 1916, Scherer & Grunewald *L'Allemagne*: 270–72. This problematic German relationship to Austria had a recent history. It was discussed from other vantage points in part one of this book, where the German perceptions of Austria-Hungary's unstable identity between the Germanic and the Slavic and between Imperial Germany and Russia were observed.
162. See Lunzer, *Hofmannsthals politische Tätigkeit*, 201.
163. See Andrian's report to Burian, 11 July 1916, in the appendix to *Hugo von Hofmannsthal—Josef Redlich. Briefwechsel*, 145f. Hofmannsthal mentions the request to hold the speech also in Germany in his letter to Andrian, 31 July 1916; see *Hugo von Hofmannsthal—Leopold von Andrian. Briefwechsel*, 235.
164. There is a mass of reports dealing with the German change of course and especially with the dismal Austrian failure to match the German-sanctioned and German-supported celebrations in Warsaw on 3 May 1916. On the German "Neue Curs," see especially Andrian's reports from 24 April (in Prutsch & Zeyringer, eds. Leopold von Andrian, 317–23) and the two reports from 17 May 1916 (with attached reports), where Andrian also strongly argues for an Austrian "counteroffensive" (HHStA, PA I, K.919). On the celebration of the Polish constitution of 1791 on 3 May 1916, see his reports from 26 and 30 April and 4 and 8 May (especially the latter) in ibid., K.919. The intense correspondence between Warsaw and Vienna over Hofmannsthal's trip (ibid., K.926) reveals the importance this trip had for Andrian's culture politics at this time as part of the Austrian "counteroffensive."

165. See Andrian's report from 11 July 1916, reprinted in the appendix to *Hugo von Hofmannsthal—Josef Redlich. Briefwechsel*, 145f.
166. See the letter from Austrian Minister President Stürgkh to Burian about having engaged Minister of Culture Hussarek on the question of sending other cultural personalities to Warsaw in agreement with Andrian's suggestion. Letter dated 1 September 1916, HHStA, PA I, K.926.
167. A few weeks before the trip, Hofmannsthal wrote to Robert Ehrhart: "Das Min[isterium] d[es] Äussern (oder Andrian durch dieses) stellt mir für einen in Warschau gleich nach meinen Ankunft zu haltenden Vortrag eine etwas schwierige Aufgabe." Letter dated Pfingst-Montag 1916, HHStA, Nachlass Sperl-Ehrhart, K.16.
168. See Hofmannsthal's letter to Ehrhart dated 10 July 1916, HHStA, Nachlass Sperl-Ehrhart, K.16.
169. See Hofmannsthal, *Reden und Aufsätze II*, 393f.
170. On Naumann and Austria-Hungary, see part one of this book.
171. Naumann had vented the question in conversation with a great many people, but had then formulated his question in writing to a smaller number of prominent German historians. The names he mentions in his letter to Max Weber are Hans Delbrück, Friedrich Meinecke, Karl Lamprecht, and Gerhard Anschütz. The latter two still remain to reply to his question at the time of writing. See the copy of Naumann's letter to Weber, 27 January 1915, BArch, Nachlass Naumann, N3001/106.
172. At least in his letters to Karl Lamprecht and Gerhard Anschütz, Naumann used these opposing Great-German and Little-German concepts. See the copy of Naumann's letter to Anschütz, appended to the Weber letter (ibid.). It seems probable that he did so throughout his contacts, since the relationship between Germany and Austria-Hungary hardly could be solved in a satisfactory way if the Germans turned their backs on their ally in the Little-German way (as Naumann described it). What Naumann here calls the Great-German solution also fits rather well with that Mitteleuropa vision he would propagate during the following years.
173. On this trip and Naumann's conclusions from it, see part one of this book.
174. See Lunzer, *Hofmannsthals politische Tätigkeit*, 171, 176. On 29 December 1915, Hofmannsthal wrote to his publisher, Kippenberg, in Leipzig, asking him to send a few of the issues from the Austrian Library to Friedrich Naumann, "den ich u.a. im Intresse unseres Unternehmens demnächst aufzusuchen gedenke. . . ." See *Hugo von Hofmannsthal. Briefwechsel mit dem Insel-Verlag*, 614–16.
175. See Rudolph, *Kulturkritik und konservative Revolution*, 94 (note 45), and Le Rider, *Hugo von Hofmannsthal*, 231. Hofmannsthal's letter, in which he thanks Naumann, is mentioned by Theodor Heuss as having been found among Naumann's papers. It does seem probable that Hofmannsthal wrote to Naumann, since he wanted to arrange a meeting with him, but I was unable to locate any letters from Hofmannsthal during my work with the Nachlass Naumann.
176. See Hofmannsthal, *Reden und Aufsätze II*, 441. Volume 17 of the Austrian Library was a selection of the correspondence of this great Austrian general.
177. Hofmannsthal used the fact that also Naumann usually talked in the Urania when in Vienna to get the identity of his opponent across. The criticism against Naumann is very indirect here and quite possible to miss if one does not look for it. See Hofmannsthal, *Reden und Aufsätze II*, 21ff.
178. See Hofmannsthal, *Reden und Aufsätze II*, 457f.
179. Hofmannsthal, *Reden und Aufsätze II*, 456f. (quotation on 457).

180. See Hofmannsthal, *Reden und Aufsätze II*, especially 21–25.
181. See Naumann, *Werke*, 4:755ff.
182. See Hofmannsthal's sketch for "Denkschrift über die czechische Frage," reprinted in Stern, "Hofmannsthal und Böhmen (2)," 117.
183. See Hofmannsthal's note, in ibid., 118.
184. On the Czech Library, see Stern, "Hofmannsthal und Böhmen (3)."
185. Hofmannsthal, in a letter to Rudolf Pannwitz on 31 July 1917, *Hugo von Hofmannsthal—Rudolf Pannwitz. Briefwechsel 1907–1926*, Gerhard Schuster, ed. (Frankfurt am Main: S. Fischer Verlag, 1994), 14.
186. Especially the articles "Boykott fremder Sprachen?" (1914) and "Bücher für diese Zeit" (1914) deal with German culture and national character without regard for the relationship to Austria. See Hofmannsthal, *Reden und Aufsätze II*, 351–55, 367–74. His anthology of German literature *Deutsche Erzähler* (1912) and his plans to reissue this work during the war is also part of this preoccupation. See the introduction to *Deutsche Erzähler* in Hofmannsthal, *Reden und Aufsätze I*, 425–31. See Hofmannsthal's letter to his publisher, Kippenberg, dated 26 November 1914, on the question of the reissue: "Es ist ja fast, als wäre sie im (geahnten) Hinblick gerade auf diesem Moment hergestellt. Die letzten Absätze der Einleitung drücken dies genau aus." See *Hugo von Hofmannsthal. Briefwechsel mit dem Insel-Verlag*, 514.
187. See Hofmannsthal, *Reden und Aufsätze II*, 453–58.
188. See Hofmannsthal, *Reden und Aufsätze II*, 459–61.
189. One very interesting parallel to this treatment of Prussian and Austrian qualities can be found in another, similar schedule Hofmannsthal made while working on his never-finished novel *Andreas*. Here, Hofmannsthal operates with a sort of split personality, which in the story appears as two different persons (Maria and Mariquita). These two women have diametrically opposed personalities, much like the Prussian and the Austrian. The challenge for the main character of the book, Andreas, is to reunite these two halves of Maria/Mariquita's personality, thus also facilitating for himself to become whole, to become "one." Behind this we can discern Hofmannsthal's perpetual problem of becoming one with himself and to unite his belonging to German culture with his Austrian identity. Richard Alewyn treats this problem in an incomparable way, also discussing it in identity terms relevant for the present approach; see Alewyn, *Über Hugo von Hofmannsthal*, 131–67.
190. For a discussion of *Der Schwierige* in a similar way as here, see, for instance, Hamburger, *Hugo von Hofmannsthal*, 116–26. On the work history, see Hugo von Hofmannsthal, *Sämtliche Werke* 12: *Dramen* 10, Martin Stern, ed. (Frankfurt am Main: S. Fischer Verlag, 1993), 147–200. The text to the play can be found in Hugo von Hofmannsthal, *Dramen IV (Lustspiele)*, in *Gesammelte Werke in zehn Einzelbänden* (Frankfurt am Main: Fischer Taschenbuchverlag, 1979) 331–439.
191. See Hofmannsthal, *Dramen IV*, 385.
192. Ibid., 399–402 (quotations from 400).
193. Ibid., 417–19.
194. Ibid., 339.
195. Ibid., 437.
196. See Broch, *Hugo von Hofmannsthal and His Time*, 86–108, on the sociocultural milieu of Hofmannsthal's upbringing and of the role of the Burgtheater therein.
197. On Andrian's directorship of the court theaters, see Steinberg, *The Meaning of the Salzburg Festival*, 49ff., and Prutsch & Zeyringer, eds. *Leopold von Andrian*, 246–49. See also the documents to this affair in *Hugo von Hofmannsthal—Leopold von Andrian. Briefwechsel*,

261–93, and Prutsch & Zeyringer, eds. *Leopold von Andrian*, 445–69. See also Andrian's own retrospective article on his directorship; Leopold von Andrian, "Meine Tätigkeit als Generalintendant der Wiener Hoftheater," *Neue Freie Presse*, 28.10, 4.11, 8.11.1928.

198. Andrian's program for the Burgtheater is discernible in several sources, see primarily Andrian, "Meine Tätigkeit als Generalintendant der Wiener Hoftheater," and Prutsch & Zeyringer, eds. *Leopold von Andrian*, 445–69 (especially 448), and *Hugo von Hofmannsthal—Leopold von Andrian. Briefwechsel*, 261–93. In Andrian, "Meine Tätigkeit als Generalintendant der Wiener Hoftheater," he describes the memorandum he wrote at the beginning of his directorship, the contents of which are reflected in documents from 1918.

199. See the Reinhardt memorandum dated 5 September 1918 and Hofmannsthal's letters from 27 August and 8 September commenting on it, in Prutsch & Zeyringer, eds. *Leopold von Andrian*, 454–64. See also Andrian, "Meine Tätigkeit als Generalintendant der Wiener Hoftheater."

200. See the letter of 27 August 1918, in Prutsch & Zeyringer, eds. *Leopold von Andrian*, 454f.

201. On the founding and early phase of the Salzburg Festival, see Steinberg, *The Meaning of the Salzburg Festival.*

202. See Prutsch & Zeyringer, eds. *Leopold von Andrian*, 489.

203. On Hofmannsthal's role in the early years of the Salzburg Festival, see Steinberg, *The Meaning of the Salzburg Festival.* See also Müller, "Hugo von Hofmannsthal's Zeit- und Kulturkritik," and Stieg, "Hofmannsthal und die Salzburger Festspiele." For a more differentiated view of Hofmannsthal's festival dramas and their ideological undercurrent and function, compare Beniston, "*Welttheater*," 200–51.

204. See "Deutsche Festspiele zu Salzburg" (1919), in Hofmannsthal, *Reden und Aufsätze II*, 255ff.

205. See "Die Salzburger Festspiele" (1919), in Hofmannsthal, *Reden und Aufsätze II*, 258–63 (quotation on 261).

206. Hofmannsthal in a letter to Efraim Frisch on 10 June 1919, "Hofmannsthal und Efraim Frisch. Zwölf Briefe 1910–1927," *Hofmannsthalblätter* 5, Max Kreutzberger, ed. (1970): 362f. Shortly after returning from Prague in the summer of 1917, Hofmannsthal wrote to Eberhard von Bodenhausen in a way that foreshadowed this stance on the Anschluss; see the letter on 10 July 1917, in *Briefe der Freundschaft*, 235f. However, compare Severin Perrig, *Hugo von Hofmannsthal und die Zwanziger Jahre. Eine Studie zur späten Orientierungskrise* (Frankfurt am Main: Peter D. Lang Verlag, 1994), 74–79, on the difficulties in pinpointing Hofmannsthal's stance on the Anschluss question.

207. See Hugo von Hofmannsthal, *Sämtliche Werke*, vol. 30, *Roman. Biographie*, Manfred Pape, ed. (Frankfurt am Main: S. Fischer Verlag, 1982), 119.

208. See especially the sketches for *Andreas* from the year 1919, in Hofmannsthal, *Sämtliche Werke* 30:179–83.

209. See Walter Brecht "Ein Romanfragment Hofmannsthals," reprinted in *Hofmannsthal-Jahrbuch* 7 (1999), 125–28. Walter Brecht had apparently discussed the novel with Hofmannsthal before the latter's death and received a very strong impression of the development of Andreas in this direction. See Walter Becht, "Fortsetzungspläne zu 'Andreas.' Mitgeteilt von Walter Brecht," *Hofmannsthalblätter* 5 (1970), 392f.

210. For an example of Hofmannsthal's evaluation of the personal effects of the disappearance of Austria-Hungary, see his letter to Josef Redlich, 28 November 1928, in *Hugo von Hofmannsthal—Josef Redlich. Briefwechsel*, 115ff.: ". . . Weil ich mit den Zusammenbruch Österreichs das Erdreich verloren habe, in welches ich verwurzelt bin, . . . weil dies mein eigenes Erlebnis ist, weil mein eigenes dichterisches Dasein in diesem Zusammensturz fragwürdig geworden ist. . . ."

211. See the libretto to *Arabella* in Hofmannsthal, *Dramen V*, 513–78. See further the commentary on the origins of *Arabella* in Hugo von Hofmannsthal, *Sämtliche Werke*, vol. 26, *Operndichtungen* 4, Hans-Albrecht Koch, ed., (Frankfurt am Main: S. Fischer Verlag, 1976), 167–99.
212. See Hamburger, *Hugo von Hofmannsthal. Zwei Studien*, 114.
213. Letter to Strauss, 13 July 1928, in *Richard Strauss. Hugo von Hofmannsthal. Briefwechsel*, Willi Schuh, ed. (Munich: R. Piper, 1990), 638–40 (quotation on 639).
214. On Andrian's protofascistic ideology, see Dorowin, *Retter des Abendlandes*, and Andrian's key work of political metaphysics, *Die Ständeordnung des Alls. Rationales Weltbild eines katholischen Dichters* (Munich: Kösel & Pustet, 1930). On his early membership in the Vaterlandsfront, see Prutsch & Zeyringer, eds. *Leopold von Andrian*, 492.
215. Andrian's diary from 1925–26, quoted in Prutsch & Zeyringer, eds. *Leopold von Andrian*, 497.
216. On the Austrian ideology of the Ständestaat, see Anton Staudinger, "Zur 'Österreich-Ideologie des Ständestaates," in *Das Juli-Abkommen 1936, Veröffentlichungen der Wissenschaftlichen Kommission des Theodor-Körner-Stiftungsfonds und des Leopold-Kunschak-Preises zur Erforschung der österreichischen Geschichte der Jahre 1927 bis 1938*, vol. 4, Ludwig Jedlicka & Rudolf Neck, eds. (Vienna: Verlag für Geschichte und Politik, 1977).
217. On Andrian's language academy, see Leopold von Andrian, "Die Sprache des Österreichers," in *Vaterland. Blätter für katholisches Österreichertum* 7:1 (1933), and Prutsch & Zeyringer eds. *Leopold von Andrian*, 497f. Except for the published articles on this subject, Andrian had apparently written a proper scientific tract on this matter, which was never published, but which was nevertheless read in the circle of active Austrian patriots in the 1930s.
218. On these activities of Andrian's, see Prutsch & Zeyringer, eds. *Leopold von Andrian*, 494–99. See also the excerpts from Andrian's *Die Grundlehren des österreichischen Glaubens. Kleiner Katechismus für Patriote*, in Prutsch & Zeyringer, eds. *Leopold von Andrian*, 627–35. The booklet was finished on 12 March 1938, but never left the printers because of the Anschluss. Parts of it had been published in different newspapers and periodicals during the spring of 1938. See also the letter from the publisher Filip Schmidt-Dengler to Andrian, 19 October 1935, ibid., 588–91.
219. See Prutsch & Zeyringer, eds. *Leopold von Andrian*, 496. Compare Ulrich Weinzierl, "Österreich als Wille und Vorstellung," *Deutschsprachige Exilliteratur: Studien zu ihrer Bestimmung im Kontext der Epoche 1930 bis 1960*, Wuld Koepke & Michael Winkler, eds. (Bonn: Bouvier, 1984), and Markus Mayr, "Leopold von Andrians 'Österreich im Prisma der Idee,'" *Geschichte und Gegenwart* 8:2 (1989).
220. See the letter from the Österreichischer Verlag für Kunst und Wissenschaft to Andrian, 7 March 1938, in Prutsch & Zeyringer, eds. *Leopold von Andrian*, 626. See also ibid., 499.
221. See the excerpt from Andrian's diary for the years 1938–40, in Prutsch & Zeyringer, eds. *Leopold von Andrian*, 647f.
222. On Andrian's biography from 1939 to 1951, see Prutsch & Zeyringer, eds. *Leopold von Andrian*, 649–61, 745–54. See also the documents in ibid., 662–707 (newspaper articles, correspondence with Otto von Habsburg and his circle, and other items).
223. See Müller, "Hugo von Hofmannsthal's Zeit- und Kulturkritik," 207ff. Compare Rudolph, *Kulturkritik und konservative Revolution*, passim.
224. See Andrian, "Hofmannsthal und die österreichische Jugend," 134–36.
225. Prutsch & Zeyringer, eds. *Leopold von Andrian*, contains correspondence from the 1930s and 1940s in part concerning the question of Hofmannsthal and his work (with publishers and historians of literature).

PART THREE

Josef Redlich (Karl Renner)

◈ The Problem of the Austrian People(s) ◈

> Already as a ten- or twelve-year-old boy, I had thoroughly and often studied the Viennese revolution and the struggles of 1848 in a multivolume work at my parents' home. However, unable to properly understand why, I instinctively felt myself to be on the side of government and the dynasty. . . . Strangely, the story of the struggle of the Austrian army in Hungary and Italy had made me feel very patriotic, and in my boyhood I dreamed that I would once collect an army and defend Austria. . . .[1]

In Josef Redlich's voluminous writing on the Austrian imperial state and its history, his personal identification with the destiny of this state constitutes a strong undercurrent. This is nowhere more evident than in the foreword to those never-finished memoirs that Redlich began writing in his new home in Cambridge, Massachusetts, in the fall of 1928, shortly after having concluded the last of a series of historical works on Imperial Austria, a preoccupation of his that stretched back to the last years before World War I. In this foreword, Redlich recounts how he strongly felt that something was lacking in these attempts of his to come to grips with the destiny of his fatherland and Heimat. The idea had slowly matured that the best vessel for reaching this goal was the story of his own life-career:

> It became increasingly clear to me that to describe old Austria—its peoples and lands—I could find no better vantage point than my own life, which was unthinkable without the particularities of the old empire and the life of its population. So intimately connected with Austria was my personal destiny and development.[2]

The fragment of Redlich's memoirs as such are quite interesting even though they are incomplete—he finished only the parts on his childhood and school years—and they do not at all address his scholarly or his political career, the two media he used to channel his engagement for Austria.[3] The fragment nevertheless contains keys for understanding crucial aspects of Redlich's development.

For one thing, his personal close identification with the destiny of the imperial state emerges clearly. Furthermore, Redlich's memory of being intensely interested in the struggle for popular and national sovereignty in 1848 signals his lifelong political and scholarly engagement in the problem of the democratization of the "multinational empire." However, Redlich here in a very short space also signals his ambivalent relationship to the imperial Austrian state when he recounts his surprise over how he instinctively took the side of the government and dynasty in the struggles of 1848–49. Normally, Redlich is very closely identified with an idealizing view of the "liberal revolution of 1848." But the contradiction here is only apparent. It is mainly because the image of Redlich has been strongly shaped by his public and controversial engagement in 1917–18 for peace and national democratic reform of the imperial state. However, this engagement came only at the end of a long, winding political development, which in its entirety contains an eminently interesting story for the investigation of the Austrian state problem.

Redlich's project was not simply a struggle for democratization; it was also a struggle for the preservation of the imperial Austrian state, which Redlich identified himself with deeply. Throughout his life, Redlich circled around the problem of how that Austrian imperial state founded by Maria Theresia in the mid-eighteenth century should develop to cope with the transition into modernity: how could a balance be struck between, on the one hand, the need for unity in such a disparate agglomeration of lands and peoples as there was in Austria and, on the other hand, the need for popular sovereignty and local autonomy to modernize this state so that it could face up to the requirements of a new age. Because Redlich in 1928 recalled how he in his youth had identified with the carriers of the historical unity of this imperial state in part reflects that in the end, the struggle for popular sovereignty and political autonomy *did* break up that multinational state that Redlich merely wanted to modernize. However, for most of his political career the problem rather seemed the opposite, i.e., the problem of devolving and modernizing an imperial state apparatus that threatened to suffocate the development of that modern democratic and multinational Austria Redlich had invested so much of his energy and personal identity in.

There is an organic relationship between Redlich's historical scholarship and his political career, insofar as the former might be said to supply the wider historical framework for understanding Redlich's political career and its development. One might say that Redlich was writing himself and his political activities into Austrian history through his scholarship just as much as he was studying Austrian history to form his judgment on the proper way of reforming the Austrian state. It is actually difficult to separate the two. Just as with Heinrich Friedjung,[4] there is an intimate relationship between Redlich's historical scholarship and his political activities. Regarding Redlich, this primarily expresses itself through an internal tension in his grand and unfinished historical work *Das Österreichische Staats- und Reichsproblem*, which preoccupied Redlich with increasing intensity from around 1906 (the year of his beginning political engagement), through a main bout of work during World War I, resulting in the publication of the first volume in 1920, and until 1926 when its second and, as it turned out, last volume was published. The nearly two thousand–page journey through the history of Austria from 1848 to 1867—which took twenty years to make—reflects Redlich's wrestling with the problem of unity and diversity, of imperial state authority and popular and national sovereignty, that also preoccupied him as an active politician and parliamentarian in the years 1906 to 1918. This work is therefore an eminent point of entry into Redlich's, in a wide sense, political biography.

1. The Problem of the Austrian State and Empire

Josef Redlich's turn to the history of the Austrian state took place in proximity to his turn to politics in 1906. Before then, Redlich's scholarship had mainly been concerned with English government and parliamentarism. With his Habilitationsschrift *Englische Lokalverwaltung* (1901), he became Privatdozent at the Faculty of Law at the University of Vienna, and his following opus *Recht und Technik des Englischen Parlamentarismus* (1905) cleared the way to an extraordinary professorship at the same university in 1906. In 1909, he attained a fixed position, an ordinary professorship at the Technical College of Vienna (Technische Hochschule), which he would uphold until 1918.[5] In its extension, this scholarly career might also be said to constitute another important trajectory in Redlich's life, one that will not be followed here: his very successful career as a scholar and lecturer in the United States, which undoubtedly became a new start for him after 1918. This career, which had already begun before 1914 with lecturing tours and other official assignments in the American university world, culminated in his professorship of comparative law at the Harvard Law School, which he upheld from 1926 and into the 1930s before retiring and moving back to Vienna during the last years of his life.[6]

In a letter to his friend Hermann Bahr in the fall of 1906, Redlich described how all his strivings and studies up to this point had been directed at understanding "the essence of the State." Now, Redlich intimates, his strivings have prepared him for an endeavor "in which also my heart is engaged."[7] What Redlich was hinting at was his beginning political engagement for the reform of the Austrian state. Only

Josef Redlich around 1910; Austrian National Library, ÖNB/Sign. NB520118B

a few weeks later he was elected to the provincial assembly of his native province Moravia as a representative of his hometown Göding (Hodonin), where in the summer of the following year he was then also elected to the Austrian parliament in the first Austrian elections with a general male franchise. It seems significant that his historical studies of the Austrian state and its institutions were intensified at this very time. Because Redlich's political engagement during the following years would find one of its primary expressions in the instigation and very active participation in the large-scale Imperial Commission for Administrative Reform, the boundary between Redlich's historical interest in the Austrian state and his political work to reform this state became blurred. Redlich's publications during the following years straddle this boundary. Some, such as *Das Wesen der österreichischen Kommunalverfassung* (1910) and Redlich's report on the Austrian finance administration (1913), part of his work in the administrative reform commission, are primarily works on administrative law and organization. But they are also very strongly historically oriented. Others, such as the articles from 1908 and 1909 on the protocols of the Kremsier parliament of 1848–49 and on Anton Schmerling and Josef Lasser,[8] two important German-Austrian liberals in the politics of the 1860s and 1870s, are more purely products of historical scholarship. These latter studies on the political history of the Austrian state after 1848 are the beginning of a preoccupation with "the Austrian problem of the state and empire" that Redlich would conclude only in 1926, and not even then conclusively, since after this time he continued to plan and undertake research for the third volume of his grand history of the Austrian state, which would have covered the years 1867 to 1890.

Under the influence of his political engagement and especially his work in the administrative reform commission, these scholarly plans of Redlich's gradually matured into a concrete project of minutely analyzing the historical development of the Austrian state and its institutions. The ultimate aim of this project was to find a solution to the problems of contemporary Austria by studying their genesis. Already in 1909, around the time he began petitioning parliament for the appointment of an administrative reform commission, Redlich complained to his German-Liberal political associate Joseph Maria Baernreither that the existing historical scholarship on modern Austria was completely useless. Nowhere could the needed study of "the origins of contemporary Austria" be found.[9] During the following years, Redlich was fully preoccupied with the work in the administrative reform commission, and with teaching and lecture tours in the United States. When the work in the commission approached the end of its three-year appointment, which would occur in the summer of 1914, Redlich was apparently expanding his field of work within it from dealing with only the finance administration, which had been his assigned field in the work of the commission, to working out also a proposal for a reform of the entire internal administration (the so-called political administration).[10] Only slightly later, after the negotiations in the commission during the late spring of 1914 had ended in intense debates and internal conflicts over the fundamentals of the reform of the Austrian state, Redlich seems to have lifted this whole plan into the scholarly sphere, where several years later it resulted in his large-scale work on *Das österreichische Staats- und Reichsproblem* (1920–26). As early as June 1914 he reported to a friend that he was working on a book about "Austrian constitutional problems," and the outbreak of war a few weeks later seems only to have spurred him on in this project.[11]

In the years 1915–18, Redlich would work on this project, and he had practically brought the first volume of the work to a close by war's end. At the beginning of 1915 he laid out his plans to Hermann Bahr in a way that makes quite clear that he, for his part, was viewing this work as a direct continuation of the work of that administrative reform commission, which according to him had failed in its historical mission of the regeneration of the Austrian state. Redlich wrote this:

> [The book about Austria] will become a work that . . . describes and explains the origins and development of "the Austrian problem" and how the rulers with the assistance of the peoples turned it into "the Austrian chaos". . . . If I succeed in properly explaining the origins, character, and effects of this "chaos," then surely it will be easy to demonstrate how we can overcome this chaos and again forge a stable and durable order.[12]

The intimate link observable between Redlich's scholarly work on the history of the Austrian state and his parallel work on the reform of this state makes it appropriate to examine these two aspects together.

As in the previous two parts of this book, the study of Redlich will be carried out within the framework of a dual biography, where the secondary character serves to highlight a problem or field of tension within the larger Austrian state problem. In the present part this role is played by Karl Renner, the well-known political theorist of the nationality problem and likewise prominent Social Democratic politician. In comparison to Redlich, Renner has been amply treated in scholarship. Despite this, the image is even more problematical than that of Redlich. In part, this has to do with the scholarship on Karl Renner being divided between several different disciplines and fields of inquiry with minimal communication between them. In part, he is viewed as a political theorist of the nationality problem. However, this is usually done in isolation from his concrete political career in the period 1899–1918, which was the period when he wrote those works that still interest political theorists. The main focus on Renner the politician lies, on the one hand, on the interwar era, when he was a leading Social Democratic politican and theorist of Austromarxism, and, on the other, on his important historical role in 1918 and 1945, when he was the founder of two Austrian republics, and in 1938 when he gave his support of Anschluss to Nazi-Germany.[13] The problem of integrating all these parts in a more or less unified historical image of Renner still eludes scholars; however, a Renner myth has been established,[14] which has made him into an integrative figure in Austrian national mythology, a sort of "father of the nation."

This Renner myth has also influenced the biographies of Renner, two out of three, those by Walter Rauscher (1995) and by Siegfried Nasko and Johannes Reichl (2000), which have a basic thrust of affirming this myth and the character of a sort of official biographies of Renner the Landesvater. The third biography, by Jacques Hannak (1965), is perhaps even more problematical in its ways; it is written from a position close to Renner's within Austrian Social Democracy and by a person, who was also his Nachlassverwalter. Despite this, Hannak's biography often cuts more deeply and confronts problems in Renner that the other two biographies avoid. The perhaps most important work on Renner is the "sketch for a political psychogram" by Anton Pelinka (1989). This work is a short critical study of Renner the politician, thus facing all the problems head-on that are often avoided elsewhere.[15] In the context of Renner studies, the present approach to Renner aims at contributing somewhat to fill out the picture of Renner before 1918 and to bridge the gulf between Renner the theorist of the nationality problem and Renner the politician.

In the context of the present study of the Austrian state problem, the parallel treatments of Karl Renner's political project and that of Josef Redlich serve to hightlight the problem of the democratization of the multinational state, what could be called the problem of the Austrian people(s). Together this whole part creates a counterpoint to part one; the projects of Karl Renner and Josef Redlich can be usefully contrasted to those of Koerber and Friedjung in several ways. The primary field of tension is that between the state and the people, between the role of monarchic Verwaltung and popular sovereignty in the modernization of the multinational state: Bureaucratic Liberal Josephism is poised against two different varieties of multinational democracy. The second important field of tension generated here is the one between the two interrelated tendencies of German nationalist hegemony and Austrian supranationalism. This field of tension, however, does not produce alternatives that are as clear: the problem of the Germanness of Imperial Austria creates four different effects in the four individuals studied. Adding the positions of Hofmannsthal and Andrian in part two, the end result is six mutually different positions on the problem of the identity of Austria. Last, but definitely not least, the parallel treatment of Renner's and Redlich's political projects in the present part results in a close examination of the possibilities and problems of Austrian multinational democracy.

In comparison with the preceeding two dual biographies, the link between Redlich and Renner is less intimate. Nevertheless, Redlich and Renner were acquainted from around the turn of the century, when they partly moved in the same left-liberal and social-democratic intellectual circles in Vienna, and they were both elected to the Austrian parliament in 1907. In some ways, this situation of two parallel intellectual and political trajectories in late Imperial Austria is striking. Considering that both their respective careers were devoted to virtually the same problem, the modernization of the Austrian state—meaning both its democratization and finding a solution that entailed the recognition of its multinational character—we find that these parallel trajectories throw light on the fundamental questions of the Austrian state problem. Furthermore, although initially very close, their two political visions contained decisive differences, which under the pressure of war after 1914 resulted in sharply divergent paths of development.

Josef Redlich's Das österreichische Staats- und Reichsproblem

In Redlich's view, the modern Austrian state had grown naturally from the "Theresian-Josephinian unitary state" founded by Maria Theresia in the 1740s. This state was roughly equal to the western half of the Dual Monarchy of Redlich's own lifetime. Besides this Austrian "state," Redlich also identifies the problem of the wider "empire," i.e., mainly the relationship to Hungary that historically is intricately interwoven with the Austrian state problem. The Austrian state was created wholly from above by tying together several lands under the Habsburg crown with a newly fashioned, unitary state apparatus. From within this apparatus in the late eighteenth century emerged the Austrian state idea, which was supported by the aristocracy and the evolving middle-class service nobility. This Austrian idea was, as Redlich emphasizes, wholly anchored in the governing classes, and this made the Theresian-Josephinian unitary state into a pure Obrigkeitsstaat. The Austrian problem, as Redlich defined it, emerged during the first half of the nineteenth century, when this state was confronted with the democratic and nationalistic ideas spawned by the French Revolution. These ideas exploded with full force on the Austrian stage during the revolution of 1848, when the first struggle of the Austrian and Hungarian peoples "for a true people's realm, a true people's state" took place.[16] At this time the fundamental question was posed whether this state could be modernized along national and democratic lines. Redlich formulates this Austrian main problem of 1848 as follows:

> Is it possible and by what means should it be done that the centuries-old common state of so many peoples and nationalities, created by absolutist rule, could . . . be maintained, when the two political principles of Liberalism and Nationalism, the one bringing individual freedom, the other the freedom of peoples, were realized simultaneously for all lands and peoples? [17]

This question might be said to guide also the whole of Redlich's following historical investigation into the struggle between government and dynasty, on the one hand, and the different groups in society, on the other, and also between these latter groups, for the control of the development of the Austrian state (and empire).

Redlich deplores that the first real chance to find a solution to the Austrian problem was missed in the Vormärz era, since at this time a more organic, slowly evolving solution could have been accomplished.[18] However, this failure was not terminal, as was demonstrated by the Kremsier parliament in 1848–49. At that time, representatives from all the peoples of Austria together worked out an Austrian constitution. This constitution was, as Redlich emphasizes, "until the end of the Habsburg dynasty the only great reform plan that built on the mutual consent of the peoples of Austria"[19] and could have served as the instrument to modernize the Theresian-Josephinian Obrigkeitsstaat.[20] The following absolutistic reaction of 1849 first brought on Interior Minister Franz Stadion's rather liberal March Constitution, which closely followed the example of Kremsier. Stadion also introduced municipal autonomy, i.e., local self-government, which Redlich calls "the strongest and most productive principle in the political and administrative development of Austria." However, Stadion was also a classical Austrian centralist who delineated an administrative reform that tied in the autonomous organs to the state administration, thus unifying and centralizing the whole political structure of Austria, something that Redlich also appreciated.[21] Redlich's strong appreciation of both the Kremsier Constitution and Franz Stadion's reform plans probably reflects his thinking that both of these plans seem to achieve a reasonable balance between unity and diversity. In fact, Redlich's appreciation of Stadion almost seems to eclipse his high evaluation of the Kremsier parliament, and it seems reasonable to judge it as an expression of Redlich's own emphasis on the need for unity in the German-Slavic state that was his Austria.

Redlich judged the following authoritarian centralism of Alexander Bach as harshly as the Kremsier and Stadion plans were judged benevolently.[22] He even goes so far as to judge the Bach system as the turning point, or pathogenesis, of the development of the Austrian state.[23] This is primarily a reflection of Bach's completely leaving the constitutional path and also abolishing local self-government, thus sharply veering the Austrian state on a course that emphasized unity very strongly. In Redlich's view, the Bach era (1849–59) meant not only the loss of ten important years in the building of a modern Austrian state, it also deeply damaged the prospects for any such development. It completely alienated large groups from the state, including the Slavic peoples who for ten years were oppressed by a German-speaking imperial bureaucracy.[24] The Bach system also had a fundamental influence on the mentality of the Austrian civil service, as well as that of the German-Austrian bürgerliche elite, giving it an authoritarian, obrigkeitliche character that it retained until the very end of the empire, a mental makeup that of course was hardly conducive to the democratization of the Austrian state.[25]

Redlich identifies the fundamental, indeed the *only* real political divide in late imperial Austria as that between centralism and federalism.[26] This divide was reflected as early as in the Kremsier parliament, where it was already conditioned by that identification of the Austrian Germans with the whole of the Austrian state and empire that Redlich traces back to the eighteenth century.[27] The Czech federalist program was also fully recognizable at this time.[28] However, Redlich observed that there was also a stable common basis for the two programs, which makes it possible to view the politics at this time of the two original peoples of Austria, the Germans and the Czechs, as a process in which the German-Slavic constitutional state could have been shaped.[29] All this promise was badly damaged by the Bach system. For one thing, the rift between the centralists and federalists had grown considerably when the neoabsolutist state was liquidated in 1860 and the political arena was reopened.[30] Under the Bach system, the process of fusing the German-Austrian Bürgerlichkeit and the centralist Beamtentum of Vienna had created a governing class with an ideology that identified all of Austria as a German empire, a development whose origins Redlich follows back to the project of a German unitary empire under Joseph II in the 1780s, but which was now, in the first half of the 1860s, embodied by the regime of Anton Schmerling.[31] Nevertheless, Redlich seems to have viewed it as possible to close the gap at this time, and it is probably in this perspective that we should see his strong condemnation of the Schmerling regime, which he judged as perpetuating the Bach inheritance, only giving it a German(-Liberal) twist and thus creating a most damaging form of German-Austrian (internal) imperialism.

This condemnation of the fusion of the German-Austrian bureaucracy with German-Austrian National-Liberalism is, in fact, one of the strongest undercurrents in the work as a whole. This undercurrent turns Redlich's *Das österreichische Staats- und Reichsproblem* into a very weighty criticism of the German-Liberal mentality in Austria, of which not least was Heinrich Friedjung an exponent. Although mainly concealed in the work as such,[32] Redlich's whole argument can be said to be directed against the view of Austrian history expressed in Friedjung's *Österreich von 1848 bis 1860* (1908–12). Redlich mentioned this work of Friedjung's as problematic already in 1909 when he complained about the lack of a proper history of "contemporary Austria."[33] When Redlich was in the midst of intensive work on his own history of contemporary Austria a few years later he sharpened this judgment considerably, condemning the work as a whole:

> It seems to me that we must teach the generation of Germans who grow up after the world war, both here and in the Reich, to view Austria in a *different* way than Friedjung does—i.e., not from the Viennese point of view, but from the *Austrian* point of view, which one can have in Salzburg and Brünn, Hermannstadt and Prague, but not in the first, second, or ninth district of Vienna.[34]

Despite this heavy criticism, Redlich was always very appreciative of Friedjung's historical craftsmanship. When the first volume of *Das österreichische Staats- und Reichsproblem* was published in 1920, Redlich was even obliged to defend himself against Hermann Bahr, who thought he been much too lenient on Friedjung. Redlich explained that during his own work in the archives, he had realized the mastery with which Friedjung had worked through the sources and analyzed the politics of the 1850s. He did concede to Bahr, though, that Friedjung's "view of the whole was absolutely wrong-headed."[35]

Redlich's critical view of the German-Liberal mentality might also be said to express itself in his almost nostalgic description of the old-Austrian culture that he viewed as having been created along with the development of the Theresian-Josephinian unitary state. With Vienna as its center, "the meeting ground of all the peoples and cultural elements of the vast empire," a special Austrian German-speaking but fundamentally culturally mixed bürgerliche culture had been cultivated and spread over the whole of the empire, even into the leading classes of Hungary. This culture was an important source of unity for the Austrian imperial state. It was "one of the strongest sources for the spread and deepening of the feeling of Austrian unity."[36] In view of the weight Redlich gives this old-Austrian culture as a support for the Austrian state idea, it follows quite logically that he would consider with special animosity the Germanization of this Austrian culture and the Austrian idea as such, a development represented most prominently by Anton Schmerling.

In the above-quoted criticism of Friedjung's Viennese, centralist view of Austrian history, Redlich's own opinion of this history is also circumscribed. It is also reflected in Redlich's appreciation of the federalist position on the Austrian state, which actually seems to be more accentuated the longer Redlich proceeds in his historical exploration. In part, this most certainly reflects Redlich's political development in this direction during the time span in which he wrote the book. Redlich did go through a development where his emphasis on the unity of the Austrian state shifted in the direction of emphasizing its diversity. In this regard his growing appreciation of the federalist position goes hand in hand with his increasing hostility to German-Austrian centralism. But it also seems to grow organically out of Redlich's minute analysis of the politics of the 1860s as a struggle between more sharply contrasting views of the political identity of the Austrian state than in 1848–49. The latter half of the first volume and the whole of the second volume of *Das österreichische Staats- und Reichsproblem* present an exploration in almost overwhelming detail of the struggle for the political identity of Austria between the centralism of Schmerling and the German-Liberals and the federalism of primarily the Hungarian and Bohemian nobility and the Czech National-Liberals. The first main (though inadvertent) result of this struggle was the Austrian dual system of separate state *and* autonomous administrations (the so-called Doppelverwaltung) that was created in 1860–62 in the struggle between the centralist Schmerling regime, on the one hand, and the Bohemian aristocrats and the Czech National-Liberal federalists, on the other. As Redlich saw it, the result of this struggle was *the* crucial event in the development of the modern Austrian state, since it contained the historically produced essence of the identity of the modern Austrian state: the Austrian municipal autonomy (the Gemeindeautonomie). The second main result of this struggle was the creation of the Dual Monarchy in 1865–67, which was also a compromise between centralism and federalism.

The personal engagement of the author grows noticeably in the parts of *Das österreichische Staats- und Reichsproblem* that deal with the question of local political autonomy, the question of self-government; for example, the sections on Franz Stadion's original idea of the Gemeindeautonomie in 1848–49 and on Hans Perthaler's implementation of these ideas in the Reichsgemeindegesetz of 1862.[37] When Redlich in the mid-1920s finished the second volume of his magnum opus, ending in 1867, he allowed himself a prospective glance. One of the aspects he fastened on in the development of the Austrian state from 1867 to 1914 was how the system of autonomous administration had de facto functioned as the basis for a gradual but far-reaching nationalization and democratization of the public life of Austria, in which the municipalities had functioned as a state-free sphere where the different peoples of Austria could unfold their political will.[38] This benevolent development in the Austrian state that Redlich could discern in retrospect was also the tendency in the Austrian political life that he had striven to reinforce during his political career.

In his *Das Wesen der österreichischen Kommunalverfassung* (1910), Redlich had made a strong pleading for the Austrian variety of local self-government as potentially a generator of power similar to its English counterpart, a generator that could propel the Austrian project of building a modern state forward. As Redlich saw it, the creation of a state-free sphere freed the inherent powers of Austrian society and put them in the service of economic and cultural progress. Even more important, Redlich saw this system of local self-government as filling an especially important function in Austria as "the true bastion of the social life of the different nations." In Austria, this system guaranteed a state-free *national* sphere, which lessened the frictions of the multinational society by leaving the nations free to unfold their political will and cultural life at the local level. In this regard, the Austrian municipal autonomy, Redlich asserted, simply embodied "the unique character of the Austrian state." The construction of his argument as a whole is very interesting because it has a strong tendency to further a historical myth of the "ideas of 1848," the ideas of the liberal revolution, as constituting the "indestructible foundation" of the local self-government in Austria. Franz Stadion's Gemeindegesetz of 1849 is paraded alongside that of Schmerling (Perthaler) of 1862 as constituting the foundation of the liberal-constitutional Austrian state. Most interesting of all is that Redlich ultimately views the local self-government as the decisive characteristic of Austria, of its identity, one might say, and then he proceeds to contrast the Austrian state to, in this regard, the "completely different" and authoritarian Prussian state.[39]

Redlich's idea of municipal self-government as the solution to the Austrian problem had two main sources. As a form it emanated from his idealization of the English state. His repeated trips to England in the 1890s were most certainly crucial in this regard.[40] In England he found already in existence the liberal state and society that seemed so distant in Central Europe. Both of his two major works on the English state in crucial ways foreshadow his vision of the self-governing, parliamentarian peoples' state of Austria that he would propagate when a member of parliament from 1907.[41] However, despite his Anglo-Saxon ideals, the concrete model for Redlich's solution to the Austrian problem must in part be sought in his Moravian background. The fragment of his memoirs, of which around half is about his childhood in Moravia, betrays a deep identification not only with Austria, but also with the history and the special culture of that which he called "my closer Heimat, my beloved Moravia." Part of this culture was quite evidently the meeting or mix of German and Slavic cultures and languages, which is also a recurring theme in his scholarly works on the Austrian problem.[42] The combination of his view on Austrian culture as essentially mixed, and his emphasis on the importance of local self-government was anchored in his experience of his closer Heimat Moravia; this was the underlying experiential matrix behind Redlich's solution to the Austrian state problem.

Karl Renner's Nationalitätenbundesstaat

In the early years of the new century, Redlich corresponded with another young doctor of law, Karl Renner, who shared his obsession with "the essence of the state."[43]

Redlich expressed his admiration of Renner's sharp analysis of the Austrian problem and also professed to sympathize with the latter's view of the reform of the Austrian state, which, he said, was very close to his own. Redlich then expressed his conviction that "there is only one truly modern state in the present, and this state is also the state of the future: i.e., a federally constructed polity whose parts rest on self-government." Redlich noted that the whole purpose of his book on English local government was to show that this was the centuries-old fundamental idea of the English state. It was exactly this characteristic that had given the English state its tremendous vitality. Sadly, Redlich admitted, you know as well as I do "how difficult it is to gain acceptance in Austria for such a simple principle."[44]

After receiving the book on English local government, Renner had written to Redlich in a euphoric tone, explaining that he had been positively enthralled by the latter's presentation of the "magical garden" of English administration. He had immediately pounced on its political potential as a model for Austria. Had he only known this book a few years earlier, Renner lamented, when he wrote his early tracts on national autonomy in Austria, he would have been able to ground his argument much better: "I will study this book for months so that I will learn every political lesson there is to learn from it, and there are many."[45] The model of English local government and the reference to Redlich's scholarly authority would indeed be constant companions to Renner in his campaign for a multinational Austria founded on democratic national autonomy all the way up to the fall of 1918.[46] Nevertheless, in 1902 Renner also noted the basic difference that separated him from Redlich's similar concerns with democratic political reform of the Austrian state. Renner was critical of Redlich's inductive method, his choice of searching for the solution to the Austrian problem in the existing historically grown institutions of this state. Renner emphasized that this mode of procedure would only lead to a perpetuation of the old system and exemplified what he meant:

> Let us recall the year 1750: Europe is a sleeping monster, buried beneath the rests of Feudalism, controlled by Absolutism. Now a man of induction comes; he describes and classifies according to Mill the existing institutions—nothing can come out of this except the apotheosis of Absolutism. Because everything that is in the process of becoming is not yet institutionalized. The method of induction can tell me only what is, but never *what I should do*. And that is the lesson of politics.[47]

Renner's mode of procedure was rather that of examining the interests and power relations of social groups, what he called the true substance of political science, and this, as he explained to Redlich, had led him to focus on the national groups of Austria with the aim of finding a working compromise between the power of the nations and the power of the Austrian state.

In this investigation, Renner had come to a conclusion that was similar to Redlich's, but not altogether the same.[48] In certain regards their solutions differed, which with time would grow into sizable differences in their views of the multinational democratic Austrian state to be created. However, at this early time Renner's view of the Nationalitätenbundesstaat, the federal multination state, as the solution to the Austrian nationalities problem was in spirit very close to Redlich's solution. Where Redlich focused on the historically grown Austrian autonomous municipality as the foundation for his model of the multinational democratic state, Renner appropriated another historical organ of Austrian state administration as the key element for his own more revolutionary scheme; Renner took the old Theresian Kreis and turned it into an institution of local self-government in a way similar to what had been planned, but never realized in the Kremsier parliament of 1848–49. Just as the original, Renner's Kreis was devised as larger than the Gemeinde. However, unlike the absolutist original, Renner devised his Kreis to fill the function of a meeting ground between the state administration and the autonomous administration, in the process doing away with the dual administration (Doppelverwaltung) of which Renner was a severe critic. The Kreise would also assume most of the functions of the old middle level of the Kronländer (the provinces), thus greatly reducing the importance of this level. The head of this new organ, the Kreishauptmann, was a crucial figure in Renner's conception because he would both lead the local state administration (fundamentally a supervisory organ) and head the local self-government, and thus in his person constitute the link between the state administration and the self-governing organs. Except for its head, the latter would be staffed entirely by nonstate civil servants appointed by the local assembly, the Kreisvertretung, and be responsible for the vast majority of the functions of the public sphere. Renner's Kreishauptmann was thus in effect the guarantor of the unity of a state built completely on local self-government. As Renner expressed it himself: "All local administration is focused on one person, the Kreishauptmann. The executive remains unitary despite the federation."[49]

Renner's Kreis was also the institution that tied together the two structures that his multinational federal state consisted of: the state structure and the nationally autonomous structure. As Renner expressed it: "The Kreis is the elementary cell of the state organism."[50] Renner's national autonomy built on the principle of personal national autonomy, which in principle meant a complete separation of national belonging from the territorial organization of the state. According to this principle, every individual belonged to a deterritorialized national political body, which culminated in a national parliament (Nationalrat) that was also the representative organ of the whole (deterritorialized) nation. In practice, though, the territorial dimension was much more to the fore because Renner used the instrument of local self-government in the territorially relatively small Kreise to ensure that 90% of the Austrian Kreise were also nationally homogeneous.[51] In effect, the personality principle came to its full use only in the 10% that was nationally mixed. For the rest, Renner's system created national-territorial organs that were tied together in a national political entity irrespective of the geographic location of the individual national *territorial* entities. The nationally autonomous structure was matched by a denationalized territorial state structure, which also culminated in a central state parliament, where all citizens, the whole denationalized population of the multinational state, were represented. These two structures, then, were joined a second time (after the Kreis) at the government level, where representatives of the national parliaments joined the parliamentary-appointed ministers under the leadership of the second key person of Renner's proposed system of government, the Austrian minister president, who was appointed by the emperor. At the top of a structure that rested on the body of Kreishauptleute, the Austrian minister president thus became the focal point of Renner's solution to the Austrian problem.[52]

Renner's whole construction of the Austrian state does, not only in a general way, look very Josephist. As noted above, its key element, the Kreis, was an old Theresian-Josephinian institution. Furthermore, as discussed later, there is also a very strong basic similarity with Alexander Bach's administrative reforms. Neither can we avoid seeing the striking resemblance, especially with regard to the key function of the Kreis, to Ernest von Koerber's administrative reform proposal discussed in part one. The fundamental difference between Renner and these two Josephists is, of course, the second dimension of Renner's reform, the nationally autonomous structure, which is absent in the traditional, nationally blind Josephist view of the Austrian state. This element was, however, present in the plans of the Kremsier parliament for utilizing the Kreis to solve the nationality problem, and also this constitutional reform plan must, just as with Redlich, be seen as an important inspiration behind Renner's plans at empire reform. Moreover, just as in Redlich's view of the Austrian state (at least as it looked before 1914), we should note the general likeness between Renner's proposal and Franz Stadion's similar intention in 1849 of using the Kreis to bind together nationally self-governing organs and a centralized unitary state administration.

The above "administrative" perspective on Renner's proposal for a reform of the Austrian imperial state is often obscured behind its revolutionary concept of personal national autonomy (Personalitätsprinzip), but it is an integrated part of a reform that at the time and in its context was devised to fill several functions. Except for the more obvious, and in the scholarship also more noted, functions of democratizing the Austrian state and securing national autonomy, Renner's reform also intended to make sure that this development furthered and indeed strengthened the Austrian unitary state. At this point we should emphasize that Renner was an imperial Austrian Beamte. He was active from 1897 to 1907 and after this time in retirement.

He recounts in his memoirs that his work as a librarian in the Austrian parliament around the turn of the century kept him in close touch with both the major issues of the Austrian state and with many of the major actors in the debates on its reform, who often discussed these matters with him in the library. Here, of course, he was also surrounded by all the central documents on the development of the Austrian state, which he could study at leisure. The most important of his contacts made at this time was with Minister President Koerber, to whom he became an informal adviser at the turn of the century. Also after his retirement, Renner was viewed, it seems, with special friendliness by the Austrian Verwaltung because he was repeatedly approached with offers to fill official functions. Most notably here was his return to state service on the invitation by Koerber as a director of the food supply authority (Ernährungsamt) in the fall of 1916 and the invitation by Emperor Karl, which he declined, to serve in the Austrian government in the last years of the war.[53] It could also be argued that the ten years of active work as a Beamte influenced Renner's thinking in a subtle way, making him prone to see the Austrian state first and foremost as an administrative apparatus, as a structure of domination. At the very least we can discern a strong dualism in Renner's thinking, which seems to go back to his dual allegiance to the Austrian state and to the Austrian labor movement.

Just like Josef Redlich, Renner was caught up in the Austrian problem of unity and diversity. His model is best viewed as his—already at an early stage—rather definite view of the ideal balance between these two poles, the balance that Redlich would spend a large part of his life unsuccessfully trying to find. Furthermore, just as with Redlich, it can sometimes be difficult to discern Renner's priorities. Sometimes it almost seems like the state, not the nations or the people, is at the center of his concerns, a reproach he had to face many times in later years. This tendency is traceable also in this early period of Renner's career, and it seems like he was painfully aware of the tension between the class-based perspective of his political party, the Austrian Social Democratic party, and his own focus on the Austrian nations and state. In 1902, a few months before criticizing Redlich for sticking too close to the existing institutions of the imperial Austrian state in his thinking about the democratic reform of this state, Renner, apparently without provocation, defended himself in a letter to Social Democratic party leader Viktor Adler against just such a reading of his new political tract *Der Kampf der österreichischen Nationen um den Staat* (1902). Renner here argued that his exclusive focus on the state was a by-product of his wish to address his bürgerliche adversaries in the field of administrative and constitutional reform and to argue the Social Democratic position in this debate. Furthermore, with almost undue emphasis Renner maintained that "nowhere in the book is an already existing institution taken for granted; the point of departure of my argument is always the noninstitutionalized facts of social reality."[54]

Indeed, it may be that the point of departure of Renner's argumentation was the interests of social groups, but he unequivocally and consistently ended up defending at least one important already-existing institution: the Austrian imperial state. So consistently, in fact, that one might wonder whether this was not Renner's real point of departure. In fact, looking at Renner's career as a whole, we can easily turn the tables on him and his criticism of Redlich's "inductive method" and tendency to work with historically grown institutions. Indeed, Anton Pelinka made exactly such a final judgment when taking an overview of Renner's political career as a whole, which spanned from the Habsburg Empire to the First Austrian Republic, via the Ständestaat and Nazi Great Germany to the Second Austrian Republic: "Renner is the theorist and practician of actual hegemony; his theory and praxis are indicators as well as instruments of legitimating the current political system."[55]

2. Democracy and Empire

The move toward democracy in imperial Austria received its first major impulse from the revolution of 1848. As Josef Redlich noted in his work on the Austrian problem, this event also disclosed the full width of the problem of popular sovereignty in an imperial state that was not only a conglomerate of different peoples, but also a conglomerate of historical lands, each with their own political institutions and constitution. The struggle for popular sovereignty would therefore never really be the cause of the Austrian people, but with a few notable exceptions it would be centered on a specific nation or specific land, or sometimes a combination of the two. The territorial dimension first resulted in the division of the empire into two main parts in 1867, "Austria" and Hungary. Although Hungary became a unitary Magyar nation-state with large non-Magyar minorities kept out of the political sphere by the small Magyar elite, Austria would go through a distinct development in a democratic direction. Significantly, this development had both a general democratic dimension and subdivisions according to nations and historic lands, i.e., a federal dimension. The milestones on this road were thus of different types. Among them can be counted such different phenomena as, first, the informal concession of expanded territorial autonomy, granted to Polish-ruled Galicia in 1868 and withheld three years later for a planned Czech-ruled Bohemia. Second, the expansion of a popular franchise in the central parliament in Vienna, begun in a series of reforms in the 1860s and continued in 1873, 1882, and 1896 until finally a general male franchise was reached in 1907 (which was the end station for this development in Imperial Austria). And third, parallel to the latter development, a move toward parliamentarization of the Imperial Austrian government could be discerned. It was begun with the so-called Bürgerministerium under Karl Auersperg in 1868–69, continued most notably with the coalition government under Alfred Windischgrätz in 1893–95 and reached its apogee in Imperial Austria in the overtly parliamentarian government of the first democratic Austrian parliament under Max Vladimir von Beck in 1907–08. Fourth, there was also a tendency toward institutionalized national autonomy, realized in Moravia (1905), Bukovina (1910), and projected both for Bosnia-Hercegovina and Galicia shortly before the outbreak of war in 1914.[56]

Within this general but hesitant move toward democracy and political autonomy, political movements and parties acted within and were shaped by the existing institutions. The examples that came closest to being Austrian people's parties were the two mass parties of Social Democracy and Christian Socialism, which grew strong in the 1880s and received their breakthrough in the 1890s and finally in the democratically elected parliament of 1907. Both these parties would, however, be strongly affected by the national and territorial divisions of Austria. In the end, Christian Socialism failed to become a Reichspartei and remained a democratic-conservative party for the German-speaking core lands of Austria. The success story of multinational Social Democracy, which culminated in the united party congress in Brünn (Brno) in 1899, where a program for national-democratic autonomy was proclaimed, ended in the federalization of the party into national subparties after 1907 and in the complete secession of the Czech Social Democrats in 1911.[57] An important part of the progressive political forces in Austria were, of course, from the very beginning channeled into national forms in different types of National-Liberal and national-democratic parties.[58] The German and Czech party spectrums were also internally strongly fragmented.[59]

As John W. Boyer has pointed out, this fragmentation meant that the move toward popular sovereignty in Austria was rather weak, and especially so when it came up against the well-entrenched Josephist bureaucracy.[60] In fact, the latter can be seen as a political force of change in its own right, as could be seen in the bureaucratic modernization project of Minister President Ernest von Koerber.[61] Any political project for the democratization of the imperial Austrian state thus found itself partly dependent on cooperation or passive consent from within the imperial regime itself. Karl Renner's close adaptation of his political project to the existing Austrian state, in combination with the general support for this project as expressed in the Social Democratic party congress of Brünn in 1899, made his program into a very real contestant in the confused political struggles of the last decades of Austria-Hungary.[62] Although not an active party member in 1899, Renner had to some degree influenced the Brünn-program from behind the scenes, and he continued to claim legitimacy for his own project by referring to this program in his campaigns until 1918, even though this party program was already obsolete in the nationally fragmented Austrian Social Democracy after around 1907.[63] As will be examined below, Renner also acted with determination to further his project by exploiting political conjunctures, such as Koerber's reform project in 1900–1904, the Hungarian crisis in 1903–06, the establishment of the new people's parliament of Austria in 1907, when Renner was elected and began his active political career, and, not least among them, the upheavals of the war in 1914–18. Karl Renner's political career until 1918 can thus be seen as a very skillful balancing act between the modernizing force of the Social Democratic mass party and the unifying force of the imperial Austrian bureaucracy. Viewed in this light, Karl Renner's early political career gives a new depth to the old cliché of the "imperial Social Democracy," the k.k. Sozialdemokratie.

In comparison, Josef Redlich's political project seems much more tenuous and centered around his own person. Redlich was elected to parliament in 1907 on the platform of the German Progressive party (Deutsche Fortschrittspartei), which was only one of several parties in the fragmented German-Liberal party spectrum in Austria.[64] Moreover, Redlich fairly immediately transcended the trappings of this party and became a sort of one-man political force in Austrian political life,[65] propagating his own liberal-democratic reform program with great determination in the Austrian parliament and elsewhere. Perhaps it was this relative isolation that drove Redlich to seek support for his political project from within the imperial regime. Moreover, he would arguably succeed in creating the ideal vessel for his projected reform of the Austrian imperial state through the realization of his own initiative of an imperial commission for administrative reform in 1911; a reform instrument that was created as being independent of both parliament and government.

In Redlich's and Renner's political projects we can generally identify a strong reliance on the structures of the Rechtsstaat. Moreover, in important regards they both merely attempted to modernize the old Josephist Rechtsstaat. And in the course of their respective projects, they demonstrated the tendency toward "bureaucratic politics" that has been observed in the previous studies of this book.

Redlich and the Allure of Empire

Redlich's engagement in Austrian politics can be traced back to the second half of the 1890s.[66] However, his direct political engagement actually commenced only around 1905.[67] It seems probable that the timing was influenced by the winds of change that were blowing in Austria in 1905 and the following years. The Russian revolution of that year markedly affected also the Austrian political scene, where the Social Democrats took the opportunity to show strength in their impressive demonstration on the Ringstrasse. This demonstration was accompanied by demands for universal suffrage, which led on to the reform of the Austrian election system of 1906–07. The Austro-Hungarian Empire was also shaken by an internal conflict in the years 1903–06, rooted in a constitutional crisis in Hungary that seemed to herald change also in the political system of the Dual Monarchy. Also in 1905, a drawn-out process was concluded to find an institutional national-political compromise between the Czech and the German parties in Redlich's home province, Moravia. So-called the Mährische Ausgleich, the solution based the provincial election system on the two national groups of the land and was a solution of national autonomy, in part inspired by the early political writings of Karl Renner. The recognition of the possibility for change carried by these developments might very well have propelled Redlich into parliamentary politics.

Redlich would develop his political engagement fully only after being elected in 1907 to the Austrian Volkshaus (people's house), as he jubilantly referred to the reformed Austrian parliament. The importance of Redlich's preoccupation with the need for reform of the Austrian bureaucracy is evident because the very first issue he would address in the forum of the Austrian parliament was that of carrying the democratization of the Austrian state also into its Verwaltung. Redlich made his debut as a speaker in parliament on 27 June 1907, as did Karl Renner, also a newly elected parliamentarian, for the Social Democratic party. Renner made a celebrated and noted speech demanding the continuation of democratic reforms also in the Austrian provinces, where the provincial parliaments (the Landtage) still retained the old interest-group election system. Renner also demanded a thought-through democratic reform of the Austrian administration, which should especially aim at solving the national problem through the introduction of nationally self-governing Kreis, a principle Renner was now publicly identified with.[68] Redlich expressed his basic agreement with "my old friend Dr. Renner" before embarking on what turned out to be the first of his many speeches on the question of the need for a thorough administrative reform in Austria. In his speech, Redlich emphasized the importance of the newly implemented democratic electoral reform, which he described as also necessitating a following administrative reform to thoroughly democratize the fabric of the Austrian state. He focused less on the national problem as such and more directly on the problem of the Austrian state. This problem he described as that of an outdated, oversized, and overstaffed and thus very expensive state administration that was completely out of touch with the population on the one hand, and an underfinanced, overburdened, autonomous administration that, for all practical purposes, managed the whole of the growing modern public sector on the other. Redlich deplored this dual administrative system, which he wanted simplified by shrinking and pulling back the centralized state administration to a supervisory function and expanding and reinforcing especially the local self-government.[69]

The new government formed in the summer of 1907 by Max Vladimir von Beck, who was also the architect behind the democratic electoral reform, was the first major attempt at a parliamentarian government in Austria. In conjunction with the electoral reform, this parliamentary Austrian government looked rather revolutionary and carried the promise of new directions in the political life of Austria.[70] Despite his doubts about the stability and aims of the Beck government, Redlich judged the constellation of a democratically elected parliament and a multinational parliamentarian government very promising. In his speech on 10 June 1908, he especially emphasized that a parliamentary government could become the instrument with which the Austrian peoples could cooperate on a democratic reform of the Austrian bureaucracy and thus in the end could truly govern the Austrian state together.[71] The radical vision of Austria as a democratic union of peoples would remain as a fundamental pattern supporting Redlich's political engagement all the way up to 1918.

Despite his political adherence to German-Austrian Liberalism, whose purest expression at this time was, arguably, Redlich's own party, the German Progressive party, Redlich wrestled with the problem of German dominance in the multinational state. Early in his political career, he succinctly delineated his basic view of the problematic relationship between the German-Austrians and the imperial Austrian state:

> The problem is actually that the role of the Germans in Austria . . . needs to be completely redefined; they must be freed from the purpose they have served since the Counter Reformation, the role of a military and bureaucratic master over the other peoples.[72]

Redlich would, indeed, stay clear of German nationalism in his political thinking and actions in the question of the regeneration of the imperial Austrian state. However, he did not shy back from enlisting support for his reform plans within the imperial regime itself. His relationship, beginning in 1909, to the retired older statesman and Austrian minister president in waiting, Ernest von Koerber, was of this type. Redlich's initiative to an imperial commission for administrative reform, which was realized in close cooperation with the Austrian government under the minister presidency of Richard von Bienerth (1908–11), is another example that will be returned to below. However, the arguably most important of these relationships was that to Foreign Minister Alois Lexa von Aehrenthal, which developed during the Bosnian annexation crisis of 1908–09.

Redlich supported Aehrenthal's policies openly during the crisis itself, and after it he remained a sort of confidante of the foreign minister; in this regard he might be said to have followed in the footsteps of Heinrich Friedjung. Redlich took upon himself minor political missions of an informal character for the foreign minister, something with which he would continue also under Aehrenthal's successor Leopold von Berchtold. He fed Aehrenthal with political analyses and programs of his own, apparently hoping that the foreign minister would function as an instrument in the regeneration of the empire and of Austria. Redlich presented perhaps the most noted of all his many parliamentary speeches in October 1908, only a few weeks after the Austro-Hungarian annexation of Bosnia-Hercegovina, at the forum of the Austrian parliamentary delegation, which convened in Budapest. In this speech he enthusiastically supported the annexation of Bosnia-Hercegovina; the gist of his argument was that Aehrenthal's deed demonstrated Austria-Hungary's will to live and to shape its own destiny.[73] In the wake of the annexation, Redlich repeatedly emphasized its importance for restoring the international status of Austria-Hungary.[74]

During the following months he stayed in close touch with Aehrenthal and also discussed developments with Heinrich Friedjung, who was soon engaged in a press campaign in preparation of the expected war against Serbia. Redlich rejoiced over these prospects, seemingly outstripping even Friedjung in his eagerness for war.[75] At the end of March, shortly before the whole crisis subsided, Redlich even approached Aehrenthal for permission to follow the development of the war from the Austro-Hungarian army headquarters, "because I want to see the war and write about it," as he explained. Aehrenthal agreed to send him there as a special diplomatic representative. Now Redlich wrote in his diary, "only the war is missing!" Regrettably, a few days later Redlich was forced to register the peaceful resolution of the crisis in his diary: "Yesterday peace finally 'broke out.' Great rejoicing in Vienna. I am not so thrilled."[76]

In the years following the Bosnian crisis, Redlich cultivated his relationship to Foreign Minister Aehrenthal, and through this relationship his political focus was also shifted from domestic Austrian politics in the direction of foreign policy and the affairs of the empire as a whole. The Hungarian question was perhaps the most central element in Redlich's political activities in this period. One of the first major political questions Redlich had to address as a parliamentarian was the new Ausgleich treaty of 1907 between Hungary and Austria. This treaty was negotiated very successfully by Austrian Minister President Beck when it came to purely economic questions, but it also brought certain constitutional changes that were regarded by many in Austria as weakening the common institutions and thus the political identity of the empire as a whole. Foreign Minister Aehrenthal belonged to these latter, and he had also a history of fighting previous changes in the constitutional relationship between Austria and Hungary;[77] this now, in 1907–08, made him take a stand on the question of the unity of the empire. During 1907, in conjunction with the Ausgleich negotiations, there took place an intense political struggle between the common foreign minister, Aehrenthal, on the one hand, and the Austrian and Hungarian minister presidents, Beck and Wékerle, on the other. Aehrenthal's objective here was to reinforce the common institutions and to tie in the two governments closer to the "common government," thus ensuring a stronger unity in the political system of the empire as a whole. But the constitutional "reform" of 1908 hardly brought with it the unified imperial state Aehrenthal had been advocating throughout his diplomatic career. Except for the constitutional recognition of the term "the common government" (Gemeinsame Regierung), this amendment (or clarification) of the Ausgleich laws of 1867 rather went in the direction of weakening the international political identity of the empire, primarily through the acceptance of the principle that the two "states" (as they were now called) of the empire would now appear also in international treaties as separate signatory powers, which was the key principle in the reform as such.[78]

In the fall of 1907, Redlich was one of the relatively few in the Austrian parliament who mainly discussed the Ausgleich not as an economic question, but in the above constitutional terms, and he did so in direct opposition to Minister President Beck's interpretation of it. In his speech in October, Redlich emphasized, in a way similar to Aehrenthal, that the new Ausgleich treaty dissolved "the unity of Austria in terms of international law." Redlich deplored this constitutional process of dissolution, which now pointed irrevocably in the direction of creating an independent Hungarian state. Significantly, he also presented in his speech the whole development represented by the Hungarian strivings, including the deplorable internal policies of the Magyar regime against the nationalities of Hungary, as destructive both for the empire and for Austria as well as for progress in general. To reverse this process Redlich therefore emphasized the need for the Austrian peoples to rally around "the great and indestructible Austrian state idea."[79]

In his following speech, in December 1907, Redlich developed his argument in a way that makes it recognizable as a call for a struggle of the newly democratized Austrian union of peoples against the reactionary Hungarian regime. Redlich asserted that the only way to ensure a harmonious, progressive development of the empire was to break the reactionary Hungarian regime.[80] Taken together, these two aspects of Redlich's argument, his emphasis on the need to restore the unity of the empire and his insistence that the multinational democratic development he saw as represented by Austria should be an ideal for the whole of the empire, function as a program for the development of the whole of the empire into a democratic union of peoples. Redlich's support of Aehrenthal's policies was therefore, in a general way, already grounded before the latter's aggressive, authoritarian annexation of Bosnia-Hercegovina, and, as peculiar as it may sound, it was grounded in a political program of multinational democracy.

During 1909 Redlich tried to use his newly won influence with Aehrenthal to make the foreign minister adopt his own plans with regard to Hungary. In March 1909, Redlich became acquainted with Joszef Kristóffy, who had been Hungarian interior minister in the Féjérváry government of 1905–06, a strictly monarchic, unparlamentarian government appointed by Franz Joseph with the mission to end the Hungarian constitutional crisis. Kristóffy's solution (never implemented) had been to introduce universal suffrage into the oligarchically ruled Hungarian state, a measure that would first have smashed the power base of the Magyar elite and second politically enfranchised the oppressed non-Magyar Hungarian nationalities. When he met him, Redlich was impressed with Kristóffy, whom he called "the first Magyar I have met who fully understands and defends the Reichsidee."[81] In the summer and fall of 1909, Kristóffy activated himself in a renewed attempt to bring about an electoral reform in Hungary. In the beginning of June, Kristóffy sent the leading Slovak opposition politician in Hungary, Milan Hodža, to see Redlich in Vienna. From Hodža, Redlich received much of the information on which he based the Hungarian memorandum he sent over to Aehrenthal a few weeks later.[82] In this memorandum, Redlich focuses on the distinct possibility in 1909 of building a new regime in Hungary, which could result in "a regeneration of the idea of imperial unity on a democratic basis."[83] There is, of course, more than a little liberal-democratic crusader mentality in the care Redlich bestowed on the internal political development of Hungary. His vision also resonates strongly with the older German-Austrian imperial mentality and with Liberal Josephism, building on the notion that Austria should be a modern unitary empire ruled from Vienna. Redlich's nurturing of hopes that "an Austro-Hungarian Bismarck" should realize this democratic union of peoples[84] only amplifies the imperialist strain in his politics during these years.

His relationship to Aehrenthal belongs to the more difficult problems of his biography. During the years 1908–12, Redlich developed a remarkably close relationship with Aehrenthal, visiting the foreign minister regularly in his office at the Ballhausplatz and even functioning as an informal adviser. They discussed domestic as well as foreign policies. These discussions, as they are recounted in Redlich's diary, relay the impression that Redlich in his political persuasions in these years veered sharply in Aehrenthal's direction.[85] Toward the end of this "political schooling," Redlich habitually speaks of the misery of Austrian parliamentarism and the need for decisive action from above to solve the unbearable situation in Austria. In April 1911, Redlich seems fully taught as *he* approaches Aehrenthal with the suggestion to solve the internal deadlock in Austria through a coup d'état.[86]

When Aehrenthal died prematurely in February 1912, Redlich confirmed in his diary the important role this Austrian statesman played for his personal political project as a whole. In what amounts to a private obituary on Aehrenthal, Redlich supplies us with a historical perspective on his own relationship with the foreign minister. Redlich had, apparently, been expecting Aehrenthal to function as a bridge between the old obrigkeitliche Austria and his own new Austria, the democratic union of peoples.[87] A historical analogy springs to mind here, one that would have made excellent sense to Redlich, though he would probably have found it disturbing. It almost seems like Redlich was hoping that Aehrenthal's basically outdated authoritarianism would make up for lost time in the creation of a modern unitary Austria in much the same way that Liberals like Alexander Bach and Franz Stadion in 1849 saw Felix Schwarzenberg's strong-willed authoritarian politics as an instrument to force Imperial Austria into a "modern" unitary shape. In fact, Redlich's growing appreciation during this same time of Ernest von Koerber, carrier of a liberal-bureaucratic program for the modernization of the unitary imperial Austrian state, also fits the pattern established with Aehrenthal.

After his first meeting with Koerber in November 1909, Redlich wrote this in his diary: "We spoke about Koerber's administrative reform plans, and I notice that I today accept many things in these plans, which I rejected at the time."[88] In fact, Redlich's relationship with Koerber became a substitute for that with Aehrenthal, insofar as Redlich nurtured hopes for a minister's post after Aehrenthal's death in 1912 in an expected renewed Austrian reform government under Koerber. Redlich also did his utmost to further such a development by keeping in close touch with Koerber and by trying to influence key decision makers to support Koerber's cause.[89] There were many points on which Redlich was in basic agreement with Koerber, but in questions on the internal reform of the Austrian state, Koerber and Redlich had before 1909 more or less represented diametrically different views about the political road to be taken. Also in the domestic politics of Austria, therefore, a marked increase in Redlich's emphasis on the unity of Austria occurs during these years. Redlich hoped Koerber would form "a powerful, able, and strong-handed government"[90] that could effectuate a decisive program for the modernization of Austria.

All in all, Redlich's activities during these years and the ideas he developed on imperial reform have strong echoes of the ideas of the 1850s; the ghost of Alexander Bach seems to hover over these liberal hopes for an authoritarian solution to the problem of unity and diversity in the multinational imperial Austrian state. Appropriately, Redlich at this time received the opportunity to work out a large-scale state reform from a position within the imperial regime. His cooperation in 1910 with Minister President Richard von Bienerth on the realization of his own idea of an imperial commission for administrative reform at last paved the way for Redlich himself to play an independent role in the political arena of Austria. When appointed in the summer of 1911, this imperial commission was given a nominally independent position as a commission appointed by and directly responsible to Emperor Franz Joseph himself; in effect, it was a type of position above both government and parliament that must have been exactly what Redlich wanted.

Renner and the Reassertion of Empire

Karl Renner's political career proper also began in 1907, when he was elected to the new democratic Austrian parliament. However, unlike Redlich, Renner had been active as a political writer for nearly ten years before this time, partaking in the events of these years from the sideline, so to speak. In retrospection, Renner would point out the Badeni conflict of 1897 as the decisive event for his entry into politics. He described how he had from his workplace in the library of the parliament, located right below the plenary hall, been an "ear witness" to the violent events of 1897, at the height of which members of parliament were involved in fistfights and demolished the furniture of the plenary hall, finally being forcefully removed by police officers.[91] Renner's first political writings were published under a pseudonym in the following years. His first full statement of his solution to the Austrian problem was *Staat und Nation* (1899). At this time his argument already had the basic shape it would retain until 1918.

In his memoirs, Renner described how he first came into contact with multinational Austria during his military service in 1889–90. His unit was based in Vienna, but it was staffed by recruits from throughout the imperial realm. Here Renner could directly experience multinational Austria without leaving Vienna, and it seems that this was a formative experience for him. He especially recalled his arguments with a Hungarian fellow recruit, who, to Renner's great astonishment, could see no need for the unity of imperial multinational Austria. During their discussions on the history and contemporary problems of the empire, this Hungarian recruit viewed the empire as an arbitrary conglomerate of acquisitions by the imperial family of the Habsburgs, with no inner cohesion of its own. As Renner wrote, "it is understandable that I was very upset by this argument, and I thought about it for a long time." Renner could simply not fathom the notion of "the dissolution of the whole imperial state . . . .whose existence I had until that time regarded as quite natural." From this time, Renner recounts, he decided to study politics and to begin with the primary question, "the problem of empire and its nations."[92] The almost naive certainty about the necessity and identity of multinational Austria Renner here recounts seems to capture well that stability in his convictions, which propelled his political project all the way up to 1918 (and in certain regards beyond).[93]

This youth experience of Renner's was markedly Vienna centered, and this is also a clear tendency in his political writings, from early on up to the last months of the empire. Although he would always criticize its democratic deficit, Renner quite clearly saw Alexander Bach's project of the 1850s of a unitary empire as an example for his own vision of a unitary, albeit democratic multination state (the federal structure in Renner's proposal was quite evidently subordinated to the unitary state structure).[94] There seems to have been something in the linear, rationalist quality of the Bach system that strongly attracted Renner, and that left clear traces in his blueprint for a new Austria. Another dimension in Renner's political writings, which is reflected in his childhood memories of nationally mixed Moravia, is the strong German dimension. The idea of the Austrian empire as a German mission appears very prominently in his earliest political writings and can be traced through the middle period,[95] after which it receives new prominence in Renner's German orientation during the war years, the results of which can especially be seen in his last weighty word on the matter of the federal multination state, *Das Selbstbestimmungsrecht der*

Nationen (1918). In the latter context, Renner's solution to the Austrian problem is explicitly described as an instrument to extend the historical German mission in Southeastern Europe into the modern age.[96]

Especially interesting here is the way Renner's own youth in the territorially fragmented, but nevertheless (at least in Renner's eyes) nationally clearly demarcated German and Czech communities in Moravia,[97] seems to have informed his vision of small nationally homogeneous territorial entities (Kreis), which are spread out geographically and interspersed with other national groups, but tied together in politically constituted, self-governing national communities. It seems that this is exactly the perception of the Moravian model and its implications for the spread-out German groups of Central Europe, projected onto the canvas of the whole empire (and in its extension on Europe), that informs Renner's political project, something that becomes clear when in 1918 he describes the Nationalitätenbundesstaat as an instrument for German unity and for the German mission in Europe:

> The consistently implemented multination state would bring the Germans of Austria much closer to the ideal of national unity than any form of the nation-state ever could. . . . Just because we are under pressure, I can see no reason for us [Austrian] Germans to abandon our historically entrusted role for the whole German cause in Europe.[98]

This clear tendency in Renner's early political writing and activities should also make his more evidently Great-German cast of mind after 1918 seem less surprising than it is normally regarded.

In its basic outline Renner's model could be described as the last descendant of the Josephist Enlightenment project of a unitary, modern, and, in an inclusive way, culturally German empire in Central Europe. Renner's project can be described as assimilating the twin tendencies of modernization into this model, the democratization and the nationalization of society. His view of the Austrian democratic federal multination state was always informed by a clear perception of the need for a true national autonomy of equality in this regard between the Germans and the other nations of Austria. However, we should also note that the final goal of Renner's model seems to have been to *neutralize* nationality as a political factor and thus, in effect, to extend the traditional supranational character of the imperial Austrian state into the age of democracy and the nation-state. Just like the historical Austrian imperial state, this modern supranational state would, of course, indirectly come to serve its socioeconomically and culturally strongest group, the German-Austrians.

Renner's German tendency would appear to be strongest during his involvement with Friedrich Naumann on the question of Mitteleuropa during the world war, and it would become dominant after 1918. But the more fundamental imperial stamp on his political thinking and actions, the Josephist inheritance as it were, came out quite unequivocally in his engagement in the political crises during the early years of the new century. Renner's early formulations of his reform vision practically calls out for a Josephist minister president such as Ernest von Koerber,[99] and it is therefore not very surprising that Renner in the following years would engage himself in the liberal-bureaucratic reform project of this Austrian statesman. This engagement has left its mark both on his early political journalism and on lectures and weightier political texts that he published in the first years after the turn of the century.[100] For a short time Renner even functioned as an informal adviser to Minister President Koerber on the question of an Austrian electoral reform, a question that was at the center of Koerber's constitutional reform plans at this time.[101] Renner also argued the case for such a reform in a lecture in 1903, where he seemingly effortlessly joined his dual allegiances with Social Democracy and the Austrian bureaucracy to win also the liberal Bürgertum for such a reform.[102]

Renner's most direct attempt to fuse the liberal bureaucratism of Koerber with his own Social Democratic persuasions had been undertaken in the political tract of a couple of years earlier, *Staat und Parlament* (1901). Superficially, this text is a fundamental criticism of the old Austrian election system of interest representation and an argument for general franchise, an eminently Social Democratic issue of these years. But the way this case is argued, by focusing on the "state-supporting" effect of such a reform,[103] also seems to make it an eminently liberal-bureaucratic issue of, for example, the contemporary Koerber government. Very near the time *Staat und Parlament* must have been written, Koerber had indeed been arguing in a very similar way for the value of a general male franchise in a memorandum to Emperor Franz Joseph, i.e., that a general franchise was no threat against the state, it would only serve to strengthen the state by breaking up those particularistic interests (for instance the nationalist parties) that *were* threatening to break up the state. In this memorandum, Koerber also argued very eloquently for the Social Democratic party as a state-supporting political force in such a multinational state as Austria.[104]

In *Staat und Parlament,* Renner thus goes a long way to approach Koerber's position. His argument goes further than Koerber's when it comes to the democratization of the imperial Austrian state, but it simultaneously goes out of its way to formulate the need for such democratization by its positive effect for this state. Renner argued that "the objective of the state is to turn diversity into unity," and this would be furthered by a democratic electoral reform. The democratic parliament, Renner emphasized, would represent the Austrian people, rather than different interest groups within it, and such a representation would be an ideal generator of "the will of the whole" ("der Gesamtwille"). Renner spelled it out: "The state itself needs the parliament as the organ of its unity." The whole text relays a message that should be somewhat controversial in Austrian Social Democratic circles, though not in the Austrian high bureaucracy. Renner himself did not beat about the bush, because he maintained that such a reform as he was suggesting would ensure "that state and people are and remain one."[105] Renner's conclusion is practically identical with the conclusion in Minister President Koerber's contemporary memorandum to the emperor on the question of constitutional reform. Here Koerber maintained that his proposed remolding of the Austrian parliament through an electoral reform would ensure that "the unity of the state is expressed more clearly and effectively in the new Lower house of parliament than it has ever been before."[106]

Looking back a few years later, Renner would describe the Koerber government very appreciatively as a truly modernizing project for the imperial Austrian state. But this did not hinder him from expressing sharp criticism against Koerber's failure to actually bring about an electoral reform, something that to Renner's satisfaction had been realized in the intervening time.[107] At an early stage, Renner also expressed disappointment over the basic bureaucratic thrust of Koerber's otherwise promising attempts at administrative reform, delivering a criticism of its democratic deficit that he would uphold until 1918.[108] However, Koerber played an important role for Renner in the Hungarian crisis, where Renner described Koerber's conflict with Tisza in the fall of 1903 as heralding the renewal of the struggle for imperial unity.[109] Renner's perception of Koerber as the upholder of imperial unity under the threat of Hungarian separatism only serves to complete Renner's picture of him as a contemporary carrier of the Bach inheritance.

The ghost of Alexander Bach hovers over the two main political texts Renner wrote during his intense engagement in the Hungarian crisis during the years 1903–06, *Die Krise des Dualismus* (1904) and *Grundlagen und Entwicklungsziele der Österreichisch-Ungarischen Monarchie* (1906). They are suffused by Renner's high expectations that the constitutional struggles in these years between Austria and Hungary, and especially between the emperor and the Hungarian elite, would lead to the breakdown of the Hungarian aristocratic regime and of the dualistic system as such. Renner's restatement in 1906 of his reform proposal from 1902 (in *Der Kampf der österreichischen Nationen um den Staat*) reflects these expectations. This is especially evident because Renner's reform proposal for a democratic Nationalitätenbundesstaat that was originally devised for only Austria was now extended to the empire as a whole.

There is a strong tension in these texts between Renner's rejoicing over the strong-handed actions of the imperial regime against Hungary and his equally strong expectations that these events will generate the creation of a unified democratic empire. The latter expectations arose because an Austrian electoral reform had already been decided, though not yet carried out, while Renner was writing in the spring of 1906, and because the imperially appointed unparliamentarian Féjérváry government in Hungary of 1905–06 was planning to democratize the Hungarian electoral system, a reform that in practical terms would have brought national autonomy also to the non-Magyar minorities of Hungary. Renner's historical discussion here of the regeneration of the imperial idea is carried by a strong pathos propelled by an almost millenarian view of the approaching electoral reform in Austria. Renner describes this reform as "a true revolution" and links it directly to the violent dispersal of the Hungarian parliament by the Féjérváry regime, which together signals the approaching reestablishment of the imperial unity lost with the fall of Alexander Bach in 1859.[110] At this point Renner even attempts to rehabilitate Bach, describing Bach's purely bureaucratic and authoritarian, rationally linear, and empirewide Kreisadministration as an ideal solution if it had only also been democratized. Renner rounds off with a lament that Bach's unitary administration was withdrawn in 1859 before the imperial regime had ensured the integration of Hungary into the empire.[111] Especially disturbing for a Hungarian reader would have been Renner's repeated references at this time to the need for a second Vilagos,[112] the place of the surrender of the revolutionary Hungarian army in 1849, an event that signaled the beginning of the authoritarian Bach system in Hungary.

Taken together, these early political writings of Renner's contain several basic elements that create a pattern of a special civilizing and modernizing mission of the imperial Austrian state in Central Europe. This pattern contained a mixture of democratic and imperialist ideas and reappeared in amplified form during World War I.

3. The Administrative Reform Commission (1911–1914)

On 27 November 1909, only a few weeks after his first meeting with Koerber, Redlich was invited to dinner by the interior minister in the Bienerth government, Guido von Haerdtl. His message to Redlich was clear and simple, as the latter recounts in his diary: "He explained to me that he—should he remain interior minister—will realize my idea of an imperial commission for administrative reform and asks me to partake in its work."[113] Redlich's profile as a Liberal reform politician in the field of administrative reform had been established firmly in his very first speech in parliament in June 1907. Two years later, in June 1909, he crowned his parliamentary campaign for administrative reform by formally petitioning the government for the appointment of an "extraordinary commission" that should prepare a complete reform of the Austrian internal administration.[114] It was this idea that Haerdtl now picked up and placed firmly on the agenda of the Austrian government. In May 1910, Redlich was invited by Minister President Richard von Bienerth to present his ideas on administrative reform more comprehensively in a memorandum, which alongside a memorandum by Interior Minister Haerdtl would supply the basic ideas on the organization and program of the planned commission. Bienerth also sent Redlich on an official mission to Berlin, where he studied the work on the current Prussian government commission on administrative reform and then reported about this directly to the Austrian minister president.[115] At the end of 1910, this matter was treated in the Austrian Council of Ministers, and during the following months the plans for the Imperial Commission for Administrative Reform were finalized. The emperor sanctioned them on 22 May 1911.[116]

A few days earlier, after returning from election campaigning in his constituency in Moravia for the general elections of 1911, Redlich received the invitation to become a member of the new commission: "That is my greatest political success!" Redlich noted in his diary.[117] He was reelected to the Austrian parliament in the beginning of June 1911, but during the following years he definitely refocused his activities in the work on the administrative reform commission.[118] Upon the appointment, the prospects were also good that this new imperial commission would receive such a position and that it would be able to make a real difference in the affairs of the Austrian state. First, it was an *imperial* commission, appointed by and directly responsible to Emperor Franz Joseph himself. Redlich always liked to call it "the first Royal Commission in Austria," viewing it as an Austrian pendant to the English system of royal commissions. This ideal also signaled the expectations Redlich had of the commission, viewing it as the first step in "a complete reform of the [Austrian] state."[119] This ambition is, in fact, also clearly written out in its founding documents, where the independence of the commission and its role as an initiator of a fundamental administrative reform is emphasized.[120] The statute regulation, which organizationally placed the commission under the bureau of the Austrian minister president (Ministerratspräsidium), also initially seemed to be more of a strength than a weakness, since the Bienerth government was indeed the initiator of the commission and could be expected to support its reform action substantially. And the resignation of the foremost advocate of the commission within the government, Interior Minister Haerdtl, a forced resignation in the midst of the preparatory work in January 1911 in the face of the growing political difficulties of the Bienerth government, was not wholly negative. He would now instead fill an important role within the commission itself. Indeed, Redlich immediately identified Haerdtl as an important ally in the commission,[121] and the two of them together actually became the motor of the whole administrative reform action in the following years. Redlich would have more trouble with the chairman of the commission, Erwin von Schwartzenau, but there was also a clear mutual appreciation between the two of them. In June 1911 Redlich seems rather to have underestimated Schwartzenau and, in any event, had a long meeting with him two days before the inauguration of the commission, during which they established "our agreement as to most questions."[122] It is with these glimmering prospects in mind that we should judge Redlich's renewed optimism in the summer of 1911.

In the weeks before the inauguration of the commission, with some determination Redlich noted in his diary that he would, most certainly "stabilize his influence" and take control of the commission.[123] This determination is also clearly reflected in his following actions. It was probably his minute preparations, and not least his meeting with the chairman, Schwartzenau, two days before the first plenary session of the commission, that first got Redlich elected to the subcommittee for drawing up the business order and working plan of the commission (Geschäftsordnungskomitee), and that second made him and Haerdtl be appointed by this subcommittee to do the actual work and to present it to the plenum of the commission.[124] The two of them therefore got off to a good start in their project of making the commission into an instrument of their vision of the reform of the Austrian Verwaltung. On 26 October, shortly after holding center stage in the negotiations of the second plenary session, Redlich also used the parliament as a platform to propagate the reform action of the commission, which he therefore became more and more publicly identified with. The parliamentary protocol containing Redlich's speech was soon out of print, and Redlich therefore had this parliamentary speech of his printed and sold as a booklet, which increased its circulation significantly.[125]

In the internal work of the commission, Redlich and Haerdtl initially took command. Their initiative is visible in many ways in the business order and working plan of the commission, which were accepted almost without amendments in the second plenary session on 16 October 1911. Especially, it was their doing that the instrument of enquêtes, i.e., making direct external inquiries among the population or specific groups therein, was incorporated into the business order. They also created the permanent committee (Ständiges Komitee), a sort of executive committee of the commission; it appeared only as optional in the statutes of the commission. Redlich then became a member of this committee. It was probably Haerdtl's influence that made the working plan distinguish between, on the one hand, the type of programmatic reform proposals of wider scope that Redlich was hoping to see realized and, on the other, the more immediate reforms of limited scope that could be implemented directly, preferably without involving legislative bodies.[126] Redlich lay behind the basic organization of the commission four subcommittees that should treat different fields of the reform and prepare concrete proposals that could then be brought together, discussed, and decided on in the plenum.[127] During the second plenary session, Redlich also saw to it that he became a member of the two most important of these subcommittees for the question of the reform of the administrative *organization* at large, subcommittees I and III. They dealt with the fundamental question of the reorganization of the whole of the internal administration (subcommittee I) and the question of the internal organization and business order of the administrative organs (subcommittee III). Redlich also became chairman of the latter subcommittee, a post that secured him membership in the permanent committee, the controlling organ of the commission. Moreover, he became a member of the commission's editorial committee, dealing with questions of publication and the spread of information about the commission. All in all, Redlich was the most ubiquitously represented member of all in the commission. Haerdtl also became a member of both the above-mentioned subcommittees.[128] With Redlich's support he would dominate the work especially of subcommittee I, where he became the motor in the work on delineating the basic reform of the administrative organization as such, laying down his vision of reform in three memoranda and a tireless defense of them in this subcommittee, as well as in several plenary sessions.

During their preparatory meeting in July 1911, Redlich and Haerdtl also agreed on the crucial need to secure permission for individual civil servants to approach the commission directly with critical observations on the administration and proposals for reforming it.[129] This latter instrument could not be anchored in the business order of the commission, however, since it conflicted with the statute that said the commission was organizationally tied to the bureau of the minister president and should also use this office as a channel for communication with the rest of the administration. Since the Bienerth government fell shortly after the inauguration of the commission, in the beginning of July 1911 this question became more acute, and therefore, arguably, Redlich and Haerdtl presented this ambition more aggressively in the working plan as a dual strategy of conducting external interview enquêtes in the wider circles of the population and sending out written questionnaires within the administration. In the latter case, the working plan also proposed that the prerogatives of the commission to freely communicate with individual civil servants should be expanded.[130]

In his presentation of the proposed working plan in the second plenary session in October, Redlich was very clear about the need for the commission to be able to act independently, to freely collect information from any quarter deemed necessary to successfully fulfill its mission. After encountering only slight resistance, Redlich made a full assault on the crucial question of the prerogatives of the commission to conduct its investigations also within the bureaucracy, demanding (more or less) that the statute about the censoring role of the bureau of the minister president should be amended. No majority could be assembled for such a far-reaching demand as the one Redlich had made, but he stubbornly maintained his position and demanded that this question of principles should receive high priority and also be presented to the minister president as a demand by the commission as a whole. The chairman, Schwartzenau, simply turned down Redlich's demand and said that he would discuss the matter with the minister president himself.[131] As newly appointed minister president, Karl Stürgkh appeared at the beginning of the third plenary session of the commission on 7 December 1911. Before leaving this session, which, when he did, was in something resembling a state of shock, he had announced that any civil servant wanting to approach the commission must first apply to his immediate superior for permission, who should also be allowed to censor the content of whatever the civil servant in question wanted to communicate to the commission. The debate that ensued in the commission would find wide agreement that this had now turned into "a question of life and death for the commission." Although some members, such as the permanent secretary, Anton Pace,[132] took the side of the minister president, arguing that a freedom such as that demanded by Redlich in the access to individual civil servants could, indeed, lead to the dissolution of discipline within the bureaucracy. The result of the debate was a decision that Schwartzenau should petition the minister president for a more open access for the commission in its dealings with the civil servants.[133]

These events turned out to be the beginning of a drawn-out conflict with the Stürgkh government, which would greatly impair the reform action of the commission. In January 1912, only weeks after this first point of conflict had openly emerged, the Stürgkh government again struck at the core of the commission by turning down the demand that the commission should be consulted in regard to all administrative reforms undertaken by the *government* during the time the commission worked out its own comprehensive reform proposal. This demand also originated in the second plenary session in October, where Redlich had engaged himself in this key question for maintaining the initiative of the commission in the planned reform action.[134] A month later it became exceedingly clear that Stürgkh was actively attempting to neutralize the commission because he declared that he would expand its membership. This time Schwartzenau sprung into action and argued that the appointment of so many new members this far into the work of the commission would seriously affect its continued work and also greatly impair its decision-making capabilities. As appointed by the Bienerth government, the commission had, arguably, been weighted in a centralist direction. The appointments made by Stürgkh were rather clearly weighted in favor of an "autonomist" or federalist direction. Three days after receiving Schwartzenau's strongly argued objections, Stürgkh simply made the new appointments public.[135]

On these questions the commission had little choice but to fold. However, on the question of the prerogatives of the commission to approach individual civil servants directly (and vice-versa), it continued to fight. The fourth plenary session on 30 March 1912 was dominated by Stürgkh's even more restrictive reply to the demands presented by the commission in December 1911.[136] This issue was also leaked and was exposed both in parliament and in the press later during 1912.[137] After the heated debate in the fourth plenary session, Schwartzenau made an emphatic attempt to turn Stürgkh around. In what amounts to an essay on the matter, Schwartzenau described the issue as crucial for the whole mission entrusted with the commission.[138] In the end, he and Stürgkh seemingly came to some sort of agreement, one that was mainly dictated by the minister president. In any event, when Interior Minister Heinold appeared at the fifth plenary session and declared himself ready to cooperate with the commission within certain bounds, Schwartzenau seems to have resigned in the question.[139] The whole affair retained an air of being unresolved, though, and festered on throughout the work of the commission, effectively curtailing its access to the bureaucracy. As expected, Redlich nearly exploded in the plenary session on 30 March when Schwartzenau read aloud Stürgkh's latest thoughts on the matter. Seconded by Haerdtl, Redlich attempted, but failed, to make the commission formulate a very sharp note in reply, in effect a declaration of war on the Stürgkh government. The matter was clinched by Schwartzenau's assurances that he stood in close contact with the minister president in this question. Instead, Redlich sulkily declared a sort of guerilla war on the government, asserting that he would most certainly see to it to get this access by other means.[140] Later, during the spring, Redlich even approached Interior Minister Heinold personally about this question, threatening to carry the conflict into the public arena if the government did not back down. At this time Redlich retained his confidence that the commission would ultimately get its way.[141]

However, it seems that Redlich and Haerdtl had drawn their conclusions at an early stage, because they soon redirected their efforts away from this bureaucratic minefield. Already on 5 March, the two of them had got a proposal for the appointment of a new subcommittee accepted in subcommittee I, and on 30 March it was accepted by the plenum. Immediately after this plenary session, the constitutive meeting was held by the new subcommittee for preparing and carrying out an enquête "in the concerned parts of the population" ("in den beteiligten Kreisen der Bevölkerung"), as the formulation reads. Redlich was promptly elected chairman, and the equally promptly elected Deputy Chairman Haerdtl swiftly presented a full draft of the questionnaire of the planned enquête.[142] As it seems from the protocols of the six meetings held by this subcommittee during the months of March through June 1912, the sheer momentum of Redlich's and Haerdtl's action swept all opposition aside. Only Schwartzenau made some trouble, coming into repeated conflict with Haerdtl, but Redlich was very successful in mediating between the two and keeping on top of things.[143] In the end, Redlich lifted the finalization of these plans and the drafting of the working plan of the enquête over into a small working group around himself, and then he and Haerdtl pressed them through the fifth plenary session on 28 June, where Haerdtl irritably discarded all substantial proposals for change in the questionnaire with the argument that it was too late now to change its basic structure.[144]

It is quite clear from the proceedings of this new subcommittee that the strategy to let the commission get into direct contact with the population was a result of the conflict with the government, which had closed the other main route, foreseen by the working plan of the commission, of letting the reform action take shape in close rapport with the Beamtentum.[145] It should also be noted here that the direct contact with groups in the population was viewed by Redlich and Haerdtl as a means to another goal: to reassert the independence of the commission vis-à-vis the government.[146] Also, the way Redlich and Haerdtl redirected their efforts to this more promising field of activity seems to bear the stamp of an attempt to regain the initiative within the commission, an initiative that had effectively been subverted by Schwartzenau and Pace: the enquête also became a vehicle to regain the lost control of the reform action. The centralization of control over the enquête in the hands of Redlich and Haerdtl was sustained from the preparatory stages until its execution in October-November 1912, when Redlich and Haerdtl chaired three weeks of continuous hearings with a wide selection of individuals representing different spheres of society and different regions and nationalities of Austria.[147] During these hearings it also becomes rather clear to what degree their own vision of reform had affected the shape of the questionnaire, which, in turn, effectively steered and controlled the interviews and left a clear mark on the large documentation of "the wishes of the concerned parts of the population" about the reform of the Austrian internal administration. This was confirmed on the very first day of the enquête, when Redlich as chairman entered into an argument with the specially invited expert on administrative law, Karl Brockhausen. Brockhausen was intimating that there was a clear bias in the question currently addressed when Redlich abruptly cut him off and warded off this view. Brockhausen immediately replied, "I do not know who has authored these questions. In any event it is a very clever man, and I see a tendency behind each and every question."[148]

Supporting Brockhausen's criticism of the questionnaire lay a fundamental disagreement on the road to be taken in any administrative reform in Austria. The program Brockhausen detected in the structure of the questionnaire was Redlich's and Haerdtl's strongly decentralizing vision of reform, where the central ministries should mainly let go of their direct control of the lower levels of the administration and resort to a slimmed-down system of supervision. To Brockhausen this was a receipt for the dissolution of the "Staatswille" (the will of the state), which was directly dangerous in such a nationally heterogeneous and geographically disparate state as Austria.[149] In the first meeting of the enquête-subcommittee, Haerdtl had openly broached what he saw as a basic problem in the work of the commission, the fact that its membership was so clearly divided into two camps: those favoring an expansion of the sphere of self-government both at the level of provinces and municipalities (the autonomists), and those favoring its restriction and subordination to the state administration (the centralists).[150] However, despite their decentralizing tendencies, Redlich and Haerdtl must both be viewed as belonging to the centralist camp in such a binary scheme. Because Brockhausen attacked Redlich and Haerdtl from a centralist direction is therefore interesting. It signals that neither was a centralist of a traditional type; they rather moved in a gray zone between the above two positions.

As Haerdtl had already declared quite openly to Redlich during their planning meeting in July 1911, he had been severely marked by his experience in the bureaucracy. Haerdtl had been a leading participant in the administrative reform action under Koerber in the early years of the century, where he had been the civil servant entrusted with working out that strongly centralist reform plan that Koerber presented in December 1904, and its failure was certainly part of this experience. Haerdtl especially described the experience as interior minister in the Bienerth government as being so unproductive that he had come to despair over the capacity of the central bureaucracy in Vienna for self-reform. As he openly let Redlich know, he was deeply critical of the organization and the way of working of the ministries in Vienna and wanted particularly to use the commission to effectuate a drastic reform at the top of the administrative system.[151] The gist of the reform action, as argued by Haerdtl throughout the work of the commission and presented in his first three memoranda, was also the decentralization of the state administration. His view is first presented in the critical study on the costs of the central bureaucracy (1912), where Haerdtl outlined an internal self-reform with simple means that needed to begin at the top, by a drastic reform of the overstaffed and grossly inefficient central ministries in Vienna. The main problem here was that the old interventionist bureaucracy had not really changed with the massive expansion of its field of activity during the modernization of society. The central bureaucracy must simply let go of its outdated system of direct control of the whole of the administrative structure and decentralize most of its functions to the lower levels and to the autonomous organs.[152]

The sharp criticism Haerdtl directed at the central bureaucracy and his preference for an expansion of the municipal self-government made him end up on the side of the autonomists in surprisingly many questions debated by the commission. The wide-ranging understanding between Haerdtl and the leading exponent of the autonomist position in the commission, Bohemian aristocrat Count Adalbert Schönborn, was especially obvious.[153] In his later memoranda, especially those two of February 1914 presenting his comprehensive reform plan for the internal administration, Haerdtl's high evaluation of the Austrian system of self-government laid down in the Austrian Gemeinde is also presented in a positive way as a value in itself. With a reference to Redlich's work on *Das Wesen der österreichischen Kommunalverfassung* (1910), Haerdtl described the Gemeinde as the widely popular carrier of the modern development of Austria, which also embodied the special, nationally heterogeneous character of the Austrian state.[154] The basic outline of his reform presented here was that of creating a wide state-free sphere for the nationalities at the lower autonomous levels and pulling back the state administration from the direct contact with the population to a supervisory function. This arrangement of separating the state and the autonomous administrations, Haerdtl argued, could fulfill the dual function of satisfying national strivings and facilitate the maintenance of the

Austrian state administration as a supranational organization. It should also considerably lessen the political confrontation and thus also the friction between this state apparatus and the national-political parties.[155]

In this latter argument, it also becomes rather obvious that Haerdtl was, after all, a centralist. His centralism also emerges in the most persistent, though not so conspicuous strain in his reform proposal, which was the need to depoliticize the autonomous organs. His argument here is strongly bureaucratic in the way it departs from the view that the self-governing organs were, after all, a sort of state organs, and he ends up with such notions as the need to "stabilize" the elections and make the regime in the Gemeinden "more conservative." He also proposes to considerably strengthen the state supervision and regulation of the self-governing organs. These elements were still present as the last stronghold Haerdtl was defending in his fourth and final memorandum in the commission of June 1914, after the core of his reform plan had been defeated in the plenary sessions during the spring of 1914.[156] There is an almost tragic strain in Haerdtl's struggle and final defeat in the commission to effectuate a modern reform of the Austrian bureaucracy, because it is quite evident that the momentum for his attempt comes from his strong identification with the Austrian Verwaltung.[157] Haerdtl's unrestrained criticism of the inefficiency of the central ministries was, regrettably, not received well in these ministries, and the attempts of the commission to receive Minister President Stürgkh's permission to publish Haerdtl's reports were unsuccessful. As late as 1917, Haerdtl's reports were treated as highly classified material in the interior ministry.[158] However, the most immediate reason for his defeat was not his confrontation with the central bureaucracy, but, arguably, his confrontation with the autonomists within the commission on the question of transferring the weight of the entire internal administration, both its autonomous and state organs, to a new intermediary level, the Kreis, in the process depriving especially the autonomous provinces, the Länder, of most of their influence. Moreover, this element becoming the core of Haerdtl's reform proposal was mainly due to the influence of Redlich.

Indeed, it was Redlich who first raised the sensitive issue of a Kreis reform in the commission and who most consistently argued its case in the negotiations of the subcommittees and the plenum of the commission.[159] The question of such a reform was also prominently represented in the questionnaire to the enquête held in the fall of 1912, and its importance was reflected in the activity of the chairmen (Redlich and Haerdtl) during the hearings themselves.[160] However, Haerdtl remained skeptical about the wisdom of including such a radical proposal as the core of the reform and seems to have preferred a more conservative and practically realizable reform, but he did finally concede to including Redlich's Kreis idea rather prominently in his own comprehensive administrative reform proposal. In any event, Haerdtl had himself advanced proposals on a Kreis reform twice before in his career, under Koerber and Bienerth, and therefore it seems probable that in the end, he identified himself with the form his reform proposal in the commission finally received.[161]

Redlich's vision of reform was indeed close to that of Haerdtl's in its basic outlines. But it was both more radical in its democratic view of the role of the self-governing organs and, strangely enough, more centralist than that of Haerdtl's. Redlich argued his position throughout the negotiations of the commission, but he presented it most clearly in the heated arguments during the spring of 1914.[162] Here he argued for the need of "a true self-government," a pure local self-government by elected civil servants. He was neither very interested in the type of depoliticization of the Gemeinden that Haerdtl wanted; he was rather of the view that the democratic principle recommended leaving these self-governing organs as free as possible to conduct their own local governments. Redlich especially criticized the provincial autonomous organs, whose mixed bureaucratic-autonomous characters he found deeply damaging to the whole of the internal administration. Just as the state administration should pull back from local affairs, so also should the provincial "autonomous" level be devolved. Redlich's suggestion here went in the direction of separating the question of the legislative autonomy from the question of administrative autonomy, leaving the provinces (Länder) as a mainly legislative body and devolving the actual administration to a lower level. The result of this strong decentralization of the administration to the local level was, though, to open up for the type of criticism that Brockhausen had delivered about the weakening of the Staatswille. This position was also strongly represented in these debates by Schwartzenau, who was of course also its chairman. Redlich was relatively receptive to this criticism, though, since his aim was not to devolve the Austrian state into a federation of municipalities, but merely to modernize and democratize it. He therefore also pleaded for the need to realign the state and the autonomous organs, thus turning the popular representations at the lower levels into state-supporting organs; he even described them as integrated parts of the state administration.[163]

Redlich's answer to the problem of realigning the state with the autonomous sphere was the Kreis reform. The way Redlich saw this new intermediate level in the administration was that it should function as the key element of the whole modernized Austrian political system. Its basis should be an elected self-government organ, the Kreisvertretung, in which, together with the old self-governing Gemeinden, practically the whole of the administration proper should be carried out. Together with its organizationally separate counterpart, the Kreisregierung, a supervisory state organ, it should assume the role of the new center of gravity in that democratized, but still unitary, Austrian state Redlich was hoping to see realized through the work of the commission. Redlich's prominent use of the Kreis idea at this time signaled a basic similarity to Karl Renner's rather strongly centralistic-democratic program for Imperial Austria.

The essential centralism of Redlich's vision was made apparent in the debates of the spring of 1914, when he came into constant conflict over the Kreis question with autonomists in the commission, such as Adalbert Schönborn, František Fiedler, and Ladislaus Jaworski. In these discussions Redlich argued heatedly that the Kreis should be acceptable also for the autonomist position, ending up in a long argument on Bohemian history with Czech parliamentarian and former minister František Fiedler in which Redlich tried to persuade a skeptical Fiedler that the Kreis was a crucial ingredient in the history of the Czech people.[164] On the other hand, Schwartzenau attacked Redlich and Haerdtl from a traditional centralist direction. Schwartzenau expressed the need for "strong state organs" centered on the person of the Landeschef (i.e., the provincial governor) to uphold the state authority in the whole of Austria.[165] As expressed here, neither Redlich nor Haerdtl could agree with Schwartzenau. But the debate on Schwartzenau's own reform proposal, presented in the summer of 1913, had made it clear that Redlich could agree with Schwartzenau to a greater extent than Haerdtl could.

Schwartzenau's work in the commission was focused on the reform of the lower level of state administrative organs, the Bezirkshauptmannschaften. He presented his proposal as an attempt to re-create the traditional character of the Theresian-Josephinian Austrian state, a character that had been lost in the top-heavy, overly centralist control implemented by Alexander Bach in the administrative reforms of the 1850s. Although Schwartzenau—very much like his former superior Koerber—presented the problem in a modern guise as furthering the economic and cultural progress of the Austrian state and people, the reform as such has strong paternalistic-bureaucratic strains. It builds on two pillars, a reform of the internal organization (Geschäftsordnung) of the Bezirkshauptmannschaften and a reform of their administrative procedures (Administrativverfahren). The first reform aimed at freeing the leading official at this level, the Bezirkshauptmann, from his suffocating clerical duties and turning him into that important presence in the local community that his pre-Bach ancestor had been. In this way he should move about among the local population, make decisions and take initiatives on the spot, and also seek out lay advisers (Amtsmänner) to help him in his now more directly governing role. The echoes of Koerber's ideas on the important role of the state authorities in the local community are strong, but Schwartzenau was a Koerber disciple. The second main part of Schwartzenau's proposal concerned the prerogatives of this local servant of the state. Through a close reading of the Austrian administrative law, Schwartzenau made a case for expanding the sphere of influence and executive power of the Bezirkshauptmannschaften, finding that the sphere of "free estimation" (freies Ermessen) of the state authorities in their interaction with the population was, indeed, much wider than had previously been thought. Schwartzenau also proposed to further expand this sphere by interpreting the Austrian administrative law to in fact making such an expansion possible wholly by administrative ordinances (Verordnungen), which needed no legislative sanction.[166]

Schwartzenau's proposal was processed in the interior ministry in 1913–14, and had it not been for the outbreak of war it might very well have been realized in some form.[167] However, the reactions within the commission were strong, and the proposal set off the first serious conflict in the plenum. It was Haerdtl and the professor of law at the University of Vienna, Edmund Bernatzik, who led the assault on Schwartzenau in the ninth plenary session on 1 and 2 July 1913. The two argued very hotly that Schwartzenau's proposal for a new administrative procedure, in which the executive power of the local state authorities was expanded, was directly unconstitutional. The debate dragged on for a long time, but several civil servants in the commission also supported Schwartzenau, and in the end it was accepted (with a minority vote against it by Haerdtl and Bernatzik). It is interesting that Redlich admitted Bernatzik was probably in the right "theoretically," but he still took Schwartzenau's side because as "a politician" he gave priority to getting manifest results in the work of the commission (!).[168] In a letter to a member of the commission, Joseph Maria Baernreither, written on the very day of this stormy plenary session, Redlich also emphasized that he really and truly appreciated Schwartzenau's proposal: "Schwartzenau's proposals are in the real and best sense of the words Liberal progress," Redlich stated.[169] Redlich's identification with this strongly bureaucratic reform proposal is a measure of the strength of his own centralism at this time. However, his marked emphasis on the creation of a truly democratic self-government as the basis for the same Austrian state that he wanted to see unified by a strong "state will" in the hands of its Josephist Beamtentum is not as paradoxical as it may seem. The result of this mixture could, indeed, in due time be the creation of a unitary democratic multinational Austria, which seems to be the most accurate description of Redlich's vision of the new Austria in the last years before 1914.

In the same plenary session, Redlich's own report on the Austrian financial administration had also been accepted, but only after Redlich had threatened to publish the report privately if it was not.[170] The new more withdrawn and more centralized financial administration proposed by Redlich also was a key element in his larger vision of reform, insofar as this reformed financial administration received a key function in the centralized state supervision and control of those self-government organs that were to carry the main burden of the Austrian state administration proper.[171] During 1913, the commission, and especially Redlich, fought hard against a not very cooperative Stürgkh government to receive permission to publish all those reports that were being finished and sanctioned by the commission. The enquête protocol was particularly problematic, and it took several months for an intransigent Stürgkh to finally issue a grudging permission for their publication, something that was viewed as a victory by Redlich, who wanted public exposure of the commission to be as wide as possible.[172] Redlich's own report on the financial administration received permission for publication at the end of September 1913, three months after its sanction in the commission, and when it was published it was also widely distributed; later in the fall of 1913 it already needed to be reprinted.[173] All in all, Redlich's strivings to let the commission tread in direct contact with the public had paid off. When Redlich in February 1914 partook in a public debate with Karl Brockhausen about his reform proposal, it also became evident that he was, indeed, the member of the commission publicly most identified with its reform action.[174]

Redlich was rather content with the work that the commission had accomplished thus far, although it was still lacking the closure that would seal the state reform. In the summer of 1913 he wrote to Baernreither that he was still hoping that a comprehensive reform of the administrative organization could be accomplished. The key element of this reform needed to be a realignment of the state and autonomous administration, a solution that by necessity, Redlich noted, would balance on the borderline between an administrative and a constitutional reform.[175] With this goal in view, Redlich, in the spring of 1914, attempted to force the commission to a conclusion. In a meeting on 16 February of the expert group of the subcommittees I and IV, where the fundamental question of the reorganization of the whole internal administration had landed, Redlich argued strongly that this fundamental question should not be buried in subcommittees any longer. It should as quickly as possible be brought to the plenum where a majority decision about the fundamentals of the administrative reform should be taken. Redlich also argued that he had observed a converging tendency in the positions of the centralists and autonomists during the course of the work in the commission and that therefore a plenary session should try to work out this common ground.[176] In the next meeting of these subcommittees, on 5–6 March, Redlich developed this argument by describing the struggle between the autonomists and centralists that dominated the commission as well as Austrian society at large as a struggle in which a new, less centralist Austrian state idea was shaped, an idea that would most certainly guarantee the unity of Austria better than the old mechanical, bureaucratic centralism simply because it would be an expression of the interests of the different groups in Austrian society and thus breathe life again into the Austrian sense of unity (Einheitsgefühl).[177]

It is interesting to note that the way Redlich here describes the process of the creation of a new Austrian state idea prefigures the basic argument of that grand history of the Austrian state he would soon begin to write, *Das österreichische Staats- und Reichsproblem*. His view in this work that the only real political line of division in Austria after 1848 was that between centralists and federalists, which was also the concrete embodiment of the Austrian problem of unity and diversity, is a perfect reflection of that microcosm of the Austrian problem he personally lived in the years 1911–14, the Imperial Commission for Administrative Reform. That unitary democratic multinational new Austria that was his vision of reform in the work in the commission is also present as a shadow behind his historical narrative of the Austrian problem. Disconcertingly enough, Redlich's vision of reform seems never again to have been as close to realization as it was in that blueprint for a German-Slavic Verfassungsstaat that in Redlich's view was the Kremsier constitution. Indeed, as described by Redlich, the constitutional subcommittee of this peoples' parliament of 1848 looks peculiarly like a historical projection of Redlich's own experience in the administrative reform commission.

Redlich might very well have received important inspiration, both for his optimism regarding the growing understanding between centralists and autonomists in the commission, and for his view of the ideal balance between unity and diversity in the solution to the historical Austrian problem of the state, from a very interesting excursion into the problem of the Austrian state idea that Schwartzenau had made in the meeting of the subcommittees I and IV on 6 March 1914. This morning Schwartzenau appeared in the meeting in a very philosophical mood and began by asking this:

> We want to reform our administration. Then I ask: What is the internal administration? The internal administration is nothing else than the realization of a certain state purpose [Staatszweck]. If I now go on asking, what is the purpose of the Austrian state? I am then confronted with a riddle.

Schwartzenau then described the national idea of most European states as their historical mission, their raison d'étre, their Staatszweck. Austria, though, had not yet found her corresponding modern "national" idea, but Schwartzenau saw its contours as slowly taking shape:

> At least since 1866, I regard the raison d'étre of Austria outside Germany as being formed by . . . Austria's many nationalities and many different languages, and they should, according to me, not be seen as an obstacle to the development of an Austrian national state idea. . . . The ultimate consequence, it seems, if Austria has eight nationalities, then its state purpose and therefore also its administrative purpose is an eightfold purpose. How this eightfold purpose of our administration can be aligned with the state idea is the Austrian problem, the solution to which we by necessity must find sooner or later.[178]

Schwartzenau's view of the Austrian problem found wide resonance. Redlich could most certainly follow the traditional centralist Schwartzenau a long way. And because he could observe how the autonomists in the commission also reacted very positively (Schönborn went out of his way in his praise of Schwartzenau),[179] he must have been reinforced in his perception that the two main political camps of the commission were finding the common ground that would make possible a successful resolution of the work on the fundamental administrative reform in Austria.

Redlich must therefore have been disappointed because he was forced to witness how his optimistic view of this common ground between the two camps turned out to be a mirage when the matter came to a head in the tenth and eleventh plenary sessions in March and May of 1914. Redlich's insistence on forcing the issue of the fundamental principles of the administrative reform through majority decisions in the plenum of the commission gave the whole reform action a certain momentum during this last phase of its work. But it also inexorably led to the result that Redlich and Haerdtl stood isolated in the midst of their disintegrating reform project; the centralists commanded by Schwartzenau and the autonomists commanded by Schönborn together shot their ambitious administrative reform proposal to pieces.[180]

It seems almost symbolic that the remnants of the concerned subcommittees, with not even a sufficient number present to conduct business, met for a last time with the aim of salvaging the remains of the defeated reform proposal on 27 June 1914, the day before the assassination of Archduke Franz Ferdinand in Sarajevo.[181] In the third annual report of the commission, where its work is summed up, the outbreak of the war in August 1914 is laconically described as "a natural interruption" of its work.[182] But in the draft Erwin von Schwartzenau brought with him to the twelfth and last plenary session of the commission on 15 December 1914, a session solely concerned with editing the third annual report of the commission, this motivation had been considerably longer. Here Schwartzenau had described the war as making the whole of the work of the commission irrelevant, since this great crisis would most certainly also reshape the Austrian state idea and thus supply the Austrian Verwaltung with a new and yet unknown purpose. The reactions against Schwartzenau's radical formulations were strong, and the debate ended by a decision to cross out this whole part of his draft. But simultaneously it emerged rather clearly that all members of the commission more or less basically agreed with Schwartzenau. They all, autonomists and centralists alike, believed that the war would bring fundamental changes in the constitution and purpose of the Austrian state.[183]

4. War as the Solution to the Austrian Problem (1914–1918)

The outbreak of war in August 1914 was greeted by many as an opportunity to break through the political deadlock in Imperial Austria, and in the empire at large. Even if we limit ourselves to the German-Austrian core of the imperial state, we find an array of political clubs and networks that sprang up during the first months of the war, all aiming to use the extraordinary conditions of the war to bring about more or less radical changes in the organization of the imperial state.[184] Although some of these networks were focusing on the imperial Austrian state as such, many and perhaps most of these groups formed in 1914 saw a crucial part of the solution in a (re)union with Imperial Germany. The name for this latter vision was Mitteleuropa, and its prophet was Friedrich Naumann.[185] These aggressive visions of political change were dominant up to 1916; at the latest after the assassination of Minister President Karl Stürgkh in October this year and the death of the old emperor Franz Joseph in November, confidence in these visions had been lost and the field of political vision became fragmented.

Josef Redlich initially greeted the outbreak of war as the return of that lost opportunity in 1909 when war with Serbia had been averted at the last moment. As if he were following a pattern set down at this earlier time, Redlich in late July 1914 wrote a letter to Foreign Minister Berchtold congratulating him on the strong-willed action of the ultimatum to Serbia, which, Redlich asserted, served to restore the belief of the empire in itself. Redlich also asked and received permission to go to the eastern front as a representative of the war press office (Kriegspressequartier). It seems like the intention behind the "war diary" Redlich wrote during these weeks at the front was to tell the story of the regeneration of Austria. However, what he actually did was to chronicle his own gradual loss of confidence in the imperial army and especially in its commander, Field Marshal Franz Conrad von Hötzendorf. Redlich met and talked to Conrad repeatedly during these weeks in the forward headquarters at the fortress of Pržmysl near the Russian border; in Conrad, Redlich was apparently hoping to find a leader able to use the war to bring political change to Austria. In the latter part of this interrupted war diary, Redlich documents his growing doubts and final disillusionment with the Austrian leadership in this, as Redlich clearly saw it, existential struggle of the old empire.[186]

Already in September 1914 Redlich seems to have lost the major part of his expectations that a successful war might bring about the wanted regeneration of Austria. Instead, he turned inward; he spent much time working on his magnum opus on the Austrian problem during the following years. In this period Redlich went through a gradual transformation with regard to his views on the Austrian problem, a process that will be returned to below. Karl Renner's trajectory during the war was, if anything, the inverse of Redlich's. Up to the beginning of 1915, Renner most of all looked like he had lost his sense of direction, not knowing where he should turn or how he should act. However, after this time he regained the kind of confidence in his political vision that he exhibited in the early years of the century. In the spring of 1915 he linked his own old political vision of the Nationalitätenbundesstaat to the new political vision of Mitteleuropa and set out on what was probably, from Renner's personal point of view, the most important political campaign of his career.

Karl Renner and Mitteleuropa

When Friedrich Naumann came to Vienna in February 1915, on the first of his many trips to Austria-Hungary during the war, he first visited Karl Renner, whom he had been acquainted with since the early years of the century.[187] Renner would later describe his contacts with Naumann during 1915 as frequent, and he would even describe himself as an Austrian counterpart to Naumann, as one of the leading figures in the Mitteleuropa movement as such.[188] In view of this self-description, it is a bit strange that Renner's Mitteleuropa engagement has not really been taken seriously in the biographical literature on Renner. It is usually quickly skipped over, as if it were a question of temporary deviation from the proper course of Renner's life career.[189] Quite on the contrary, I believe it to be one of the most central elements of his life career, and *the* most central element in his pre-1918 life. In Renner's political campaign during the war years, several crucial elements came together that had earlier been only loosely joined in his campaigns for the federal multination state: his adherence to the imperial state, his ideological loyalty to Social Democracy, his strong German identification, and his theoretical advocacy of Marxism. The magic formula that could join all these disparate strands of Renner's self was Mitteleuropa.[190] I would argue that Renner never again in his life came so close to seeing his political vision realized to the full.

Renner's activities during World War I add up to an impressive political and ideological balance act. Renner during these years made no less than a very serious and initially successful attempt to wed Austrian and Reichs-German Social Democracy to the Mitteleuropa project. The aim of this mind-boggling attempt to turn Central European Social Democracy into the willing instrument of empire building was to further Renner's own vision of a Nationalitätenbundesstaat. In the shape this vision took during the war years, its central element snapped into place, that of sustaining into the modern era the historical role of the Germans as the masters and bringers of civilization to Central and southeastern Europe. The development of Renner's vision during the world war was mirrored in an opposite movement in Redlich's political project; in 1914 these two formerly parallel political trajectories began to diverge, and in crucial regards they ended up in 1918 as two contrasting visions of what Imperial Austria should and could have become.

From his basis inside the executive committee of the German-Austrian Social Democratic party, Renner acted with great determination to set this party on the course toward Mitteleuropa, a point of destination that was also propagated from his position as a coeditor of the ideological party paper, the monthly *Der Kampf*, and as a member of the editorial staff of the daily party organ, the *Arbeiter-Zeitung*. Renner had slowly begun to develop parts of his coming war program already in the fall of 1914 in the internal idea conferences of the executive committee of the party on the official stance of the party toward the war. Here Renner in a neutral manner delineated the two fundamental positions on this question: The "old" position, which had, in practice, been defeated by the breakdown of the International in August 1914, (so Renner) and the "new" position, which viewed the war as fundamentally changing the preconditions for the Social Democratic movement.[191] At this time Renner did not openly argue the latter position. However, from the spring of 1915 until 1917, Renner more and more openly and aggressively tried to reformulate the Social Democratic ideology so that it should fit the "new" position. The aim of this was to make it possible for the movement to take advantage of geoeconomic and geopolitical changes that according to Renner were going to take place in any event.[192] His meeting with Friedrich Naumann in early February 1915 was probably a crucial event in this development. Renner's period of success ended in the fall of 1917; in the first party-congress since the beginning of hostilities, his position was assaulted head on from the left of the party, which brand-marked him as a "social patriot."[193] After this congress, Renner's influence in the party was more restricted, but up to this time he seems actually to have been supported by the main part of the German-Austrian Social Democratic leadership, including its head Viktor Adler.[194]

Karl Renner in Berlin in 1917; Verein für Geschichte der Arbeiterbewegung, Vienna, VGA/Sign. 4/0/0/179

Renner's development can be followed in his actions in the party's executive committee, where he carefully gauged the powerbalance and, with an eye on Viktor Adler, tested the limits of acceptability of the notions of geopolitical "restructuring" in Eastern Europe, even propagating annexations to Austria in the east.[195] Renner was also the driving force in the party discussion of a "closer union" between Germany and Austria-Hungary. Parallel in time to the development of this question on the government level and between the bürgerliche parties of Germany and Austria, Renner was instrumental in also making it into a high priority question for the Social Democratic sister parties in the allied empires. In the fall of 1915, several meetings were held in Vienna and Berlin between the leadership of the German Social Democracy and the German-Austrian Social Democracy, where Renner presented the case for an economic union between the two Central European empires.[196] His attempt to build "eine kleine Internationale" around the program of Mitteleuropa culminated on 9 January 1916, when he held center stage in an expanded Social Democratic party and trade union conference on this issue in Berlin. In his keynote speech in Berlin, Renner very subtly rehabilitated Naumann by arguing that his bürgerliche rhetoric did not really affect the substance of what he said. Rather, Renner continued less subtly, Mitteleuropa was firmly grounded first in an inexorable development toward larger economic entities in the globalizing economy, a development that had only been speeded up by the war, and second in a very long historical development in which the interruption of mitteleuropäische unity beginning in 1866 was only a historical episode. The objective forces working for Mitteleuropa were simply irresistible. Although the organization of Mitteleuropa that was realized during the war would not necessarily meet the expectations of the Social Democrats, it should be welcomed, Renner maintained, as a "shell" within which the Social Democratic vision of society could "mature." He concluded that the Social Democrats had no reason to obstruct the movement toward a closer union between the two empires, "but should on the contrary function as a pushing factor."[197]

During the spring of 1916 Renner turned back toward the internal Austrian scene and attempted to secure the support for Mitteleuropa on the home front. In the party conference (Reichskonferenz) of March 1916, he was successful in calming the internal criticism that had grown from his overly enthusiastic support of Naumann's Mitteleuropa in the party organs. In the end, Renner even succeeded in getting the program of the economic integration in Mitteleuropa integrated into the political platform of the German-Austrian Social Democratic party.[198] Slightly later, in May 1916, Renner had a key role in a delicate meeting between leading representatives of German-Austrian Social Democracy and the German-Liberal party grouping (Deutsche Nationalverband) centered around the question of Mitteleuropa. In the meeting, the question of a common platform between these German-Austrian parties on the question of a closer union with Germany was broached. It actually seems like the proposal of the chairman of the German-Liberals, Gustav Gross, to engage in parallel actions on certain key questions was tacitly taken under consideration by the Social Democrats.[199] This impression is reinforced because Renner at this time was working out what adds up to a war aims program of the German-Austrian Social Democratic party, a program that seems to have been consciously constructed along the basic lines of the corresponding official war aims programs of the German-Liberals and the Christian Socials, in effect facilitating a common German-Austrian national platform.[200] Its content, though, is unmistakably constructed around Renner's old program of the Nationalitätenbundesstaat, now expanded into a democratic imperialist vision of a Central European federal multination state that is closely tied to Imperial Germany. Renner visualizes "a middle European community of peoples" ("mitteleuropäische Völkergemeinschaft") arranged around the core of the Dual Monarchy restructured as a Bundesstaat with national autonomy internally. This federal multination state should first be united with Germany. Second in the northeast and the southeast, this federal state should integrate Bosnia-Hercegovina "as well as all future acquisitions" as imperial provinces (Reichslande)—this means primarily Poland, but the formulation is open. Before being integrated, though, these lands should receive a constitution, a democratic representation, and a democratic administrative organization built on national autonomy (Renner's Kreis organization).

Renner's concept of an originally Austrian (western half of the empire) democratic federal multination state, which during the Hungarian crisis in 1903–06 was imperialistically expanded into encompassing the empire as a whole, was, during the political conjunctures of World War I, thus expanded a second time into the imperialistic democratic multinational federation of Mitteleuropa. To sustain such an ideologically overextended position something had to give way. Renner's choice was to subordinate socialism to his geopolitical vision. In *Marxismus, Krieg und Internationale* (1917), Renner, in a rather sophisticated argument, reformulated Marxism to adapt it to what he views as an evolution of the global economic system that has been made apparent during the war. In essence, Renner tries to make Marxism into a state-supporting ideology that can be instrumentalized in furthering the development of large juridically and politically structured "economic spheres," a development he describes as part of the recent evolution of the world economy. Renner describes the end station of this development as the "world state," which should frame in that "world economic community" that Renner poetically calls the *Ökumene*. But the present intermediate stage in this development is that of the evolution of fewer large economic spheres. In the world economic competition between the Russian empire, the United States, the French and the British colonial empires, and the rising Japanese empire, Mitteleuropa is, very cursorily in this mainly theoretical discussion, described as a potential contestant.[201] *Marxismus, Krieg und Internationale* can thus be read as Renner's ambitious attempt to anchor the vision of Mitteleuropa in Marxist theory and in the ideology of Central European Social Democracy.

At the time *Marxismus, Krieg und Internationale* was published, Renner's position within the Social Democratic party was already weakened. The book would even become a weapon against him at the party congress of October 1917, where it was an important piece of evidence in the case against Renner the social-patriot. Soon thereafter Karl Kautsky published his *Kriegsmarxismus* (1918), a scathing criticism of Renner's theoretical reformulation of Marxism,[202] obliterating the carefully constructed ideological foundation to the political position that the Social Democratic party congress had already seriously weakened. In the last year of the war, Renner's influence in the party was increasingly restricted by the rise of the left wing of the party under Otto Bauer.[203] However, Renner retained some support and continued to propagate a less expansive version of the Nationalitätenbundesstaat as a reform of Austria and possibly of the empire as a whole. This vision was stated in *Das Selbstbestimmungsrecht der Nationen* (1918), a work with continuing theoretical relevance.[204] During the fall of 1918, Renner, under a growing German, Anschluss-oriented tendency in the executive committee, a faction led by Otto Bauer, remained firm on his vision of the federal multination state as the solution that should be attempted after the end of hostilities.

As is well known, Renner became chancellor of state in the provisional government of the new republic. From this position Renner had a strong influence on shaping the foundations of the new state. One of the most important documents authored by Renner in this phase is the declaration of the territorial extension of the Republic of Austria of 22 November 1918.[205] Compared to Renner's earlier writings, this document most of all looks like the German national skeleton of his Nationalitätenbundesstaat in its attempt to collect all territorially contiguous German groups in the new polity, one that is then also presented as a guardian of all those German minorities dispersed outside of this perimeter, and, finally, that lays claims to the economic interests of this German-Austrian state on the Balkans and in the Orient. However, this skeleton would hardly stick together without the "sinews" and "flesh" of the Nationalitätenbundesstaat and subsequently Renner's vision mutated into a German national or Gesamtdeutsche project that was typical of German-oriented circles in Austria in the interwar era.

In a speech Renner held in Berlin in 1922, he supplied us with the key for understanding his political project as basically continuous in this way. Here he made the connection between his early political writings on national autonomy, the Mitteleuropa plans of the war years, his own plans for a Nationalitätenbundesstaat presented in its final version in 1918, and his post-1918 engagement for the cause of Germandom in Europe. Renner here describes his plans for a federal multination state as from early on containing the notion of a special role for the German-Austrian national group: "I departed from the notion that when German-Austria had become one of eight member-states of the Danube Reich, it would present no difficulties also to later join this German-Austrian member-state with the German Empire." [206] In view of this model with German-Austria as a link between Germany and the eastern dominions of the federalized Habsburg Empire, that which might look like a continuous vacillation by Renner between Anschluss and different renewed attempts at realizing some variety of Mitteleuropa or Danube confederation during the interwar era, looks more like a strategy aiming at the reconstruction of the special historical role of the German-Austrians, indeed, as an imprint of that imperial experience that continued to guide the actions of many an Austrian politician during the interwar era.[207]

Josef Redlich and the Transformation of the Austrian Problem

During the last years before the breakout of World War I, Redlich was preoccupied with the problem of the relationship between the inner cohesion of the empire on the one hand, and its ability to act on the international arena on the other. During this time, he made an interesting comparison between Austria-Hungary and the other Great Powers: "The difference between us and these states is great because all other states can always withdraw to an instinctive national standpoint in foreign policy; however, for us the internal strife makes it impossible to find any common standpoint."[208] With Redlich's actions in the administrative reform commission as a backdrop, we can see that this perspective on foreign policy was only another aspect of that same problem he addressed in the commission. If the Austrian state purpose could be formed as a true expression of its multinational composition, then the empire as a whole stood a much better chance to appear also outwardly as one and united.

If Redlich before 1914, in a way similar to Karl Renner, had emphasized the state as the focal point, the guarantor of unity in multinational Austria, after this year he moved away from such a position. The definite shift came during 1916, when Redlich observed how the "war absolutism" of Austrian Minister President Karl Stürgkh was rapidly losing all support and legitimacy in Austrian society. Redlich's skepticism toward Stürgkh was noticeably intensified in early 1916. At this time Redlich received information about the centralist "reform" plans of the Stürgkh government. During the following months, with accelerating agitation he followed the development of a plan to implement constitutional changes through imperial decree. One part of these changes was designed to reinforce the German identity of the imperial Austrian state (a German-oriented official languages act); another was aiming at centralizing the Austrian Verwaltung by abolishing the autonomous administration. Redlich reacted strongly against the whole centralistic-authoritarian thrust of these plans and engaged himself publicly in a political cause for the first time during the war, holding speeches at political meetings during the spring in defense of the autonomous administration and against the rallying political forces of German-Austrian centralism.[209]

One result of Redlich's hostility against this reassertion of bureaucratic centralism was that he promised that he would move to the United States as soon as the war was over, but before doing so, "I will indulge in writing a little book about 'The poverty of ideas of 1914 in Europe with special emphasis on Austria.'"[210] It actually seems like this idea, born out of the agitation against Stürgkh and all the German-Austrians that supported him, is the embryo to that extremely critical account Redlich would write on the *Austrian War Government* (1929) in the years immediately following the end of the war.[211] This book is written with the type of verve and critical incisiveness that one would expect from a strong personal reaction against that German-Austrian bureaucratic centralism into which the book is a genealogical inquiry. The work is streamlined around that earlier-discussed central strain of Redlich's *Das österreichische Staats- und Reichsproblem* (1920–26), the view of the fusion of the German-Liberal elite in Austria with that centralistic-authoritarian bureaucracy founded by Alexander Bach in the 1850s as the pathogenesis of the imperial Austrian state. Redlich's historical exposition practically collapses the "war-absolutism" of Karl Stürgkh into "the defeat of the revolution of 1848" and the Germanizing, authoritarian Bach centralism that Redlich judges was born in this reaction. Between these periods, Redlich draws a straight line of inexorable historical development, which is highlighted here and there. So, for instance, with regard to the Koerber administration of 1900–1904, which is credited with perfecting the Austrian system of the "bureaucratic dictatorship" of the minister president, which would be operated so successfully by Stürgkh in 1914.[212] A long central section of Redlich's work is a catalog of the content of that war absolutism, which during the early war years operated wholly independently of any political control.[213] The result of this system by 1916, as Redlich saw it, was that the Austrian government and bureaucracy were politically completely isolated, hovering over the Austrian society completely detached from it.[214]

Later in 1916 another event moved this whole problem to the personal level. The eagerly awaited offer in late October 1916 to finally partake in an imperial reform government under Koerber served as a litmus test on Redlich's changing priorities. During the war years, his contacts with Koerber had been close, and it seems that he had expectations that this Austrian statesman could serve as the vessel for his own engagement in the renewal of Austria. Because of this, and because of his long relationship with Koerber, Redlich must have been rather excited when he was summoned to Koerber's office on 28 October, the very day of the latter's official appointment as Austrian minister president.[215] But three days later, Redlich mailed a letter to Koerber and declined to accept the offer made, to partake in a leading position in an administrative reform action to be launched by the new Koerber government. This seems somewhat surprising, especially since this was a marvelous opportunity to carry out what he had spent so much energy trying to do in the administrative reform commission only a couple of years earlier.

One could suppose, and many did at the time, that Redlich's declining answer was because the job offered a post as Sektions-Chef in the interior ministry in immediate charge of the planned administrative reform action was not prestigious enough. Redlich had wanted a ministry for himself and was deeply disappointed that Koerber offered him a "mere" leading civil service function, this view of the affair says. Redlich was most certainly to some extent disappointed, but he himself emphatically maintained afterward that this was not the reason for his declining answer.[216]

Therefore we should perhaps take his given reasons into account, which together are actually different expressions of the one true reason why Redlich declined: that during his historical studies of the Austrian problem in the years 1914 to 1916, and in his parallel observation of the behavior of the Austrian government during the war, he had come to the conclusion that the Austrian problem could (no longer) be solved unilaterally from above.

In his declining letter to Koerber, Redlich began by stating that his long experience in Austrian politics, and especially in studying and actively working for an administrative reform, had taught him that the Austrian problem was no "administrative-technical" problem, as Koerber had presented it when offering him the job, but rather a political one. Redlich continued: "The necessary precondition for a solution to this great problem is a comprehensive program building on a well-thought-out view of the Austrian state and its terms of existence. . . ." He added that such a program must be anchored in the people and in state-supporting parties, then implemented with great determination.[217] Redlich could not see the government Koerber had put together as answering these requirements.

His sense of the problematic character of the renewed and aggressive German-Austrian centralism in 1916 had probably been sharpened by his observation of Karl Renner's prominent engagement in this political campaign. Hermann Bahr wrote to Redlich in February 1916 of the magnificent spectacle of Renner's press campaign: "By the way, I find this mix between Alexander Bach and Karl Marx wonderful!" Bahr exclaimed.[218] Redlich agreed with Bahr about the strangeness of the phenomena they were witnessing, but he found it rather more serious than his friend did. Renner's campaign, Redlich replied curtly, is geared toward abolishing the political autonomy. Furthermore, Redlich asserted, Renner's press campaign is coordinated with Stürgkh's centralistic-authoritarian plans to restructure the Austrian state, and he has the support of the Social Democratic leadership in this.[219] However, this may have been Bahr's description of Renner as a fusion of Alexander Bach and Karl Marx is, indeed, an accurate description of Renner's dual press campaign at this time. In the theoretical organ of the Social Democrats, *Der Kampf*, Renner was simultaneously reformulating Marxism into a state- and empire-supporting ideology as in the daily *Arbeiter-Zeitung* he was propagating a Bach-inspired administrative reform of the Austrian state.[220] Redlich should not have been so surprised, since the administrative reform he was propagating at this time was basically the same as what he had been advocating all along. However, in Renner's campaign during the war, the centrality of the state came to the fore more strongly, and Renner now clearly devalued political autonomy as a value in itself, arguing openly for the subordination of the autonomous organs under the state administration.[221] Joining the devaluation of political autonomy was the strange definition of democracy that Renner advocated in these articles; it contains the essence of what could be called his "democratic centralism." After criticizing the "anarchic" (in effect liberal-individualist) definition of democracy "current" in the debate, Renner continued with his own definition:

> Democracy wants to concentrate a multiplicity of men in an acting unit; the important part here is the unit, not the individual. Unity means organization and the subordination of the individual; it means putting the interest of the organization higher, and this demands discipline, meaning subordination and sacrifice.[222]

This definition is, in fact, not much different from his argument in *Staat und Parlament* (1901), discussed earlier, where Renner approached the position of the current Minister President Koerber. Furthermore, in his definition of democracy as liberty within the state, not liberty from the state, Renner also came close to the concept used in Imperial Germany during the world war, the Deutsche Freiheit, as a special German form of liberty "through the state." Indeed, Anton Pelinka noted in his overview of Renner's political career, that Renner throughout his life discussed only democracy in the context of "order" and the unity of the state.[223]

Redlich's experience in 1916 of the broad support of German-Austrian centralism and the study of Renner's modulation of the principle of self-government into a form of neo-Josephist democratic centralism were probably decisive for his turn away from the emphasis on the unity of the Austrian state to a new sense for the diversity of its peoples and lands as the foundation of the new Austria. The last part of Redlich's letter to Koerber in November 1916 reflects this positive part of his turn, insofar as Redlich here adds as the last and most "personal" of his reasons for declining, that he is unwilling to give up his seat in parliament to enter into state service.[224] From the late summer of 1916, Redlich joined the movement for the reopening of the Austrian parliament, and in the following time this institution would be at the center of his political project. In September of this year he was invited to join the executive committee of the recently formed Austrian Political Society (Österreichische Politische Gesellschaft, ÖPG), a political club that superseded the Marchet-Baernreither group and many other similar clubs in Vienna. Soon thereafter, Redlich partook prominently in the society, the first public engagement of which was the manifestation planned for 22 October on the question of the reopening of parliament by a group around the university professors Edmund Bernatzik, Heinrich Lammasch, and Ludo Moritz Hartmann, officially supported by the Social Democratic party. The Austrian Political Society held a meeting shortly before this planned manifestation, mobilizing its members to participate in it, and in this meeting Redlich held a one-hour speech propagating the need to reactivate the parliament. Shortly afterward the manifestation was prohibited by the government, and it was this government action that triggered Friedrich Adler's assassination of Minister President Stürgkh on 21 October.[225]

When parliament was reassembled much later in the spring of 1917, Redlich successfully turned it into a vessel for a political campaign for parliamentarization of the government and a constitutional national political reform that brought him an offer from Emperor Karl to form a government. The program Redlich propagated publicly during the summer of 1917 shows remarkable similarities with that program for the creation of an Austrian democratic union of peoples, which Redlich had propagated so insistently almost exactly ten years earlier upon his election to the first Austrian Volkshaus in the summer of 1907. It actually looks like Redlich during these ten years made a full circle in his movement from initially building his program squarely on the diversity of the Austrian peoples and lands, through an intervening period of a belief in the unifying force of the Austrian imperial state and reform from above, and back to his original position.

In the beginning of 1917, Redlich documents a definite move in the autonomist, or federalist direction of his arch-Austrian friend Hermann Bahr, as he recounts his fundamental agreement with several articles Bahr has lately published.[226] In one of these articles, Bahr delineated the difference between Prussia and Austria and the need for Austria to distance itself from the Prussian misconception of the state as a mechanic organization, and to mobilize a belief in the historically grown organic quality of Austria as the foundation of the Austrian state. In another set of articles, Bahr had described the Austrian centralist state founded by Alexander Bach as a uniform, wholly artificial and mechanical, and therefore, arguably, a Prussian construction, which rested heavily on the true Austria, embodied in its nationally mixed historical lands and with its core in the autonomous Austrian Gemeinde. To renew itself, Bahr argues in these articles, Austria must free itself from this Bach uniform and reconceptualize itself on the basis of its true identity.[227] In early 1917, Redlich had accepted the basic analysis of the Austrian problem as presented by Bahr. He now argued that the foundations for an organic, legitimate Austrian administration can be found only in the historical communities, formed over long stretches of time by geography and nature; among these Redlich emphasizes the Gemeinden and the historical lands, the Kronländer.[228] The Austrian state must be rebuilt from below, not from above, Redlich emphatically concluded at this time.

Another source of inspiration for Redlich's shift was Friedrich Wilhelm Foerster, the German educational pedagogue. Foerster was in 1916 becoming a rallying point for the anti-Prussian, antimilitaristic forces of Austria.[229] Foerster had a concrete solution to the Austrian problem, perhaps the type of program for the regeneration of Austria that Redlich had lacked in Koerber. Foerster's solution lay in an active move away from the destructive Prusso-centric German nationalism that had also infected the German-Austrians toward an affirmation of Austria as the carrier of an old-German and Great-German, Catholic, and supranational mission in Europe. Furthermore, in the present circumstances of the war, Foerster maintained, this mission should receive an immediate expression as an antimilitaristic, anti-Prussian program for peace.[230]

Foerster's solution to the Austrian problem was an integrated part of the political program that Redlich propagated in the summer of 1917 in a series of speeches at the reopened Austrian parliament[231] and in several meetings at the Austrian Political Society.[232] The central elements of this program were, first of all, Redlich's strong focus on the Austrian political autonomy as the embryo of the modern Austrian multinational state, and second, the need to realize this new Austria of the autonomous peoples through a peaceful understanding. The latter vision was especially propagated in the speech he held at the peace manifestation of 17 July, where Redlich focused on Emperor Karl's recent amnesty to all political prisoners as a "great deed" that had done wonders for clearing the way to a new political atmosphere of conciliation between the peoples in Austria.[233]

The central element of Redlich's speeches at this time is the view of Schmerling's reform of the 1860s as creating a peculiar, unresolved mix of the old and the new Austria, of the centralist Zwangsstaat ("coercive state") and the autonomous Volksstaat ("people's state"). Redlich describes the road to be followed as that of pulling back the former and putting it under the strict control of the parliament, but retaining the idea of a unitary state. This idea must then be transferred to the rudimentary institutions of the Volksstaat, the historical lands, and the Gemeinden, which should now step in as the full realization of the liberal tendency of the 1860s. The Austrian state idea, Redlich concludes, should hereafter be: "Emperor, Land, and Municipality" ("Der Kaiser, das Land, die Gemeinde").[234]

It is interesting that apparently Redlich at this time even put special emphasis on the first of the above, Der Kaiser. In his deeply critical retrospective view of the German-Austrian bureaucratic centralism (*Austrian War Government*, 1929), Redlich would split the war era into two fundamentally contrasting periods: the period of war absolutism, 1914–17, and the period of the attempt of Emperor Karl "to heal the terrible political wounds that the Austrian war absolutism of 1914 to 1917 had inflicted on the internal coherence of the Austrian peoples and on the Austrian administration by breathing new life into the Austrian constitution and parliamentarism."[235] The contrast that comes from this rather idealistic view of Emperor Karl's somewhat confused imperial regime being lodged within a bitingly critical account of Austrian government is an effect of Redlich's personal involvement with Emperor Karl in the summer of 1917. Redlich's celebrated speech in parliament on 12 June had resulted in a visit by Karl's first chamberlain (Obersthofmeister), Konrad Hohenlohe, who sounded him out on his views of the political situation and especially discussed the ideas Redlich had expressed in his speech on the need for a parliamentarian peoples' government. And a few days after his speech at the Austrian Political Society on

27 June, where he launched his new version of the Austrian state idea, Redlich was summoned to the first of his two audiences with Emperor Karl in early July.[236]

On the morning of 3 July 1917, Redlich appeared before Karl in Laxenburg outside of Vienna, where in a one-and-a-half-hour meeting they apparently discussed the situation in Austria rather openly. Karl especially queried Redlich on his stance regarding the question of administrative reform, on the Autonomie, and he raised the issue of the reception of his political amnesty of the day before, which Redlich had publicly supported. They seem to have found much common ground, especially when Redlich developed his view of the fundamental difference between the Austrian and the Prussian states, with autonomy being the crucial characteristic of the Austrian state. Redlich described the Prussian state as an authoritarian state built on conquest and the Austrian state being built on contractual agreements between its peoples and lands, historically governed "with mildness" ("mit Milde"). Karl was apparently quite taken in by Redlich's elaborations because he added this: "Yes, tu felix Austria nube? Thus you understand these words! You are quite right!"[237]

In the second audience on 5 July, Karl queried Redlich further, testing on him a government program building on peace and national political reform, a program that Karl had partly formed during several contacts with the leading members of the Austrian peace movement, most prominently Heinrich Lammasch, Julius Meinl, and Friedrich Wilhelm Foerster. Karl then asked Redlich: "Now, my dear friend, would you take it upon yourself to form such a government?" Redlich replied that it would be an honor to serve Karl and the fatherland in this way. While discussing the details of the formation of the government, Redlich also claimed the interior ministry for himself, which he said was necessary to have full control of the constitutional and administrative reforms that his government would carry out.[238]

With hindsight, we can understand that this was in effect the culmination of Redlich's political campaign in the summer of 1917. Already at midnight on the day of the second audience, Redlich was telephoned by Arthur Polzer-Hoditz, the director of the imperial chancellery, and asked to come to the palace on the next day to receive some additional instructions on the mode of procedure in forming a new Austrian government. The meeting in question resulted in a postponement of Redlich's mission to form such a government and then its abortion. However, Redlich continued to appear in several other combinations during July, since Heinrich Lammasch, Julius Meinl, and Friedrich Wilhelm Foerster were repeatedly consulted about the question of forming a new government on the same program of peace and national political reform during this time.[239]

The climax of the campaign of the larger Lammasch-Meinl group was, arguably, the manifestation for peace, national conciliation, and reform of the empire on 17 July 1917, in which Redlich took a prominent part. During the manifestation,

Meinl, Foerster, and Redlich all spoke and developed its basic themes of peace and national conciliation in Austria-Hungary. Redlich especially emphasized the need for this program to be carried out by a parliamentarian government that was firmly anchored in the different peoples of Austria, adding a critical remark on the disdainful way the Czechs had been treated by the Austrian government during the war.[240] Remarks such as the latter had contributed to making leading German-Liberals increasingly critical of Redlich during the summer of 1917, and his participation in the peace manifestation of the Meinl group made the German national radicals around Karl Hermann Wolf initiate a campaign against him. After another appearance by Redlich in the Austrian Political Society on 4 October, where he criticized the submarine warfare of imperial Germany and the whole "crazy war mongering" emanating from Berlin and finding such "foolhardy disciples" in Austria, his enemies made an emphatic attempt to have him thrown out of the German-Liberal parliamentary club. It was only the collapse of the German-Liberal party group as such, the Deutsche Nationalverband, a few weeks later, that inhibited the process of having Redlich formally excluded.[241]

After the dust from the political campaign in the summer of 1917 had settled, Redlich found himself just as distant from power as he had been before this episode and only even more pessimistic about the future of Austria. Nevertheless, he would once more be lured into engaging himself on behalf of the Austrian state. In the early days of October 1918, when the contours of the military breakdown of the central powers were already discernible, Redlich, together with Heinrich Lammasch, started to figure prominently in the discussion on a new Austrian government that could handle the imminent passage into a new state of being for the union of peoples about to be freed from their imperial shackles. Redlich remained very active in his contacts with representatives from a wide spectrum of parties, from which he seems to have been strengthened in his convictions that it was still possible to reconstruct Austria. In a mid-October entry in his diary, he expressed that his intention was to get a nationally mixed imperial government appointed, "a transitional government led by me that will execute the transformation of the centralist Obrigkeitsstaat to the democratic federal peoples' state." Redlich was hoping for and believing in support from Emperor Karl in this undertaking, which was essential, since he saw the emperor as the only guarantor for a successful passage into the renewed life of the Austrian multinational state.[242]

However, on 16 October Redlich's hopes were drastically diminished when he heard of the imminent publication of Emperor Karl's manifesto, in which the Austrian nationalities were invited to form themselves politically as the first step on the road to reshape Austria as a federal union of peoples. Redlich was even more disappointed because he had received signals that a Lammasch-Redlich government was in the making with the aim of gaining recognition both internationally and among the Slavic peoples of Austria. If only such a government had *first* been appointed, Redlich lamented, the federal principle could have been established *before* the Austrian peoples were released from their bonds to the imperial state. With the present mode of procedure, Redlich concluded, the imperial regime had rescinded all authority, and any following imperial government had lost all moral support.[243] Despite this unfavorable point of departure, Redlich would partake in the formation of a government under Heinrich Lammasch in the last days of October 1918, a government that initially had the ambition to act as a true imperial government above the already forming national governments, the embryo of a federal multination state as it were, but which soon retreated into the function of a caretaker cabinet with the mission to ease the process of dissolution.[244]

5. The End of the Austrian Problem

Although the ghost of the empire would continue to haunt the political and intellectual elites of republican Austria throughout the interwar era and beyond,[245] the Austrian problem as defined by Josef Redlich was resolved by the decapitation of the imperial state. Now the people's states could enfold freely and realize the democratic political order that Redlich had also striven for, albeit in plural. But the achieved solution was hardly to Redlich's satisfaction, and also he was plagued by a Phantomschmerz of the empire for the remaining part of his life. He had struggled politically to achieve a *balance* between the historically established state machinery of the Habsburg dynasty and the second, new Austria that he so strongly felt was growing from below, to modernize the old imperial bureaucratic Theresian-Josephinian state and let it evolve into the multinational democratic Volksstaat of Austria. This was the Austria Redlich identified himself with, and the complete disappearance of this polity was a heavy blow.

Redlich's estrangement and disbelief at the whole situation is quite evident when two days after his resignation as the last imperial Austrian finance minister he visited the provisional national assembly of the state of "German-Austria." "The whole thing makes a peculiar, unreal impression: Renner as chancellor of the state on the seat of the minister president, and right and left from him the secretaries of state." Redlich followed the debate on the new law regarding the territorial extension of this new state, noting that the idea of the Austrian Völkerbund was completely dead, that Karl Renner of all people had abandoned this vision and now led the struggle to collect as large a portion of the German-speaking areas as possible within the new German-Austrian state, which was then also defined as part of the German Republic.[246] A few weeks later Redlich reflected on this: "Renner must have given up his Austrian program of the supranational state after an inner struggle. This was indubitably the precondition for becoming 'chancellor of the state.'"[247]

This need to explain Renner's turn in the fall of 1918, from an advocate of the Austrian Nationalitätenbundesstaat to an adherent of Anschluss and an outspoken Great-German, has become endemic in the literature on an Austrian statesman, who at this time had just begun his historical career as the father of two Austrian republics. The most usual explanation is also the one put forward above by Redlich, that Renner made this turn out of opportunism. Because of the massive consensus on Karl Renner's opportunism, as expressed not only in 1918, but throughout his life and most prominently in 1938 and 1945, I would not like to differ here. There was a strongly pragmatic, even opportunist trait in Renner's personality that cannot be disregarded.[248]

Nevertheless, I would like to suggest that his turn in 1918 was not of the fundamental character it is often viewed as. I would like to substitute the view of the clean break contained in many attempts at understanding Renner's actions in 1918, with a view that emphasizes more strongly the continuity of his thinking before and after this year. As demonstrated above, there is a strong strain from early on in Renner's writings to view the Habsburg Empire as a German mission in southeastern Europe. In its political context, his Nationalitätenbundesstaat most of all comes across as the modern political solution to the problem of the geographically dispersed German groups in Central Europe; it represents perhaps the only way to collect and house all or most of these groups in a modern, democratic polity where, despite their territorial fragmentation, they can still fill the role of the leading national group in a large and internationally powerful polity. This, I would argue, was the underlying motive force of Renner's political project, which reached its apex during the Mitteleuropa euphoria of World War I.

However, Renner's project was also a direct descendant of Josephism and the Bach system. A supranational, multination federation of Renner's proposed type, where nationality has been politically neutralized by embedding it institutionally, most of all looks like a democratized variety of the old Josephist unitary state, which viewed its population as an atomized mass of individuals who could be of any nationality they liked as long as they did not insist on the state seeing them in this capacity. After the greater part of the population of this polity, formerly simply imperial subjects, has been politically enfranchised, this state needs exactly such a solution as that propagated by Renner to sustain itself. This solution was one that would facilitate democratic participation by many different nationalities and also, in effect, screen out nationality from the political process, institutionalizing it as an integrated part of the unitary, centralized, democratic neo-Josephist state that was Renner's Nationalitätenbundesstaat. The two strands of Renner's project, the German national and the Josephist, are joined in their combined effect of giving the German-Austrians a dominant cultural and economic position in such a state as envisioned by Renner;

it was this quality of the old Josephist state that Renner wanted to salvage over into the age of democracy.

What happened with Renner's project in 1918 was that the institutional foundation for the union of all the German groups of Central Europe, the Habsburg Empire, disappeared, and consequently the German dimension in Renner's project was laid free: Renner "became" a Great-German. This is exceedingly clear in his actions and writings during the First Republic and was not either controversial in "the state that no one wanted." However, Renner's publicly expressed option for Anschluss to the rising political force of Nazi Germany in 1938 was much more controversial. However, Renner's actions here can be viewed against the background of his expectations of the military might of Imperial Germany to realize Mitteleuropa during the world war. I believe we can safely say that Renner had a strong tendency to think in terms of fundamental historical categories and processes, and in such a perspective both Emperor Wilhelm and Adolf Hitler could bring about changes, which in the short term were of a doubtful nature, but in the long run were good. Renner's public endorsement of Anschluss was also followed later in 1938 by a deeply compromising pamphlet, though at the time never published, that historically justified the Nazi-German annexation of the Sudetenland. Disregarding its complicity with the cause of Nazi Germany, this pamphlet actually contains a rather consequential restatement of the position that Renner had taken in 1918, that all the Germans of Imperial Austria who lived in a contiguous territory should rightly have been joined to the German-Austrian republic. Now his position had only changed insofar as in the absence of an Austrian republic, these Germans should be joined directly to Germany.[249]

The diverging political trajectories of Karl Renner and Josef Redlich became increasingly obvious during the interwar era. When Renner retreated into a Great-German position, Redlich made serious plans to make a new life in the republic of Czechoslovakia, where his homeland, Moravia, now lay and where many of his family were residents. During this period he also figured in political combinations in Czechoslovakia, not the least because of his personal friendship with the Czechoslovak president, Tomas G. Masaryk.[250] This interest in Czechoslovakia as a political heir to Imperial Austria was also mirrored in the tendency of Redlich's historical writings in the 1920s, where the appreciation and affirmation of the federal strain in Austrian history grew noticeably. In the second part of *Das österreichische Staats- und Reichsproblem* (1926) and in Redlich's last work on Imperial Austria, his biography of Franz Joseph of 1929, his long-standing theoretical adherence to the federal idea completed its naturalization to Austrian history. In the first of the above works, his older affirmation of the Austrian political autonomy was complemented by an open appreciation of the federalism of the Hungarian Liberals around Ferenc Déak during the 1860s. In the second, where he continues beyond the 1867 end point of the former, he judges benevolently the failed Hohenwart plan of 1870–71 to continue the federalization of the empire by granting also Bohemia far-reaching political autonomy. Parallel to this, Redlich also evaluates that perennial outsider in German-Austrian Liberalism, Adolf Fischhof, and his program of national federalism for Austria at this same moment in history as the major lost opportunity of the German-Liberals to find "the way to a working reconstruction of the dynastic unitary state as a monarchic union of peoples on the basis of national autonomy."[251]

The explicit federalist view on Austrian history in Redlich's Franz Joseph biography, and especially his view of the Hohenwart plan, disturbed his friend the publisher, Berthold Molden. Redlich therefore did his utmost to clarify his position:

> My view of federalism is so to speak the center of my political thinking. It goes way beyond the special case of the Austrian problem and dominates my whole theoretical and practical political development, since more than thirty years and my convictions in this matter have only been reinforced by the results of the world war. That the federalist plan of 1871, with its historical romanticist foundation, cannot be compared with modern federalism is most certainly true: However, under the historically given conditions, it was the only possible federalist policy at the time.[252]

Redlich even concluded that the failure to grasp this historical opportunity was crucial for the following decline and fall of the Habsburg Empire. Redlich's conclusion here is a result of research he had done during the previous years on the planned but never realized third volume of *Das österreichische Staats- und Reichsproblem*,[253] in which the Hohenwart government would have been the first major subject. The continuing tendency of Redlich's magnum opus seems clear, to affirm the federalist tendency in Austrian history as the road never taken, the road that could have led to the modern democratic Austrian union of peoples.

In the above quote, Redlich also concisely describes his political road, a road that has been followed here in rather more detail. One can easily agree with him about the continuity in his search for a federal solution to the Austrian problem, but within this paradigm there were also considerable changes. Redlich began with a theoretical idea of state-free local self-government after the English model as the motor for a regeneration of the Imperial Austrian state. He also viewed the Austrian municipal autonomy created in 1862 as the embryo of such an organization of the Austrian state. On such a foundation, Redlich wanted to rebuild the Austrian state largely through an administrative reform in which the centralist state apparatus was devolved into a democratic self-governing administration, something that preoccupied him from around 1906 to 1914. The culmination of this development was his prominent engagement in the Imperial Administrative Reform Commission (1911–14), in which it also became quite evident that Redlich at this early stage was primarily aiming at modernizing the Austrian centralist state, not to federalize it in a political way. Redlich's position at this early stage in his career was closely related to that democratic centralism that was Karl Renner's Nationalitätenbundesstaat.

As Redlich himself emphasized in his above-quoted letter to Berthold Molden, his decisive experience was the world war. It has been demonstrated above that Redlich had already undergone a marked change during the war. In 1917 and 1918, he completed this turn as he propagated an Austrian Völkerbund built on Kaiser, Land, Gemeinde, a model with parts of its root system in the Austrian Vormärz rather than in the liberal revolution of 1848, which had been his guiding star throughout his political career. At the core of this major turn lay Redlich's deeply grounded hostility toward the fusion between German-Austrian bureaucratic centralism and German-Austrian National-Libe:alism. As Redlich saw it, this system was in effect a sort of internal German-Austrian imperialism with the intent of ruling over the other peoples of Central Europe, and as such it contained the seed of the final destruction of Austria. In this core of Redlich's political views can also be seen its diametrical difference to Karl Renner's affirmation and refinement of just this political-cultural inheritance of German-Austrian centralism. This difference can also be seen in the differing perceptions Redlich and Renner had of their common homeland, Moravia: where Renner could see only cleanly separated German and Czech groups, Redlich saw a mixed German-Slavic land. The diametrical difference in this perception of Moravia is also reflected in their deeply differing models for multinational democracy in Austria.

While the dissolution of the empire resulted in a political configuration of Central Europe that could be assimilated and even affirmed by Renner, who continued to participate productively in Austrian and German politics, Redlich was left on the sidelines. However, history also had an ironic twist in readiness for the conclusion of Karl Renner's political career. The man who had spent his whole life theorizing on large states and economic spheres, and who had throughout his life been shaped by his fundamental sense of belonging to the German nation, would conclude his political career as the head of state in that occupied, unfree small-state Austria, which in the late 1940s was vehemently denying its German heritage. In the last years of his life, Karl Renner was presiding over what more or less looks like the complete negation of his political vision.

Notes

1. Josef Redlich, *Aus dem alten Österreich. Erinnerungen und Einsichten. Fragmente der Lebenserinnerungen*, 89f, in Nachlass Josef Redlich.
2. Ibid., 4.
3. Despite Redlich's rather prominent political career in late Imperial Austria, and especially his widely observed political engagement for peace and internal reform of Austria in 1917–18,

the scholarship on him has remained very limited. The only important work done on Redlich until very recently is that of Austrian historian Fritz Fellner, who is also in the possession of Redlich's Nachlass. Fellner has primarily published a great deal of source material in connection with Redlich. Most important are his diary for the years 1909–19; see Josef Redlich, *Schicksaalsjahre Österreichs 1908–1919. Das politische Tagebuch Josef Redlichs* (2 vols.), Fritz Fellner, ed. (Graz: Böhlau Verlag, 1953–54), and his correspondence with Hermann Bahr (see *Dichter und Gelehrter*). Fellner has also published other correspondence involving Redlich. Fellner's article on the plans of the Austro-Hungarian foreign ministry to send Redlich on a propaganda mission to the United States in 1914–15 should be mentioned in this context; see Fritz Fellner, "Der Plan einer 'Vortragsmission Redlich-Apponyi' in den Vereinigten Staaten von Amerika," in *Beiträge zur neueren Geschichte Österreichs*, Heinrich Fichtenau & Erich Zöllner, eds. (Vienna: Böhlau Verlag, 1974). As an introduction and epilogue to Redlich's diary, Fellner has also published the only, as far as I know, biographical article on Josef Redlich thus far (see Redlich, *Schicksaalsjahre*, vols. 1:XI–XIX and 2:351–58). Parallel to my own work, Amy Ng of Oxford University has written a dissertation (2001), which is a dual biographical approach to Josef Redlich and Lewis Namier. It has later been published slightly revised as *Nationalism and Political Liberty. Redlich, Namier, and the Crisis of Empire* (Oxford: Clarendon Press, 2004). I have mainly found it useful as a broad exposition of Redlich's intellectual and political career. It also contains a long section (ibid., 11ff.) on Redlich's family background and early years, matters that I do not go deeper into. On the questions that I focus on, I found Ng's work especially helpful in its recognition of the importance of Redlich's early scholarship on the English state for our understanding of his later work on Austria (see 19–34). John W. Boyer has not least well noted the important work of Redlich in the administrative reform commission 1911–14; see the formerly quoted Boyer, *Culture and Political Crisis*, 357–63, and idem. "The End of an Old Regime," 176–83.

4. See part one of this book.
5. See the acts on Redlich in the ministry of education (AVA, MKU). See also Redlich's personnel file in the archive of the Technische Universität in Vienna (TU). Some basic data here can be found also in Fritz Fellner, "Josef Redlich. Leben und Werk," in Redlich, *Schicksaalsjahre*, 1:XI–XIX.
6. The outlines of this career of Redlich's are sketched in Fellner, "Josef Redlich. Leben und Werk," and in Fritz Fellner, "Josef Redlich. Leben und Werk, Ausklang," in Redlich, *Schicksaalsjahre*, 2:351–58.
7. See Redlich's letter to Bahr from 17 October 1906, in *Dichter und Gelehrter*, 48–50.
8. See Josef Redlich, "Die Originalprotokolle des Verfassungsauschuß im Kremsierer Reichstag," *Österreichische Rundschau* 17 (1908), and idem, "Lasser und Schmerling, Nach ihren Briefen," *Österreichische Rundschau* 19 (1909).
9. See Redlich's letter to Baernreither from 29 July 1909, in HHStA, Nachlass Baernreither, K.47.
10. On 25 July 1913, Redlich wrote to Joseph Maria Baernreither, who was also a member of the commission, that he had begun to write "eine Denkschrift . . . über die Reform der politischen Behörden" (HHStA, Nachlass Baernreither, K.49). Redlich also wrote to Hermann Bahr about this on 13 October 1913 (*Dichter und Gelehrter*, 92): "Im Frühjahr hoffe ich, eine bereits begonnene Denkschrift über die Reform unserer politischen Behörden zu vollenden. . . ." I have been unable to find any trace of this memorandum in Redlich's papers.
11. See Redlich's letter to Flora Darkow-Singer from 19 June 1914, in WStLB/HS (Sign. IN 198.646). Compare also Redlich's letter to Bahr, 20 November 1914, in *Dichter und Ge-*

lehrter, 101. Professor Fritz Fellner of Vienna has made transcriptions of Redlich's letters to Flora Darkow-Singer, which have been incorporated into the Nachlass Redlich, and I want to thank Professor Fellner for the kindness to let me use these transcriptions. The originals of these letters lie in WStLB/HS (Sign. IN 198.547–743). Redlich's correspondence with his friend of youthful years, Flora Darkow-Singer, spanning 1887–1936, is one of the most complete sources to Redlich's development from his youger days all the way up to the last year of his life.

12. See Redlich's letter to Bahr, 31 January 1915, in *Dichter und Gelehrter*, 104 (also quoted at the top of the introduction above).
13. Important general works treating Renner in his context of Austrian Social Democracy and Austromarxism are Mommsen, *Die Sozialdemokratie und die Nationalitätenfrage*, Norbert Leser, *Zwischen Reformismus und Bolchewismus. Der Austromarxismus als Theorie und Praxis* (Vienna: Europa-Verlag, 1968), and Kulemann, *Am Beispiel des Austromarxismus.* Other more specialized works on Renner will be quoted in the relevant contexts below. However, one more work must be mentioned here: Ernst Panzenböck, *Ein deutscher Traum. Die Anschlußidee und Anschlußpolitik bei Karl Renner und Otto Bauer* (Vienna: Europa-Verlag, 1985), is one of the few works that follows Renner (and Otto Bauer) from 1900 all the way up to 1945 (focusing on the Anschluss question) and is therefore a very important work. The biographies are quoted below.
14. See Anton Pelinka, *Karl Renner zur Einführung* (Hamburg: Junius Verlag, 1989), 14f.
15. See the biographies of Renner: Hannak, *Karl Renner und seine Zeit*; Rauscher, *Karl Renner*; Nasko & Reichl, *Karl Renner*; see especially Pelinka, *Karl Renner zur Einführung.*
16. Redlich, *Das österreichische Staats- und Reichsproblem*, 1:87.
17. Ibid., 1:89.
18. Ibid., 1:85f.
19. Ibid., 1:92. Redlich discusses the work of the Kremsier parliament thoroughly on 1:221–323.
20. For this argument, see for example, ibid., 1:232f.
21. Redlich discusses the Schwarzenberg-Stadion cabinet and Stadion's reform plan in ibid., 1:323–82. See especially 1:375–82 (quotation on 1:381).
22. On Bach, see ibid., 1:382–459.
23. Ibid.,1:396ff.
24. Ibid., 1:452–59.
25. Ibid., 1:405–12.
26. See, for example, ibid., 1:244.
27. Ibid., for example, 1:36f., 84. On the German centralist program in 1848, see, for example, 1:124–32, 172–74.
28. On the Czech position, see ibid., 1:109–17, 174–76.
29. Ibid., 1:139f.
30. For an evaluation of the Bach system in this regard, see ibid., 1:410–22.
31. See, for example, ibid., 1:37f., 84f., 125f., 173f., 527f.. On Schmerling, see especially 1:689–701.
32. There are several references to Friedjung's historical works in *Das österreichische Staats- und Reichsproblem*, particularly to Friedjung's *Österreich von 1848 bis 1860.* Redlich is usually very appreciative of Friedjung's work, and he always avoids polemics (see, for example, the high estimation of Friedjung's work in Redlich, *Das österreichische Staats- und Reichsproblem*, 1:146 and 2:500). In ibid., 2:398, however, Redlich very concisely identifies the fundamental difference between himself and Friedjung on the subject of Schmerling and German-Austrian centralism.

33. See Redlich's letter to Joseph Maria Baernreither, 29 July 1909, HHStA, Nachlass Baernreither, K.47.
34. See Redlich's letter to Bahr, 1 June 1915, *Dichter und Gelehrter*, 119.
35. See Redlich's letter to Bahr, 15 November 1920, *Dichter und Gelehrter*, 430.
36. See especially Redlich, *Das österreichische Staats- und Reichsproblem*, 1:49–55 (quotations on 49f.). Redlich returns throughout his work to this question of the special Austrian culture.
37. See ibid., especially 1:375–82 and 715–32.
38. See ibid., 2:679.
39. As interesting as this latter aspect is, it must also be viewed in its context: Redlich's publication on the Austrian municipal constitution was originally held as a lecture in Berlin in 1908. On the above quoted characteristics, see especially Josef Redlich, *Das Wesen der österreichischen Kommunal-Verfassung* (Leipzig: Duncker, 1910), 23, 52ff, 61–65, and 71f (quotations on 62–63).
40. On Redlich's contacts with England, see Fellner, "Josef Redlich. Leben und Werk." On the influence of the English experience and his work on English administration and parliamentarism on his view of the Austrian state problem, see Ng, *Nationalism and Political Liberty*, 19–34.
41. See Josef Redlich, *Englische Lokalverwaltung. Darstellung der inneren Verwaltung Englands in ihrer geschichtlichen Entwicklung und in ihrer gegenwärtigen Gestalt* (Leipzig: Duncker, 1901), and ibid. *Recht und Technik des Englischen Parlamentarismus. Die Geschäftsordnung des House of Commons in ihrer geschichtlichen Entwicklung und gegenwärtigen Gestalt* (Leipzig: Duncker, 1905), which between them also demonstrate an evolution in Redlich's thinking in the direction of emphasizing the need for unity, the need for a uniting state idea above the peoples. The reason for this evolution was most certainly the destructive obstruction of the Austrian as well as the English parliament by national minorities Redlich could observe at the time. See here, Ng, *Nationalism and Political Liberty*, 32–34.
42. Redlich, *Erinnerungen* (Nachlass Redlich). Redlich had a Slavic nanny, and up to the age of seven he seems to have spoken Slovakian or Moravian, as he termed it himself, only turning definitely to German as his primary language when he began school. See, for instance, ibid., 52. Later he retained this special identification with the Slavic culture of his Heimat, and in 1902 he noted in his diary that in him "unverkennbar das Herz für das slawische schlägt." (Quoted in Fellner, "Josef Redlich. Leben und Werk," 1:XII.) See here also Ng, *Nationalism and Political Liberty*, 30f.
43. See Renner's letters to Redlich from around the turn of the century, in Nachlass Redlich. This correspondence has only survived in parts. There are several letters from Karl Renner to Redlich from the same period and one from 1918, in Nachlass Redlich, but only one letter from Redlich to Renner (from 1903) in VGA, Teilnachlass Renner. From the existing correspondence, it is possible to deduce that several letters are missing. The few surviving letters, though, are crammed full of political and scholarly reflections on the Austrian state and the empire.
44. See Redlich's letter to Renner, 23 December 1903, VGA, Teilnachlass Renner.
45. See Renner's letter to Redlich, 23 May 1902, Nachlass Redlich.
46. The model of English local government (and the references to Redlich) was especially conspicuous in Renner's campaign for a reform of the Austrian state during World War I. For an example of this tendency, see Karl Renner, *Österreichs Erneuerung. Politisch-programmatische Aufsätze*, 3 vols. (Vienna: Brand, 1916), 1:115–18.
47. See Renner's letter to Redlich, 23 May 1902, Nachlass Redlich.
48. Because of his civil service position as a librarian in the library of the Austrian parliament, Renner wrote under pseudonyms at this early stage in his career, until his election

to the Austrian parliament in 1907 (when he moved upstairs from the library into the session hall of the parliament!). It was, though, from early on an open secret in political and scholarly circles in Vienna that "Rudolf Springer" was Karl Renner. His most overtly political early works are Karl Renner, *Staat und Nation. Staatsrechtliche Unter-suchung über die möglichen Principien einer Lösung und die juristischen Voraussetzungen eines Nationalitätengesetzes* (Vienna: Dietl, 1899) [pseudonym Synopticus]; idem, *Staat und Parlament. Kritische Studie über die Österreichische Frage und das System der Interessenvertretung* (Vienna: Genossenschafts-Buchdruckerei, 1901) [Rudolf Springer]; idem, *Der Kampf der österreichischen Nationen um den Staat. Das nationale Problem als Verfassungs- und Verwaltungsfrage* (Leipzig: Deuticke, 1902) [Rudolf Springer]; idem, *Die Krise des Dualismus und das Deákistische Episode in der Geschichte der habsburgischen Monarchie. Eine politische Skizze* (Vienna: Genossenschafts-Buchdruckerei, 1904) [Rudolf Springer]; and idem, *Grundlagen und Entwicklungsziele der Österreichisch-Ungarischen Monarchie. Politische Studie über den Zusammenbruch der Privilegienparlamente und die Wahlreform in beiden Staaten, über die Reichsidee und ihre Zukunft* (Vienna: Deuticke, 1906) [Rudolf Springer].

49. Quoted from Renner, *Der Kampf der österreichischen Nationen*, 197.
50. See ibid., 154.
51. That it would be possible to make 90% of the Kreise nationally homogeneous in the many nationally strongly mixed provinces of Imperial Austria is Renner's own evaluation. This view builds, for instance, on discounting small minorities, whose interests would be guarded through other means. On the general problem of even identifying national identity in late Imperial Austria in this way, see Brix, *Die Umgangssprachen in Altösterreich*, and Stourzh, *Die Gleichberechtigung der Nationalitäten*.
52. Renner's model for a federal multination state (Nationalitätenbundesstaat) is presented in its basic outline several times throughout his career with minor changes and development of the argument, beginning with Renner, *Staat und Nation* (1899) and idem, *Der Kampf der österreichischen Nationen um den Staat* (1902), through idem, *Grundlagen und Entwicklungsziele der Österreichisch-Ungarischen Monarchie* (1906), to *Das Selbstbestimmungsrecht der Nationen (*1918). Renner (1902) and (1918) contains the most complete statements of his argument. It is also expressed in its entirety and its parts in Renner's very active political journalism from 1900 to 1918, some of which will be returned to below.
53. On Renner's work as a civil servant and his contacts with Koerber, see the autobiographic fragment *Memoiren 1896–1897*, KA, Nachlass Renner, E/1731:18. See also the last sections in Renner, *An der Wende zweier Zeiten*, where he treats his entrance into state service. On his general closeness to bureaucratic circles during World War I, see, for example, Pelinka, *Karl Renner zur Einführung*, 45.
54. See Renner's letter to Viktor Adler, 22 February 1902, VGA, Nachlass Viktor Adler, Mappe, 147/1.
55. See Pelinka, *Karl Renner zur Einführung*, 99.
56. For a treatment of the democratization of Austria in a long perspective, see Karl Ucakar, *Demokratie und Wahlrecht in Österreich. Zur Entwicklung von politischer Partizipation und staatlicher Legitimationspolitik* (Vienna: Verlag für Gesellschaftskritik, 1985), and Ernst Hanisch, *Der lange Schatten des Staates. Österreichische Gesellschaftsgeschichte im 20. Jahrhundert, 1890–1990* (Vienna: Ueberreuther, 1994). Kann, *The Multinational Empire*, remains a standard work on the problem of the democratization of the multinational empire.
57. On Christian Socialism, see Boyer, *Political Radicalism in Late Imperial Vienna*, and idem, *Culture and Political Crisis in Vienna*, and on Social Democracy, see Mommsen, *Die Sozialdemokratie und die Nationalitätenfrage*. See also the very interesting discussion on the view of imperial reform in these two mass parties, Boyer, "The End of an Old Regime."

58. For a broad overview of the different national party systems in imperial Austria, see *Die Habsburgermonarchie 1848–1918*, vol. 3, *Die Völker des Reiches*, Wandruszka & Urbanitsch, eds.
59. On the German-Liberal party spectrum, see Höbelt, *Kornblume und Kaiseradler*. On the problem of the secessionist Alldeutschen, see Andrew Whiteside, *The Socialism of Fools. Georg Ritter von Schönerer and Austrian Pan-Germanism* (Berkeley: University of California Press, 1975). The Czech parties have been treated by, for instance, Garver, *The Young-Czech Party*, and Křen, *Die Konfliktgemeinschaft*.
60. See Boyer, "The End of an Old Regime."
61. See above, part one of this book.
62. It should be noted that Karl Renner's reformism was widely shared in Austrian Social Democracy and especially so in its leadership.
63. See Panzenböck, *Ein deutscher Traum*, 1–10, on Renner and the Brünner program. It should be added here that the Brünner program built on a national-territorial solution, not on Renner's personality principle. It did, however, contain the program of national autonomy, which Renner usually emphasized.
64. See Höbelt, *Kornblume und Kaiseradler*, on the German-Liberal party spectrum, especially 116–41 for the creation in 1896 and early history of the Deutsche Fortschrittspartei.
65. On Redlich's individualism as a member of parliament, see Fellner, "Josef Redlich. Leben und Werk," XVII.
66. On this early political engagement, see Fellner, "Josef Redlich. Leben und Werk," and Ng, *Nationalism and Political Liberty*, 17–19. Redlich partook in the founding of the Social Political party in 1896; on this party, see Eva Holleis, *Die Sozialpolitische Partei. Sozialliberale Bestrebungen in Wien um 1900* (Vienna: Verlag für Geschichte und Politik, 1978). He was at this time also involved in starting a newspaper with political ambitions, *Die Zeit*; see Edith Walter, *Österreichische Tageszeitungen der Jahrhundertwende. Ideologischer Anspruch und ökonomische Erfordernisse* (Vienna: Böhlau Verlag, 1994), 51–67.
67. Fellner, "Josef Redlich. Leben und Werk," XVI, quotes a few entries in Redlich's early (unpublished) diary, which concerns his political turn. Also, Redlich's letters to Flora Darkow-Singer during these years contain indications for the coming turn to politics. See especially his letters to her on 11 October 1900 and 16 October 1905, WStLB/HS (Sign. IN 198.592 and 198.610).
68. Renner's speech in *Stenographische Protokolle des Abgeordnetenhauses, Session XVIII (1907–09)*, 120–124.
69. Redlich's speech in *Stenographische Protokolle des Abgeordnetenhauses, Session XVIII (1907–09)*, 125–131.
70. On the Beck government, see Johann Christoph Allmayer-Beck, *Ministerpräsident Baron Beck. Ein Staatsman des alten Österreich* (Vienna: Verlag für Geschichte und Politik, 1956), 122–246, and Boyer, *Culture and Political Crisis in Vienna*, 111–134. On the sense of revolutionary change brought on by the franchise reform, see Kann, *The Multinational Empire*, 2:221–27.
71. Redlich's speech in *Stenographische Protokolle des Abgeordnetenhauses, Session XVIII (1907–09)*, 5549–5560.
72. See Redlich's letter to Bahr, 2 June 1909, in *Dichter und Gelehrter*, 63–64.
73. *Protokolle der Delegation des österreichischen Reichsrates vom 27. Oktober in Budapest, Wiener Zeitung*, 28 October 1908, 2–3, 5–10.
74. See for instance Redlich's speech on 17 December 1908 in the Lower house of the Austrian parliament, in *Stenographische Protokolle des Abgeordnetenhauses, Session XVIII (1907–09)*, 8116–28.

75. On Friedjung's engagement with Aehrenthal at this time, see part one of this book.
76. See Redlich, *Schicksaalsjahre*, 1:5–11 (entries for the period January-March 1909). Quotations on 10f.
77. See part one of this book for a discussion of Aehrenthal's previous constitutional politics.
78. On Aehrenthal's constitutional politics of 1907/08, see Somogyi, "Aehrenthals Reformbestrebungen 1906–1907," and Wank, "Aehrenthal's Programme for the Constitutional Transformation of the Habsburg Monarchy." See also the protocols to the common ministerial council of 1907, in *Protokolle des Gemeinsamen Ministerrates der Österreichisch-Ungarischen Monarchie, 1896–1907*, Éva Somogyi, ed. (Vienna: Österreichischer Bundesverlag, 1991), as well as Aehrenthal's and Wékerle's memoranda on this question, in *Aus dem Nachlass Aehrenthal*, 2:433–60 (this volume also contains additional correspondence of interest in regard to this question, not the least between Aehrenthal and Beck). The long-time importance of this question to Aehrenthal can be traced in several sources, including especially *Aus dem Nachlass Aehrenthal*. Another important source here is Heinrich Friedjung's notes on conversations with Aehrenthal during the years 1898–1909, Friedjung, *Geschichte in Gesprächen*. On this question, see also Wank, "Varieties of Political Despair."
79. See Redlich's speech in the Lower house of parliament on 30 October 1907, *Stenographische Protokolle des Abgeordnetenhauses, Session XVIII (1907–09)*, 2359–68 (quotations on 2359 and 2366).
80. Redlich's speech in the Lower house of parliament on 18 December 1907, *Stenographische Protokolle des Abgeordnetenhauses, Session XVIII (1907–09)*, 3595–99.
81. Redlich on Kristóffy, see Redlich, *Schicksaalsjahre*, 1:8 (entry for 10 March 1909).
82. Redlich, *Schicksaalsjahre*, see especially 1:17–19, 24–25 (entries for 5, 23 and 25 June and for 24 October 1909). The memorandum and the accompanying letter from Redlich to Aehrenthal (dated 26 June 1909) lie in HHStA, Nachlass Szápary, K.6 (the text of Redlich's Hungarian memorandum is reprinted under the entry for 23 June 1909, in Redlich, *Schicksaalsjahre*, 1:17–18). At the very time Redlich wrote his memorandum and sent it to Aehrenthal, there were negotiations between Franz Joseph and the leading Liberal Hungarian politician Ladislaus Lukács for a renewed attempt at a mixed parliamentarian/imperial government with an electoral reform on its program.
83. The text of the memorandum is reprinted in Redlich, *Schicksaalsjahre*, 1:17–18.
84. Redlich, *Schicksaalsjahre*, 1:152 (entry for 13 September 1912).
85. There are many recorded conversations between Aehrenthal and Redlich during the years 1908–12, Redlich, *Schicksaalsjahre*, 1. For a few examples of the above-mentioned tendency, see 1:24 (entry on 20 October 1909), 1:26 (entry on 28 October 1909), and 1:31 (entry on 6 November 1909).
86. Redlich, *Schicksaalsjahre*, 1:82 (entry on 18 April 1911).
87. See Redlich, *Schicksaalsjahre*, 1:125 (entry on 18 February 1912).
88. Redlich, *Schicksaalsjahre*, 1:28–30 (entry on 5 November 1909).
89. The possibility of Koerber's return as minister president especially arose during the summer and fall of 1912 (accompanied by rumors of Redlich's appointment in his government). See Redlich, *Schicksaalsjahre*, for instance 1:141ff., 145, 148, 153.
90. See Redlich, *Schicksaalsjahre*, 1:143 (entry on 28 July 1912). At this time Redlich also developed ideas on "the impossibility of parliamentarian governments" in Austria and the need to prepare multinational Austria for its future by conducting "a sort of social development policy . . . for half a man's age." Only by helping the masses, and the peripheries of Austria, to attain a high level of economic development can we pave the way, Redlich concluded, for a progressive political development of the Austrian state and society. See Redlich, *Schicksaalsjahre*, 1:146–48 (entry on 28 August 1912).

91. See Renner, *Memoiren 1896–1897*, 1–2, KA, Nachlass Renner, E/1731:18. For a very vivid description of the tumultuous events of 1897, see Gerschenkron, *An Economic Spurt*, 16–20.
92. See Renner, *An der Wende zweier Zeiten*, 181–206 (quotations on 194–95).
93. This view of the empire is reflected in several of Renner's main texts on the Austrian problem, which have a long section describing the "natural" necessity of the empire, its historical, geographic, and economic "naturalness." See, for instance, Renner, *Die Krise der Dualismus*, 20–36.
94. For Renner's appreciative view of the Bach system, see, for instance, Renner, *Der Kampf der österreichischen Nationen*, 231, idem, *Die Krise der Dualismus*, 39f., idem, *Grundlagen und Entwicklungsziele*, 37f.
95. See, for instance, Renner, *Staat und Parlament*, 30–31; idem, *Der Kampf der österreichischen Nationen*, 96, 170; idem, *Die Krise der Dualismus*, 30; idem, *Grundlagen und Entwicklungsziele*, 238–39.
96. See, for instance, Renner, *Das Selbstbestimmungsrecht der Nationen*, 134f., 156, 250–53.
97. See Renner's description of his Moravian homeland and the strong focus on the German and Czech communities as living in peace, but wholly and cleanly separated from one another throughout a long history of several hundred years, in Renner, *An der Wende zweier Zeiten*, 7f., 20, 45ff., 148ff., 275.
98. Quoted from Renner, *Das Selbstbestimmungsrecht der Nationen*, 134, 156.
99. This can be discerned, for instance, in the major early political tract, Renner, *Staat und Nation* (1899).
100. Renner, for instance, published himself in Friedrich Naumann's *Die Hilfe*, Paul Barth's *Die Nation* (both Berlin), and in Engelbert Pernerstorfer's *Deutsche Worte* (Vienna) in these years. Many of these articles also went into his weightier political texts, which appear here and there in footnotes and forewords to these texts and thus constitute a strong connection to day-to-day politics in these more high-flying political tracts of Renner's.
101. See Renner's autobiographical sketch, *Biographie (Lebensläufe)*, in KA, Nachlass Renner, E/1731:304, where he especially focused his political activism around the turn of the century, part of which was his cooperation with Koerber (because of its contents and adjacent material in the Nachlass, it appears to have been written in 1931). On Koerber's constitutional reform plan, see above in part one of this book.
102. This lecture was held in the bürgerliche forum of the Viennese Fabian Society, where Redlich was also a member, and it was published as a brochure in the following year; see Karl Renner, *Mehrheits- oder Volksvertretung. Zur Aufklärung der intellektuellen und bürgerlichen Klassen über ihr Interesse an einer Wahlreform, sowie über Wesen, Arten und Bedeutung der Proportionalwahl* (Vienna: Deuticke, 1904) [Rudolf Springer].
103. See Renner, *Staat und Parlament*, 5.
104. See part one of this book regarding Koerber's constitutional reform plan of 1900. The memorandum itself has been published in *Briefe und Dokumente*, 2:371–442.
105. See Renner, *Staat und Parlament*, quotations on 5 and 7.
106. See Koerber's report in *Briefe und Dokumente*, 2:396. See also part one above.
107. See Renner, *Was haben die Sozialdemokraten geleistet? Zehn Jahre parlamentarischer Arbeit für das Wohl der arbeitenden Klasse* (Vienna: Brand, 1907), 9–21.
108. This criticism has surfaced already in Renner, *Der Kampf der österreichischen Nationen um den Staat* (1902), where he thoroughly discusses and criticizes Koerber's proposal of 1900 for a new Kreis-administration in Bohemia (136–44). It can be traced in the intervening period, and then it resurfaces in Renner, *Das Selbstbestimmungsrecht der Nationen* (1918), 67f., 219–24.

109. Renner, *Die Krise der Dualismus*, 68f.
110. See Renner, *Grundlagen und Entwicklungsziele*, especially 1–4, 95, 103f., 139, 151, 160, and 226–32 (quotation on 2.) See also Renner's long exposé on the history of the Reichsidee, ibid., 5–47, which gives the whole text its strong thrust toward renewed imperial unity.
111. On Bach, see Renner, *Grundlagen und Entwicklungsziele*, especially 37f., 41. Compare also Renner, *Die Krise der Dualismus*, 39f. (and note 13).
112. See, for instance, Renner, *Die Krise der Dualismus*, 59, and Renner, *Grundlagen und Entwicklungsziele*, 149.
113. Redlich, *Schicksaalsjahre*, 1:35 (entry on 27 November 1909).
114. The speech of 27 June 1907, in *Stenographische Protokolle des Abgeordnetenhauses, Session XVIII (1907–09)*, 125–31 (this speech is discussed above), and the petition of 15 June 1909, in *Stenographische Protokolle des Abgeordnetenhauses, Session XIX (1909)*, 1579, and Beilage 723.
115. See Redlich, *Schicksaalsjahre*, 1:57–64 (entries for 2 and 18–20 May 1910).
116. See Hasiba, "Die Kommission zur Förderung der Verwaltungsreform," 241.
117. Redlich, *Schicksaalsjahre*, 1:84 (entry for 13 May 1911).
118. In his diary for this period are intertwined pessimistic reflections about Austrian parliamentary politics and equally optimistic thoughts on the potential of the new commission. See, for example, Redlich, *Schicksaalsjahre*, 1:84f. (entries for 21 April and 20 May 1911).
119. Redlich had high expectations of the commission from the day of its inception; see Redlich, *Schicksaalsjahre*, 1:84 (entry on 13 May 1911), and his late retrospective glance, Redlich, *Austrian War Government*, 54.
120. See *Grundsätze für die Tätigkeit der Kommission zur Förderung der Verwaltungsreform* (1911) and the appended *Communiqué* (of the minister president) and imperial declaration (*Kaiserliches Handschreiben*), in AVA, MRP/VRK, K.1. This material also is found in AVA, MRP, K.289 (Z.5302/1916).
121. Redlich, *Schicksaalsjahre*, 1:89f. (entry on 6 July 1911).
122. Ibid., 1:88 (entry on 26 June 1911).
123. Ibid., 1:85, 86 (entries on 20 May and 3 June 1911).
124. See the protocol to the constitutive session of the commission on 28 June 1911, MRP/VRK, K.4. See also Redlich, *Schicksaalsjahre*, 1:89–90 (entry on 6 July 1911), regarding Redlich's and Haerdtl's discussion on the business order and working plan. See also Hasiba, "Die Kommission zur Förderung der Verwaltungsreform," 245.
125. See Josef Redlich, *Zustand und Reform der österreichischen Verwaltung. Rede des Reichsratsabgeordneten Professor Dr. Josef Redlich gehalten in der Budgetdebatte des Abgeordnetenhauses des österreichischen Reichsrates vom 26. Oktober 1911* (Vienna: Manz Verlag, 1911). See also *Stenographische Protokolle des Abgeordnetenhauses, Session XXI (1911–1914)*, 1217–41, and Redlich, *Schicksaalsjahre*, 1:107 (entry on 28 October 1911).
126. See *Arbeitsplan für die Kommission zur Förderung der Verwaltungsreform*, in MRP/VRK, K.1, and the protocol to the second plenary session of the commission on 16 October 1911, MRP/VRK, K.4. Compare also Redlich's notes to his meeting with Haerdtl on 6 July 1911, Redlich, *Schicksaalsjahre*, 1:89–90.
127. This idea had already surfaced during Redlich's meeting with Haerdtl in July 1911 (see Redlich, *Schicksaalsjahre*, 1:89).
128. See the protocol to the second plenary session on 16 October 1911, in MRP/VRK, K.4, especially 266–267. See also the overview of the subcommittee elections, in Z.71/VRK (dated 18 October 1911) MRP/VRK, K.1. The four subcommittees were Ausschuss I: Organization der Verwaltungsbehörden; Auschuss II: Heranbildung und Fortbildung der Staatsbeamten; Auschuss III: Innere Einrichtung und Geschäftsgang der Behörden;

Ausschuss IV: Verfahren vor den Verwaltungsbehörden. For a type of fundamental reform that Redlich wanted to bring about, the subcommittees I and III were, arguably, the two most important to control.

129. Redlich, *Schicksaalsjahre*, 1:90.
130. See *Arbeitsplan für die Kommission zur Förderung der Verwaltungsreform*, MRP/VRK, K.1, 8–9.
131. See the protocol to the second plenary session 16 October 1911, MRP/VRK, K.4, 146–161.
132. On Anton Pace's role under Koerber in the years 1900–1904, see part one above.
133. See the protocol to the third plenary session on 7 December 1911, MRP/VRK, K.4, especially 2, 26–31. See also Schwartzenau's letter to Stürgkh on this matter, 25 December 1911 (Z.119/VRK), MRP/VRK, K.1.
134. See the correspondence on this issue between Schwartzenau, Stürgkh, and Interior Minister Heinold, AVA, *Ministerium des Innern*, Präs. K.1265. See also the protocol to the second plenary session on 16 October 1911, in MRP/VRK, K.4, especially 166–175, where government opposition to the commission in this question is already discussed.
135. See the correspondence between Schwartzenau and Stürgkh from February 1912, in MRP/VRK, K.1. The new appointments were made public on 25 February, see Hasiba, "Die Kommission zur Förderung der Verwaltungsreform," 246 (also containing a list of the new members in note 52).
136. See the protocol to the fourth plenary session on 30 March 1912, MRP/VRK, K.4, especially 9–28, and Stürgkh's reply to the demands of the commission, dated the day before this plenary session (!), 29 March 1912.
137. See the press cutting appended to Z.194/VRK, in MRP/VRK, K.1. See also the debate in the enquête-subcommittee (Enquete-Ausschuss) on 14 May (MRP/VRK, K.6) on the question of the widely known rumors about the conflict between the government and the commission in this regard.
138. See Schwartzenau's letter to Stürgkh from 3 May 1912 (Z.194/VRK), MRP/VRK, K.1.
139. See the protocol to the fifth plenary session, 28 June 1912, MRP/VRK, K.5, especially 24–34.
140. See the protocol to the fourth plenary session, 30 March 1912, MRP/VRK, K.4, 9–28 (on Redlich's "guerilla war," see 24).
141. Redlich recounts his contacts with Interior Minister Heinold in the enquête subcommittee on 7 June 1912, MRP/VRK, K.6, 16f.
142. See the protocol to the meeting of subcommittee I on 5 March 1912, MRP/VRK, K.1; the protocol to the fourth plenary session on 30 March 1912 (especially 29–36), MRP/VRK, K.4; and the protocol to the constitutive meeting of the enquête-subcommittee, also on 30 March 1912, MRP/VRK, K.6.
143. See the protocols to the meetings of the enquête-subcommittee on 30 March, 22 and 30 April, 14 May, and 7 and 27 June 1912, all in MRP/VRK, K.6.
144. See the protocol to the last meeting of the enquête-subcommittee on 27 June 1912, MRP/VRK, K.6, and the protocol to the fifth plenary session on 28 June 1912, MRP/VRK, K.5 (on Haerdtl's stance, see especially 60–62).
145. On the direct, rather uninformed (or perhaps consciously provocative) question of commission member Baernreither why there were no civil servants among those to be interviewed in the enquête, Haerdtl quite clearly stated that this enquête had a completely different purpose, because the conflict between commission and government for the time being blocked all access to the civil service, (see the meeting of the enquête-subcommittee on 7 June 1912, 14–16, MRP/VRK, K.6).

146. This is particularly obvious from the argumentation of both Haerdtl and Redlich in the first two meetings of the enquête-subcommittee. See the protocols to the meetings on 30 March and 22 April 1912, MRP/VRK, K.6. Compare also the open argumentation to use the results of the enquête to further public discussion of the administrative reform action and to rally support for the reform action of the commission in the "public sphere." (See the protocol to the sixth plenary session on 10 January 1913, MRP/VRK, K.5, especially Redlich's argument on 12–13.)
147. See the impressive protocol to the *Enquete der Kommission zur Förderung der Verwaltungsreform veranstaltet in der Zeit vom 21. Oktober bis 9. November 1912 zur Feststellung der Wünsche der beteiligten Kreise der Bevölkerung in bezug auf die Reform der inneren und Finanzverwaltung* (Vienna: k.k. Hof- und Staatsdruckerei, 1913). Redlich relinquished the chairmanship for a few days in the beginning of November 1912 when he went on a special mission for Foreign Minister Berchtold to Belgrade (see Redlich, *Schicksaalsjahre*, 1:166–76).
148. See the *Enquete der Kommission zur Förderung der Verwaltungsreform*, 16.
149. See the interview with Brockhausen in ibid., 14–20 (especially 15 on the Staatswille). Compare also the much later criticism of Redlich's vision of reform delivered by Brockhausen at the meeting of the Industrial Association (Industrielle Vereinigung) on 4 February 1914. See "Die Vorschläge Prof. Redlichs zur Reform der Finanzverwaltung. Referent: Regierungsrat Professor Dr. Karl Brockhausen. Gemeinsame Zusammenkunft am 4 Februar 1914," in *Mitteilungen der Industriellen Vereinigung*, no. 23, (1914), where Brockhausen's argument about the subversion of the Staatswille brought about by Redlich's plans resurfaces.
150. See the protocol to the constitutive meeting of the enquête subcommittee on 30 March 1912, MRP/VRK, K.6, especially 8–9.
151. See Redlich, *Schicksaalsjahre*, 1:89 (entry for 6 July 1911). Compare also part one of this book on Haerdtl's role in Koerber's administrative reform action in the years 1900–04.
152. On this first report of Haerdtl's in the commission, see the report itself, *Bericht über die Steigerung der Kosten der staatlichen inneren Verwaltung 1890–1911* (1912), MRP/VRK, K.5, and his very lucid presentations of it in the protocol to the common meeting of subcommittees I and III on 17 and 18 October 1912, MRP/VRK, K.1, and on the sixth plenary session on 10 January 1913, MRP/VRK, K.5. On Haerdtl's reports in the commission, see also Boyer, "The End of an Old Regime," 177–78.
153. This tendency is clear throughout the work of the commission and visible in many of the debates.
154. See Haerdtl's report, *Die Beziehungen der Gemeindeverwaltung zur Staatsverwaltung* (1914), especially 1, 27, MRP/VRK, K.12.
155. See Haerdtl's report, *Bericht über Grundzüge einer Reform der Organisation der inneren Verwaltung* (1914), MRP/VRK, K.12, and his three-stage presentation of this reform plan in the meeting of the expert-committee appointed by subcommittees I and IV on 16 February 1914, MRP/VRK, K.13, in the combined subcommittees I and IV on 5 and 6 March 1914, MRP/VRK, K.12, and, finally, in the tenth and eleventh plenary sessions on 27–28 March and 8 May 1914. These latter protocols are missing in the archive of the commission in AVA. They are treated by Hasiba, "Die Kommission zur Förderung der Verwaltungsreform," 259–60, who had access to these protocols (through the Nachlass of commission member Edmund Bernatzik), and also in the third annual report of the commission (*Dritter Jahresbericht*, 1914), MRP/VRK, K.3. Haerdtl sums up the debate in his fourth and last report during the commission of June 1914, *Bericht über die Reform der Organisation der inneren Verwaltung* (1914), MRP/VRK, K.12.

156. On this, compare the sections on the autonomous administration in Haerdtl's two comprehensive reports on the internal administration, *Bericht über Grundzüge einer Reform der Organisation der inneren Verwaltung* (February 1914) and *Bericht über die Reform der Organisation der inneren Verwaltung* (June 1914). See also his defense of the proposals aiming at stabilizing and depoliticizing the Gemeinden in the last meeting of the combined subcommittees I and IV on 27 June 1914, MRP/VRK, K.12, especially 12ff. and 19f.

157. See the protocol to the sixth plenary session on 10 January 1913, MRP/VRK, K.5. When Haerdtl presented his first memorandum to the plenum of the commission, which was severely critical of the gross inefficiency of the central ministries, he concluded with something resembling a credo of the Austrian high bureaucracy: "Es handelt sich darum, langsam wieder . . . jene hohe Bürokratie zu schaffen, die in Oesterreich so glänzende Dienste geleistet hat und die temporis tractu zum Teile leider zerstört wurde. Es handelt sich darum, die hohen Beamten von den Strömungen der Zeit dadurch unabhängig zu machen, dass man sie in ihren persönlichen Verhältnissen freier und zufriedener macht, dass man ihnen aber auch eine amtliche Stellung gibt, mit der sie ausreichend zufrieden sind. . . ." (100)

158. See Schwartzenau's request for permission to publish Haerdtl's report and his own on 17 October 1913, which was answered two months later, on 10 December, with a permission to publish only his own report, Haerdtl's was not even mentioned. Compare also the protocol to the meeting in the *Ständiges Komitee für Verwaltungstechnik und Verfahren* of the interior ministry, the sad remnants of the administrative reform commission, on 17 December 1917: ". . . streng vertraulich zu behandeln das Referat Haerdtls an den verstorbenen Kaiser . . . .die Publikation dieses Referates wurde verboten. Der Grund lag darin, daß Haerdtl ein Bekämpfer des Präsidialsystems war." (All in MRP/VRK, K.3)

159. Redlich first raises this key issue in the constitutive meeting of the enquête subcommittee on 30 March 1912 and returns to it during nearly all of the following meetings during the spring of 1912 of this subcommittee (all the protocols in MRP/VRK, K.6). He also argues this case strongly in the combined meetings of subcommittees I and IV in the spring of 1913 and then again in the spring of 1914 (the protocols to these meetings lie in MRP/VRK, K.12, and K.13). He ultimately defended this position together with Haerdtl in the tenth and eleventh plenary session in the spring of 1914. (See the third annual report of the commission [*Dritter Jahresbericht*, 1914], in MRP/VRK, K.3, and Haerdtl's last report in the commission of June 1914, *Bericht über die Reform der Organisation der inneren Verwaltung* [1914], in MRP/VRK, K.12.)

160. This is quite evident from the protocol of the hearings in October-November 1912. For one illuminating episode, see *Enquete der Kommission zur Förderung der Verwaltungsreform*, 161–70.

161. Haerdtl consistently argued in the commission to keep the reform as simple as possible and not to tamper too much with the established administrative organization, not least to make the reform realizable wholly outside of the legislative process. Despite this, he included Redlich's Kreis-proposal in his own comprehensive reform proposal in the spring of 1914. Simultaneously, he repeatedly distanced himself from this element in the following debate in the combined subcommittees I and IV, saying that he had given in to the pressure from the expert committee, ostensibly from Redlich; see particularly the protocols to the meetings on 16 February 1914 (15, MRP/VRK, K.13) and on 5–6 March 1914 (4–5, MRP/VRK, K.12). After his reform proposal had been defeated, though, he vehemently described the Kreis as its core (see especially the debate about this in the twelth plenary session, the protocol lies in MRP/VRK, K.6).

162. See especially Redlich's argumentation in the meetings of the combined subcommittees I and IV on 16 February 1914 (the expert-group of the subcommittee), MRP/VRK, K.12,

and on 5–6 March 1914, MRP/VRK, K.13. Compare also his argumentation in the meetings of the expert-group of these subcommittees on 31 March and 8 May 1913, MRP/VRK, K.12.

163. See the protocol to the meeting in the expert-group of the combined subcommittees I and IV on 16 February 1914, 12, MRP/VRK, K.13: "Worauf es in Österreich ankomme, sei, den zweifellos in Umbildung begriffenen *Staatsbau* so zu gestalten, daß die Selbstverwaltung ein den Gesamtstaat mittragendes Organ der Volksgesamtheit werde, die der Staat vorstelle." (Emphasis in original.) See also the protocol to the meeting of the combined subcommittees I and IV on 5–6 March 1914, 18–20, 29–33, 36–37: "Wohl aber halte ich es für wünschenswert und möglich, durch andere Einrichtungen—es ist schwierig den Ausdruck zu finden—die Autonomie wieder mehr in das Staatsgefüge als ganzes hereinzubringen und sie als ein Stück der staatlichen Tätigkeit überhaupt wirken zu lassen." (Quotation on 37.)

164. See especially the protocol to the meeting of the combined subcommittees I and IV on 5–6 March 1914, 5–9, MRP/VRK, K.12.

165. See Schwartzenau's argumentation in ibid., 10–11.

166. See Erwin von Schwartzenau, *Anträge der Kommission zur Förderung der Verwaltungsreform betreffend die Erlassung einer Geschäftsordnung der k.k. Bezirks-hauptmannschaften und die Feststellung von Grundsätzen für das Verfahren von den politischen Behörden samt Erläuterungen und einem Bericht über die Kanzleireform bei den politischen Behörden* (Vienna: k.k. Hof- und Staatsdruckerei, 1913).

167. After its acceptance in the plenum of the commission on 2 July 1913 and Stürgkh's permission to publish the report on 10 December 1913, Schwartzenau's proposal became the subject of extensive treatment in the interior ministry during the years 1913 and 1914. See the large collection of documents in a folder dated 15 January 1915 (Z.1353/1915/MI, AVA, Ministerium des Innern, Präsidiales, K.1286). Among these documents also lies Interior Minister Heinold's letter to Schwartzenau from 10 December 1913, where he intimates that Schwartzenau's reform could indeed be implemented on a trial basis in some Bezirkshauptmannschaften. Compare also the documentation in MRP/VRK, K.3 (Z.388 and Z.396/VRK).

168. See the excerpt of the protocol to the ninth plenary session on 1 and 2 July 1913, in MRP/VRK, K.1. (See especially Redlich's appearance on 11–13.) The protocol in its entirety is missing in the archive of the commission in AVA. Compare also Redlich's description of this plenary session in Redlich, *Schicksaalsjahre*, 1:203 (entry for 3 July 1913).

169. See Redlich's letter to Baernreither from 3 July 1913, HHStA, Nachlass Baernreither, K.49.

170. See the protocol to the meeting of the combined subcommittees I and III on 12 June 1913, 14–20, MRP/VRK, K.11.

171. See Redlich's report: Josef Redlich, *Bericht des Mitgliedes der Kommission zur Förderung der Verwaltungsreform Professor Dr. Josef Redlich über die Entwicklung und den gegenwärtigen Stand der österreichischen Finanzverwaltung sowie Vorschläge der Kommission zur Reform dieser Verwaltung* (Vienna: k.k. Hof- und Staatsdruckerei, 1913). Compare also the debate in the combined subcommittees I and III on 12 June 1913, protocol in MRP/VRK, K.11. See especially Redlich's description of the reformed financial administration as a key instrument in the supervision of the administration, in the protocol to the meeting of the expert group of the combined subcommittees I and IV, 12–13, in MRP/VRK, K.13. On Redlich's report, see also Boyer, "The End of an Old Regime," 178–81.

172. On the affair of the publication of the enquête protocol, see the correspondence between Schwartzenau and Stürgkh, March through May 1913, MRP/VRK, K.2. See also Redlich, *Schicksaalsjahre*, 1:194, 199–201.

173. See Stürgkh's permission, MRP/VRK, K.3 (Z.384/VRK). Compare Redlich, *Schicksaalsjahre*, 1:213 (entry for 31 December 1913).
174. See the protocol to the meeting of the Industrial Association (Industrielle Vereinigung) on 4 February 1914, "Die Vorschläge Prof. Redlichs zur Reform der Finanzverwaltung," 6. Brockhausen said, ". . . ich verrate wohl kein Geheimnis, wenn ich sage, der spiritus rector dieser Reformbewegung sei Professor Redlich."
175. See Redlich's letter to Baernreither on 3 July 1913, HHStA, Nachlass Baernreither, K.49.
176. See the protocol to the meeting in the expert group of the combined subcommittees I and IV on 16 February 1914, 5, MRP/VRK, K.13.
177. See the protocol to the meeting of the combined subcommittees I and IV on 5–6 March 1914, 42, MRP/VRK, K.12.
178. See the protocol to the meeting of the combined subcommittees I and IV on 5–6 March 1914, 21–22, MRP/VRK, K.12.
179. See the protocol to the meeting of the combined subcommittees I and IV on 5–6 March 1914, 25, MRP/VRK, K.12.
180. On this last phase of the work of the commission, see Hasiba, "Die Kommission zur Förderung der Verwaltungsreform" 259–60, and the third annual report of the commission (*Dritter Jahresbericht*, 1914), MRP/VRK, K.3. Haerdtl also very lucidly sums up the debate in these plenary sessions in the last report in the commission of June 1914, *Bericht über die Reform der Organisation der inneren Verwaltung* (1914), MRP/VRK, K.12. Compare also the debate in the subcommittee meeting on 27 June 1914 (MRP/VRK, K.12), where the attempt was made to rescue the remnants of the reform proposal.
181. See the protocol to the meeting of the combined subcommittees I and IV on 27 June 1914, MRP/VRK, K.12. This was the last working meeting of the commission.
182. See the third annual report of the commission, 15, MRP/VRK, K.3.
183. See the protocol to the twelth and last plenary session of the commission on 15 December 1914, MRP/VRK, K.6.
184. On this political development in Austria during the war years, see part one above and the references therein.
185. On Naumann, see above part one.
186. Redlich's letter to Berchtold has been published in Fritz Fellner, "Der Plan einer 'Vortragsmission Redlich-Apponyi'," 475. Redlich's "war diary" (Kriegstagebuch) has been published as part of his political diary, in Redlich, *Schicksaalsjahre*, 1:247–72.
187. See Naumann's notes on his conversation with Renner on 11 February 1915, BArch, Nachlass Naumann, N 3001/217. *Die Hilfe* was one of the media Renner used for his publishing campaign for internal reform of the Habsburg Empire at the beginning of the century. In the midst of the Hungarian crisis, in August 1905, Renner wrote jubilantly to Naumann about the promising strong-handed "imperialist policies" of Emperor Franz Joseph against the intransigent Hungarians, and he also tried to enlist Naumann in his current campaign for the constitutional restructuring of the Dual Monarchy. See Renner's letter to *Die Hilfe*/Naumann, 29 August 1905, BArch, Nachlass Naumann, N 3001/211. On Renner's early cooperation with Naumann, see Renner's *Biographie (Lebensläufe)*, KA, Nachlass Renner, E/1731:304.
188. See especially Karl Renner, *Deutschland, Oesterreich und die Völker des Ostens* (Berlin: Verlag für Sozialwissenschaft, 1922), 18–21. Compare the concept to Renner's letter to director Strencioch of the Mitteleuropäischer Wirtschaftstag, from 10 April 1930 (KA, Nachlass Renner, E/1731:67): "Ich setze voraus, dass Sie wissen, dass ich seinerzeits zusammen mit Naumann einer der theoretischen und praktischen Vorkämpfer für Mitteleuropa gewesen bin."

189. Renner's Mitteleuropa engagement has usually been deemphasized in the literature about him; see Nasko & Reichl, *Karl Renner*, 163, and Rauscher, *Karl Renner*, 87. However, compare Hannak, *Karl Renner und seine Zeit*, 224–32.
190. Practically all of the articles in Renner's press campaign during 1915–16 in the *Arbeiter-Zeitung* and *Der Kampf* are collected in Renner, *Österreichs Erneuerung* 1–3. The articles on Mitteleuropa are collected in 1:3–73, 127–60, 2:83–109, and 3:2–119. The attempt to anchor the political vision in Marxist theory was made in Karl Renner, *Marxismus, Krieg und Internationale. Kritische Studien über offene Probleme des wissenschaftlichen und des praktischen Sozialismus in und nach dem Weltkrieg* (Stuttgart: Dietz, 1917).
191. See the protocols to the internal idea conferences of the German-Austrian Social-Democratic party in the fall of 1914, in VGA, APA (I), Mappe 109 (Weltkrieg 1914–1918). Renner's presentation took place on 30 October 1914.
192. Renner published a series of articles in *Der Kampf* in these years, which were then also worked into his major theoretical and ideological statement during the war years, Renner, *Marxismus, Krieg und Internationale* (1917). On this, see further below.
193. See the protocol to the party congress, *Protokoll der Verhandlungen des Parteitages der Deutschen sozialdemokratischen Arbeiterpartei in Oesterreich in Wien, 19–24. Oktober 1917* (Vienna: Brand, 1917). See especially "Die Erklärung der Linken" on 113–17. On the party congress of 1917 and the wider problem of the conflict between the left and right wings in German-Austrian Social Democracy during the world war, see, for instance, Leser, *Zwischen Reformismus und Bolschewismus*, 263–87; Kulemann, *Am Beispiel des Austromarxismus*, 159–211; and Berthold Unfried, *Zu Politik und Theorie der 'Linken' innerhalb der österreichischen Sozialdemokratie während des 1. Weltkrieges* (University of Vienna, Unpublished Diplomarbeit, 1978), passim.
194. For a scathingly critical treatment of the Social Democratic leadership (including Renner) during the war years, see Michael Siegert, "Sozialdemokratie und Imperialismus: Kriegsziele und Beutehoffnungen 1914–1918 (Teil 1)," *Neues Forum* (September 1975). The relative congeniality of Renner's position to the mainstream of the executive committee of the party can be followed in the protocols of this organ (Parteivorstandsprotokolle), in VGA, APA (I), Mappe 1–2. Almost only Friedrich Adler took a deviating position (from the left) from this mainstream, whereas Engelbert Pernerstorfer was sometimes castigated for his German-national (rightist) tendency.
195. A selection of instances when Renner in the party-executive-ventured "imperialist" ideas can be found in Siegert, "Sozialdemokratie und Imperialismus," who also demonstrates that Viktor Adler expressed himself in much the same way in the early war years. On Viktor Adler's "open mindedness" with regard to annexations, see also Philipp Scheidemann, *Der Zusammenbruch* (Berlin: Verlag für Sozialwissenschaft, 1921), 28f., and idem, *Memoiren eines Sozialdemokraten*. 2 vols. (Dresden: Carl Reissner Verlag, 1928), 1:342, 376. See Erich Matthias, *Die deutsche Sozialdemokratie und der Osten 1914–1945* (Tübingen University, Working paper, 1954), on similar tendencies in Reichs-German Social Democracy. Only at one point, on 13 July 1915, during the debate on the question of annexations, Renner seems to have gone too far when Karl Seitz attacked his openly affirmative elaboration on this question, which had been supported by German-national "bad-boy" Pernerstorfer: "Seitz polemisiert gegen Renner und sagt, daß er seine Strafe durch die Anerkennung Pernerstorfers erhalten habe. . . . Pernerstorfer hat sich am weitesten von dem entfernt, was wir bisher einen Sozialdemokraten nannten." (Quoted in Siegert, "Sozialdemokratie und Imperialismus," 37.)
196. See Siegert, "Sozialdemokratie und Imperialismus," 36–38. See also the party executive protocols for 1915, in VGA, APA (I), Mappe 1, and Scheidemann, *Der Zusammenbruch*, 29.

197. See *Die Bestrebungen für eine wirtschaftliche Annäherung Deutschlands und Oesterreich-Ungarns. Protokoll der Verhandlungen die am 9. Januar 1916 zwischen der sozialdemokratischen Fraktion des deutschen Reichstages, dem sozialdemokratischen Parteivorstand und Parteiausschuß, der Generalkommission und den Vorständen der deutschen Gewerkschaften, einer Vertretung der Zentralverbandes deutscher Konsumvereine und einer Vertretung der sozialdemokratischen Partei Oesterreichs und der österreichischen Gewerkschaften in Berlin über die wirtschaftliche Annäherung Deutschlands und Oesterreich-Ungarns stattfanden. Herausgegeben vom Vorstand der sozialdemokratischen Partei Deutschlands* (Berlin: Paul Singer, 1916). Renner's speech is reproduced on 3–22, and he sums up his case on 58–63 (quotation on 19). Renner's case for Naumann is presented on 15ff. On Reichs-German Social Democracy during the war years, see Susanne Miller, *Burgfrieden und Klassenkampf: Die deutsche Sozialdemokratie im ersten Weltkrieg* (Düsseldorf: Droste, 1974), and Carl Schorske, *German Social Democracy 1905–1917. The Development of the Great Schism* (Cambridge, Mass: Harvard University Press, 1955).
198. See the resolution of the Reichskonferenz (25–28 März 1916), published in *Protokolle der Verhandlungen des Parteitages der Deutschen sozialdemokratischen Arbeiterpartei in Oesterreich* (1917), 57–63. See also the protocol to this party conference itself, in VGA, APA (I), Mappe 57 (Reichskonferenz März 1916).
199. See the letter of Ferdinand Skaret, Social Democratic party secretary, to Gustav Gross from 1 May 1916, HHStA, Nachlass Gross, K.2, and the protocol to the meeting of the executive committee of the Social Democratic party on 31 May 1916, VGA, APA (I), Mappe 1.
200. See Renner's "Politische Leitsätze," VGA, APA (I), Mappe 109 (Weltkrieg 1914–18). The handwritten original to this memorandum lies in KA, Nachlass Renner, E/1731:14. Together with Renner's memorandum in the party archive lie the war aims programs of the German-Liberals and the Christian Socials, which are indeed very similar to Renner's in structure and in the arrangement of the basic elements, though not in its political substance.
201. See Karl Renner, *Marxismus, Krieg und Internationale*, passim. Mitteleuropa is discussed on 224–25. For a poetic description of the *Ökumene*, see 112ff. Large parts of this work actually originated as articles published during the previous years, mainly in the ideological organ of the party, *Der Kampf*, where Renner was a coeditor together with Friedrich Adler. *Marxismus, Krieg und Internationale* is generally recognized as a key work in Renner's oeuvre. For a critical perspective, see Kulemann, *Am Beispiel des Austromarxismus*, especially 182–185. For a sympathetic account, see Leser, *Zwischen Reformismus und Bolschewismus*, 33–100 and particularly 280–82. For a perceptive analysis of this work and its wider meaning for Renner's thinking, see Pelinka, *Karl Renner zur Einführung*, 39–49.
202. See Karl Kautsky, *Kriegsmarxismus. Eine theoretische Grundlegung der Politik des 4. August* (Vienna: Brand, 1918). The criticism against Renner had been building up for some time. In this regard, compare also Kautsky's criticism of Naumann's *Mitteleuropa*, in Karl Kautsky, *Die Vereinigten Staaten Mitteleuropas* (Stuttgart: Dietz, 1916), and the debate between Rudolf Hilferding and Renner on Naumann's book in *Der Kampf*, November/December issue of 1915 (Hilferding), and the January issue of 1916 (Renner).
203. On this shift in the German-Austrian Social Democracy during 1917 and 1918, see, for instance, Kulemann, *Am Beispiel des Austromarxismus*, 197–211, and Leser, *Zwischen Reformismus und Bolschewismus*, 280–87. See also Panzenböck, *Ein deutscher Traum*, 67–91, for a view more strongly emphasizing Renner's continuing strong position in the party, at least until the beginning of 1918 and in certain regards until mid-October 1918.
204. See Renner, *Das Selbstbestimmungsrecht der Nationen*, passim. On the Nationalitätenbundesstaat in the above perspective, see particularly 28–32.

205. See *Staatserklärung über Umfang, Grenzen und Beziehungen des Staatsgebietes von Deutschösterreich* (22 November 1918), reprinted in *Aussenpolitische Dokumente der Republik Österreich 1918–1938*, vol. 1: *Selbstbestimmung der Republik*, Klaus Koch, Walter Rauscher, and Arnold Suppan eds. (Vienna: Verlag für Geschichte und Politik, 1993), 171f.
206. See Renner, *Deutschland, Oesterreich und die Völker des Ostens*, 20.
207. On this, see Fellner, "Die Historiographie zur österreichisch-deutschen Problematik."
208. See Redlich's letter to Baernreither from 12 August 1910, HHStA, Nachlass Baernreither, K.47.
209. This engagement of Redlich's during the spring of 1916 against the reform action of the Stürgkh government is documented in Redlich, *Schicksaalsjahre*, 2:94, 96f., 110–12, and in *Dichter und Gelehrter*, 151, 153, 156, 157–61, 167.
210. See Redlich's letter to Bahr from 18 July 1916, in *Dichter und Gelehrter*, 182.
211. See Redllich, *Austrian War Government*. This book is a slightly reworked translation of the German original: See Josef Redlich, *Österreichische Regierung und Verwaltung im Weltkriege* (Vienna: Hölder-Pichler-Tempsky AG/New Haven: Yale University Press, 1925).
212. See Redllich, *Austrian War Government*, passim. On Koerber, see especially 43ff., 50f. (quotation on 43).
213. See ibid., 77–106.
214. Ibid., 96.
215. See Redlich, *Schicksaalsjahre*, in particular 2:150–53 (entries for 28 October—1 November 1916). The diary for the first years of the war chronicles a great many conversations with Koerber.
216. Redlich defends himself against this apparently widespread view of the affair in a letter to Hermann Bahr from 22 November 1916, in *Dichter und Gelehrter*, 197–98. Compare also his diary (Redlich, *Schicksaalsjahre*, 2:156; the entry of 22 November 1916).
217. See the concept to Redlich's letter to Koerber dated 1 November 1916, Nachlass Redlich. I was unable to trace the original letter, which was apparently sent to Koerber on this day (see Redlich, *Schicksaalsjahre*, 2:153).
218. See Bahr's letter to Redlich, 20 February 1916, *Dichter und Gelehrter*, 158.
219. Redlich's letter to Bahr, 24 February 1916, *Dichter und Gelehrter*, 159.
220. These articles later went into Renner, *Marxismus, Krieg und Internationale* (1917) and Renner, *Österreichs Erneuerung* 1–3 (1916–17). Administrative reform is the second main theme besides Mitteleuropa in the articles of the *Arbeiter-Zeitung* published in Renner, *Österreichs Erneuerung*.
221. Renner's articles in the *Arbeiter-Zeitung* on the Austrian administrative reform are reprinted in *Österreichs Erneuerung*, 1:57–118 and 2:131–200.
222. See Renner, *Österreichs Erneuerung*, 1:69–73 (quotation on 70).
223. On the Deutsche Freiheit as a concept during the World War I, see Wolfgang Mommsen, "Die 'deutsche Idee der Freiheit,'" in idem, *Bürgerliche Kultur und politische Ordnung. Künstler, Schriftsteller und Intellektuelle in der deutschen Geschichte 1830–1933* (Frankfurt am Main: Fischer Taschenbuchverlag, 2000). On Renner and democracy, see Pelinka, *Karl Renner zur Einführung*, 45f.
224. See Redlich's letter to Koerber, 1 November 1916, Nachlass Redlich.
225. On the Austrian Political Society (ÖPG), see Birgitt Morgenbrod, *Wiener Großbürgertum im Ersten Weltkrieg. Die Geschichte der 'Österreichischen Politischen Gesellschaft' 1916–1918* (Vienna: Böhlau Verlag, 1994), 64f., on Redlich's beginning engagement in the ÖPG. On this see also Redlich, *Schicksaalsjahre*, 2:141–43, 148.
226. See Redlich's letter to Bahr, 22 January 1917, *Dichter und Gelehrter*, 209–11.

227. A representative selection of Bahr's wartime articles were published in Hermann Bahr, *Schwarzgelb* (Berlin: S. Fischer Verlag, 1917); see, for example, 53–67 and 74–76 for his basic argument. On Bahr's Austrian ideology and politics, see Fritz Fellner, "Austriaca: Ideologi und Politik in den Tagebüchern Hermann Bahrs," in *Hermann-Bahr-Symposion "Der Herr aus Linz." Bericht*. Margret Dietrich, ed. (Linz: Linzer Veranstaltungsgesellschaft, 1987).
228. See Redlich's letter to Bahr, 22 January 1917, *Dichter und Gelehrter*, 209–211.
229. See Redlich's letter to Bahr, 19 October 1916, *Dichter und Gelehrter*, 193.
230. See Friedrich W. Foerster, *Das österreichische Problem vom ethischen und staatspädagogischen Standpunkte* (Vienna: Hugo Heller, 1914), passim, and idem, *Erlebte Weltgeschichte 1869–1953. Memoiren* (Nürnberg: Glock & Lutz, 1953), 215–57, 344–74.
231. See Redlich's speech in the Lower house of parliament on 12 June 1917, *Stenographische Protokolle des Abgeordnetenhauses, Session XXII (1917–1918)*, 161–68. See also Redlich, *Schicksaalsjahre*, 2:209.
232. See Redlich's speeches in the ÖPG on 27 June 1917, excerpts reprinted in the brochure *Das Nationale Problem in Österreich. Auszug aus den im Juli 1917 gehaltenen Reden der Herren Reichsratsabgeordneten Professor Dr. Josef Redlich, E.O. Zenker, Dr. R. Von Lodgmann und Dr. K. Renner an den Diskussionsabenden über das Thema Das nationale Problem in Österreich. Österreichische Politische Gesellschaft* (Vienna: Carl Fromme, 1917), and his speech on the peace manifestation of the Meinl group on 17 July 1917, excerpts reprinted in the brochure *Österreich und der Friede. Verständigung unter den Völkern Österreichs. Versammlung vom 17. Juli 1917 in der 'Österreichischen Politischen Gesellschaft'* (Vienna: Herrmann, 1917). Both these meetings and Redlich's speeches in them are extensively treated in Morgenbrod, *Wiener Großbürgertum im Ersten Weltkrieg*, 111–38. See also Redlich, *Schicksaalsjahre*, 2:212, 222.
233. See Morgenbrod, *Wiener Großbürgertum im Ersten Weltkrieg*, 116–18, and *Das Nationale Problem in Österreich.*
234. Quoted from *Das nationale Problem in Österreich*, 7. Besides the three speeches quoted above (footnotes 231–33), Redlich expressed this vision of the new Austrian state in his speech in parliament on 20 November 1917, in *Stenographische Protokolle des Abgeordnetenhauses, Session XXII (1917–1918)*, 2076–81.
235. Redlich, *Austrian War Government*, xi–xii. See also ibid., 136ff.
236. On Hohenlohe's visit and the summons to the first audience with Karl, see Redlich, *Schicksaalsjahre*, 2:210–13, and *Dichter und Gelehrter*, 232–34.
237. On the audience with Karl on 3 July, see Redlich, *Schicksaalsjahre*, 2:213–15.
238. Redlich, *Schicksaalsjahre*, 2:216–18 (entry for 6 July 1917).
239. The continuing affair of the formation of a government building on the combination Lammasch-Meinl-Redlich-Foerster is treated extensively in Morgenbrod, *Wiener Großbürgertum im Ersten Weltkrieg*; see particularly 119–28. It can also be followed in Redlich, *Schicksaalsjahre*, 2:210–33 (July-August 1917). Hermann Bahr was closely involved with Heinrich Lammasch, and Redlich's correspondence with Bahr is therefore an important source here; see *Dichter und Gelehrter*, in particular 233–56. On the wider context of the Lammasch-Meinl-Foerster campaign for peace during the summer of 1917, see Heinrich Benedikt, *Die Friedensaktion der Meinlgruppe 1917/18. Die Bemühungen um einen Verständigungsfrieden nach Dokumenten, Aktenstücken und Briefen* (Graz: Böhlau Verlag, 1962). See also Foerster, *Erlebte Weltgeschichte*, 237–42.
240. Excerpts from the protocol of this meeting were published in *Österreich und der Friede* (1917), see 3–8 for Redlich's speech. This manifestation is treated extensively in Morgenbrod, *Wiener Großbürgertum im Ersten Weltkrieg*, 129–39. Compare Benedikt, *Die Frie-*

densaktion der Meinlgruppe, 123–26. See also Redlich, *Schicksaalsjahre*, 2:222 (entry of 20 July 1917), and Foerster, *Erlebte Weltgeschichte*, 239.

241. The conflict between Redlich and the German-Liberals and German Nationals can be followed in his diary and in his letters to Hermann Bahr; see Redlich, *Schicksaalsjahre*, 2:209–39, and *Dichter und Gelehrter*, 226, 228–29, 237–38, 253–54, 260, 267–71. See also Morgenbrod, *Wiener Großbürgertum im Ersten Weltkrieg*, 153–61 (on Redlich's appearance at the meeting on 4 October, see ibid., 159–61).
242. Redlich's activity in the first half of October 1918 is chronicled in his diary; see Redlich, *Schicksaalsjahre*, 2:295–301 (quotation on 300).
243. See Redlich, *Schicksaalsjahre*, 2:301–03 (entries for 15 and 16 October).
244. Redlich discusses the short-lived Lammasch government thoroughly in Josef Redlich, "Heinrich Lammasch als Minister-Präsident," in *Heinrich Lammasch. Seine Aufzeichnungen, sein Wirken und seine Politik*, Marga Lammasch & Hans Sperl, eds. (Vienna: Deuticke, 1922).
245. On this imperial legacy in republican Austria, see Fellner, "Die Historiographie zur österreichisch-deutschen Problematik," and Klemperer, "Das nachimperiale Österreich." On its reproduction in the Austrian ideology after 1945, see Fellner, "The Problem of the Austrian Nation."
246. See Redlich, *Schicksaalsjahre*, 2:319 (entry of 14 November 1918).
247. See Redlich, *Schicksaalsjahre*, 2:323 (entry of 4 December 1918).
248. See, for example Panzenböck, *Ein deutscher Traum*, 163–65, for an insightful discussion of this problem of Renner's opportunistic or pragmatic personality. This discussion can be found in practically every work on Renner.
249. For a very insightful treatment of Renner's political psyche and his position on the Anschluss in 1938, see Pelinka, *Karl Renner zur Einführung*. See also Renner's political pamphlet of November 1938 justifying the Nazi-German annexation of the Sudetenland, Karl Renner, *Die Gründung der Republik Deutschösterreich der Anschluß und die Sudetendeutschen. Dokumente eines Kampfes ums Recht*, edited and introduced by Eduard Rabofsky (Vienna: Globus Verlag, 1991). In the year before writing this political pamphlet, Renner finished a theoretical work on the nation as a juridical category, and in this work Renner is still maintaining that the Habsburg Empire with national autonomy had been the ideal solution for Central Europe. See Karl Renner, *Die Nation: Mythos und Wirklichkeit. Manuskript aus dem Nachlaß*. Jacques Hannak, ed. (Vienna: Europa Verlag, 1964) [manuscript dated 1937], 104. Arguably, a clean Anschluss was for Renner in the late 1930s still only second best.
250. Redlich's attraction to the Czech Republic remained until his death, but it was at its strongest during the first years after 1918. On this, see, for example, Redlich, *Schicksaalsjahre*, 2:325–49 (December 1918–December 1919), and *Dichter und Gelehrter*, 371–73, 518. See also his letter to Flora Darkow-Singer, 30 October 1919, WStLB/HS (Sign. IN 198.655). See also his manuscript for a speech on the occasion of Masaryk's 70th birthday in 1920, "Thomas G. Masaryk als Geschichtsphilosoph und seine historische Sendung," Nachlass Redlich.
251. On Fischhof and the Hohenwart plan, see Josef Redlich, *Kaiser Franz Joseph von Österreich. Eine Biographie* (Berlin: Verlag für Kulturpolitik, 1929), 325–33 (quotation on 328).
252. See Redlich's undated letter to Berthold Molden (early 1930s), in ÖNB/HS (Sign. 1022/46–11).
253. On this work, see Redlich's letter to Hermann Bahr, 5 April 1927, in *Dichter und Gelehrter*, 559–561.

Conclusion

> The Wilson note should in the next few days lead to the forming of all the Austrian Volksstaaten. The strange thing about this is that the army, the police, and the civil administration so far work like normal also in the Slavic lands: the "state" has thus been reduced to its true nature, as the function of a historically established power structure![1]
>
> Josef Redlich (1918)

In October 1918, Josef Redlich made this sharp observation about how the Josephist state continued functioning fully right through the "dissolution" process; viewed thus, "transition" would probably be a better term to describe this process. However, the view implicit in the observation of a parallel existence of the two Austrias—the old Josephist Zwangsstaat and the new multinational Volksstaat—had been part of Redlich's perception of things for some time. Indeed, I would argue that this division constitutes an important key to understanding the development of late Imperial Austria and its dissolution. By shifting the perspective from the nationality problem to this vertical field of tension, a new view on late Imperial Austria will be opened, one that shifts focus from nationalism and national identity to the state, the political system, and the hesitant emergence of a multinational democratic politics.

There have been two very interesting perspectives on Austria presented in later years that focus one on each side of this field of tension. Gary B. Cohen has convincingly argued that we need "new narratives on society and government in late Imperial Austria." Cohen presented a broad, empirewide perspective on the development of political participation on different levels in the constitutional monarchies of Austria and Hungary after 1867, arguing that the internal political development in Austria-Hungary needs to be considered anew.[2] While Cohen's perspective focuses on the emerging multinational Volksstaat of Austria (and that of Hungary), James Shedel's complementary perspective focuses on the perseverance of the Josephist Rechtsstaat in Austria until the very last phase of the monarchy. Shedel emphasizes that the Josephist state functioned as a very stable framework for the sometimes turbulent political life of the multinational state. Parliamentary life was to a degree irresponsible exactly because it could be; the Rechtsstaat and its Verwaltung guaranteed stability and continuity.[3]

This field of tension had been institutionalized in the Austrian constitutional monarchy since 1860–62, when the October-Diploma and the Reichgemeindegesetz created the famed "dual administration" (Doppelverwaltung) of Austria, one state structure and one autonomous structure. In his study of the Beamte in late Imperial Austria, Karl Megner makes the very interesting empirical observation that there were even two parallel, sometimes competing and opposing political cultures that had evolved around these two administrative structures. However, Megner also notes how in the later phases of the parallel developments of mass politics *and* a growing administrative apparatus, the average Beamte also increasingly acquired an integrative function between these two political cultures.[4]

The long-term development here seems to be that of the Rechtsstaat and its Verwaltung filling the role of a paternalistic educator, and supporting structure, of an emerging system of political participation. Dressed in Max Weber's terminology, a central process in the state and society of late Imperial Austria was the interaction between a strong and firmly established bureaucratic leadership and an emerging political leadership. In Weber's view, the balance between them in late Imperial Austria would not have been ideal. However, because of the problem noted in the introduction, that the overshadowing question of unity in diversity in Austria probably necessitated a stronger bureaucratic leadership than in the average nation-state, this process might indeed have been exactly what could have secured the long-term survival of the multinational state. In my view, this perspective on the development of state and society needs to be considered more closely in Habsburg scholarship.

In the present biographical studies, the state side of this problem has been focused on; in a wide sense, for all the political projects examined here, the Josephist Rechtsstaat was more or less central, but it played different roles. Koerber, Renner, and Redlich focused on the need for this state to move with the times. Ernest von Koerber's solution was the most traditionally Josephist, aiming to buttress the state and to shape the Verwaltung into an efficient instrument for bureaucratic leadership in the modernization of Austria. I would simply characterize Karl Renner's approach as neo-Josephist: his solution aimed at democratizing the Josephist Rechtsstaat while simultaneously maintaining it virtually intact. Because Renner (as a leading Social Democrat) belonged to the political leadership capabilities in late Imperial Austria, this may look like a surprising conclusion; perhaps we should emphasize that he was also a Josephist Beamte. Nevertheless, in Renner's project political leadership was ultimately subordinated to the bureaucratic leadership of the Josephist state. Indeed, in comparison Josef Redlich's solution was more thoroughly democratic, insofar as he consistently aimed to reinforce the political leadership capabilities of Imperial Austria. However, like so many Austrian Liberals, Redlich did not fully withstand the temptation to seek support from the state in his endeavors to modernize Austria. Nevertheless, in the end he firmly came down on the side of political leadership.

From around 1916, Redlich's critique of the Josephist tradition of bureaucratic leadership became ferocious, and after 1918 he pointed out the bureaucratic "absolutism" of this tradition as being directly responsible for the destruction of Imperial Austria.

The three remaining political projects related more indirectly to the state. At the center of Leopold von Andrian's concerns was the more conservative vision of ensuring the continued existence of the dynastic union of peoples. However, Andrian chose the bureaucratic path and worked within the structures of the Josephist state in his attempt to realize his vision. Heinrich Friedjung came from the political sphere; he belonged to the leading strata of Austro-German National-Liberalism up to the mid-1890s. But in his later career, focused on here, he moved very close to the state, seeking to anchor his project of German hegemony in Austria (and Austria-Hungary) in the bureaucratic leadership. Hofmannsthal's project was a similar balancing act; he was repeatedly seeking to anchor his political project of the cultural revitalization of Habsburg Austria in the state structures. However, in the end, Hofmannsthal's quest for an Austrian identity transcended the Austrian state problem.

One central strain in these studies has been, following James Shedel, to observe the centrality of the state for politics and individual life careers in late Imperial Austria; at least at the center of the imperial state, the Rechtsstaat was considered more as a supporting structure and instrument for reform—or personal advancement—than as a hindrance to development. Another central aspect that followed has been that of Austrian identity. In the late imperial period, it encompassed a broad spectrum of positions, and to place too much emphasis on the two extreme positions taken here by Friedjung and Andrian would be misleading. As Jörg Kirchhoff has demonstrated, there was a broad mainstream in the view of Austria that was characterized by an adherence to the special culture and institutions created by the long historical experience of Habsburg rule in Central Europe; this view was "German-Austrian," rather than either "German" or "Austrian."[5]

Also, in all the political projects reviewed here, the closeness to an old imperial structure of domination created an imperialist tendency, both political and cultural.[6] However, it did so in very different ways. Most interesting to note, perhaps, is the strongly Josephist tendency of a civilizing mission in the east and southeast that colored practically all the projects reviewed here (excepting Andrian). In regard to Renner and Redlich, this old Josephist tendency transformed itself into an interesting variety of Liberal-Democratic crusader mentality: Austrian multinational democracy should be exported eastward.

No matter how the imperial legacy was sublimated, it personally affected all the individuals reviewed here. The special historical role—whatever it was—accorded to the Habsburg Empire by these individuals also became closely integrated with their personal identities. Hofmannsthal integrated the search for an Austrian identity with his personal identity quest, which made him feel the results of the dissolution of the empire in his own self—already in 1900 he foresaw the personally devastating effects a defeat in this quest would have. For Andrian, the dissolution was a completely shattering experience, because his identification with Imperial Austria, with the Austrian idea, was all-embracing. Josef Redlich was completely lost after 1918, compulsively indulging in the self-therapy of trying to make sense of his life by writing a series of books on the history of Imperial Austria. Arguably, Friedjung and Renner were less severely struck by the dissolution because they both had their identities firmly anchored in the German nation.

Ernest von Koerber was arguably the one hit hardest by the dissolution of the empire in 1918; Koerber was fully identified with the Josephist state, which disappeared in this year. However, we could also say that although Koerber's work on reinforcing the supranational Josephist Rechtsstaat ultimately failed, it had created the foundation for a different kind of success; the existence of the stable framework of the Rechtsstaat was crucial to the peaceful and ordered transition into a system of nation-states in 1918. After fulfilling this last civilizing duty, the Josephist state quietly dissolved itself. As Josef Redlich noted in retrospect, ". . . History [will not] see it as a mean achievement that . . . the dissolution of the Habsburg Empire took place in a legal fashion, that there were no internal conflicts, no civil wars or war; and that the new states, suddenly called into being, found themselves at once supplied with state governments and the indispensable administrative machinery for carrying them on by the one effective available instrument—the national civil service of the empire that had passed away."[7] Perhaps the time has now come when this achievement of the Josephist bureaucracy and the Imperial Austrian state can at last be recognized. And perhaps this recognition in turn can open up new perspectives on the role of the state and the bureaucracy in late Imperial Austria.

Notes

1. Redlich, *Schicksaalsjahre*, 2:305 (entry on 21 October 1918).
2. See Gary B. Cohen, "Neither Absolutism nor Anarchy: New Narratives on Society and Government in Late Imperial Austria," *Austrian History Yearbook* 29, part 1 (1998): 37–61.
3. See Shedel, "*Fin de Siècle* or *Jahrhundertwende.*"
4. See Megner, *Beamte*, 209–213.
5. See Kirchhoff, *Die deutschen in der Österreichisch-Ungarischen Monarchie*, passim.
6. On this problem, see the contributions in Johannes Feichtinger, Ursula Prutsch & Moritz Csáky, eds. *Habsburg postcolonial. Machtstrukturen und kollektives Gedächtnis* (Innsbruck: StudienVerlag, 2003).
7. Redlich, *Austrian War Government*, 174f.

Sources and Literature

I. Archival sources

Allgemeines Verwaltungsarchiv, Vienna (AVA)
- Finanzministerium
- Handelsministerium
- Ministerium des Innern
- Ministerratspräsidium (MRP)
- Ministerratspräsidium /Verwaltungsreformkommission (MRP/VRK)
- Ministerium für Kultus und Unterricht (MKU)
- Nachlass Robert Davy

Bundesarchiv, Berlin (BArch)
- Reichskanzlei (R 43)
- Nachlass Friedrich Naumann (N 3001)

Czech State Archives (Prague)
- Ministerratspräsidium (PMR)

Freies Deutsches Hochstift, Frankfurt am Main (FDH)
- Hofmannsthal-Archiv (Nachlass Hugo von Hofmannsthal)

Haus-, Hof-, und Staatsarchiv, Vienna (HHStA)
- PA I (Politisches Archiv)
- Kabinettsarchiv
- Nachlass Alois Lexa von Aehrenthal
- Nachlass Joseph Maria Baernreither
- Nachlass Heinrich Friedjung
- Nachlass Gustav Gross
- Nachlass Gustav Marchet
- Nachlass Lasser von Zollheim
- Nachlass Ernst von Plener
- Nachlass Sperl-Ehrhart
- Nachlass Friedrich Szápary

Kriegsarchiv, Vienna (KA)
- Kriegsministerium (KM)
- Militärkanzlei Seiner Majestät (MKM)
- Nachlass Karl Renner (E/1731)

National Museum, Prague (Archiv Národního Musea)
– Bedřich Pacák papers
– Josef Kaizl papers
National Literary Archive, Prague (Literárni Archiv Památníku Národního Písemnictví)
– Antonín Rezek papers
Österreichische Nationalbibliothek, Vienna (ÖNB)
– Handschriftensammlung (HS)
Österreichische Theatermuseum, Vienna (ÖTM)
– Nachlass Hermann Bahr
Politisches Archiv des Auswärtigen Amts, Bonn/Berlin (PAAA)
– PA Österreich
Technische Universität, Vienna (TU)
– Personalakt Josef Redlich (Index No. I/374)
Verein für die Geschichte der Arbeiterbewegung, Vienna (VGA)
– Altes Partei-Archiv I/II (APA I/II)
– Nachlass Viktor Adler
– Teilnachlass Karl Renner
Wiener Stadt- und Landesbibliothek, Handschriftensammlung,Vienna (WStLB/HS)
– Nachlass Heinrich Friedjung
– Briefsammlung Friedjung
Privately owned by professor Fritz Fellner (Vienna)
– Nachlass Josef Redlich
Bibliothek des Österreichischen Staatsarchivs
– *Reden und Schriftsstücken des Ministerpräsidenten Dr. Ernest von Koerber 1900–1904* (2 vols.)

II. Newspapers and periodicals

Allgemeine Zeitung
Arbeiter-Zeitung (AZ)
Der Kampf
Mitteilungen des Dorotheum
Neue Freie Presse (NFP)
Neues Wiener Tageblatt (NWT)
Vossische Zeitung
Wiener Zeitung (WZ)

III. Published primary sources

Die Aehrenthals. Eine Familie in ihrer Korrespondenz 1872–1911. 2 vols., Franz Adlgasser, ed. Vienna: Böhlau Verlag, 2002.

Andrian, Leopold von. "Meine Tätigkeit als Generalintendant der Wiener Hoftheater." *Neue Freie Presse*, 28 October, 4 November, 8 November 1928.

Andrian, Leopold von. *Die Ständeordnung des Alls. Rationales Weltbild eines katholischen Dichters.* Munich: Kösel & Pustet, 1930.

Andrian, Leopold von. "Die Sprache des Österreichers." *Vaterland. Blätter für katholisches Österreichertum* 7 (1933/34): 4–8, 24–27.

Andrian, Leopold von. "Hofmannsthal und die österreichische Jugend." *Vaterland. Blätter für katholisches Österreichertum* 8 (1934–35): 130–36.

Andrian, Leopold von. *Österreich im Prisma der Idee. Katechismus der Führenden.* Graz: Schmidt-Dengler, 1937.

Andrian, Leopold von. "Erinnerungen an meinen Freund." In *Hugo von Hofmannsthal. Die Gestalt des Dichters im Spiegel der Freunde.* Helmut Fiechtner, ed. Vienna: Humboldt Verlag, 1949, 52–64.

Andrian, Leopold von. *Der Garten der Erkenntnis. Mit Dokumenten und Zeitgenössischen Stimmen.* Walter H. Perl ed. Frankfurt am Main: S. Fischer Verlag, 1970. [*Der Garten der Erkenntnis* was originally published in 1895 and reissued in 1919.]

"Leopold Andrian über Hugo von Hofmannsthal. Auszüge aus seinen Tagebüchern." Ursula Renner, ed. *Hofmannsthalblätter* 35/36 (1987): 3–49.

Aus dem Nachlass Aehrenthal. Briefe und Dokumente zur österreichisch-ungarischen Innen- und Aussenpolitik 1885–1912, 2 vols., Salomon Wank, ed. Graz: Wolfgang Neugebauer Verlag, 1994.

Aussenpolitische Dokumente der Republik Österreich 1918–1938. Vol. 1: *Selbstbestimmung der Republik.* Klaus Koch, Walter Rauscher, and Arnold Suppan, eds. Vienna: Verlag für Geschichte und Politik, 1993.

Bahr, Hermann. *Schwarzgelb.* Berlin: S. Fischer Verlag, 1917.

Benedikt, Heinrich. *Die Friedensaktion der Meinlgruppe 1917/18. Die Bemühungen um einen Verständigungsfrieden nach Dokumenten, Aktenstücken, und Briefen.* Graz: Böhlau Verlag, 1962.

Berchtold, Klaus, ed. *Österreichische Parteiprogramme 1868–1966.* Munich: Oldenbourg Verlag, 1967.

Die Bestrebungen für eine wirtschaftliche Annäherung Deutschlands und Oesterreich- Ungarns. Protokoll der Verhandlungen die am 9. Januar 1916 zwischen der sozialdemokratischen Fraktion des deutschen Reichstages, dem sozialdemokratischen Parteivorstand und Parteiausschuß, der Generalkommission und den Vorständen der deutschen Gewerkschaften, einer Vertretung der Zentralverbandes deutscher Konsumvereine und einer Vertretung der sozialdemokratischen Partei Oesterreichs und der österreichischen Gewerkschaften in Berlin über die wirtschaftliche Annäherung Deutschlands und Oesterreich-Ungarns stattfanden. Herausgegeben vom Vorstand der sozialdemokratischen Partei Deutschlands. Berlin: Paul Singer, 1916.

Bihl, Wolfdieter. "Zu den österreichisch-ungarischen Kriegszielen 1914." *Jahrbücher für Geschichte Osteuropas*, Wiesbaden: Verlag Otto Harrassowitz, 1968: 505–30.

Brecht, Walter. "Fortsetzungspläne zu 'Andreas,' Mitgeteilt von Walter Brecht." *Hofmannsthalblätter* 5 (1970): 392–93.

Brecht, Walter. "Ein Romanfragment Hofmannsthals." *Hofmannsthal-Jahrbuch* 7 (1999): 125–28.

Briefe 1890–1909. Hugo von Hofmannsthal, 2 vols. Berlin: S. Fischer Verlag, 1935–37.

Briefe der Freundschaft. Hugo von Hofmannsthal. Eberhard von Bodenhausen. Berlin: Eugen Diedrich, 1953.

Briefe und Dokumente zur Geschichte der österreichisch-ungarischen Monarchie. Der Verfassungstreue Großgrundbesitz 1880–99/1900–1904, 2 vols. Ernst Rutkowski, ed. Munich: Oldenbourg Verlag, 1983–91.

Brockhausen, Carl. *Österreichs Kriegsziel.* Vienna: Hölzel, 1915.

Dichter und Gelehrter. Hermann Bahr und Josef Redlich in ihren Briefen 1896–1934. Fritz Fellner, ed. Salzburg: Wolfgang Neugebauer Verlag, 1980.

Ein Briefwechsel. Eberhard von Bodenhausen—Harry Graf Kessler. Ein Briefwechsel 1894–1918. Hans-Ulrich Simon, ed. Stuttgart: Klett, 1978.

Enquete der Kommission zur Förderung der Verwaltungsreform. Enquete der Kommission zur Förderung der Verwaltungsreform veranstaltet in der Zeit vom 21. Oktober bis 9. November 1912 zur Feststellung der Wünsche der beteiligten Kreise der Bevölkerung in bezug auf die Reform der inneren und Finanzverwaltung. Vienna: k.k. Hof- und Staatsdruckerei, 1913.

Foerster, Friedrich W. *Das österreichische Problem vom ethischen und staatspädagogischen Standpunkte*. Vienna: Hugo Heller, 1914.

Foerster, Friedrich W. *Erlebte Weltgeschichte 1869–1953. Memoiren*. Nürnberg: Glock & Lutz, 1953.

Friedjung, Heinrich. *Der Ausgleich mit Ungarn. Politische Studie über das Verhältnis Österreichs zu Ungarn und Deutschland*. Leipzig: Otto Wiegand, 1877.

Friedjung, Heinrich. *Ein Stück Zeitungsgeschichte*. Vienna: Genossenschafts-Buchdruckerei, 1887.

Friedjung, Heinrich. *Der Kampf um die Vorherrschaft in Deutschland 1859–1866*, 2 vols. Stuttgart: J. G. Cotta, 1897–98.

Friedjung, Heinrich. *Benedeks Nachgelassene Papiere. Herausgegeben und zu einer Biographie verarbeitet von Heinrich Friedjung*. Leipzig: Grübel & Sommerlatte, 1901.

Friedjung, Heinrich. *Österreich von 1848 bis 1860*, 2 vols. Stuttgart: J. G. Cotta, 1908–12.

Friedjung, Heinrich. *Denkschrift aus Deutsch-Österreich.* Leipzig: S. Hirzel, 1915 (in cooperation with Michael Hainisch, Eugen Philippovich, and Hans Uebersberger).

Friedjung, Heinrich. *Historische Aufsätze.* Stuttgart: J. G. Cotta, 1919.

Friedjung, Heinrich. *Das Zeitalter des Imperialismus 1884–1914*, 3 vols. Berlin: Neufeld & Henius, 1919–22.

Friedjung, Heinrich. "Ernest von Koerber." *Neue österreichische Biographie*, Anton Bettelheim, ed. Vienna: Amalthea Verlag, 1923, 23–43.

Friedjung, Heinrich. *Geschichte in Gesprächen. Aufzeichnungen 1898–1919*, 2 vols. Herausgegeben und eingeleitet von Franz Adlgasser und Margret Friedrich. Vienna: Böhlau Verlag, 1997.

Die Grosse Politik der Europäischen Kabinette 1871–1914. Sammlung der diplomatischen Akten des Auswärtigen Amtes, Johannes Lepsius, Albrecht Mendelssohn-Bartholdy & Friedrich Thimme, eds. 40 vols. Berlin: Deutsche Verlags Gesellschaft für Politik und Geschichte, 1922–27.

Hofmannsthal, Christiane von. *Tagebücher und Briefe des Vaters an die Tochter.* Frankfurt am Main: S. Fischer Verlag, 1991.

Hofmannsthal, Hugo von. *Dramen IV (Lustspiele)*, in *Gesammelte Werke in zehn Einzelbänden.* Frankfurt am Main: Fischer Taschenbuchverlag, 1979.

Hofmannsthal, Hugo von. *Dramen V (Operndichtungen)*, in *Gesammelte Werke in zehn Einzelbänden.* Frankfurt am Main: Fischer Taschenbuchverlag, 1979.

Hofmannsthal, Hugo von. *Reden und Aufsätze I (1891–1913)*, in *Gesammelte Werke in zehn Einzelbänden.* Frankfurt am Main: Fischer Taschenbuchverlag, 1979.

Hofmannsthal, Hugo von. *Reden und Aufsätze II (1914–1924)*, in *Gesammelte Werke in zehn Einzelbänden.* Frankfurt am Main: Fischer Taschenbuchverlag, 1979.

Hofmannsthal, Hugo von. *Reden und Aufsätze III (1925–1929), Aufzeichnungen,* in *Gesammelte Werke in zehn Einzelbänden.* Frankfurt am Main: Fischer Taschenbuchverlag, 1980.

Hofmannsthal, Hugo von. *Erzählungen, Erfundene Gespräche und Briefe, Reisen*, in *Gesammelte Werke in zehn Einzelbänden.* Frankfurt am Main: Fischer Taschenbuchverlag, 1979.

Hofmannsthal, Hugo von. *Sämtliche Werke,* vol. 26. *Operndichtungen* 4. Hans-Albrecht Koch, ed. Frankfurt am Main: S. Fischer Verlag, 1976.

Hofmannsthal, Hugo von. *Sämtliche Werke,* vol. 29. *Erzählungen* 2. Ellen Ritter, ed. Frankfurt am Main: S. Fischer Verlag, 1978.

Hofmannsthal, Hugo von. *Sämtliche Werke,* vol. 30. *Roman. Biographie.* Manfred Pape. ed. Frankfurt am Main: S. Fischer Verlag, 1982.

Hofmannsthal, Hugo von. *Sämtliche Werke,* vol. 12. *Dramen* 10. Martin Stern, ed. Frankfurt am Main: S. Fischer Verlag, 1993.

Hofmannsthal, Hugo von. *Sämtliche Werke,* vol.19. *Dramen* 17. Ellen Ritter, ed. Frankfurt am Main: S. Fischer Verlag, 1994.

Hugo von Hofmannsthal-Leopold von Andrian. Briefwechsel. Walter H. Perl, ed. Frankfurt am Main: S. Fischer Verlag, 1968.

Hugo von Hofmannsthal—Richard Beer-Hofmann. Briefwechsel. Eugene Weber, ed. Frankfurt am Main: S. Fischer Verlag, 1972.

"Hofmannsthal und Efraim Frisch. Zwölf Briefe 1910–1927." In *Hofmannsthal-blätter* 5, Max Kreutzberger, ed. (1970): 356–370.

Hugo von Hofmannsthal. Briefwechsel mit dem Insel-Verlag, 1901–1929. Gerhard Schuster, ed. Frankfurt am Main: Buchhändler-Vereinigung, 1985.

Hugo von Hofmannsthal—Harry Graf Kessler. Briefwechsel 1898–1929. Hilde Burger, ed. Frankfurt am Main: Insel Verlag, 1968.

Hugo von Hofmannsthal—Max Mell. Briefwechsel. Margret Dietrich & Heinz Kindermann, eds. Heidelberg: Lambert Schneider, 1982.

"Hugo von Hofmannsthal—Yella, Felix und Mysa Oppenheimer. Briefwechsel. Teil II: 1906–1929." Nicoletta Giacon, ed. in *Hofmannsthal-Jahrbuch*, 8 (2000): 7–156.

Hugo von Hofmannsthal—Rudolf Pannwitz. Briefwechsel 1907–1926. Gerhard Schuster, ed. Frankfurt am Main: S. Fischer Verlag, 1994.

Hugo von Hofmannsthal—Josef Redlich. Briefwechsel. Helga Ebner-Fußgänger, ed. Frankfurt am Main: S. Fischer Verlag, 1971.

Hugo von Hofmannsthal—Arthur Schnitzler. Briefwechsel. Therese Nickl & Heinrich Schnitzler, eds. Frankfurt am Main: S. Fischer Verlag, 1964.

Hugo von Hofmannsthal. Richard Strauss. Briefwechsel. Willi Schuh, ed. Munich: R. Piper, 1990.

Hugo von Hofmannsthal—Christiane Gräfin Thun-Salm. Briefwechsel. Mit Briefen Hofmannsthals an Paul Graf Thun-Hohenstein. Renate Moering, ed. Frankfurt am Main: S. Fischer Verlag, 1999.

Hugo von Hofmannsthal. Anton Wildgans. Briefwechsel. Norbert Altenhofer, ed. Heidelberg: Lothar Stiehm Verlag, 1971.

Kautsky, Karl. *Die Vereinigten Staaten Mitteleuropas.* Stuttgart: Dietz, 1916.

Kautsky, Karl. *Kriegsmarxismus. Eine theoretische Grundlegung der Politik des 4. August.* Vienna: Brand, 1918.

Kielmannsegg, Erich. *Kaiserhaus, Staatsmänner, Politiker. Aufzeichnungen des k.k. Statthalters Erich Graf Kielmannsegg.* Walter Goldinger, ed. Vienna: Oldenbourg Verlag, 1966.

Lemke, Heinz. "Die deutsche Polenpolitik 1914 bis 1916 in der Sicht eines österreichisch-ungarischen Diplomaten. Der Bericht Baron Andrians vom 30. Dezember 1916." *Jahrbuch für Geschichte der UdSSR und der volksdemokratischen Länder Europas*, vol.7. Berlin: Rütten & Loening, 1963: 495–504.

Das nationale Problem in Österreich. Auszug aus den im Juli 1917 gehaltenen Reden der Herren Reichsratsabgeordneten Professor Dr. Josef Redlich, E.O. Zenker, Dr. R. Von

Lodgmann und Dr. K. Renner an den Diskussionsabenden über das Thema Das nationale Problem in Österreich. Österreichische Politische Gesellschaft. Vienna: Carl Fromme, 1917.

Naumann, Friedrich. *Werke.* 6 vols., Thomas Nipperdey & Wolfgang Schieder, eds. Opladen: Westdeutscher Verlag, 1964–69.

Österreich-Ungarns Außenpolitik von der bosnischen Krise 1908 bis zum Kriegsausbruch 1914. Ludwig Bittner, Heinrich von Srbik and Hans Uebersberger, eds. 9 vols., Vienna: Österreichischer Bundesverlag, 1930.

Österreich und der Friede. Verständigung unter den Völkern Österreichs. Versammlung vom 17. Juli 1917 in der 'Österreichischen Politischen Gesellschaft'. Vienna: Herrmann, 1917.

Pace, Anton. *Ernst Mayerhofers Handbuch für den politischen Verwaltungsdienst.* 8 vols., Anton Pace, ed. 5th ed., Vienna: Manz, 1895–1913.

Plener, Ernst von. *Erinnerungen.* 3 vols., Stuttgart: Deutsche Verlagsanstalt, 1911–21.

Protokolle des Gemeinsamen Ministerrates der Österreichisch-Ungarischen Monarchie, 1896–1907. Éva Somogyi, ed. Vienna: Österreichischer Bundesverlag, 1991.

Protokolle des Gemeinsamen Ministerrates der Österreichisch-Ungarischen Monarchie, 1914–1918. Miklós Komjáthy, ed. Budapest: Akademie Kiado, 1966.

Protokoll der Verhandlungen des Parteitages der Deutschen sozialdemokratischen Arbeiterpartei in Oesterreich in Wien, 19–24. Oktober 1917. Vienna: Brand, 1917.

Prutsch, Ursula & Klaus Zeyringer, eds. *Leopold von Andrian (1875–1951). Korrespondenzen, Notizen, Essays, Berichte.* Ursula Prutsch & Klaus Zeyringer, eds. Vienna, 2003.

Redlich, Josef. *Englische Lokalverwaltung. Darstellung der inneren Verwaltung Englands in ihrer geschichtlichen Entwicklung und in ihrer gegenwärtigen Gestalt.* Leipzig: Duncker, 1901.

Redlich, Josef. *Recht und Technik des Englischen Parlamentarismus. Die Geschäftsordnung des House of Commons in ihrer geschichtlichen Entwicklung und gegenwärtigen Gestalt.* Leipzig: Duncker, 1905.

Redlich, Josef. "Die Originalprotokolle des Verfassungsauschuß im Kremsierer Reichstag." *Österreichische Rundschau* 17 (1908): 163–81.

Redlich, Josef. "Lasser und Schmerling. Nach ihren Briefen." *Österreichische Rundschau* 19 (1909):79–93.

Redlich, Josef. *Das Wesen der österreichischen Kommunal-Verfassung.* Leipzig: Duncker, 1910.

Redlich, Josef. *Zustand und Reform der österreichischen Verwaltung. Rede des Reichsratsabgeordneten Professor Dr. Josef Redlich gehalten in der Budgetdebatte des Abgeordnetenhauses des österreichischen Reichsrates vom 26. Oktober 1911.* Vienna: Manz Verlag, 1911.

Redlich, Josef. *Bericht des Mitgliedes der Kommission zur Förderung der Verwaltungsreform Professor Dr. Josef Redlich über die Entwicklung und den gegenwärtigen Stand der österreichischen Finanzverwaltung sowie Vorschläge der Kommission zur Reform dieser Verwaltung.* Vienna: k.k. Hof- und Staatsdruckerei, 1913.

Redlich, Josef. *Das österreichische Staats- und Reichsproblem. Geschichtliche Darstellung der inneren Politik der habsburgischen Monarchie von 1848 bis zum Untergang des Reiches.* 2 vols., Leipzig: Der neue Geist Verlag, 1920–26.

Redlich, Josef. "Heinrich Lammasch als Minister-Präsident." In *Heinrich Lammasch. Seine Aufzeichnungen, sein Wirken und seine Politik.* Marga Lammasch & Hans Sperl, eds. Vienna: Deuticke, 1922.

Redlich, Josef. *Österreichische Regierung und Verwaltung im Weltkriege.* Vienna: Hölder-Pichler-Tempsky AG/New Haven: Yale University Press, 1925.

Redlich, Josef. *Austrian War Government.* New Haven: Yale University Press, 1929.

Redlich, Josef. *Kaiser Franz Joseph von Österreich. Eine Biographie.* Berlin: Verlag für Kulturpolitik, 1929.

Redlich, Josef. *Schicksaalsjahre Österreichs 1908–1919. Das politische Tagebuch Josef Redlichs.* Bearbeitet und herausgegeben von Fritz Fellner, Graz: Böhlau Verlag, 1953–54.

Renner, Karl (Synopticus). *Staat und Nation. Staatsrechtliche Untersuchung über die möglichen Principien einer Lösung und die juristischen Voraussetzungen eines Nationalitätengesetzes.* Vienna: Dietl, 1899.

Renner, Karl (Springer, Rudolf). *Staat und Parlament. Kritische Studie über die Österreichische Frage und das System der Interessenvertretung.* Vienna: Genossenschafts-Buchdruckerei, 1901.

Renner, Karl (Springer, Rudolf). *Der Kampf der österreichischen Nationen um den Staat. Das nationale Problem als Verfassungs- und Verwaltungsfrage.* Leipzig: Deuticke, 1902.

Renner, Karl (Springer, Rudolf). *Die Krise der Dualismus und das Déakistische Episode in der Geschichte der habsburgischen Monarchie. Eine politische Skizze.* Vienna: Genossenschafts-Buchdruckerei, 1904.

Renner, Karl (Rudolf Springer). *Mehrheits- oder Volksvertretung. Zur Aufklärung der intellektuellen und bürgerlichen Klassen über ihr Interesse an einer Wahlreform, sowie über Wesen, Arten und Bedeutung der Proportionalwahl.* Vienna: Deuticke, 1904.

Renner, Karl (Springer, Rudolf). *Grundlagen und Entwicklungsziele der Österreichisch-Ungarischen Monarchie. Politische Studie über den Zusammenbruch der Privilegienparlamente und die Wahlreform in beiden Staaten, über die Reichsidee und ihre Zukunft.* Vienna: Deuticke, 1906.

Renner, Karl. *Was haben die Sozialdemokraten geleistet? Zehn Jahre parlamentarischer Arbeit für das Wohl der arbeitenden Klasse.* Vienna: Brand, 1907.

Renner, Karl. *Österreichs Erneuerung. Politisch-programmatische Aufsätze.* 3 vols. Vienna: Brand, 1916.

Renner, Karl. *Marxismus, Krieg, und Internationale. Kritische Studien über offene Probleme des wissenschaftlichen und des praktischen Sozialismus in und nach dem Weltkrieg.* Stuttgart: Dietz, 1917.

Renner, Karl. *Das Selbstbestimmungsrecht der Nationen in besonderer Anwendung auf Österreich.* Leipzig: Deuticke, 1918.

Renner, Karl. *Deutschland, Oesterreich und die Völker des Ostens.* Berlin: Verlag für Sozialwissenschaft, 1922.

Renner, Karl. *Die Nation: Mythos und Wirklichkeit. Manuskript aus dem Nachlaß.* Jacques Hannak, ed. Vienna: Europa Verlag, 1964 [Manuscript dated 1937].

Renner, Karl. *Die Gründung der Republik Deutschösterreich der Anschluß und die Sudetendeutschen. Dokumente eines Kampfes ums Recht.* Edited and introduced by Eduard Rabofsky. Vienna: Globus Verlag, 1991 [Manuscript dated November 1938].

Renner, Karl. *An der Wende zweier Zeiten. Lebenserinnerungen von Karl Renner.* Vienna: Danubia-Verlag, 1946.

Riezler, Kurt. *Tagebücher—Aufsätze—Dokumente.* Karl Dietrich Erdmann, ed. Göttingen: Vandenhoeck & Ruprecht, 1972.

Scheidemann, Philipp. *Der Zusammenbruch.* Berlin: Verlag für Sozialwissenschaft, 1921.

Scheidemann, Philipp. *Memoiren eines Sozialdemokraten.* 2 vols. Dresden: Carl Reissner Verlag, 1928.

Scherer, André & Jacques Grunewald. *L'Allemagne et les problèmes de la paix pendant la première guerre mondiale. Documents extraits des archiv de l'Office allemand des Affaires étrangères,* vol. 1: *Des origines la déclaration de la guerre sous-marine a outrance (août 1914—31 janvier 1917).* Publiés et annotés par André Scherer et Jacques Grunewald, Paris: Presses universitaire de France, 1962.

Schwartzenau, Erwin von. *Anträge der Kommission zur Förderung der Verwaltungsreform betreffend die Erlassung einer Geschäftsordnung der k.k. Bezirkshauptmannschaften und die Feststellung von Grundsätzen für das Verfahren von den politischen Behörden samt Erläuterungen und einem Bericht über die Kanzleireform bei den politischen Behörden.* Vienna: k.k. Hof- und Staatsdruckerei, 1913.

Stenographische Protokolle des Abgeordnetenhauses, Session XVI–XXII (1897–1918). Vienna: k.k. Hof und Staatsdruckerei, 1897–1918.

Stern, Martin. "Hofmannsthal und Böhmen (1). Der Briefwechsel mit Jaroslav Kvapil und das Projekt der 'Ehrenstätten Österreichs'." *Hofmannsthalblätter* 1 (1968): 3–30.

Stern, Martin. "Hofmannsthal und Böhmen (2). Die Rolle der Tschechen und Slowaken in Hofmannsthals Österreich-Bild der Kriegszeit und seiner Prager Erfahrung im Juni 1917." *Hofmannsthalsblätter* 2 (1969): 102–135.

Stern, Martin. "Hofmannsthal und Böhmen (3). Hofmannsthals Plan einer 'Tschechische Bibliothek' (1918). Ein Aufklärungswerk für die Deutschen." *Hofmannsthalsblätter* 3 (1969): 195–215.

"Die Vorschläge Prof. Redlichs zur Reform der Finanzverwaltung. Referent: Regierungsrat Professor Karl Brockhausen. Gemeinsame Zusammenkunft am 4. February 1914." *Mitteilungen der Industriellen Vereinigung*, no. 23 (1914): 3–40.

IV. Secondary sources

Ableitinger, Alfred. *Ernest von Koerber und das Verfassungsproblem im Jahre 1900. Österreichische Nationalitäten- und Innenpolitik zwischen Konstitutionalismus, Parlamentarismus und oktroyiertem allgemeinem Wahlrecht.* Vienna: Böhlau Verlag, 1973.

Adlgasser, Franz & Margret Friedrich. "Einleitung." In *Heinrich Friedjung. Geschichte in Gesprächen. Aufzeichnungen 1898–1919.* Franz Adlgasser & Margret Friedrich, eds. Vienna: Böhlau Verlag, 1997.

Alewyn, Richard. *Über Hugo von Hofmannsthal.* Göttingen: Vandenhoeck & Ruprecht, 1958.

Allmayer-Beck, J.C. *Ministerpräsident Baron Beck. Ein Staatsman des alten Österreich.* Vienna: Verlag für Geschichte und Politik, 1956.

Anderson, Benedict. *Imagined Communities: Reflections on the Origin and Spread of Nationalism.* London: Verso, 1983.

Beller, Steven. *Vienna and the Jews 1867–1938. A Cultural History.* Cambridge: Cambridge University Press, 1989.

Beller, Steven, ed. *Rethinking Vienna 1900.* New York: Berghahn Books, 2001.

Bendix, Reinhard. *Max Weber—Das Werk. Darstellung—Analyse—Ergebnisse.* Munich: Piper, 1964,

Beniston, Judith. *"Welttheater": Hofmannsthal, Richard von Kralik, and the Revival of Catholic Drama in Austria, 1890–1934.* London: Maney, 1998.

Berger Waldenegg, Georg Christoph. *Mit vereinten Kräften! Zum Verhältnis von Herrschaftspraxis und Systemkonsolidierung im Neoabsolutismus am Beispiel der Nationalanleihe von 1954.* Vienna Böhlau Verlag, 2002.

Berlepsch, Hans Jürgen von. "Der Wiederkehr des 'wirklichen Menschen' in der Geschichte. Neue biographische Literatur." In *Archiv für Sozialgeschichte* 29 (1989): 488–510.

Blanning, T.C.W. *Joseph II.* London & New York: Longman, 1994.

Blanning, T.C.W., ed. *History and Biography. Essays in Honour of Derek Beales.* Cambridge: Cambridge University Press, 1996.

Bluhm, William, T. *Building an Austrian Nation. The Political Integration of a Western State.* New Haven: Yale University Press, 1973.

Böckenförde, Ernst Wolfgang. "Der Verfassungstyp der deutschen konstitutionellen Monarchie im 19. Jahrhundert." In idem., *Moderne deutsche Verfassungsgeschichte (1815–1918).* Cologne: Kiepenhauer & Witsch, 1972.

Böckenförde, Ernst Wolfgang, ed. *Probleme des Konstitutionalismus im 19. Jahrhundert.* Berlin: Duncker & Humblot, 1975.

Bödeker, Hans Erich, ed. *Biographie Schreiben.* Göttingen: Wallstein Verlag, 2003.

Bödeker, Hans Erich. "Biographie. Annäherungen an den gegenwärtigen Forschungs und Diskussionsstand." In idem., ed. *Biographie Schreiben.* Göttingen: Wallstein Verlag, 2003.

Botz, Gerhard & Gerald Sprengnagel, eds. *Kontroversen um Österreichs Zeitgeschichte. Verdrängte Vergangenheit, Österreich-Identität, Waldheim und die Historiker.* Frankfurt am Main: Campus Verlag, 1994.

Boyer, John, W. *Political Radicalism in Late Imperial Vienna. Origins of the Christian Social Movement 1848–1897.* Chicago: University of Chicago Press, 1981.

Boyer, John, W. "The End of an Old Regime: Visions of Political Reform in Late Imperial Austria." *Journal of Modern History* 58:1 (1986): 159–193.

Boyer, John, W. *Culture and Political Crisis in Vienna. Christian Socialism in Power, 1897–1918.* Chicago: University of Chicago Press, 1995.

Brandt, Harm-Hinrich. *Der österreichische Neoabsolutismus: Staatsfinanzen und Politik, 1848–1860.* Göttingen: Vandenhoeck & Ruprecht, 1978.

Brauneder, Wilhelm. "Die Verfassungsentwicklung in Österreich 1848–1918." Peter Urbanitsch and Helmut Rumpler, eds. *Die Habsburgermonarchie, 1848–1918,* vol. 7: *Verfassung und Parlamentarismus.* Vienna: Verlag der österreichischen Akademie der Wissenschaften, 69–237.

Brauneder, Wilhelm. *Österreichische Verfassungsgeschichte.* 8th ed., Vienna: Manz, 2001.

Brix, Emil. *Die Umgangssprachen in Altösterreich zwischen Agitation und Assimilation.* Vienna: Böhlau Verlag, 1982.

Broch, Hermann. *Hugo von Hofmannsthal and His Time. The European Imagination 1860–1920.* Translated, edited, and with an introduction by Michael P. Steinberg, Chicago: University of Chicago Press, 1984. [Originally published in German in 1955.]

Broucek, Peter. *Karl I. (IV.). Der politische Weg des letzten Herrschers der Donaumonarchie.* Vienna: Böhlau Verlag, 1997.

Bruckmüller, Ernst. *Nation Österreich. Sozialhistorische Aspekte ihrer Entwicklung.* Vienna: Böhlau Verlag, 1984.

Bruckmüller, Ernst. "Die Frage nach dem National-Bewußtsein in der österreichischen Geschichte unter sozialhistorischem Aspekt." In *Probleme der Geschichte Österreichs und ihrer Darstellung.* Herwig Wolfram & Walter Pohl, eds. Vienna: Verlag der österreichischen Akademie der Wissenschaften, 1991.

Bruckmüller, Ernst. "Österreichbegriff und Österreich-Bewußtsein in der Franzisko-Josephinischen Epoche." In *Was heisst Österreich? Inhalt und Umfang des Österreichbegriffs vom 10. Jahrhundert bis heute.* Richard G. Plaschka, Gerald Stourzh & Paul Niederkorn, eds. Vienna: Verlag der österreichischen Akademie der Wissenschaften, 1995, 255–88.

Bruckmüller, Ernst. *Nation Österreich. Kulturelles Bewußtsein und gesellschaftlich-politische Prozesse.* Vienna: Böhlau Verlag, 1996.

Bruckmüller, Ernst. "Die Entwicklung des Österreich-Bewußtsein." In *Österreichische Nationalgeschichte nach 1945. Die Spiegel der Erinnerung: Die Sicht von innen* (vol. 1). Robert Kriechbaumer, ed. Vienna: Böhlau Verlag, 1998.

Charmatz, Richard. *Österreichs innere Geschichte, 1848–1907.* 2 vols., Leipzig: Teubner, 1909–11.

Charmatz, Richard. "Ein moderner Ministerpräsident. Dr. Ernest von Körber." In idem., *Lebensbilder aus der Geschichte Österreichs.* Vienna: Danubia-Verlag, 1947, 165–77.

Cohen, Gary, B. *The Politics of Ethnic Survival: Germans in Prague, 1861–1914.* Princeton, N.J.: Princeton University Press, 1981.

Cohen, Gary, B. "Neither Absolutism nor Anarchy: New Narratives on Society and Government in Late Imperial Austria." *Austrian History Yearbook* 29, part 1 (1998): 37–61.

Conze, Werner. *Polnische Nation und deutsche Politik im ersten Weltkrieg.* Cologne: Böhlau Verlag, 1958.

Cord Meyer, Henry. *Mitteleuropa in German Thought and Action, 1815–1945.* The Hague: Nijhoff, 1955.

Czedik, Alois. *Zur Geschichte der k.k. österreichischen Ministerien, 1861–1916.* 4 vols., Vienna: Prochaska, 1917–20.

Daviau, Donald G. *Der Mann von Übermorgen. Hermann Bahr 1863–1934.* Vienna: Österreichischer Bundesverlag, 1984.

Dechel, Alfred. *Das 'Linzer Programm' und seine Autoren. Seine Vorgeschichte unter besonderer Berücksichtigung der Rolle des Historikers Heinrich Friedjung.* Unpublished dissertation, University of Salzburg, 1975.

Doppler, Bernhard. "Konkurrenz um das katholisch-österreichische. Hofmannsthal, Richard von Kralik und das Haus Habsburg. Eine Dokumentation." *Hofmannsthalblätter* 40 (1990): 73–92.

Dorowin, Hermann. *Retter des Abendlandes. Kulturkritik im Vorfeld des europäischen Fascismus.* Stuttgart: J.B. Metzlersche Verlagsbuchhandlung, 1991.

Duff, Tim. *Plutarch's Lives: Exploring Virtue and Vice.* Oxford: Clarendon Press, 1999.

Eisenmann, Louis. "Austria-Hungary." *Cambridge Modern History*, vol. 12: *The Latest Age.* Cambridge: Cambridge University Press, 1910.

Erdmann, Karl Dietrich. "Kurt Riezler—ein politisches Profil (1882–1955)." Introduction to Kurt Riezler, *Tagebücher—Aufsätze—Dokumente.* Karl Dietrich Erdmann, ed. Göttingen: Vandenhoeck & Ruprecht, 1972.

Erdmann, Karl Dietrich. *Die Spur Österreichs in der deutschen Geschichte. Drei Staaten, zwei Nationen, ein Volk?* Zürich: Manesse Verlag, 1989.

Fellner, Fritz. "Josef Redlich. Leben und Werk." In Josef Redlich, *Schicksaalsjahre*

Österreichs, 1908–1919. Das politische Tagebuch Josef Redlichs. 2 vols. Bearbeitet und herausgegeben von Fritz Fellner, Graz: Böhlau Verlag, 1953, 1: XI–XIX.

Fellner, Fritz. "Josef Redlich. Leben und Werk, Ausklang." In Josef Redlich, *Schicksaalsjahre Österreichs 1908–1919. Das politische Tagebuch Josef Redlichs.* 2 vols. Bearbeitet und herausgegeben von Fritz Fellner, Böhlau, Graz-Köln, 1954, 2:351–58.

Fellner, Fritz. "Der Plan einer 'Vortragsmission Redlich-Apponyi' in den Vereinigten Staaten von Amerika. Ansätze und Vorschläge zum Aufbau einer österreichisch-ungarischen Propaganda-aktion im neutralen Ausland während des Ersten Weltkrieges." Heinrich Fichtenau & Erich Zöllner, eds. *Beiträge zur neueren Geschichte Österreichs.* Vienna: Böhlau Verlag, 1974, 469–88.

Fellner, Fritz. "Die Historiographie zur österreichisch-deutschen Problematik als Spiegel der nationalpolitischen Diskussion." In *Österreich und die Deutsche Frage im 19. und 20. Jahrhundert.* Heinrich Lutz & Helmut Rumpler, eds. Munich: Oldenbourg Verlag, 1982, 33–59. [Reprinted in Fritz Fellner, *Geschichtsschreibung und nationale Identität.* Vienna: Böhlau Verlag, 2002, 145–72.]

Fellner, Fritz. "The Problem of the Austrian Nation after 1945." *Journal of Modern History* 60:2 (1988): 264–89.

Fellner, Fritz. "Austriaca: Ideologi und Politik in den Tagebüchern Hermann Bahrs." In *Hermann-Bahr-Symposion "Der Herr aus Linz." Bericht.* Margret Dietrich, ed. Linz: Linzer Veranstaltungsgesellschaft, 1987, 51–58.

Fellner, Fritz. "Heinrich Friedjung—Ein österreichischer Ahnherr des 'Oral History.'" In Fritz Fellner, *Geschichtsschreibung und nationale Identität.* Vienna: Böhlau Verlag, 2002, 293–322. [Reprinted. Originally published in1988].

Fellner, Fritz. "Denkschriften aus Österreich. Die österreichische Mitteleuropa-Diskussion in Wissenschaft und Politik, 1915/16." In idem, *Vom Dreibund zum Völkerbund: Studien zur Geschichte der internationalen Beziehungen, 1882–1919.* Heidrun Maschl und Brigitte Mazohl-Wallnig, eds. Vienna: Verlag für Geschichte und Politik, 1994, 221–240.

Fellner, Fritz. "Die Mission Hoyos." In idem., *Vom Dreibund zum Völkerbund: Studien zur Geschichte der internationalen Beziehungen, 1882–1919.* Heidrun Maschl & Brigitte Mazohl-Wallning, eds. Vienna: Verlag für Geschichte und Politik, 1994: 112–41.

Fellner, Fritz. "Heinrich von Srbik—'Urenkelschüler Rankes.'" In Fritz Fellner, *Geschichtsschreibung und nationale Identität.* Vienna: Böhlau Verlag, 2002, 330–45.

Fellner, Fritz. *Geschichtsschreibung und Nationale Identität. Probleme und Leistungen der österreichischen Geschichtswissenschaft.* Vienna: Böhlau Verlag, 2002.

Fewster, Colin. "Hugo von Hofmannsthal and the Cavalry," *Seminar. A Journal in Germanic Studies* 32:2 (May 1996): 115–28.

Gall, Lothar. *Europa auf dem Weg in die Moderne, 1850–1890.* Munich: Oldenbourg Verlag, 1997.

Garver, Bruce M. *The Young Czech Party, 1874–1901, and the Emergence of a Multi-Party System.* New Haven: Yale University Press, 1978.

Gellner, Ernest. *Nations and Nationalism.* Oxford: Blackwell, 1983.

Gerschenkron, Alexander. *An Economic Spurt That Failed. Four Lectures in Austrian History.* Princeton, N.J.: Princeton University Press, 1977.

Gilbert, Mary F. "Hofmannsthal's essays, 1900–1908: A poet in transition." In *Hofmannsthal. Studies in Commemoration.* F. Norman, ed. London: Publications of the Institute of Germanic Studies, University of London, 1963, 29–52.

Glaubauf, Karl. *Bismarck und der Aufstieg des Deutschen Reiches in der Darstellung Heinrich Friedjungs.* Unpublished dissertation, University of Vienna, 1979.

Godsey, William D. Jr. *Aristocratic Redoubt. The Austro-Hungarian Foreign Office on the Eve of the First World War.* West Lafayette, Ind.: Purdue University Press, 1999.

Goldinger, Walter. "Die Zentralverwaltung in Cisleithanien—Die Zivile gemeinsame Zentralverwaltung." In *Die Habsburgermonarchie, 1848–1918.* Vol. 2: *Verwaltung und Rechtswesen.* Adam Wandruszka & Peter Urbanitsch, eds. Vienna: Verlag der österreichischen Akademie der Wissenschaften, 1975, 100–189.

Gradmann, Christoph. "Geschichte, Fiktion und Erfahrung—kritischen Anmerkungen zur neuerlichen Aktualität der historischen Biographie." *Internationales Archiv für Sozialgeschichte der deutschen Literatur* 17:2 (1992): 1–16.

Gratz, Gustav & Richard Schüller. *Die Äussere Wirtschaftspolitik Österreich-Ungarns. Mitteleuropäische Pläne.* New Haven: Yale University Press, 1925.

Grupp, Peter. *Harry Graf Kessler. Eine Biographie.* Frankfurt am Main: Insel Verlag, 1999.

Hadamowsky, Franz. *Hugo von Hofmannsthal. Katalog der Ausstellung im Prunksaal der Österreichischen Nationalbibliothek (11. Juni bis 16. Oktober 1971). Bearbeitet von Franz Hadamowsky.* Vienna: Österreichische Nationalbibliothek, 1972.

Hamburger, Michael. *Hugo von Hofmannsthal. Zwei Studien.* Göttingen: Sachse & Pohl Verlag, 1964.

Hanisch, Ernst. *Der lange Schatten des Staates. Österreichische Gesellschaftsgeschichte im 20. Jahrhundert, 1890–1990.* Vienna: Ueberreuther, 1994.

Hannak, Jacques. *Karl Renner und seine Zeit. Versuch einer Biographie.* Vienna: Europa-Verlag, 1965.

Hasiba, Gernot D. *Das Notverordnungsrecht in Österreich (1848–1917). Notwendigkeit und Mißbrauch eines 'staatserhaltenden Instrumentes'.* Vienna: Verlag der österreichischen Akademie der Wissenschaften, 1985.

Hasiba, Gernot D. "Die Kommission zur Förderung der Verwaltungsreform (1911–1914)." In *Recht und Geschichte. Festschrift Hermann Baltl zum 70. Geburtstag.* Helfried Valentinitsch, ed. Graz: Leykam Verlag, 1988, 237–62.

Häusler, Wolfgang. "Kaiserstaat oder Völkerverein? Zum österreichischen Staats- und Reichsproblem zwischen 1804 und 1848/49." In *Was heisst Österreich? Inhalt und Umfang des Österreichbegriffs vom 10. Jahrhundert bis heute.* Richard G. Plaschka, Gerald Stourzh & Paul Niederkorn, eds. Vienna: Verlag der österreichischen Akademie der Wissenschaften, 1995, 221–54.

Heer, Friedrich. *Der Kampf um die österreichische Identität.* Vienna: Böhlau Verlag, 1981.

Heerde, Jeroen Bastiaan van. *Staat und Kunst. Staatliche Kunstförderung 1895–1918.* Vienna: Böhlau Verlag, 1993.

Heindl, Waltraud. *Gehorsame Rebellen: Bürokratie und Beamte in Österreich 1780 bis 1848.* Vienna: Böhlau Verlag, 1991.

Hellbling, Ernst. *Österreichische Verfassungs- und Verwaltungsgeschichte.* 2nd ed. Vienna: Springer, 1974.

Heuss, Theodor. *Friedrich Naumann: Der Mann, das Werk, die Zeit.* Stuttgart: Rainer Wunderlich, 1949.

Hinrichs, Eibe. *Die Wirtschaftspolitik Ernest von Koerbers als Integrationsfaktor für die Nationalitäten des Habsburgerreiches (1900–1904).* Unpublished dissertation, University of Vienna, 1998.

Höbelt, Lothar. *Kornblume und Kaiseradler. Die deutsch-freiheitlichen Parteien Altösterreichs 1882–1918.* Vienna: Verlag für Geschichte und Politik, 1993.

Höbelt, Lothar. *1848: Österreich und die deutsche Revolution.* Vienna: Amalthea-Verlag, 1998.

Hobsbawm, Eric. *Nations and Nationalism since 1780.* Cambridge: Cambridge University Press, 1990.

Holleis, Eva. *Die Sozialpolitische Partei. Sozialliberale Bestrebungen in Wien um 1900.* Vienna: Verlag für Geschichte und Politik, 1978.

Ingrao, Charles. *The Habsburg Monarchy 1618–1815,* Cambridge: Cambridge University Press, 1994.

Jefferson, Alan. *Richard Strauss. Der Rosenkavalier.* Cambridge: Cambridge University Press, 1985.

Judson Pieter, M. *Exclusive Revolutionaries: Liberal Politics, Social Experience and National Identity in the Austrian Empire, 1848–1914.* Ann Arbor: University of Michigan Press, 1996.

Judson Pieter, M. *Wien brennt! Die Revolution von 1848 und ihr liberales Erbe.* Vienna: Böhlau Verlag, 1998.

Kann, Robert A. *The Multinational Empire: Nationalism and National Reform in the Habsburg Monarchy, 1848–1918.* 2 vols., New York: Columbia University Press, 1950.

Kann, Robert A. *A History of the Habsburg Empire, 1526–1918.* Berkeley: University of California Press, 1974.

Kann, Robert & Friedrich Prinz, eds. *Deutschland und Österreich. Ein bilaterales Geschichtsbuch*. Vienna: Jugend und Volk, 1980.

Kapp, Richard W. "Bethmann Hollweg, Austria-Hungary and Mitteleuropa, 1914–1915." *Austrian History Yearbook* 19–20 (1983–84) Part I: 215–36.

Katzenstein, Peter J. *Disjoined Partners: Austria and Germany since 1815*. Berkeley: University of California Press, 1976.

Kirchhoff, Jörg. *Die deutschen in der Österreichisch-Ungarischen Monarchie. Ihr Verhältnis zum Staat, zur deutschen Nation und ihr kollektives Selbstverständnis (1866/67–1918)*. Berlin: Logos Verlag, 2001.

Klabouch, Jirí. *Die Gemeindeselbstverwaltung in Österreich 1848–1918*. Vienna: Verlag für Geschichte und Politik, 1968.

Klemperer, Klemens. "Das nachimperiale Österreich, 1918–1938: Politik und Geist." In *Österreich und die Deutsche Frage im 19. und 20. Jahrhundert*. Heinrich Lutz & Helmut Rumpler, eds. Munich: Oldenbourg Verlag, 1982, 300–317.

Klieneberger, H. R. "Hofmannsthal and Leopold Andrian." *The Modern Language Review* 80 (1985): 619–36.

Kohler, Alfred. "Die europäische Bedeutung des Begriffs 'Casa de Austria'." In *Was heisst Österreich? Inhalt und Umfang des Österreich-begriffs vom 10. Jahrhundert bis heute*. Richard G. Plaschka, Gerald Stourzh & Paul Niederkorn, eds. Vienna: Verlag der österreichischen Akademie der Wissenschaften, 1995, 135–47.

Kolmer, Gustav. *Parlament und Verfassung in Österreich*. 8 vols., Graz: Akademische Druck- und Verlagsanstalt, 1974–80 [Originally published in 1902–14].

Koralka, Jirí. *Tschechen im Habsburgerreich und in Europa, 1815–1914: sozialgeschichtliche Zusammenhänge der neuzeitlichen Nationsbildung und der Nationalitätenfrage in der böhmischen Ländern*. Vienna: Verlag für Geschichte und Politik, 1991.

Kramer, Lloyd S. *Lafayette in Two Worlds: Public Cultures and Personal Identities in an Age of Revolutions*. Chapel Hill, N.C.: University of North Carolina Press, 1996.

Kreissler, Felix. *Der Österreicher und seine Nation: Ein Lernprozeß mit Hindernissen*. Vienna: Böhlau Verlag, 1984.

Křen, Jan. *Die Konfliktgemeinschaft. Tschechen und Deutsche 1780–1918*. Munich: Oldenbourg Verlag, 1996.

Kulemann, Peter. *Am Beispiel des Austromarxismus. Sozialdemokratische Arbeiterbewegung in Österreich von Hainfeld bis zur Dollfuß-Diktatur*. Hamburg: Junius Verlag, 1979.

La Vopa, Anthony, J. "Doing Fichte. Reflections of a Sobered (but Unrepentant) Contextual Biographer." In Hans Erich Bödeker, ed. *Biographie Schreiben*, Göttingen: Wallstein Verlag, 2003, 107–71.

Leitgeb, Herwig. *Die Ministerpräsidentschaften Dr. Ernest v. Körbers in den Jahren 1900–1904 und Oktober-November 1916*. Unpublished dissertation, University of Vienna, 1951.

Le Rider, Jacques. "Hugo von Hofmannsthal and the Austrian Idea of Central Europe." In *The Habsburg Legacy. National Identity in Historical Perspective. Austrian Studies 5*. Robert Robertson & Edward Timms, eds. Edinburgh: Edinburgh University Press, 1994, 121–35.

Le Rider, Jacques. *Hugo von Hofmannsthal. Historismus und Moderne in der Literatur der Jahrhundertwende*. Vienna: Böhlau Verlag, 1997.

Leser, Norbert. *Zwischen Reformismus und Bolschewismus. Der Austromarxismus als Theorie und Praxis*. Vienna: Europa-Verlag, 1968.

Leslie, John. "Österreich-Ungarn vor dem Kriegsausbruch. Der Ballhausplatz in Wien im Juli 1914 aus der Sicht eines österreichisch-ungarischen Diplomaten." In *Deutschland und Europa in der Neuzeit. Festschrift für Karl Otmar Freiherr von Aretin zum 65. Geburtstag*. 2 vols., Stuttgart: Steiner Verlag Wiesbaden, 1988, 2:661–84.

Levi, Margaret. *Of Rule and Revenue*. Berkeley: University of California Press, 1988.

Levi, Margaret. *Consent, Dissent, and Patriotism*. Cambridge: Cambridge University Press, 1997.

Liebel-Weckowicz, Helene. "Auf der Suche nach neuer Autorität: Raison d'Etat in den Verwaltungs- und Rechtsreformen Maria Theresias und Joseph II." In *Österreich im Europa der Aufklärung. Kontinuität und Zäsur in Europa zur Zeit Maria Theresias und Joseph II. Internationales Symposion in Wien 20–23 Oktober 1980*. 2 vols., Plaschka, Richard G. & Grete Klingenstein, eds. Vienna: Verlag der österreichischen Akademie der Wissenschaften, 1985, 339–64.

Lindström, Fredrik. "Ernest von Koerber and the Austrian State Idea: A Reinterpretation of the Koerber Plan (1900–1904)." *Austrian History Yearbook* 35 (2004): 143–84.

Loew, Hans. *Alexander Freiherr von Bach*. Unpublished dissertation, University of Vienna, 1947.

Lunzer, Heinz. *Hofmannsthals politische Tätigkeit in den Jahren 1914–1917*. Frankfurt am Main: Verlag Peter D. Lang, 1981.

Lutz, Heinrich & Helmut Rumpler, eds. *Österreich und die deutsche Frage im 19. und 20. Jahrhundert. Probleme der politisch-staatlichen und soziokulturellen Differenzierung im deutschen Mitteleuropa*. Munich: Oldenbourg Verlag, 1982.

Malfér, Stefan. "Der Konstitutionalismus in der Habsburgermonarchie—Siebzig Jahre Verfassungsdiskussion in 'Cisleithanien.'" In *Die Habsburgermonarchie 1848–1918*, Band VII: *Verfassung und Parlamentarismus*. Helmut Rumpler & Peter Urbanitsch, eds. Vienna: Verlag der österreichischen Akademie der Wissenschaften, 2000.

Mann, Michael. *The Sources of Social Power*. 2 vols. Cambridge: Cambridge University Press, 1986–93.

Matthias, Erich. *Die deutsche Sozialdemokratie und der Osten 1914–1945.* Tübingen University, Working paper, 1954.

Mayer, Matthias. *Hugo von Hofmannsthal.* Stuttgart: Metzler, 1993.

Mayr, Markus. "Leopold von Andrians 'Österreich im Prisma der Idee'." *Geschichte und Gegenwart* 8:2 (1989): 96–126.

McGrath, William J. *Dionysian Art and Populist Politics in Austria.* New Haven: Yale University Press, 1974.

Megner, Karl. *Beamte. Wirtschafts- und sozialgeschichtliche Aspekte des k.k. Beamtentums.* Vienna: Verlag der österreichischen Akademie der Wissenschaften, 1985.

Miller, Susanne. *Burgfrieden und Klassenkampf. Die deutsche Sozialdemokratie im 1. Weltkrieg.* Düsseldorf: Droste, 1974.

Mommsen, Hans. *Die Sozialdemokratie und die Nationalitätenfrage im habsburgischen Vielvölkerstaat.* Vienna: Europa-Verlag, 1963.

Mommsen, Wolfgang. "Die 'deutsche Idee der Freiheit'." In idem., *Bürgerliche Kultur und politische Ordnung. Künstler, Schriftsteller und Intellektuelle in der deutschen Geschichte 1830–1933.* Frankfurt am Main: Fischer Taschenbuchverlag, 2000, 133–57.

Morgenbrod, Birgitt. *Wiener Großbürgertum im Ersten Weltkrieg. Die Geschichte der 'Österreichischen Politischen Gesellschaft' 1916–1918.* Vienna: Böhlau Verlag, 1994.

Müller, Achim. *Zwischen Annäherung und Abgrenzung: Österreich-Ungarn und die Diskussion um Mitteleuropa im Ersten Weltkrieg.* Marburg: Tectum-Verlag, 2001.

Müller, Karl. "Hugo von Hofmannsthal's Zeit- und Kulturkritik seit dem Ersten Weltkrieg," *Austriaca* 18/37 (1993): 193–214.

Nasko, Siegfried & Johannes Reichl. *Karl Renner. Zwischen Anschluß und Europa.* Vienna: Holzhausen, 2000.

Ng, Amy. *Nationalism and Political Liberty: Redlich, Namier, and the Crisis of Empire.* Oxford: Clarendon Press, 2004.

Novotny, Alexander. "Ministerpräsident Ernest von Koerber (1850–1919)." In *Gestalter der Geschicke Österreichs.* Hugo Hantsch, ed. Innsbruck: Tyrolia Verlag, 1962, 485–500.

Ogris, Werner. "Zwischen Absolutismus und Rechtsstaat." In *Österreich im Europa der Aufklärung. Kontinuität und Zäsur in Europa zur Zeit Maria Theresias und Joseph II. Internationales Symposion in Wien 20–23 Oktober 1980.* 2 vols., Plaschka, Richard G. & Grete Klingenstein, eds. Vienna: Verlag der österreichischen Akademie der Wissenschaften, 1985, 365–76.

Pantenburg, Isabel F. *Im Schatten des Zweibundes. Probleme österreichisch-ungarischer Bündnispolitik 1897–1908.* Vienna: Böhlau Verlag, 1996.

Panzenböck, Ernst. *Ein deutscher Traum. Die Anschlußidee und Anschlußpolitik bei Karl Renner und Otto Bauer.* Vienna: Europa-Verlag, 1985.

Pape, Matthias. *Ungleiche Brüder. Österreich und Deutschland 1945–1965*. Cologne: Böhlau Verlag, 2000.

Pelinka, Anton. *Karl Renner zur Einführung*. Hamburg: Junius Verlag, 1989.

Perrig, Severin. *Hugo von Hofmannsthal und die Zwanziger Jahre. Eine Studie zur späten Orientierungskrise*. Frankfurt am Main: Peter D. Lang Verlag, 1994.

Plaschka, Richard G. & Grete Klingenstein, eds. *Österreich im Europa der Aufklärung. Kontinuität und Zäsur in Europa zur Zeit Maria Theresias und Joseph II. Internationales Symposion in Wien 20–23 Oktober 1980*. 2 vols., Plaschka, Richard G. & Grete Klingenstein, eds. Vienna: Verlag der österreichischen Akademie der Wissenschaften, 1985.

Plaschka, Richard G., Gerald Stourzh, & Paul Niederkorn. *Was heisst Österreich? Inhalt und Umfang des Österreichbegriffs vom 10. Jahrhundert bis heute*. Vienna: Verlag der österreichischen Akademie der Wissenschaften, 1995.

Prutsch, Ursula & Klaus Zeyringer. "Einleitung." In *Leopold von Andrian (1875–1951). Korrespondenzen, Notizen, Essays, Berichte*. Ursula Prutsch & Klaus Zeyringer, eds. Vienna: Böhlau Verlag, 2003. (19–28, 91–105, 235–49, 485–502, 649–61, 745–54)

Ramhardter, Günther. *Geschichtswissenschaft und Patriotismus. Österreichische Historiker im Weltkriege 1914–1918*. Vienna: Verlag für Geschichte und Politik, 1973.

Rauscher, Walter. *Karl Renner. Ein österreichischer Mythos*. Vienna: Ueberreuther, 1995.

Reinhard, Wolfgang. *Geschichte der Staatsgewalt. Eine vergleichende Verfassungsgeschichte Europas von den Anfängen bis zur Gegenwart*. Munich: Verlag, C. H. Beck, 1999.

Renner, Ursula. *Leopold Andrians 'Garten der Erkenntnis'. Literarisches Paradigma einer Identitätskrise in Wien um 1900*. Frankfurt am Main: Verlag Peter Lang, 1981.

Rieckmann, Jens. *Aufbruch in die Moderne. Die Anfänge des Jungen Wiens. Österreichische Literatur und Kritik im Fin de Siècle*. Königstein/Ts: Athenäum, 1985.

Rieckmann, Jens. "Zwischen Bewusstsein und Verdrängung. Hofmannsthals jüdisches Erbe." In *DVjs* 67 (1993): 466–83.

Rieckmann, Jens. "Knowing the Other. Leopold von Andrian's *Garten der Erkenntnis* and the Homoerotic Discourse of the Fin de Siécle." In *Gender and Politics in Austrian Fiction (Austrian Studies 7)*, Ritchie Robertson and Edward Timms, eds. Edinburgh: Edinburgh University Press, 1996.

Rieckmann, Jens. *Hugo von Hofmannsthal und Stefan George. Signifikanz einer 'Episode' aus der Jahrhundertwende*. Tübingen: Franke, 1997.

Ritter, Ellen. "Hugo von Hofmannsthal: 'Die Briefe des Zurückgekehrten'." In *Jahrbuch des Freien Deutschen Hochstifts*, Tübingen: Max Niemeyer Verlag, 1988: 226–52.

Ritter, Harry. "Progressive Historians and the Historical Imagination in Austria: Heinrich Friedjung and Richard Charmatz." *Austrian History Yearbook* 19/20 (1983/84): 45–90.

Robertson, Ritchie & Edward Timms, eds. *The Austrian Enlightenment and its Aftermath. Austrian Studies* 2. Edinburgh: Edinburgh University Press, 1991.

Rudolph, Hermann. *Kulturkritik und konservative Revolution. Zum kulturell-politischen Denken Hofmannsthals und seinem problemgeschichtlichen Kontext.* Tübingen: Niemeyer, 1971.

Rumpler, Helmut, ed. *Innere Staatsbildung und gesellschaftliche Modernisierung in Österreich und Deutschland 1867/71–1914. Historikergespräch Österreich—Bundesrepublik Deutschland 1989.* Vienna: Verlag für Geschichte und Politik, 1991.

Rumpler, Helmut & Peter Urbanitsch, eds. *Die Habsburgermonarchie 1848–1918.* Vol. 7: *Verfassung und Parlamentarismus.* Vienna: Verlag der österreichischen Akademie der Wissenschaften, 2000.

Rutkowski, Ernst. "Aehrenthal über die Innenpolitische Lage Österreich-Ungarns im Sommer 1899." *Südost-Forschungen* 23 (1964): 284–97.

Schorske, Carl. *German Social Democracy 1905–1917. The Development of the Great Schism.* Cambridge, Mass: Harvard University Press, 1955.

Schorske, Carl. *Fin-de-Siècle Vienna. Politics and Culture.* London: Weidenfeld & Nicolson, 1980.

Schorske, Carl. "Grace and the Word: Austria's Two Cultures and Their Modern Fate." *Austrian History Yearbook* 22 (1991): 21–34.

Schumacher, Horst. *Leopold von Andrian. Werk und Weltbild eines österreichischen Dichters.* Vienna: Bergland Verlag, 1967.

Shanafelt, Gary W. *The Secret Enemy: Austria-Hungary and the German Alliance, 1914–1918.* Boulder & New York: Columbia University Press, 1985.

Shedel, James. "*Fin de Siècle* or *Jahrhundertwende*. The Question of an Austrian Sonderweg." In *Rethinking Vienna 1900.* Steven Beller, ed. New York & Oxford: Berghahn Books, 2001, 80–104.

Shedel, James. *Art and Society. The New Art Movement in Vienna 1897–1914.* Palo Alto, CA: Society for the Promotion of Science and Scholarship, 1981.

Siegert, Michael. "Sozialdemokratie und Imperialismus: Kriegsziele und Beutehoffnungen 1914–1918 (Teil 1)." *Neues Forum* (September 1975): 31–38.

Sieghart, Rudolf. "Ernest von Körber." In *Deutsches Biographisches Jahrbuch.* Vol. 2: 1917–20. Stuttgart: Deutsche Verlags Anstalt, 1928, 426–34.

Sked, Alan. *The Decline and Fall of the Habsburg Empire 1815–1918.* London: Longman, 1989.

Söderqvist, Thomas. "Wissenschaftsgeschichte á la Plutarch. Biographie über Wissenschaftler als Tugendethische Gattung." In Hans Erich Bödeker, ed. *Biographie Schreiben.* Göttingen: Wallstein Verlag, 2003.

Söderqvist, Thomas. *Science as Autobiography: The Troubled Life of Niels Jerne*. New Haven: Yale University Press, 2003.

Somogyi, Éva. "Aehrenthals Reformbestrebungen 1906–1907." *Österreichische Osthefte* 30 (1988): 60–75.

Somogyi, Éva. *Der gemeinsame Ministerrat der österreichisch-ungarischen Monarchie 1867–1906*. Vienna: Böhlau Verlag, 1996.

Staudinger, Anton. "Zur 'Österreich-Ideologie des Ständestaats." In *Das Juli-Abkommen 1936. Veröffentlichungen der Wissenschaftlichen Kommission des Theodor-Körner-Stiftungsfonds und des Leopold-Kunschak-Preises zur Erforschung der österreichischen Geschichte der Jahre 1927 bis 1938* (vol. 4). Ludwig Jedlicka & Rudolf Neck, eds. Vienna: Verlag für Geschichte und Politik, 1977, 198–240.

Steinberg, Michael P. *The Meaning of the Salzburg Festival. Austria as Theater and Ideology, 1890–1938*. Ithaca: Cornell University Press, 1990.

Stieg, Gerald. "Hofmannsthal und die Salzburger Festspiele." *Austriaca* 18/37 (1993): 287–98.

Stourzh, Gerald. *Die Gleichberechtigung der Nationalitäten in der Verfassung und Verwaltung Österreichs, 1848–1918*. Vienna: Verlag der österreichischen Akademie der Wissenschaften, 1985.

Stourzh, Gerald. *Vom Reich zur Republik. Studien zum Österreichbewusstsein im 20. Jahrhundert*. Vienna: Edition Atelier, 1990.

Stourzh, Gerald. "Der Dualismus 1867 bis 1918: Zur staatsrechtlichen und Völkerrechtlichen Problematik der Doppelmonarchie." In *Die Habsburgermonarchie 1848–1918*, vol. 7: *Verfassung und Parlamentarismus*. Helmut Rumpler and Peter Urbanitsch, eds., Vienna: Verlag der Österreichischen Akademie der Wissenschaften, 2000, 1177–1230.

Sutter, Berthold. *Die Badenischen Sprachenverordnungen von 1897*. 2 vol., Graz: Böhlau Verlag, 1960–65.

Sutter Fichtner, Paula. "Schorske's Garden Transformed Again: War Propaganda, Aesthethics, and the Conservative Revolution." In Samuel Williamson Jr, & Peter Pastors, eds. *Essays on World War I: Origins and Prisoners of War*. New York: Columbia University Press, 1983, 83–102.

Thaler, Peter. *The Ambivalence of Identity. The Austrian Experience of Nation-Building in a Modern Society*. West Lafayette, Ind.: Purdue University Press, 2001.

Theiner, Peter. *Sozialer Liberalismus und deutsche Weltpolitik. Friedrich Naumann im Wilhelminischen Deutschland (1860–1919)*. Baden-Baden: Nomos Verlagsgesellschaft, 1983.

Tilly, Charles, ed. *The Formation of National States in Western Europe*. Princeton N.J.: Princeton University Press, 1975.

Tilly, Charles. *Coercion, Capital, and European States, A.D. 990–1990*. Oxford: Blackwell, 1990.

Tilly, Charles. *European Revolutions 1492–1992*. Oxford: Blackwell, 1993.

Ucakar, Karl. *Demokratie und Wahlrecht in Österreich. Zur Entwicklung von politischer Partizipation und staatlicher Legitimationspolitik*. Vienna: Verlag für Gesellschaftskritik, 1985.

Unfried, Berthold. *Zu Politik und Theorie der 'Linken' innerhalb der österreichischen Sozialdemokratie während des 1. Weltkrieges*. Unpublished Diplomarbeit, University of Vienna, 1978.

Unowsky, Daniel. *The Pomp and Politics of Patriotism: Imperial Celebrations in Habsburg Austria, 1848–1916*. West Lafayette, Indiana: Purdue University Press, 2005.

Velek, Luboš . "Koerberovy Česko-Německé smiřovací konference 1900" [Koerbers Czech-German conciliation conferences in 1900]. *Časopis Národního muzea—řada historická* 168/1–2 (1999): 28–54.

Velek, Luboš. "Sestavení Vlády Ernesta von Koerbera a obnovení Úřadu Českeho ministra krajana roku 1900" [Koerber's formation of government and restoration of a Czech *Landesmann* ministry]. *Paginae historiae* 6 (1998): 38–63.

Volke, Werner. *Hugo von Hofmannsthal. Mit Selbstzeugnissen und Bilddokumenten dargestellt von Werner Volke*. Reinbek bei Hamburg: Rowohlt Taschenbuch Verlag, 1967.

Walter, Edith. *Österreichische Tageszeitungen der Jahrhundertwende. Ideologischer Anspruch und ökonomische Erfordernisse*. Vienna: Böhlau Verlag, 1994.

Walter, Friedrich. *Die österreichische Zentralverwaltung*. Veröffentlichungen der Kommission für neuere Geschichte Österreichs. Vols. 29, 32, 35, 36, 42, 43, 49, 50, 54, 55. Vienna: Holzhausen, 1934–1971.

Walter-Klingenstein, Grete. "Was bedeuten 'Österreich' und 'österreichisch' im 18. Jahrhundert? Eine begriffsgeschichtliche Studie." In *Was heisst Österreich? Inhalt und Umfang des Österreichbegriffs vom 10. Jahrhundert bis heute*. Richard G. Plaschka, Gerald Stourzh & Paul Niederkorn, eds. Vienna: Verlag der österreichischen Akademie der Wissenschaften, 1995, 149–220.

Wandruszka, Adam & Peter Urbanitsch, eds. *Die Habsburgermonarchie 1848–1918*. Vol. 3: *Die Völker des Reiches*. Vienna: Verlag der österreichischen Akademie der Wissenschaften, 1980.

Wank, Solomon. "Aehrenthal's Programme for the Constitutional Transformation of the Habsburg Monarchy: Three Secret Mémoires." *Slavonic and East European Review* 41, No. 97 (June 1963): 513–36.

Wank, Solomon. "Zwei Dokumente Aehrenthals aus den Jahren 1898–99 zur Lösung der inneren Krise in Österreich-Ungarn." *Mitteilungen des Österreichischen Staatsarchivs* 19 (1966): 339–62.

Wank, Solomon. "Varieties of Political Despair: Three Exchanges between Aehrenthal and Goluchowski, 1898–1906." In *Intellectual and Social Developments in the*

Habsburg Empire from Maria Theresia to World War I. Stanley Winters & Joseph Held, eds. New York: Columbia University Press, 1975, 203–39.

Was blieb von Joseph II? Eine Dokumentation Internationales Symposion Melk 1980. St.Pölten-Wien: Niederösterreichisches Pressehaus, 1980.

Weinzierl, Ulrich. "Österreich als Wille und Vorstellung." *Deutschsprachige Exilliteratur: Studien zu ihrer Bestimmung im Kontext der Epoche 1930 bis 1960.* Wulf Koepke & Michael Winkler, eds. Bonn: Bouvier, 1984, 242–59.

Weinzierl, Ulrich. *Hofmannsthal. Skizzen zu einem Bild.* Vienna: Zsolnay Verlag, 2005.

Whiteside, Andrew G. *The Socialism of Fools. Georg Ritter von Schönerer and Austrian Pan-Germanism.* Berkeley: University of California Press, 1975.

Wistrich, Robert S. *The Jews of Vienna in the Age of Franz Joseph.* Oxford: Oxford University Press, 1990.

Wolfram, Herwig & Walter Pohl, eds. *Probleme der Geschichte Österreichs und ihrer Darstellung.* Vienna: Verlag der österreichischen Akademie der Wissenschaften, 1991.

Zailer, Erich. *Heinrich Friedjung. Unter besonderer Berücksichtigung seiner politischen Entwicklung.* Unpublished dissertation, University of Vienna, 1949.

Zöllner, Erich, ed. *Österreich im Zeitalter des Aufgeklärten Absolutismus.* Vienna: Österreichischer Bundesverlag, 1983.

Zöllner, Erich. *Der Österreichbegriff. Formen und Wandlungen in der Geschichte.* Vienna: Verlag für Geschichte und Politik, 1988.

Index

Page references in italics refer to illustrations.